# Rock Climbing
## Virginia, West Virginia, and Maryland

Eric J. Hörst

**FALCON**GUIDES ®

GUILFORD, CONNECTICUT
HELENA, MONTANA
AN IMPRINT OF THE GLOBE PEQUOT PRESS

Copyright © 2001 by The Globe Pequot Press

Cover photo by Eric J. Hörst
Photo bases for photo topos by Stewart M. Green and Eric J. Hörst

**Library of Congress Cataloging-in-Publication Data**
Hörst, Eric J.
    Rock climbing Virginia, West Virginia, and Maryland / Eric J. Hörst.—1st ed.
    p. cm. — (A Falcon guide)
    Includes bibliographical references and index.
    ISBN 978-1-56044-812-9
    1. Rock climbing—Virginia—Guidebooks. 2. Rock climbing—West Virginia—Guidebooks. 3. Rock climbing—Maryland—Guidebooks. 4. Virginia—Guidebooks. 5. West Virginia—Guidebooks. 6.Maryland—Guidebooks. I. Title. II. Series.

GV199.42.V8 H67 2001
917.52—dc21

                                                                    2001024666

Printed in the United States of America
First Edition/Sixth Printing

# DEDICATION

To my son Cameron, whose adventures in the world are just beginning.

# ACKNOWLEDGMENTS

First, I want to thank all my climbing partners of the last twenty-four years who have explored and climbed with me at "Type-A" speed across the Mid-Atlantic states and from coast to coast. I especially want to thank my brother, Kyle, for introducing me to this wonderful sport and for input on the guide; my first hardman climbing partner and inspiration over the years, Jeff Batzer; my long-time "team machine" partner, Rick Thompson; and my favorite climbing companion of all, my wife Lisa Ann. Thanks to you all for the many great times both on and off the rock—I look forward to many more!

Writing this guide would have never happened if it weren't for Stewart Green proposing the project. Stewart helped me from beginning to end, and his excellent action photography and photo topos are featured throughout the book. Also thanks to Martha Morris for her world-class cliff topos and contributions to the photo topos and maps. This guide would not be half as good without both your efforts.

My sincere thanks and appreciation go out to all the climbers (or others) who contributed in some way to this guide: Eric Angel, Tony Barnes, Jeff Batzer, Eddie Begoon, Tom Cecil, Chris Clarke, Greg Collins, Guy and Karen deBrun, Kelly Dinneen, Howard Doyle, Adam Ehrlich, Sandy Fleming, Pete Grant, Fabrizia Guglielmetti, Cindy Mai, Stewart Hammett, Darell Hensley, Khanh and Kyle Hörst, Tom Isaacson, Kris Kirk, Gene Kistler, Mark Kochte, Keith McCallister, Mike McGill, Steve Muzyka, Kenny Parker, Karen and Stuart Pregnall, Scott Ridenour, Jason Roberts, Carl Samples, Rob Savoye, Harrison Shull, Taylor Smith, and Rick Thompson. Special thanks to Eric McCallister for his help on several aspects of this guide, including last-minute road trips to dial-in missing details, and to John Burbidge and everyone at Falcon for their efforts in bringing this monsterous project to fruition.

Finally, I'd like to thank my parents, Bob and Ethel, for all their love, support, and prayers over the two-thirds of my life I've been involved in this sport.

# CONTENTS

# VIRGINIA, WEST VIRGINIA, MARYLAND CLIMBING AREAS OVERVIEW

1 Old Rag Mountain
2 Great Falls, VA
3 Hidden Rocks
4 Hone Quarry
5 Rawley Springs
6 Crescent Rock
7 Iron Gate
8 Skyline Drive
9 McAfee's Knob
10 Carderock
11 Great Falls, MD
12 Rocks State Park
13 Patapsco Valley State Park
14 Annapolis Rock
15 Sugarloaf Mountain
16 Maryland Heights
17 Coopers Rock
18 Seneca Rocks
19 Nelson Rocks
20 Summersville Lake
21 New River Gorge
22 Bozoo
23 Franklin

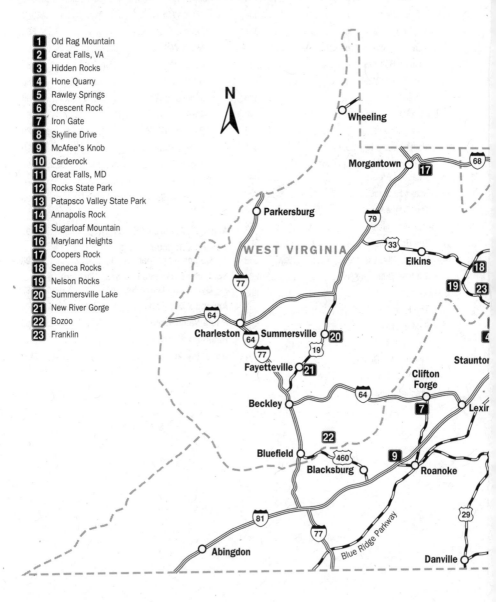

# MAP LEGEND

# TOPO LEGEND

| | |
|---|---|
| Interstate Highway | |
| Paved Road (major) | |
| Paved Road (minor) | |
| Gravel Road | |
| Dirt Road | |
| Trail | |
| Railroad | |
| Fence | |
| Gate | |
| River/Creek | |
| Lake | |
| Camping | |
| Building | |
| Parking | |
| Interstate Highway | |
| U.S. Highway | |
| State/County Roads | |
| Forest Service Road | |
| City/Town | O Charleston |
| Bridge | |
| Peak/Elevation | x |
| Waterfall | |
| River Flow | |

| | |
|---|---|
| Face climbing | |
| Chimney or crack | |
| Obscured route | |
| Fixed bolt(s) or piton | X  XX |
| One-piece fixed anchor | |
| Two-piece fixed anchor | |
| Three-piece fixed anchor | |
| Natural gear belay | |
| Descent route | 150' |
| Difficulty rating | .11a |
| Route number | 16 |

| | |
|---|---|
| Project | P |
| Crag/Boulder | |
| Cliff | Cliff face |
| Route Number | 28 |
| Compass | N |
| Scale | 0  1  2  Miles |

# INTRODUCTION

In 1977, a thirteen-year-old boy from southern Pennsylvania was introduced to the vertical challenge of rock climbing, and the 200-foot hometown cliffs of Chickies Rock became his after-school playground. In the years that followed, that youth used every available opportunity to explore the crags of the eastern United States, including almost every famous and obscure crag in the states of Virginia, Maryland, and West Virginia. One year he climbed over 300 days, and over the next two decades he would climb thousands of routes across America and in Europe. However, he always returned to the climbing areas of his home region—the magical crags that helped shape him as a climber and a person.

Without a doubt, this basic story line has been played out by hundreds, even thousands, of different people who live or have grown up in this region. It is estimated that about 30 percent of the U.S. climbing population lives in the Mid-Atlantic—an area not recognized as having any "real" mountains—and, fortunately, excellent rock climbing exists in the states of Virginia, Maryland, and West Virginia. From the granite peaks of Old Rag Mountain to the miles of glowing Nuttall Sandstone in the New River Gorge, this region offers many different climbing opportunities and so much potential to experience this world of wonder.

The goal of *Rock Climbing Virginia, West Virginia, and Maryland* is to distill nearly twenty-five years of exploring and climbing into a regional guide that can introduce countless new climbers to our diverse selection of climbing resources. Covering twenty-three different areas and organized into thirteen chapters, this guide will get you to the best climbs at the best areas, as well as some hidden gems on out-of-the-way hillsides that only a few "in the know" were aware of until recent years.

Surely everyone knows of the New River Gorge and its nearly 2,000 traditional and sport climbs—but where should you begin when visiting such an expansive area the first few times? Quite possibly you've heard about the granite crags on Old Rag Mountain, but its reputation for hard-to-find areas and a heinous approach have scared you away. Is Old Rag worth the effort to visit? (You bet!) Or what about the smaller crags, previously without a guidebook, like Rocks Maryland, Annapolis Rock, Sugarloaf Mountain, and Coopers Rock—how good are these areas, and are there enough quality climbs to justify a trip? Then there is the handful of relatively unknown areas that possess good rock and a lack of crowds—have you heard of Crescent

Rock, Hidden Rocks, Iron Gate, Bozoo, or the recently founded Nelson Rocks Preserve? If not, read on!

The fact is, there is nearly a lifetime of good climbing packed into the rolling hills of Virginia, West Virginia, and Maryland. Still, the region is commonly disparaged by some with a low tolerance for adventure or the unwillingness to be flexible or create a "Plan B" when faced by a sudden rainstorm. Clearly, the weekend destinations for many climbers are the world-class crags of Seneca Rocks and the New River Gorge. However, some of the beauty of climbing in the Mid-Atlantic is the close proximity of good training crags to metropolitan areas like Washington, D.C., and Baltimore, as well as to mid-sized towns such as Frederick, Hagerstown, Cumberland, Charlottesville, Harrisonburg, Lynchburg, Roanoke, Blacksburg, Beckley, Charleston, Martinsburg, and Morgantown. With good rock less than an hour from all of these towns, there's no excuse not to squeeze in a half-day of climbing before the rain begins, or as soon as the skies start to clear. Not every perfect day of climbing has to begin with perfect weather.

So get out and explore the wonderful resources we're blessed with in the Mid-Atlantic region. Decide that any day that you can be out moving over stone—whether it's a 30-foot toprope at Great Falls or a 300-foot, multipitch classic at Seneca Rocks—is a great day. Make it a goal to visit each of the twenty-three areas in this guide at least once in the next year or two—not only is variety the jalapeño of a climber's life, but take it from an authority that climbing at a wide range of crags is the fastest way to improve your climbing ability. Savor each day, each climb, and each move, and vow to enjoy the process of climbing regardless of the outcome (or the weather).

## CLIMBING HISTORY

Climbing in the Mid-Atlantic region dates back almost to the genesis of the sport in North America. In the late 1920s and 1930s, a small group of climbers, including Gus Gambs, Don Hubbard, and Paul Brandt, climbed at Carderock using a manila rope tied around their waists with a bowline knot (please don't try this at home!), a few soft-iron pitons, and stiff-soled hiking boots. Washington, D.C.–area climbers also began to visit the daunting cliffs at Seneca Rocks, and in 1939, Brandt, Hubbard, and Sam Moore climbed to the South Peak via *Skyline Traverse* (5.3). A few years later at Carderock, Herb Conn pushed the limits sky high with his amazing 1942 toprope ascent of *Herbie's Horror,* one of the country's first 5.9s.

Seneca Rocks and Carderock continued as the primary areas for climbers to ply their trade through the 1940s, and during World War II Seneca Rocks was the main proving ground for the U.S. Army's 10th Mountain Division. The post-war era saw a marked increase in climbing activity with recreational groups like the Pittsburgh Explorers Club and the Potomac Appalachian Trail

*The author on an early lead of Bushwhack Crack (5.10c), Old Rag Mountain (circa 1985).* PHOTO HÖRST COLLECTION

Club (PATC) hitting the rocks most weekends. The 1950s saw climbers exploring more out-of-the-way areas like Old Rag Mountain, Coopers Rock, and Sugarloaf Mountain. Still, the hardest routes were being climbed at Carderock and Seneca Rocks. In 1951, Tony Soler toproped *Jam Box* at Carderock (the area's first 5.10), and at Seneca Rocks he led an imposing line known today as *Soler* (5.7+). These two ascents established Soler as one of the leading climbers of the decade.

The psychedelic 1960s featured even more wild ascents, especially at Seneca Rocks. George Livingstone led Seneca Rock's first 5.10 *Madmen Only* and Joe Faint climbed 12-foot *Faint's Roof* (5.10a) at Annapolis Rock. As the 1960s gave way to the 1970s, new talent was developing with the likes of Howard Doyle, Matt Hale, Eric Janoscrat, Herb Laeger, and Hunt Prothro leading the way. A growing pool of Washington-based talent was climbing weekdays at Carderock and Great Falls, then applying their well-honed face-climbing skills to the steep faces at Seneca Rocks and Nelson Rocks. One powerful D.C.–area climber named John Stannard—better known for his 1970s dominance at the Gunks—freed the impressive *Totem* roof, giving Seneca Rocks its first 5.11 in 1971. Herb Laeger, Howard Doyle, and others soon added harder, more sustained 5.11s that are still "necky" leads today (even with superior shoes and protection). As the 1970s wound down, a new area was just beginning to be explored along the New River in southern West Virginia; though, big-time climbing at the New would take a few more years to come to fruition.

The 1980s started with a bang as Cal Swoager free-climbed the first half of the old *Satisfaction #1* aid route at Seneca Rocks. This short climb established 5.12 in the region, a feat that would soon be equaled by Hugh Herr at Rocks Maryland and by Greg Collins and John Bercaw at Great Falls and Carderock. Meanwhile, energetic climbers were beginning to flood into the New River Gorge, cranking out over 400 new routes in a few seasons during the mid-1980s. In 1986, Alex Karr and Andrew Barry climbed the first 5.12 routes at the New, and in October 1987 Eric Hörst climbed *Diamond Life,* the region's first 5.13.

Quickly, the emphasis of climbing in the region shifted from all other areas to the New River Gorge. High-end climbers arrived from a variety of cities to contribute to the development of this soon-to-be climbing mecca. A few of the more notable players were Mike Artz and Eddie Begoon (Harrisonburg, Virginia), Eric Hörst and Rick Thompson (Pennsylvania), Doug Reed and Porter Jarrard (powerful southerners), Kenny Parker and friends (from Roanoke/Blacksburg, Virginia), and Doug Cosby and Gary Beil (Washington, D.C., area). Together, the nine climbers listed above are responsible for more than 1,000 climbs at the New River Gorge and nearby Summersville Lake!

Climbing history during the most recent decade is hard to track, as the 1990s "climbing boom" thrust thousands of new climbers into the scene.

Some of these gym-bred climbers quickly progressed through the grades, and they have gone on to make significant contributions here in the Mid-Atlantic region and beyond. During this time, several smaller crags were developed into worthwhile areas (though, of mainly local interest), including places like Iron Gate, Bozoo, Franklin, and Hidden Rocks. Meanwhile, some of the region's aging hardmen (thirty somethings) returned to the "older areas" to up the ante at places like Nelson Rocks, Old Rag, and Seneca Rocks. To date, the two hardest climbs in the region are Scott Franklin's *Mango Tango* (at The Meadow) and Brian McCray's *Proper Soul* (at the New), both 5.14a.

# GEOLOGY AND GEOGRAPHY

Rocks exposed in the Mid-Atlantic region are the result of a variety of forces, including ancient volcanoes, colliding continents, and eons of erosion and weathering. These climbing areas lie in four different geological provinces— from east to west: the Piedmont Plateau, Blue Ridge, Valley and Ridge, and Appalachian Plateau provinces.

The piedmont province of east-central Maryland and Virginia possesses a variety of igneous and metamorphic rocks; however, the popular crags, such as Carderock, Great Falls, and Rocks Maryland are composed primarily of metamorphic mica schist. When you climb at these areas, you'll notice frequent quartz veins that protrude from the weathered schist outcrops. These quartz knobs and edges are, of course, many of the "thank god" hand- and footholds you come upon on these typically smooth faces.

The Blue Ridge province is home of Old Rag Mountain, Crescent Rock, Annapolis Rock, and the multitude of outcrops along Skyline Drive. Most notable is the ancient granite on Old Rag Mountain, which dates back over one billion years. Its distinctive, coarse grain (and sharp crystals) developed as massive magma intrusions slowly cooled deep below the earth's surface. The crags we now climb on were revealed after millions of years of erosion of the overlying rocks. Elsewhere, the sedimentary rocks that comprise many of the other crags in the province are most commonly greenstone (primarily along Skyline Drive), as well as sandstone and quartzite.

West of the Blue Ridge province is the Valley and Ridge province, consisting of elongated parallel valleys and ridges that are found in extreme western Virginia and the eastern third of West Virginia. The dramatic landscapes are the result of repeated folding of the underlying sedimentary rock. Many of the cliffs in this region—including Champe, Seneca Rocks, Nelson Rocks, and North Fork Mountain—are very hard, fine-grained quartzite, specifically known as Tuscarora Sandstone.

Farthest west is the Appalachian Plateau province, which encompasses the western two-thirds of West Virginia. Best known as West Virginia's "coal country," climbers know this area as home of the New River Gorge. Here, the

*Jeremy Rhee on The Pod (5.13a/b), The Coliseum, Summersville Lake, West Virginia.*
PHOTO BY STEWART GREEN

rock formations have remained relatively flat (not folded like in the Valley and Ridge province), and the exposed rock is mainly found along the prominent rivers in the region. In the New River Gorge, there has been plenty of time to reveal the layers of hard Nuttall sandstone and underlying coal—the New River is believed to be the second oldest river on earth.

## CLIMBING DANGERS AND SAFETY

Rock climbing, while safer than driving your car around the Washington beltway, is a dangerous recreational activity. The perils of rock climbing are, however, often overstated. The only risks we climbers take are those we choose to take. Most climbers assume the risks of their vertical sport, but also do everything possible to mitigate the effects of gravity and minimize the danger. Still, H. L. Mencken's astute observation of hot air balloonists also holds true for rock climbers: "They have an unsurpassed view of the scenery, but there is always the possibility that it may collide with them."

Remember the above maxim, no matter how much fun you're having or how benign a climb appears to be. Every route has the potential to kill or injure you or your partner. Every climber, no matter what his or her level of experience or skill, can and will make stupid, potentially life-threatening mistakes. Every time you step into your rock shoes, buckle up your harness, and tie onto the rope, you or your partner might die as a direct result of your actions or by an act of God (see Objective Dangers). Rock climbing, despite all the fun and hype, is serious business, and you need to treat it seriously. The fun quickly drains out of the vertical game when your buddy is hauled off in a body bag.

It is totally up to you to minimize the risks of rock climbing. If you are inexperienced or out of shape, get help. Don't jump onto the sharp end and lead some horrendously runout route because you think you might lose face with your pals. The worst case scenario sees you in that body bag, or at least hauled off to the hospital with a broken back. Safe rock climbing takes lots of real-life experience. At one time, tyros served an apprenticeship under the watchful eye of a more experienced hand; but now, with the burgeoning growth of rock gyms, those with basic climbing know-how and a handful of hard gym routes under their harnesses think they're rock jocks. In reality, indoor climbing and outdoor climbing are barely the same sport. Just because you can swing up a gym 5.12 doesn't mean you can jam a 5.9 crack outside. Ratings of climbing routes are subjective grades arrived at by the consensus opinion of experienced climbers—if you are not experienced at a certain type of climbing, then the route will feel much harder than graded. Finally, consider that every outdoor climb is potentially X-rated—a fixed anchor could fail, a piece of gear you placed could pull out, or your belayer could drop you.

This guidebook, as well as other climbing guides and instruction books, is no substitute for your own experience and good judgment. Do not depend or rely on the information in this book to get you safely to the top of the crag and back to the parking lot. Guidebook writing is by necessity a compilation of information obtained by the author through his experience at a given crag, as well as information obtained from experienced climbers. Errors can and do creep into route descriptions, cliff topos, gear recommendations, anchor placements, fixed gear notes, and descent routes and rappels. Things change out there on the rocks. Rockfall might obliterate that crucial set of rappel anchors, or that fixed piton at the crux move might have pulled out on the last leader fall. You must rely solely on your own experience and judgment to ensure your own personal safety and that of your partner. There's an old saying that "bad judgment is a result of a lack of experience, and experience is a result of bad judgment." Hopefully you will survive your times of bad judgment and gain your experience at a variety of crags and in a wide range of mountain situations.

Indeed, most accidents and fatalities are the result of bad judgment and carelessness—thus, most climbing accidents are preventable! The well-trained, experienced climber develops rituals that help minimize the risks. For instance, always check and recheck both your and your partner's harness buckles and knots. Always double-check your belayer's set-up and the belay anchor.

Below is a partial list of things to consider every time you visit the crags.

- Always protect yourself near the start of a route by placing lots of gear or stick-clipping a high bolt to avoid groundfalls.
- Always double-check your harness and tie-in knot before climbing, as well as your harness and rappel device before rappelling.
- Do not climb below other parties. Rockfall can be fatal.
- Wear a helmet for cranial protection from falling or rockfall.
- Do not solo routes (without a rope). Even a 30-foot fall is deadly.
- Place protection whenever possible to keep yourself and your partner safe.
- Use a rope when descending in wet, snowy, or dark conditions.
- Tie knots in the end of your ropes to avoid rappelling off the ends of the ropes.
- Tie in properly after completing a sport pitch and double-check your knot and rope before downclimbing or lowering.
- Remember that the belay is a crucial part of the safety link. Belayers need to be alert, competent, and anchored. Expect and remind your belayer to pay attention while you climb and not to visit with the neighbors or fix lunch.
- Tie a knot in the end of your rope to avoid being dropped by inattentive belayers while they're lowering you.

# OBJECTIVE DANGERS

Objective dangers—those that you have no control over—are found while you're hiking to the cliff, climbing your route, descending, and returning to your car. It's a good rule to never consider the climbing day over until you're safely back at the car. Many accidents happen on descents, due to rockfall, carelessness, fatigue, loose or wet rock, and darkness. Always rope up on any descent you are the least bit uneasy about. Pay attention to your intuition.

**Loose rock.** Loose blocks and flakes are found on many Mid-Atlantic routes, perched on ledges or wedged in cracks and chimneys. Use extreme caution around any suspect rock. Falling rocks are deadly to your belayer and friends at the cliff base, and they can even chop your lead rope. Warn your partners if you feel a block is unstable so they can be prepared for possible rockfall. Consider that thawing and freezing cycles of winter and spring can loosen flakes and blocks. The movements of your climbing rope can also dislodge loose rocks. Use care when pulling rappel ropes, because you can also pull a stone missile down as well. Wear a helmet while climbing and belaying to reduce the risk of serious head injury or death from rockfall and falling.

**Fixed gear.** Use fixed gear with caution. The high precipitation and range of temperatures in the Mid-Atlantic region accelerates the deterioration of pitons and bolts. Metal fatigue, rust, and age affect the useful life of fixed gear. Always back up fixed pieces whenever possible, and always back them up at belay and rappel stations. Never rely on a single piece of gear for your safety—build redundancy into the system so the failure of one piece will not affect the overall safety of the system. Never rappel or lower from a single bolt and don't lean straight out on a bolt—it may have been placed improperly and is just waiting to pull out! Don't trust your life to questionable anchors, worn coldshuts, or rotten rappel slings, and please don't be so cheap that you're unwilling to leave a piece of gear to safeguard your life.

**Noxious plants, bugs, and snakes.** Poison ivy, beehives and wasp nests, ticks, black flies, and poisonous snakes are all found in the Mid-Atlantic region. Poison ivy, the most common poisonous plant, causes a severe, itching reaction that can take weeks to heal. Learn to identify their shiny "leaves of three." Poison ivy often grows along the cliff base, along the access and descent trails, and often on the cliff itself. Products are available at drugstores that provide some pre-exposure protection from poison ivy. Otherwise, wear long pants and sleeves and shoes to avoid body contact. Bees and wasps live on many crags. Take note of possible hive locations and avoid them.

Ticks are tiny, blood-sucking arachnids that are often found in brush, meadows, and forests. They're usually active in spring and early summer. Ticks can carry tick fever and the more serious Lyme disease. Avoid tick-infested areas whenever possible; otherwise, wear clothing that fits tightly around the neck, ankles, waist, and wrists; use lots of bug dope; and always

*Taylor Smith on Black Crack (5.9), Annapolis Rock, Maryland.* PHOTO BY ERIC J. HÖRST

check your clothes and pack before getting into your car. Ticks usually crawl around on you for a few hours before settling down to a blood feast, so they're usually found before damage is done.

Rattlesnakes and copperheads are found at all the Mid-Atlantic climbing areas but are seldom seen. Watch out for them in boulderfields or along the cliffbase, and be especially cautious when scrambling and bushwhacking. Snakes are usually most active between May and October.

**Weather.** Lastly, keep an eye on the western sky for approaching storms. Thunderstorms can move in at up to 50 miles per hour, so it would be most prudent to bail off your route at the first sight of lightning. In cold weather, rainy or snowy conditions can lead to hypothermia. Be prepared for wet weather by carrying a good raincoat, gloves and hat, and extra clothes.

## ACCESS AND ENVIRONMENTAL CONSIDERATIONS

Rock climbers have long been a maverick bunch, doing their own thing at the crags like it was their God-given right. Now, however, climbers have a growing responsibility to minimize their impact on the rock and the surrounding environment, and realize that rock climbing is a privilege, not a right. America is a fragile landscape that is being damaged by insensitive and inconsiderate users, including loggers, miners, ranchers, mountain bikers, horsemen, rafters, and yes, rock climbers. Climbers need to focus more on preserving and protecting our many climbing areas, rather than battling over old ethics or putting up new routes at tired cliffs.

The increasing numbers of climbers in the United States are creating pressures that never existed twenty years ago. Many common climbing practices, such as bolting and aid climbing, are viewed as high-impact activities by land managers. Federal law requires land management agencies, such as the National Park Service, to protect and preserve the areas they manage. They are consequently designing comprehensive management plans that regulate recreational land uses, such as climbing, to minimize human impact and to preserve the natural resources.

Fortunately, an excellent climber-advocate organization, The Access Fund, is working with governmental agencies and private landowners to ensure that our precious crags are kept open and generally free from bureaucratic red-tape regulations. If you are not a member of The Access Fund, please consider joining. There is strength and power in numbers. We climbers need to be involved in the decision-making process regarding climbing regulations, rather than leaving it to the politicians and political appointees in Washington, D.C.

*Eric Hörst on Notch Up Another One (5.10d/5.11a), Nelson Rocks, West Virginia.*
Photo by Stewart Green

To ensure climbing freedom, we need to adopt an environmental ethic that reflects our concern and love for the rock. We need to be more sensitive and caring toward the limited rock resources and minimize our impact at the crags. We need to establish positive partnerships with landowners and land managers, as well as climbing organizations, to actively preserve our rock resources. We need to be active stewards and caretakers of our local areas—think globally, act locally—by investing in "sweat equity." Devote your time to building proper trails, restoring trampled cliffbase ecosystems, picking up trash at the crags, and replacing colored slings with muted colors.

We can begin the process by doing all the little things that add up to a big difference. Look at the various impacts that climbers have at the crags and begin mitigating them by changing your own habits. Here are a few suggestions on how you can help:

- Pick up all your trash at the crags, including cigarette butts, burned matches, tape, soda and beer cans, and candy wrappers.

- Bury human waste away from the base of the cliff, or leave it in the open where it will rapidly deteriorate. Burn your toilet paper in arid environments, or better yet, pack it out in a plastic baggie and dispose of it properly. Don't leave human feces on access trails or below routes—as unbelievable as it sounds, it does happen! And use established toilets whenever possible.

- Use existing approach and descent trails. Avoid taking shortcuts on switchbacks and causing additional erosion. Stay off loose talus and scree slopes that easily erode. Soil erosion destroys plants and ground cover. Use a longer approach or descent route to protect sensitive ecological areas.

- Do not leave cheater slings on bolts, or brightly colored slings on rappel anchors. Instead, use slings that match the rock's color. Bolt hangers should be camouflaged with paint that matches the rock.

- Respect wildlife closures. Some cliffs, like at the New River Gorge, have been temporarily closed for nesting raptors. Climbing near an active nest can cause the birds to abandon the nest.

- Practice clean camping ethics, especially when primitive camping. Put out your fire cold before leaving or going to sleep. Use a stove for cooking. Use only campsites that show signs of previous use.

- Join and contribute money and time to worthwhile climbing organizations like The Access Fund and the New River Alliance of Climbers.

**Ethics.** Ethics are at the very heart of our sport. Every climber and every area has a unique and individual ethic regarding how routes are put up, ascended, and rated, but we need to remember to disagree about ethics only to the point where the rock itself doesn't become an innocent victim of ethical wars and monstrous egos gone crazy. There have been too many "bolt wars" that solved nothing, but left irreparable damage to the crags. A schism, although now healing, has existed in American climbing for the last couple of decades between traditional climbers and sport climbers. This us-versus-them mentality benefits no one. Respect and enjoy the challenges of both schools and leave the petty ethical grievances behind.

The style employed on a route is a personal choice. How you climb is entirely up to you. There is purity, beauty, and adventure in climbing from the ground up, placing gear, route finding, leaving the topo behind, and accepting what the rock offers for both protection and technique. Most of the Mid-Atlantic region's classic routes were established in this traditional fashion. Conversely, modern gymnastic routes require working, memorizing, and hangdogging before the coveted redpoint ascent from the ground to the anchors is achieved. Toproping is a legitimate tactic on some hard routes as well as high-ball boulder problems. It not only saves the climber from a serious fall, but also saves the rock from extra bolts. Accept that there is value in both approaches to climbing.

**Bolting.** Bolting is the most controversial ethical dilemma of modern climbing, and it has played a major role in the route development at popular Mid-Atlantic areas like the New River Gorge and Summersville Lake. While bolts allow more difficult routes to be climbed in a relatively safe manner, they can also been misused. Overbolted routes are an eyesore, and they anger land managers as well as other users. In other parts of the country, crags have been subjected to bolt wars, with the offended faction either chopping or placing bolts. The placement, as well as the removal of bolts, however, doesn't solve the problem; instead it only damages the rock and creates more climbing restrictions. Common sense, dialogue between climbers, and some civility and manners go a long way toward resolving bolting issues. Many climbing areas have limitations on the placement of new bolts, while others have a bolting moratorium that allows only for the replacement of existing, unsafe anchors and bolts. Always check with land managers to learn about bolting restrictions and concerns.

The Access Fund has worked with many management agencies to resolve the use of fixed anchors (i.e., bolts) on public lands. Climbers should support the work they have done to create a broad national policy for fixed anchors on our crags. They are working to allow fixed anchors at many climbing areas, recommending that their use be determined on an area-by-area basis by climbers who rely on them for their personal safety. Climbers, not the government, should bear the responsibility for the placement and upkeep of fixed protection. The Access Fund is also working to permit the use of fixed anchors in designated wilderness areas to safeguard climbers and to minimize the impact of climbing on soils, vegetation, wildlife, and fragile environments on top of the cliffs.

Climbers who establish bolt-protected routes need to think long and hard about the bolt placement before they begin to drill. Toprope the proposed line to determine if it is indeed worthy of creation. If it is, place the bolts with a safe, yet minimalist approach. Do not place bolts next to cracks and, whenever possible, follow the natural line up the rock. Don't force the route up the hardest, most contrived path, because everyone else will surely follow the natural weakness. In the end, it really doesn't matter if a route was established ground-up or on rappel—the important thing is properly placed (and located) fixed anchors and the aesthetic qualities of the route. Don't let the ease of rap bolting lead to over-protecting the route. Finally, respect the style of other first ascent parties and don't add bolts to existing routes.

**Defacement.** Chipping and manufacturing holds is a growing problem at many American crags. As climbers push ratings higher, they aspire to climb harder routes to test their abilities. As many indoor gym climbers, often newcomers to the climbing world, spread outward from their insulated world of plywood walls and plastic holds, they see the real rock as a malleable medium ready for their route sculpting. Please don't chip or chisel any holds on natural cliffs (find a quarry and go to town). If you can't do the route with what is already there, either you aren't good enough, or that section of rock wasn't meant to be climbed.

In the quest for your own personal ethic, remember that neither the rock nor the route belongs to you. You're only a transient traveler across the vertical terrain. Be sensitive to both the cliff and the landscape, and consider each route as a precious gift for every climber to open, enjoy, and share.

# USING THIS GUIDE

The climbs in this book have been described using text, maps, photographs, and topos. A series of overview maps at the beginning of the book and more localized maps accompanying each chapter aid in locating each climbing area.

Each area's chapter includes an **Overview**, which incorporates a general description of the area; included in the Overview is a section on the area's **Climbing history.**

Next comes a section called **Trip planning information**, which includes data in the following categories:

**General description:** A summary of the area.

**Location:** A general description of where the area is located relative to the nearest town (or easily-located geographical feature).

**Camping:** The names and locations of the nearest campgrounds, including federal, state, and private campgrounds or other nearby lodgings.

**Climbing season:** A description of the best times to visit the area, including note of any conditions that should be anticipated.

**Gear:** Recommendations on what type of gear you will want at that area. Note that these are recommendations only; it's up to you to decide what gear you need to safely climb any given route.

**Fees, restrictions, and access issues:** A description of any physical, social, or managerial considerations that could affect current or future access to the area, including issues of special concern to climbers.

**Guidebooks:** A listing of any guidebooks describing the area, whether in print, out of print, or still to be published.

**Nearby mountain shops, guide services, and gyms:** A listing of those sources for gear, local beta, and instruction nearest the area being described. Complete name and address listings are included in Appendix C.

**Services:** A list of any amenities or services available at the crag or within a short distance of it.

**Emergency services:** A listing of whom to contact in the event of an emergency, as well as the name and phone number of the nearest hospital.

**Nearby climbing areas:** A list and capsule description of the nearest climbing areas, if any.

**Nearby attractions:** For non-climbing days, a list of additional points of interest.

**Finding the crags:** A brief but complete set of driving and hiking directions to the crag or crags.

The **Route descriptions** section of each chapter identifies each route numerically and lists the routes in either left-to-right or right-to-left order, whichever sequence is appropriate for clarity. Generally, the routes appear in the order they would be encountered along the usual approach route. Each description gives the route's name, its difficulty rating, a brief description of how to find the starting point, a description of the actual climb, a list of any additional gear needed, and other information considered helpful in the interests of safety. In many cases, photos or topos depict the routes being described. Multipitch routes are described pitch-by-pitch whenever possible. If a crag is very complex, or if a climbing area consists of several separate formations, the route descriptions are grouped for ease of use. A key to topo symbols used in these descriptions is located in the front of this book.

At the end of the book comes a series of **Appendices.** Appendix A is a bibliographic listing of other sources of information. Appendix B is a comparison chart of several different systems of rating climbing difficulty. Appendix C is a state-by-state listing of the names, addresses, and telephone numbers of mountain shops, guide services, and climbing gyms. Appendix D is a listing of miscellaneous climbing organizations.

An **index** at the end of the book provides page references for all routes, formations, and climbing areas, listed alphabetically.

This book covers a large and diverse region, and in several cases represents the first written description of some of the crags. Climbs vary greatly in both length and difficulty, and nature itself can create changes in routes. It is therefore inevitable that some errors will find their way into print. Although the author has personally visited and climbed on every crag described here, it is physically impossible to have climbed all the routes. Therefore, the reader should not accept all the information presented here at face value. What seems doable in print can take on a different face entirely in the field. This book is intended to direct you to climbing opportunities and give you some idea of which way to go. Beyond that, you must rely on your own skill and experience to safely make the climb. This book is not a substitute for experience and good judgment; only you can determine what you can safely do.

Although I have climbed in this region for nearly twenty-five years, a few errors or outdated information is inescapable. Climbing areas are in constant flux—access, parking, routes, anchors, grades, and descents can change. Certainly all guidebooks eventually become dated as these changes occur and new routes are developed. Fortunately, the areas in this guide are fairly "mature," so such changes will be very gradual and this guide should be useful throughout your climbing career.

Contact the author with feedback or new routes at: e-mail: Eric@Training ForClimbing.com or Internet: www.TrainingForClimbing.com.

## RATING SYSTEM

The rating system used in this guide is the time-honored Yosemite Decimal System (YDS), which, cumbersome as it is, has gained nationwide acceptance. One should note at this point that there is no absolute measure of climbing difficulty; each climb's rating is the result of local consensus. While there is a general correlation of ratings among areas, the nature of the rock and the abilities of the climbers who habituate any given area can affect that area's rating. As a result, the "moderate" routes at one area may be somewhat more difficult than their counterparts at another area; further, a muscular and acrobatic 5.10d at an area known for steep rock may seem easier or harder than a 5.10d friction climb at a slab area, depending upon the climber's past experience. For a Rating Systems Comparison Chart that compares YDS ratings with British, French, and Australian ratings, please see Appendix B.

The YDS is an outgrowth of an earlier system developed by German climber Willo Welzenbach, who described mountain travel ratings so:

**Class 1:** Easy walking, no special footwear required.

**Class 2:** Off-trail hiking requiring boots; hands occasionally used for balance.

**Class 3:** Scrambling; handholds and footholds come into play; exposure increases, making a rope a good idea for less experienced members of the party.

**Class 4:** Smaller holds and steeper terrain encountered; anchored belays are likely necessary for the safety of all members of the party. Descents may require rappels.

**Class 5:** Steeper rock, smaller holds, and the need for more specialized technique are encountered, necessitating anchored belays and the use of specialized hardware to safeguard the leader. Descents may require rappels.

**Class 6:** Rock unclimbable by use of the holds available; the party must resort to the use of specialized hardware and slings for progress (i.e., "aided," or "aid" climbing).

American climbers in the 1930s discovered that most of their climbing was "Class 5," but that there was a big range of difficulty within that class. They therefore subdivided the class into decimals to produce 5.0 to 5.9 climbs. Similarly, they determined that Class 6 was inappropriate in this system because it was not necessarily harder than Class 5, just different. They accordingly replaced the Class 6 with Class A1 to A5, which signified climbs that required direct aid.

In 1960, climbs were accomplished that were distinctly harder than 5.9, but were not "aided" climbs. The climbing community jokingly referred to these as "5.10" climbs. With the psychological and logical rating barrier broken, the former decimal-based Class 5 became an open-ended system that currently stops at 5.14. To further complicate matters, in the early 1970s, climbers in Yosemite Valley began to further subdivide routes at and above 5.10 into sub-grades of a, b, c, or d to indicate relative difficulty within the rating. We now must deal with ratings such as 5.11c, which, according to the original proponents, is as much harder than a 5.11b as a 5.9 is than a 5.8.

Most of the routes in this guide are one-pitch climbs, but some run as long as four pitches. Clearly, length has some bearing on the overall seriousness of the climbs as does the quality and quantity of protection available. Some of the routes listed include protection or danger ratings. R-rated routes possess marginal protection and a fall could result in serious injury. X-rated climbs have little or no protection, so a ground fall and death is the likely consequence of a fall.

# OLD RAG MOUNTAIN

## OVERVIEW

Old Rag Mountain (3,268 feet) is one of the highest peaks in the Blue Ridge Mountains of northern Virginia and offers breathtaking views of the Skyline Drive to the west and the Piedmont to the east. The mountain is also covered with myriad rock outcrops that offer stunning landscapes and the only major granite climbing in the Mid-Atlantic region. Well-utilized by hikers (over 100,000 people hike on Old Rag per year), this wonderful resource continues to be avoided by climbers despite its position between the densely populated I–81 and I–95 corridors. Skip Old Rag and you'll be missing some of the best climbing in the eastern United States!

If you've been climbing in the East for even a short time, odds are that you've heard about Old Rag and the long rap sheet of alleged reasons *not* to climb there: heinous approaches, major bushwhacks, snake habitat, lack of "good routes," classic climbs that are hard to find, and no good guide to the area. While there may be a bit of truth to some of these, those who diss Old Rag are either misguided or not of the make that should venture to such a wilderness climbing area.

Here are a few facts that may help dispel the above. 1) Most people use the long approach to the mountain, adding one mile and an extra 500 feet of elevation gain to the hike in—the approach from Berry Hollow, compared to Weakley Hollow, is actually not bad; 2) Climbers' trails improve a little each year, though a few areas remain difficult to reach during peak undergrowth season; 3) Over eighteen years on the mountain I've had only one close encounter with a snake—climbing during cool weather diminishes the odds of this; 4) There are more than one hundred good routes on the mountain; and 5) There are many quality routes that can be easily accessed from the main trail.

Clearly, the lack of good information about the area has caused many first-time visitors to have an excessively adventurous or even unpleasant climbing experience filled with bushwhacking and uncertain approaches. Knowing this (first hand!), I've spent more time developing this chapter than

# OLD RAG MOUNTAIN

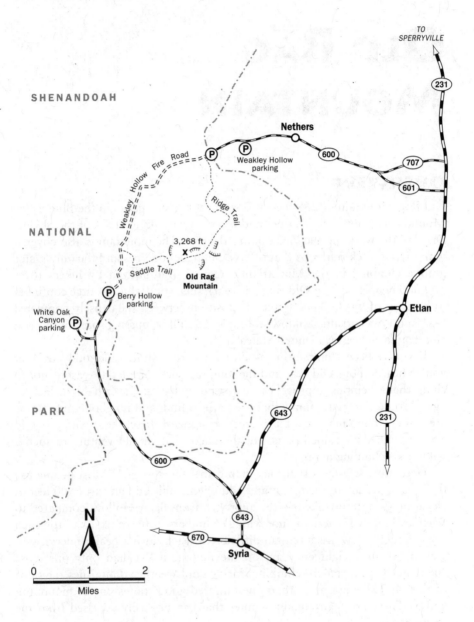

TO
SPERRYVILLE

231

SHENANDOAH

Nethers

Weakley Hollow Fire Road

P  P
Weakley Hollow
parking

600

707

601

Ridge Trail

NATIONAL

3,268 ft.
X

Saddle Trail

Old Rag
Mountain

P
Berry Hollow
parking

White Oak
Canyon
parking
P

Etlan

231

PARK

643

600

643

N

670

Syria

0        1        2

Miles

OLD RAG MOUNTAIN OVERVIEW
(EAST SIDE VIEW)

To Summit

Reflector Oven

Jabba

God's Area

Eagle's Gift

Whale's Lip

Seldom Seen Area

Wall That Dreams Are Made Of

Ridge Trail routes

Ridge Trail

Lower Ridge Trail Slab

Ridge Trail To Weakley Hollow Parking

any other in the book, and many days were spent mapping the mountain in painstaking detail to help you find—first try—the crag and route you desire to climb. This book provides overview maps, cliff topos, cliff photos, and detailed route descriptions that will hopefully allow you to confidently locate and send your route of choice.

But do be sure to come prepared when you climb on Old Rag; it is a true wilderness area, and climbing here can quickly become a drastically different experience from cragging at Great Falls or the New River Gorge. Two things to always keep in mind as you prepare for a trip to Old Rag: there is no accessible water on the mountain, and you'll drink part of your supply during the hike up, so bring a minimum of two quarts on a cool day and three quarts on a warm day; and always pack a raincoat *and* a pair of long pants—the latter will come in handy if you decide to venture to one of the more remote areas. Be sure also to bring a first-aid kit, and do everything with greater-than-usual caution—a rescue would take many hours to arrange and longer to achieve.

The mild climate of the Mid-Atlantic allows climbing at Old Rag almost year-round. The best months are February through May and October through November. Good winter climbing is possible at the southeast-facing Reflector Oven and the southwest-facing Sunset Walls areas. Best in hot weather is the north-facing Skyline (a.k.a. PATC) Wall; although many other areas, such as Sunset Walls and Summit Area, have sections that remain in the shade much of the day. Another seasonal consideration is undergrowth that becomes rampant on sunny eastern and southern exposures. Poison ivy, briars, and snakes are most common around the sunny exposures of the Whale's Lip, Eagle's Gift, Reflector Oven, and God's areas. The north- and west-facing Skyline Wall, Summit Area, and Sunset Walls seem to be more user-friendly with regard to these objective dangers.

The diverse offering of granite routes at Old Rag is an ideal training ground for Mid-Atlantic climbers planning trips to other granite areas. If you're planning a trip to New Hampshire, the Adirondacks, North Carolina, or the West, consider putting in a few days at Old Rag. There are Cannon Cliff–like cracks and corners, South Platte–like slabs, and Joshua Tree–like crystal-pinching face climbs. And all just ninety minutes from Washington, D.C.!

**Climbing history:** As with many areas in the Mid-Atlantic region, the first technical climbers at Old Rag were members of the Potomac Appalachian Trail Club. The first known roped ascents likely occurred in the 1940s, and in 1951 Arnold Wexler climbed *Jaws Chimney* (5.6) in the Reflector Oven area, the earliest named and rated climb here. Other cracks were climbed (both aid and free) during the 1950s and 1960s, and in 1970 Dieter Klose freed the classic *Strawberry Fields* (5.9+) hand crack pitch. Unfortunately, records of route names and first ascent parties for many of the moderate routes established during this period have yet to be uncovered. (Rather than listing these routes with "unknown" title, generic names have been assigned. Please contact the author if you have route name or grade information.)

Development in the 1980s resulted primary from the efforts of Greg Collins and Sandy Fleming. Sandy pioneered many impressive slab routes on the Whale's Lip and Eagle's Gift. These routes require not only friction climbing proficiency, but also a cool head. Greg Collins explored some of the more remote areas and made impressive ascents on The Wall Dreams Are Made Of, including *Bushwhack Crack* (5.10c), a 50-foot splitter hand crack that would be a classic anywhere. He also began working the steep finger crack to its right, a radical line that became known as *The The* (5.13a/b), led free in 1989 by John Bercaw.

With many of the known cracks already freed, the small number of Old Rag climbers shifted their focus to the blank faces on the mountain. From the mid 1980s to the late 1990s, approximately forty bolt-protected face routes were established; many of these were climbed with a ground-up ethic established, bolts being drilled by hand on lead, often from a desperate stance or skyhooks. Climbs established in this fashion are much more "sporty" than "sport routes," and you can credit area hardmen Eddie Begoon, Darell Hensley, Howard Clark, Bob Berger, Larry Gieb, and Sandy Fleming for many of these routes. Be prepared for long runouts between bolts, the occasional bad bolt placement, homemade or missing hangers, and rusty coldshuts. One can only hope that the most dubious-looking fixed placements will be replaced as route traffic increases; regardless, always examine everything you clip, and consider the consequences of its failure.

The vast majority of bolt-protected routes are found at the God's, Reflector Oven, and Sunset Walls areas. Some of the more recent routes, established over the last five years or so, were established as sport routes and tend to be better protected with bigger and more abundant bolts, hangers, and anchors. Rappel anchors have also been added to a handful of existing routes to facilitate descents; thus far Old Rag climbers have faithfully avoided placing bolts next to natural gear placements. Old Rag today remains a fairly serious adventure climbing area, and it is not a good proving ground for inexperienced climbers or those pushing their limits.

# TRIP PLANNING INFORMATION

**General description:** Rare Mid-Atlantic region granite climbing. Splitter cracks, corners, thin face, and slab routes up to 150 feet in height.

**Location:** Forty-five minutes south of Front Royal and just within the eastern boundary of Shenandoah National Park.

**Camping:** Camping is allowed below 2,800 feet on Old Rag Mountain, but sites can be difficult to find and a backcountry permit is required. A few good sites are located near the Old Rag Shelter and Byrd's Nest Shelter, and along the Ridge Trail when approaching from Weakley Hollow. In-season camping is tough, though, as hikers tend to capture all the sites. Backcountry camping permits are available at either the White Oak Canyon (near Berry Hollow) or Weakley Hollow parking areas. Several public campgrounds are located nearby along Skyline Drive. In the end, most climbers visit Old Rag on day-trips—its central location in northern Virginia means it's within a two-hour drive of the most highly populated parts of the Mid-Atlantic region.

**Climbing season:** February to April and September to November are ideal, although a few good climbing days are possible during each month of the year.

**Gear:** A 165-foot rope and a standard crag rack of wired stoppers, TCUs, and cams to 4 inches are sufficient for most traditional routes. Bring ten quickdraws for the mixed climbs and the handful of sport routes.

**Fees, restrictions, and access issues:** A $5.00 day-use fee is required to hike or climb on Old Rag. A ranger will collect your fee on weekends at the Weakley Hollow parking area; otherwise there is a self-pay tube located at both Berry Hollow and Weakley Hollow Trailheads. If you possess a Golden Eagle Pass, you need not pay the day-use fee. Consider making this investment ($50), as the Golden Eagle Pass allows free entry to Carderock, Great Falls, Harpers Ferry, and Old Rag, as well as all other national parks.

**Guidebooks:** No other guidebooks are available, although some route information has been published on the Internet and in a couple of climbing magazines. Greg Collins and Darell Hensley wrote articles that appeared in *Rock & Ice* magazine in 1983 and 1991, respectively. Jeff Watson's *Virginia Climber's Guide* has a brief section on Old Rag, but the information is unusable. Send new route information and corrections to the author at P.O. Box 8633, Lancaster, PA 17604 or e-mail Eric@TrainingForClimbing.com.

**Nearby mountain shops, guide services, and gyms:** Mountain Trails (540–667–0030) in Winchester, Wilderness Voyagers (800–220–1878) in Harrisonburg, and numerous shops in the Washington, D.C., area. Guide services and indoor climbing are available at Rocky Top Climbing Club (804–984–1626) in Charlottesville.

**Services:** Gasoline and some food are available in Sperryville, just fifteen minutes from the Old Rag trailheads. A full array of restaurants and other accommodations can be found forty-five minutes from Old Rag in Front Royal, Warrenton, and Charlottesville.

**Emergency services:** Call 911 or dial 800–732–0911 to report fires, accidents, and other urgent situations. The nearest hospital is Warren Memorial Hospital at 1000 North Shenandoah Avenue in Front Royal (540–636–0300).

**Nearby climbing areas:** Some so-so climbing can be found along Skyline Drive between the Thornton Gap and Swift Run Gap entrance stations. See the chapter on Skyline Drive for details.

**Nearby attractions:** Skyline Drive is the crown jewel of Shenandoah National Park. The winding 105-mile drive provides many awesome vistas that are worth more than the price of admission. The park also offers fishing, numerous beautiful picnic grounds, and hundreds of miles of hiking trails. An excellent 7.2-mile Old Rag Mountain Loop Trail begins and ends at the Weakley Hollow parking area, and provides great views (and a great workout) any month of the year.

**Finding the crags:** Locate Sperryville, the nearest small town with accommodations, on a Virginia map and navigate your way to this sleepy community. From the Washington, D.C., area, take I–66 west to Gainesville (22 miles). Exit on US 29 South and proceed to Warrenton (13 miles). Just before Warrenton, bear right to exit on US 29 Business/US 211 South. Drive through Warrenton (1 mile) and turn right onto US 211. Follow US 211 to Sperryville (28 miles).

From Sperryville, drive to one of the two Old Rag Mountain trailheads. While the Weakley Hollow parking area is most popular with day hikers, the Berry Hollow parking area provides the easiest access to most climbing areas.

**From Sperryville to Berry Hollow Parking Area and Saddle Trail:**
At Sperryville, bear left on US 522 South and go one block (0.1 mile) to a stop sign. Turn left on US 522 and go 0.6 mile to VA 231. Turn right on VA 231 and drive 9.7 miles to VA 643. Take a right onto VA 643 and continue for 4.3 miles to the intersection with VA 601. Turn right and drive the final 5.3 miles on VA 601 to the trailhead for Saddle Trail.

*Saddle Trail:*
This nice trail is devoid of the scrambling and tiring rock-hopping found on the Ridge Trail. It's also shorter, and begins a full 500 feet higher on the mountain. The car-to-summit distance is 2.8 miles with a vertical gain of about 1,760 feet. Typical hiking time to the summit is 1 to 1.25 hours. From the Berry Hollow parking area, hike up the Berry Hollow Fire Road for 0.8 mile, then bear right onto the Saddle Trail and continue for 2.0 miles to the summit. From the end of the fire road (beginning of Sadder Trail), the Saddle Trail passes the "Old Rag Shelter" at 0.4 mile and reaches the Byrd's Nest Shelter at 1.5 miles. The summit is just 0.5 mile beyond the Byrd's Nest Shelter.

**From Sperryville to Weakley Hollow Parking Area and Ridge Trail:**
At Sperryville, bear left on US 522 South and go one block (0.1 mile) to a stop sign. Turn left on US 522 and go 0.6 mile to VA 231. Turn right on VA 231 and drive 7.6 miles to a right turn onto VA 601 at Old Rag sign. Follow VA 601 for 0.3 mile and bear right onto VA 601/VA 707. Continue for 3.0 miles to the main parking area on your left. The trailhead is another 0.8 mile down the road and features a small parking lot. If you arrive early, you may find a parking space available at the trailhead; otherwise you'll need to hike

# OLD RAG MOUNTAIN—WEST SIDE

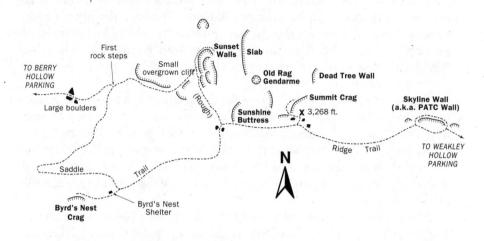

up the road the 0.8 mile to reach the trailhead. On weekends, a gate may prevent you from driving the final stretch to the trailhead.

*Ridge Trail:*

Steep and strenuous with a 2,260-foot elevation gain over 2.8 miles from the trailhead. Plus, you may need to hike the additional distance from the main parking area, making for a total approach of 3.6 miles. Depending on your pace and parking location, the hike to the Old Rag summit will take seventy-five minutes to two hours. The Ridge Trail is popular with day hikers, and you may find the parking lots and trail packed—get an early start. Although climbers have traditionally used this approach, it is faster and easier to use the Berry Hollow and Saddle Trail approach to all areas except, possibly, the Ridge Trail routes and lower Ridge Trail Slabs.

## SUNSET WALLS

This area offers a variety of traditional and sport routes up to 50 feet in length, as well as the shortest approach to roped climbing on the mountain. From the Berry Hollow parking lot, it's a reasonable 2.2-mile approach that takes less than an hour from car to crag. Ironically, Sunset Walls has not been well-traveled since it is the farthest crag from the more-popular Weakley Hollow parking area. However, Sunset possesses some great climbing, and the approach trail becomes more well-defined each year as more and more climbers become familiar with the benefits of parking at Berry Hollow. In addition to the twenty-three routes described below, there are up to a dozen

# SUNSET WALLS

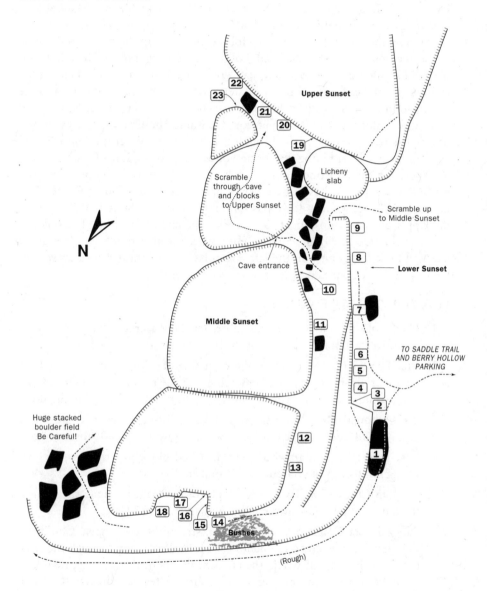

more routes located behind the Sunset Walls on a series of northwest-facing blocks and faces. One area contains several 5.11 crack climbs, including *Vice Squad,* a thin diagonal line, and a half-dozen mixed and sport routes.

**Finding the cliffs:** Park at Berry Hollow and hike up the fire road 0.8 mile to the beginning of the Saddle Trail. Follow the smooth, but steady uphill Saddle Trail about 1.2 miles to a long series of "rock steps" at a right bend in the trail. Near the beginning of the rock steps (where the main trail curves to the right), follow a faint trail on the left into the woods. In 75 yards, the trail turns uphill along a small rock outcrop. Continue uphill about 150 yards and follow the trail as it cuts left through a break in the outcrop. Another 100 yards of nearly level hiking will bring you to the base of Lower Sunset Wall.

There are three distinct tiers of rock at Sunset Walls. The approach trail leads directly to the base of Lower Sunset near *Sunset Super Crack.* Just uphill, you'll find a short 4th-Class scramble to Middle Sunset Wall. To gain the Upper Sunset climbs, locate a cave-like opening between the huge blocks on the right side of Middle Sunset. Hike back through the "cave" about 30 feet and look for a cairn on the left. From here, it's a short 4th-Class scramble to gain the Upper Sunset ledges. Proceed carefully!

## LOWER SUNSET WALL

1. **Phil's Solo** (5.10a) Climb the short, left-facing crack and corner that begins off a sloping slab left of the *Mae Day* roof (30 feet).

2. **Mae Day** (5.12a) Start under the right side of a low roof at the base of a large, right-facing corner. Undercling out the roof (stick-clip first bolt) and ascend delicate moves to finish in a short crack. 3 bolts to anchors.

3. **The Arborist** (5.6) Climb the prominent right-facing corner and crack past a small tree to ledge (35 feet). Belay or lower from anchors on right.

4. **Easy Project** (5.5) Start at a small detached block just right of the corner. Scramble up the flared crack (30 feet).

5. **No Jam Crack** (5.8) Twenty feet right of the right-facing corner, climb the left-slanting crack to the ledge and anchors (35 feet).

6. **Super Sunset Crack** (5.12c) Technical, strenuous, *and* super! Climb the thin, left-slanting crack to anchors (50 feet). Protection through the crux is extremely difficult where the crack seals. As of this writing, there are a couple of fixed stoppers and a pin. Bring a few small cams (0.5 to 1 inch) for the beginning and end of the route.

7. **Sunset Crack** (5.11b/c) Climb the hand crack near the middle of the face. The first 30 feet of this route is a classic 5.10c hand crack—the crack then ends in 15 feet of difficult face moves past a lone bolt (fortunately,

the original rusty 0.25-inch bolt has been replaced). A great lead if you're up to the 5.11 finish. Otherwise, set up a toprope through the anchors and run a lap or two. **Variation Start** (5.10a): Start 8 feet right of the hand crack and lieback up the smaller, left-slanting crack. Move on to the regular route after about 20 feet.

8. **Crystal Whipped** (5.11c) Beginning 20 feet right of *Sunset Crack,* crank up the thin face and flakes past 3 bolts to anchors.

9. **Swimming with the Karp** (5.8+) A nice warm-up with a tricky conclusion. Climb the right line of 3 bolts to shared anchors.

## MIDDLE SUNSET WALL

10. **Mosaic** (5.10b) Short, but very good! Start on blocks below a shallow, left-facing, left-leaning corner. Climb the corner to its end, then move up and right to anchors. 4 bolts.

11. **Sunburn** (5.11c/d) A technical, crystal-pinching face route. Beginning from blocks below the pretty white streak of rock, dance up the face and over the right side of the overhang to anchors. 4 bolts.

12. **Priapus Verde** (5.11a) Begin at a small, 3-foot-high, right-facing flake. Climb up past a series of flakes and 3 bolts to anchors.

13. **Sunset Gun** (5.12a/b) Power up a short, left-facing, left-slanting corner, then fire through a bulge and move right to anchors on *Priapus Verde.* 3 bolts.

14. **Project (steep flake)**

15. **Dark Side of the Moon** (5.11a/b) Good face climbing up the cool, north-facing wall on the west face of Middle Sunset. Start at the chockstone in the base of the *Frigid Air* corner and boulder up and right onto the face. Face climb along a right-slanting line of bolts, then finish back left along a low-angle arête to anchors. 4 bolts.

16. **Frigid Air** (5.8) A great lieback crack, and with natural air-conditioning! Climb the wide crack up the prominent corner to anchors on the left wall (50 feet). **Gear:** Medium to large cams.

17. **Stone Cold** (5.11?) Toprope. Climb the short, overhanging crack (sometimes wet) located just left of *Frigid Air.* Finish up along a short arête to anchors.

18. **Gone Fishing** (5.11c/d) Classic! Opposite *Dark Side of the Moon* is a nice sport route up the steep, south-facing wall. Climb along the left-slanting line of bolts to anchors. Maybe the best 5.11 face climb at Old Rag.

*Kelly Dinneen on Mosaic (5.10b), Sunset Walls, Old Rag Mountain.* PHOTO BY
STEWART GREEN

## UPPER SUNSET WALL

19. **The Streak** (5.5) Often wet. On the right side of Upper Sunset Wall is a dark waterstreak up a low-angle face. Climb on good holds along the streak, then move left to anchors above a large ledge. 2 bolts.

20. **Cliché** (5.8+) Begin 5 feet right of *Upper Sunset Crack*. Face climb up to a short crack that begins about 25 feet up. Jam up the crack to a dicey exit onto the ledge. Rappel from anchors (40 feet).

21. **Upper Sunset Crack a.k.a. *USC*** (5.6) Start on the left side of the blocky, comfy ledge below a juggy crack with a small ledge 20 feet up. Climb the crack to a stance, then work up a few awkward offwidth moves to a slabby finish (40 feet). Rappel from anchors on the large ledge.

22. **Green Face** (5.9R) Begin in the base of the large gap just left of *USC*. Climb up the vertical green face and crack located about 10 feet left of *Upper Sunset Crack* (55 feet).

23. **Charmed Life** (5.12a) One of the best sport routes of its grade at Old Rag. Start in the base of the large gap just left of *USC* and at the base of a steep, clean face opposite *Green Face*. Lieback a short, wide crack to an overhang and the first bolt. Continue up slightly overhanging and increasingly difficult moves past 3 more bolts to a ledge and anchors.

## SUMMIT AREA CRAGS—WEST FACE

There are a few roped climbs and some good bouldering near the Old Rag summit proper. The roped climbs are up to 100 feet in length and face roughly to the west. At over 3,000 feet above sea level, though, the summit of Old Rag can be up to 15 degrees cooler than the major metropolitan areas to the east. Pack a sweater or jacket when climbing here during all but the summer months.

**Finding the cliff:** From Berry Hollow, take the blue-blazed Saddle Trail all the way to the "Attention Hiking Leaders" sign at the summit. About 20 yards before this sign, walk left (west) toward the summit boulders and locate a small corridor between two boulders (the right boulder has an obvious diagonal crack). Walk through the short corridor and scramble down a short chimney. Follow a faint trail down and right about 50 yards to the cliff base.

24. **Pedestal** (5.6) Start from a square pedestal at the base of a left-facing corner. Pitch 1: Climb up past a piton to a statice on a slabby ledge. Move left and up along a large flake until you can rig a belay. Pitch 2: Wander up broken rock until you can scramble left and up to the top.

25. **Pure Fun** (5.7) Start below a 1-foot overhang with a crack about 15 feet above. Climb face and crack to lower angle rock (pin) below roof. Work through roof and up to the top.

SUMMIT AREA CRAGS

26. **Twin Cracks** (5.7) Begin up short twin cracks to black streak, then around right side of roof system to summit slabs.

27. **Groovy** (5.9) Climb a low-angle groove to a stance. Finish up a short, vertical crack.

28. **Beginner Crack** (5.4) Climb the 12-foot hand crack located near the top of the Summit Area Crags descent trail

# SKYLINE WALL

Also known as the PATC Wall, this north-facing wall is a popular refuge when it's too warm to climb at the nearby God's or Reflector Oven areas. Although there are a couple of bolted climbs, Skyline Wall is known for its numerous moderate crack climbs. The routes here are easily accessed from the Ridge Trail and can be led or toproped. Consider taping up before diving into the typically gritty granite cracks.

**Finding the cliff:** From the "Attention Hiking Leaders" sign at the summit, hike the blue-blazed Ridge Trail for about five minutes until it crosses a series of slabs and boulders—this is the top of the Skyline Wall, and you can descend at either end of the cliff. From the Berry Hollow direction, watch on your left for a huge boulder sitting on rock slabs near the beginning of the rocky section of trail. Below this boulder is a narrow, chimney-like corridor that leads

# OLD RAG MOUNTAIN—EAST SIDE

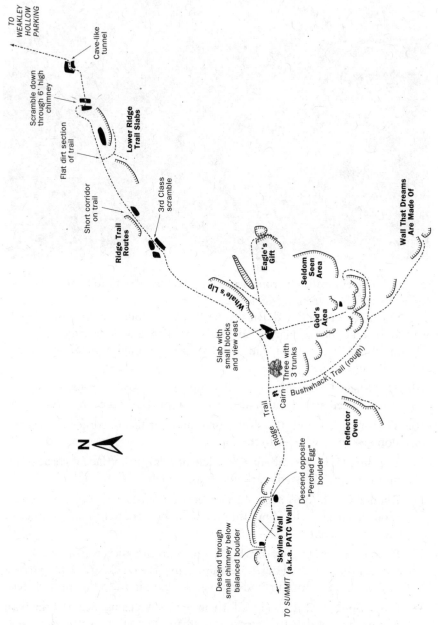

**SKYLINE WALL**

to a short descent trail. The routes are described from right to left as you walk along the cliff base from this descent.

You can also scramble down on the Weakley Hollow end of the Skyline Wall. Descend opposite a large, balanced, egg-shaped rock near the beginning of the rocky section of trail. This descent drops through a break in the cliff next to *Picture Perfect.*

29. **The Ragged Edge** (5.10c R) Recommended as a toprope. Climb the steep, jagged arête located at the bottom of the descent trail (60 feet).

30. **Thrash** (5.7) Climb the short crack and left-facing corner to a green, sloping ramp. Wander to the top.

31. **Vegemite** (5.5) Start about 8 feet left of a large, left-facing corner. Jam up the short, fist-sized crack and finish to left.

32. **Rhodey Crack** (5.6) Begin 12 feet left of a left-facing corner at a small rhododendron bush. Climb the crack and broken, right-facing corner to the top (50 feet).

33. **Piton Crack** (5.7) A worthwhile route. Start at a nice 4-inch-wide crack that leads to a slab about 12 feet up. Climb the crack and slab up to the headwall, then move up and left past several pitons to the top (70 feet).

34. **Rusty Bong** (5.8) A good lead if you have large cams. Begin at the base of a prominent, left-facing corner with an old bolt just left of the crack. Climb the crack and corner (70 feet).

35. **Fern Crack** (5.7) Beginning 20 feet left of *Rusty Bong,* jam up the hand/fist crack through a blocky roof (70 feet).

36. **Hemlock Crack** (5.9) Just right of a nice hemlock, climb the crack and finish left around a bulge to the top (75 feet).

37. **PATC Lieback** (5.8) Lieback the beautiful 25-foot crack on the right side of a large detached flake. Finish up along the bomb-bay chimney.

38. **Bombay Crack** (5.8) Scramble up gully to ascend along a serious bomb-bay chimney.

39. **Psychobabble** (5.10b) Features a nice, technical face sequence after the second bolt. Start at a shallow, left-facing corner and green crack. Work up easy moves to the first of two bolts. Continue up and left on increasingly thin moves, passing the second bolt, to shared anchors on the left (60 feet).

40. **Waste Age** (5.12a/b) Left of *Psychobabble,* wander up very thin face moves past five bolts to shared anchors below the roof (50 feet).

41. **The Dobie Gillis Route** (5.8) A Skyline Wall classic. Start at a right-facing corner with a nice crack system. Climb the crack and corner to its end (bolt), then move up and right to anchors on *Waste Age* (60 feet).

42. **Duckwalk** (5.10c) Great climbing, but a somewhat dicey lead. Start up through a low roof, then along a crack until you can work up and right to a bolt. Continue up to and through final overhang to finish on the right (90 feet).

43. **Moonshadow** (5.12?) Left of *Duckwalk* is a steep, bolted face climb. Currently all but one bolt hanger are missing. Use wired stoppers on the studs, or toprope the climb.

44. **#10 Hex Offwidth** (5.9) A good lead if you bring cams or Big Bros up to 6 inches. Start on broken rock at the base of a tall, right-facing corner and crack system. Climb the cracks and corner all the way to the top (75 feet).

45. **Crack Back** (5.8) Begin below the left side of a low, broken overhang (about 15 feet up). Climb through broken overhang and up a somewhat vegetated crack to finish up and right (70 feet).

46. **Keyhole Right** (5.6) Just right of the "keyhole" opening, lieback up the short, nice, right-facing corner.

47. **Keyhole Left** (5.5) On the left side of the "keyhole" opening, climb a short, left-facing corner to a stance 20 feet up. Wander up easy rock to the top.

48. **Picture Perfect** (5.8) Just left of the cliff break down (descent), locate an obvious, right-facing flake and cracks near the top of the face. Start

# SKYLINE WALL

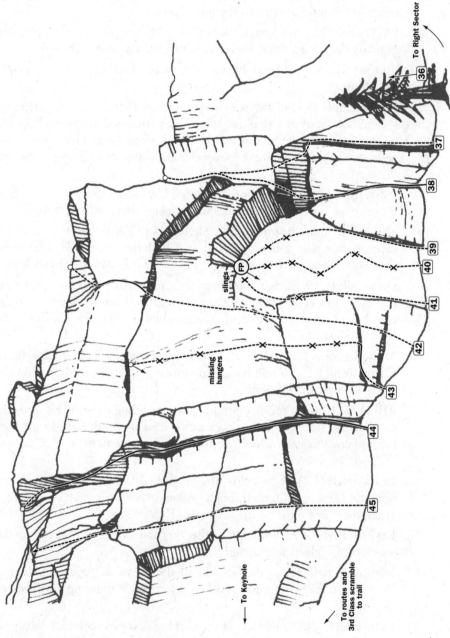

To Right Sector

36

37

38

39

40

41

42

43

44

45

FP

slings

missing
hangers

To Keyhole

To routes and
3rd Class scramble
to trail

directly below this feature on a short arête or in a left-facing corner. Climb up to a ledge with a bush, then move up to the crack above. Stretch left to reach the crack in the right-facing flake and lieback to the top (50 feet).

## REFLECTOR OVEN

Named for its southeast exposure, Reflector Oven is an excellent cold weather crag. Best known as the location of the classic *Strawberry Fields* crack, the area also possesses several other good sport and traditional lines. The cliff base becomes overgrown during the summer, so stay away from this area from May through September.

**Finding the crag:** From the "egg" on the main trail above Skyline Wall, follow the Ridge Trail downhill about 300 yards (five minutes in the direction of Weakley Hollow). The descent to Reflector Oven, Lower God's, and Bushwhack Crack areas drops off to the right at a cairn located about 25 yards before a tree with three trunks. If you come to a large slab and clearing on your right, you've gone too far. Follow the Bushwhack Trail downhill (this trail can be impossible to locate from May to early October) about 100 yards to a split. Bear right to gain the base of Reflector Oven, or follow the left branch of the trail farther downhill toward the Lower God's and Bushwhack Crack areas.

# REFLECTOR OVEN AND GOD'S AREA

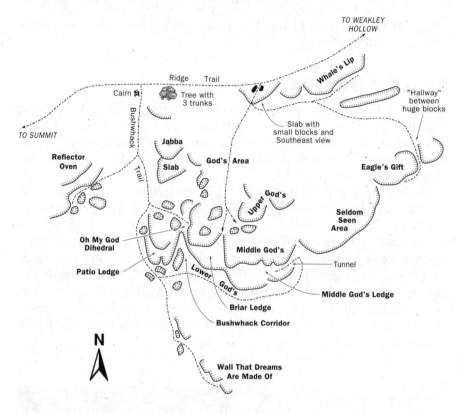

Coming from the Weakley Hollow direction, locate the large rock slab and clearing at the beginning of the descent to the Whale's Lip and Upper God's Area descent and hike uphill just about 50 yards. You'll pass a tree with three trunks, then turn left (cairn) onto a faint trail downhill. From here, the Bushwhack Trail drops downhill about 100 yards to a split. Bear right to gain the base of Reflector Oven (just another 50 yards), or follow the left branch of the trail farther downhill toward the Lower God's and Bushwhack Crack areas.

49. **The Crackin'** (5.11c/d) Start up a short, left-facing corner, then move left and fire up the nice crack to finish on the slab above.

50. **Sheds of Wonderland a.k.a. Old Duffer's Route** (5.12a) Right of the cave, climb up broken rock to reach a left-arching crack. Follow this to the break in the roof, pull through, and finish up to the slab.

51. **B & H Route** (5.11c) Start atop boulders above the cave. Climb a thin seam and face moves along a line of bolts to anchors high on the wall.

*Keith McCallister on Strawberry Fields (5.9+/5.11a), Reflector Oven.* Photo by Stewart Green

52. **Yellow Jacket** (5.11b) Begin in a large, slabby, left-facing corner. Scramble up this to attain a crack and right-facing corner. Jam it up.

53. **Mystery Move** (5.11d/5.12a) Start up the large left-facing corner as in *Yellow Jacket;* however, move left to a bolt and follow a ramp up past a couple more bolts above.

54. **Strawberry Fields** (5.9+/5.11a) A must-do classic! Climb the beautiful hand crack up to a ledge and two-bolt belay (5.9+ and 65 feet). Rap from here, or continue up the thin crack to a second set of anchors (5.11a and 35 feet). Direct Finish: **Strawberry Tart** (5.11a) Begins from the low-angle slab above the top of *Strawberry Fields*. Climb the water-streaked face past two bolts and a dirty finish.

55. **Blue Begoonias** (5.10a) Starting from a low block ledge, climb the thin, licheny crack.

56. **The Vegetated Crack** (5.7) Climb a right-slanting crack to tree.

57. **Report to Sickbay** (5.10c) Work your way up the prominent chimney and hand crack. A long and beautiful route that is unfortunately often a bit wet and dirty near the top. (100 feet)

58. **Project**—Two Bolts to Nowhere.

59. **Project**—5.13 micro face. 5 bolts.

60. **The Jaws Chimney** (5.6) Reflector Oven's first route—put up in 1951 by Arnold Wexler. Climb up the right-facing flake and chimney system. You may find this dirty and awkward.

61. **Chasm Crack** (5.10a) This route begins where the trail drops down a 15-foot chimney. From above the chimney, step across the cliff face and move left to a small stance (place gear in horizontal crack!). Move up and left to climb a crack and face to lower-angle rock.

62. **The Parker Route** (5.11b) Begin just beyond the base of the chimney where the trail drops down about 15 feet. Ascend the left-facing flake and incipient crack.

63. **Obstacle Illusion** (5.12a) Start 15 feet left of where the trail descends a chimney. Boulder up on broken rock to a small overhang, then send the line of six bolts.

## GOD'S AREA CRAGS

Named after the incredible, 60-foot *Oh My God Dihedral*, this area contains nearly a quarter of Old Rag's routes. Unfortunately for the first time visitor, the area is somewhat difficult to navigate since its climbs lie on three different tiers. See the overview topo and photo for access tips and landmarks to help locate the route of your choice. The best approach for each sub-area is

GOD'S AREA OVERVIEW

Upper God's Area

Oh My God Dihedral

Middle God's Area

Patio Routes

To Lower God's Area

Jabba The Hutt

Bushwhack Trail

described below; however, all the approach trails become choked with vegetation during the summer months. The best months for climbing at God's Area Crags are from late October through April.

## UPPER GOD'S AREA

**Finding the area:** These three routes are just a few minutes off the Ridge Trail, just beyond the Whale's Lip Slab descent. Drop off the Ridge Trail at the east-facing clearing and slab with several small resident blocks. At the lowest point on the slab, a trail into the woods will split—take the right trail, which goes straight through the woods. In about 75 yards you'll come to a series of rocky outcrops. The three routes described here are on a 45-foot, east-facing wall on the left.

64. **Don't Bother Calling Home** (5.9 R) On the left side of the face, start up a short, left-facing corner and crack. Step left and up to a bolt, then run it out up to a second bolt. Easier moves lead to the top (40 feet).

65. **The Latest Trick** (5.11c/d) The nicest and best-protected route on the wall. Climb the very thin middle section of the wall past 4 bolts to a horizontal. Continue up past a fifth bolt to the top (45 feet).

66. **Alchemy** (5.10b) Climb the arête and right face past 4 bolts to a horizontal crack. Move right and finish up a crack to the top (45 feet).

## MIDDLE GOD'S AREA—LEFT

From the Ridge Trail, descend along the Bushwhack Trail and stay left at the split. Soon you'll see the *Oh My God Dihedral* through the trees on the left. To approach the base of the dihedral, exit the main trail and scramble through a narrow hallway between boulders to gain the base of the wall. The three Patio Ledge routes are below the dihedral, so continue down the Bushwhack Trail about 50 yards to a short wall on the left. Here, you'll find the two-bolt *Toothe 'n' Nail,* or scramble over a block and walk out onto the "patio" to the start of *The Ragged Edge #2* and *Climbers in Torpor.* You can also climb up to Patio Ledge from one of the routes on the left side of the Bushwhack Corridor.

67. **Oh My God Dihedral** (5.10c) One of the best climbs in the Eastern U.S. If there's one must-do route at Old Rag, this is it! From below the dihedral, climb a 15-foot, 5.6 crack to gain a nice ledge at the base of the corner (belay here). Now, send the huge, left-facing corner and enjoy every minute of it! **Gear:** A full set of camming units from 1 to 4 inches.

## PATIO LEDGE ROUTES

68. **Toothe 'n' Nail** (5.9) Not actually on the "patio," but along the short gray wall that leads to the patio. Climb along a narrow dike past two bolts. Finish on a crack and easier rock to a ledge.

*Climbers on Oh My God Dihedral (5.10c).* PHOTO BY STEWART GREEN

# GOD'S AREA CRAG

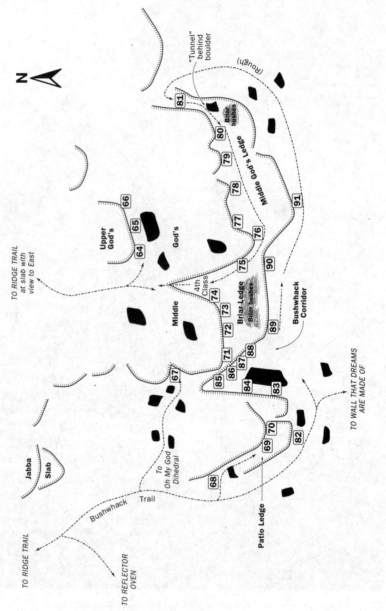

69. **The Ragged Edge #2** (5.10c) Start on the left side of Patio Ledge (near a pair of Metolius rap anchors). Climb the face just right of the arête past two bolts.

70. **Climbers in Torpor** (5.10b) Climb along the line of three bolts above the "patio."

## MIDDLE GOD'S AREA—RIGHT

There are three possible ways to approach routes beginning from the Briar and Middle God's Ledges, though neither is straighforward or easy. From the Ridge Trail, descend to the Upper God's Area routes and continue down and right a short distance to a 4th-Class downclimb along a gully to Briar Ledge. From here you can scramble around a small buttress to Middle God's Ledge. The second approach is from Lower God's Area by hiking past the farthest-right route. Scramble over a few boulders and bushwhack a short distance to a cliffbreak down between a gray slab on the right (Seldom Seen Area) and a bright orange, vertical wall above on the left. Scramble up and left to the ledge below the orange wall (the 8-bolt *Tombstone Shadow* route begins from this ledge). Walk left across the ledge and locate a narrow passageway behind a detached block. Squeeze through to Middle God's Ledge. The third option is to climb one of the routes up the right wall of Bushwhack Corridor.

## BRIAR LEDGE ROUTES

71. **God Knows** (5.11a) At the left end of the briar-covered ledge, start up slabby rock to a high first bolt. Continue up the steeper nose above past five bolts to a horizontal crack. Traverse right to the anchors on *The Untamed* (65 feet). You may want to attempt a stick clip of the high first bolt, and bring a few cams to protect the traverse. Otherwise, a nice route.

72. **The Untamed** (5.10d) Lots of great climbing, but bring a light rack of small wires and small cams for the beginning and end of the route. Climb the middle of the face past three bolts, then finish up along a flake to anchors above (55 feet).

73. **The Unchained** (5.11b/c) On the right side of the low-angle buttress, climb difficult moves to gain the first bolt (or stick clip), then finish up much easier, right-facing flake to anchors on *The Untamed* (50 feet).

74. **House Broken** (5.8) Along the left side of the gully, climb a low-angle hand crack to its end. Step left, and continue up the nose to anchors.

75. **Dayglow** (5.9+) Start up the offwidth crack on the right wall near the base of the gully. Finish up the lower-angle face above past two bolts.

## MIDDLE GOD'S LEDGE ROUTES

76. **Golden Showers** (5.9 R/X) Climb the low-angle nose of rock on the left

side of Middle God's Ledge. Hang on through steeper moves above with more poor protection (60 feet).

77. **Scared Seamless** (5.10b/c) A beautiful slab route with reasonable gear. Bring a few small stoppers and cams. Near the left side of the large ledge, slab up the face past two bolts to a nice right-facing flake. Follow this feature, then up past one more bolt to belay at slings (55 feet). Variation: **Praying Mantle** (5.9 R) After the second bolt, stay right of the prominent flake and climb straight up the face, past a series of small right-facing flakes to slings through fixed pins.

78. **Leitmotif** (5.9) Start below bush-filled offwidth cracks and boulder up and right to a small, right-facing flake. Continue up past 2 bolts to a slabby finish (40 feet).

79. **Alpenglow** (5.11a) Classic. Boulder up on blocks to left side of orange face. Move right out a horizontal crack to a bolt on the nose and continue straight up past 4 more bolts. **Direct Start** (5.12?): Not yet freed. Try to climb straight up through the bulge, past two bolts, to finish up the regular route along a line of 5 bolts (50 feet).

80. **Midlife Crisis** (5.9) On the face right of *Alpenglow,* climb up to the left side of a large roof, then move right and around the right side of the roof to the top.

81. **Tombstone Shadow** (5.11c/d) This 8-bolt line is located about 50 feet around the right side of the buttress from *Alpenglow*. A tight squeeze through a hole behind a boulder enables you to skirt a major briar patch.

## LOWER GOD'S AREA

Lower God's Area and its "bushwhack corridor" possess a number of high-quality routes in an isolated, yet comfortable, setting. Definitely worth the ten-minute approach off the Ridge Trail.

**Finding the area:** Descend the Bushwhack Trail roughly five to ten minutes to gain the left side of Lower God's Area.

82. **Vanishing Act** (5.12b/c) This bolted route is located where the Bushwhack Trail bends left to meet the Lower God Area wall. Climb the prominent, gray buttress past 7 or 8 bolts to Metolius rap anchors on Patio Ledge (70 feet). Originally rated 5.11d, many face holds have crumbled this route into the solid 5.12 range.

83. **Finger Four** (5.11d/5.12a) On the left side of Bushwhack Corridor, climb the beautiful, 25-foot finger crack to its end. Now switch gears and climb thin face moves past four bolts (55 feet).

84. **Earth Tones** (5.11c) Start behind a tree along the left wall and dance up delicate crystal moves past 3 bolts to a horizontal crack (gear). Finish up easier rock to a tree (45 feet).

85. **Bermuda Triangle** (5.9) Begin at a thin, left-slanting crack way back on the right wall of the Bushwhack Corridor. Climb the crack and small, left-facing dihedral to a triangular roof with anchors on the right.

86. **Assemblage Point** (5.11b) A short, but nice, slabby sport route. Begin left of a gross-looking crack, and climb the slabby face past 4 bolts to anchors right of a triangular roof. Provides access to left side of Briar Ledge and the Middle God's Area routes.

87. **Left Crack** (5.11a/b) Start at triple vertical seams on right wall. Boulder up to and follow the main left-slanting crack to stance and top (40 feet).

88. **Right Crack** (5.10b) Begin 5 feet right of triple vertical seams and climb up a short, left-facing flake to a good crack. Finish up into a large fracture with a bush to a ledge (40 feet).

89. **Unfinished** (5.12c) Just outside the right side of the corridor, climb the bulging face past 5 bolts to a good horizontal crack. The route ends here, so you'll need to lower from the last bolt or two. Good 5.12 face climbing to this point (45 feet).

90. **Ungodly Offwidth** (5.8+) Right of Bushwhack Corridor is an overhanging offwidth crack. Grunt up this grungy, 40-foot crack.

91. **Short 'n' Schweet** (5.9) This is the last route on the right side of Lower God's Area. Climb a slabby face with two bolts to a crack finish.

# WALL THAT DREAMS ARE MADE OF

If you dream of a pair of world-class cracks, then this wall is made for you. While the approach is Old Rag's longest (and carries a nightmarish reputation), I believe it's 100 percent worth the effort just to climb the wonderful *Bushwhack Crack* (5.10c). The approach is only passable from November through April—it's a jungle in the summer.

**Finding the crag:** Descend from the Ridge Trail via the Bushwhack Trail. Stay left at the split and continue down to Lower God's Area. From here the trail becomes increasingly faint on its way downhill—pass along the right side of a small, undeveloped crag and continue down about another 100 yards to the awesome *Bushwhack* and *The The* cracks (on left).

92. **Bushwhack Face** (5.11c) Start in the corner left of *Bushwhack Crack* and find your way up the thin face just left of the crack. Consider toproping this after sending the crack.

93. **Bushwhack Crack** (5.10c) *The* classic Old Rag splitter crack! Hand-jam through the low roof and up to a good belay ledge (50 feet).

94. **The The** (5.13a/b) This stunning, 45-foot, off-fingers crack is Virginia's *Supercrack*. Bring extra camming units in the .75 to 1.5 inch range. Note: The route can be made somewhat easier by traversing right below the roof for a rest. F.F.A. John Bercaw, 1989.

# WHALE'S LIP

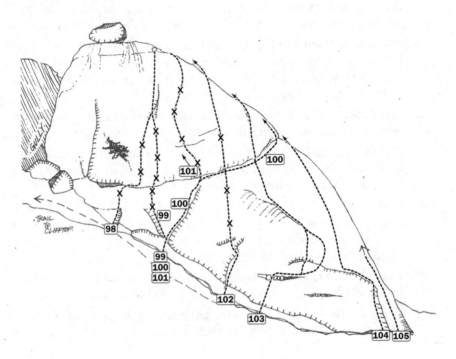

95. **Banana Crack** (5.11a) Climb the offwidth crack and corner just right of *The The.*

96. **Swan Song** (5.12a) Next to *Banana Crack,* climb the nice face and arête past 3 bolts and finish up a thin crack (crux) to the top. Bring a light rack of stoppers, TCUs, and small cams.

97. **Potato Chips** (5.11d/5.12a) Just right of the arête, climb thin edges up to finish along a dihedral.

## WHALE'S LIP

This South Platte–like granite outcrop possesses a few of Old Rag's most classic (and bold) slab routes. The fact is, a few of these traditionally established routes could be life-threatening if you blow it. The bolted routes on the left side of the wall are certainly safer, yet still a bit sporty. Make sure you're up to the grade if you take the sharp end at Whale's Lip.

    **Finding the crag:** Drop off the Ridge Trail at the east-facing clearing and slab with serveral small resident blocks above God's Area. Stroll down the slab, and upon entering the woods, immediately take the left trail downhill along the base of the Whale's Lip slab.

98. **Autumn Harvest** (5.10c) A nice climb, but bring a light rack of small-to-medium cams and stoppers. Start on a small, detached block on the left side of the face. Climb up and right past a bolt to a small overlap (place gear). Continue straight up past two more bolts to a left-facing flake and easier slab moves to top.

99. **Thar She Blows** (5.11b) Begin at a short, left-facing corner, and boulder up sporty moves to the first bolt. (Consider a long stick clip, or maybe place some gear in the *Crab Walk* flake.) Fire up past a second bolt to a horizontal crack, then up past three more bolts before stepping left to finish up the flake and slab near *Autumn Harvest*. A light rack and a good spotter would be helpful.

100. **Crab Walk** (5.8) The easiest, but certainly not most-direct, line up the Whale's Lip slab. Bring a moderate rack of small to medium gear. Start as in *Thar She Blows,* but move right as soon as possible to the obvious flake. Climb the flake to the horizontal crack, then follow the crack all the way right until you can slab up to the top.

101. **Pincer Perfect** (5.9+) This nice mixed-gear route climbs the first portion of *Crab Walk* to the horizontal crack, then fires up the face past four bolts to the top.

102. **Introspection** (5.10b) This route ascends the middle of the wall along an all-too-obvious line of homemade hangers. Start at a right-facing corner and boulder up steep moves to a stance below the first bolt. Friction up to the second bolt, move a bit right, and run up to a right-facing flake and horizontal crack. Finish up the face above past a bolt to the top.

103. **Archful Dodger** (5.9 X) Start below some wild vertical slots about 12 feet up the wall. Climb up to the slots and place what may be your best piece of gear on the climb. Now, traverse way right (below and past a shallow overhang) until you come upon more featured rock that can be followed up to the left-slanting crack above. Follow this feature left to near its end, where you can move up lower-angle rock to the top. **Direct Variation** (5.9 R/X) From the "slots" move right just a few moves, then climb straight up through the arching overlap to the slanting crack. Finish along the regular route.

104. **Another Green World** (5.7 R) Begin downhill, near the right end of the wall and climb a flake up to a tree. Traverse left to attain a cool dike, which is climbed up to the slabby finish.

105. **Sold to the Highest Buddha** (5.6) Right of *Another Green World,* climb the path of least resistance up a right-facing flake and an obvious crack to a slab finish.

WHALE'S LIP AREA OVERVIEW
(VIEW FROM NORTH)

PATC/Skyline Wall

Ridge Trail Routes

Whale's Lip

Trail

Eagle's Gift Slab

Ridge Trail Slab

# EAGLE'S GIFT SLAB

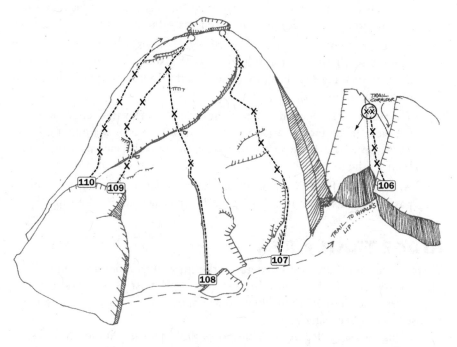

# EAGLE'S GIFT AREA

This huge, southeast-facing slab is plainly visible when viewing the Old Rag crags from VA 231. No doubt, the routes here are classic slab climbs with great position. Unfortunately, there are two major drawbacks to the area—the descent trail is usually overgrown, and worse yet, the climbs are marginally protected.

**Finding the crag:** From the large slab and east-facing clearing along the Ridge Trail, walk down the slab to the wood's edge and take the left trail, which drops downhill along the Whale's Lip wall. After about 50 yards, exit the Whale's Lip descent trail and bushwhack right around a small rock outcrop that parallels the Whale's Lip wall. Descend the vegetated hillside right of the small outcrop for approximately 100 yards until you spot a "hallway" corridor between huge blocks on the right. Pass through this corridor to gain the base of the large Eagle's Gift slab (on right).

106. **The Celebrated Crystal Crank** (5.11c) This short, 4-bolt route is on the right wall of the hallway. It appears a bit dirty and lichen-covered near the top.

107. **The Eagle's Gift** (5.10a R) Classic, but run-out, this is the first route on the right as you exit the "hallway." Start up a short, right-facing corner, then wander up the face past four well-spaced bolts to the top (150 feet).

108. **Muscle Memory** (5.11d R) Left of *Eagle's Gift,* climb up a series of right-facing flakes, past a bolt to a pin at a small overlap. Continue up the face past another bolt, then run it out a long way (past a bad bolt) to the top (150 feet).

109. **The Ally** (5.11a) Start near the right edge of an elevated ledge along the left side of the face. Start up past a bolt to a pin in the angling seam. Move up past a flake to another bolt, then up the face past two more bolts to the top.

110. **A Visit from Juan** (5.9-) Begin on the ledge left of *The Ally.* Climb up past four bolts, then run it out up a much easier slab to the top.

## RIDGE TRAIL AREA

There are several routes scattered about the small cliffs along the Ridge Trail. The two routes described below are the nicest and most obvious. Both routes are better and harder than they first appear. The descent scramble is exposed—consider using a belay.

**Finding the crag:** If you're hiking downhill from the Summit, God's, or Whale's Lip areas, locate a smooth, clean face (with a few bolts) on your left, just beyond a short downclimb on the Ridge Trail. The downhill hike from the God's and Whale's Lip area is just over five minutes, or about fifteen minutes below the Summit area.

When approaching from Weakley Hollow, the Ridge Trail Area will be the first popular climbing spot you'll come upon. The hike along the Ridge Trail takes you through a cavelike tunnel, then around the right side of a huge, box-car-size block. In another 100 yards or so, you come to a rare flat section of trail and a passage between a tall block on the left and a clean, 45-foot face (with a few bolts) on the right. The hike in is about 2.3 miles from the Weakley Hollow trailhead and about 3.1 miles from the main Weakley Hollow parking lot. Plan on a sixty- to ninety-minute approach, depending on your pace and where you park.

111. **Ridge Trail Direct** (5.12b/c) Very hard! Formerly a nice 5.11, several broken holds have increased the grade significantly. Begin on a small boulder near the left side of the face. Boulder up to an incipient crack (bolt), then continue up the face past two more bolts. Stick-clip the first bolt, and bring a 0.75-inch TCU for a slot below the second bolt.

112. **The Stud** (5.8-) Good, moderate face climbing. Start where the trail passes through the corridor between the main face and a tall boulder. Climb up past an old bolt (no hanger, so loop the stud with a wired stopper) to a flake, then up an easy crack and corner to the top.

**RIDGE TRAIL ROUTES**

# LOWER RIDGE TRAIL SLABS

This area offers the closest roped climbs to the Weakley Hollow parking lot. As with all the southeast-facing walls on the mountain, the Ridge Trail slabs provide good cool-weather climbing. However, as the farthest area from the preferable Berry Hollow trailhead, the routes are not as popular with the area's regular climbers.

**Finding the crag:** Park at Weakley Hollow trailhead and follow the Ridge Trail about 2 miles (2.8 miles from lower parking lot) to the first prominent, rocky overlook facing to the east. Continue along the Ridge Trail, through a few scramble sections, to a 6-foot downclimb into a narrow chimney. Follow the trail for roughly another 50 to 100 yards to a flat dirt section of trail. Here, a faint trail descends southeastward (left) into the woods. Follow this downhill about 75 yards, then cut right or left to access either of the two Lower Ridge Trail slab areas.

# GREAT FALLS

## OVERVIEW

Fourteen miles upriver of Washington, D.C., the Potomac River plunges over the Great Falls and races through the narrow channel of Mather Gorge. The cliffs lining the channel offer excellent climbing, particularly on the Virginia side of the river, and a breathtaking view of the falls. In addition to climbing, the park offers excellent kayaking, fishing, horseback riding, picnicking, biking, and hiking along the many miles of historic trails and canals. Entrance to the park costs four dollars per vehicle, though; regular visitors typically purchase an annual pass.

The rock type at Great Falls, Virginia, is the same schist featured at Carderock, Maryland; however, the character of the crags on the Virginia side is significantly different. The 30- to 60-foot cliffs here tend to be less featured, steeper, and, at times, they drop straight into the churning Potomac River. The climbing areas are more spread out than at Carderock and the approach to these areas is from the top, not the bottom, making routefinding a bit more difficult. All this aside, most people consider this the best climbing area in the Capital region.

There are eight distinct cliff areas that possess high concentrations of high quality routes. Included in this guide and described from the parking lot on downstream are Microdome, Dihedrals, Juliet's Balcony, Romeo's Ladder, Aid Box, Bird's Nest, Cornice, and Dr. Needlepoint. The blue-blazed River Trail wanders along the clifftop and provides easy access from one area to the next. From the parking area, the approach ranges from just five minutes to Microdome up to twenty minutes to reach Dr. Needlepoint.

Although a few climbs here allow natural protection and lead climbing, most people utilize toprope rigs and apply a "training" philosophy to their climbing activites. While the lower-angle walls of Carderock are more popular with beginner-level climbers, the high concentration of 5.8 to 5.12 routes at Great Falls is perfect for experienced climbers looking to push their limits. Diverse climbing at a wide range of difficulty levels can be found at Diherdals, Juliet's Balcony, and Romeo's Ladder areas, with classics such as *Layback Dihedral* (5.4), *Romeo's Ladder* (5.6), *Left Stuff* (5.7), *Nylons* (5.9+), and *Entropy* (5.11b). Higher concentrations of harder routes are located at Microdome, Aid Box, and Bird's Nest areas, with popular testpieces such as *Armbuster* (5.9), *Two-Lane Highway* (5.10a), *Lost Arrow* (5.10c), *Z-Slash* (5.11c/d), and *P.V.O.* (5.12b/c).

# WASHINGTON, D.C., AREA CRAGS

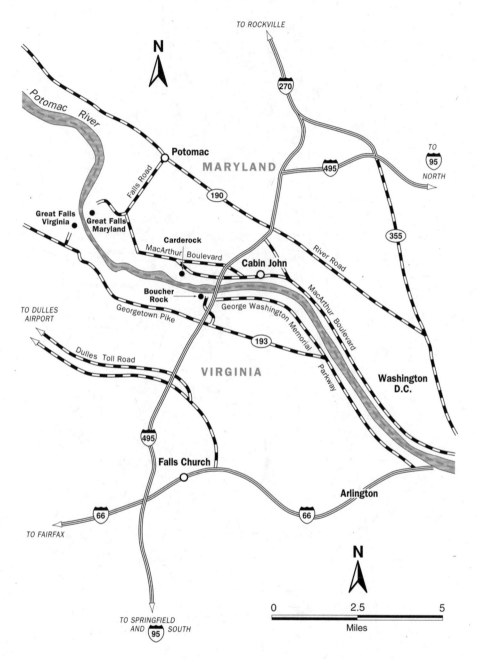

# GREAT FALLS, VIRGINIA

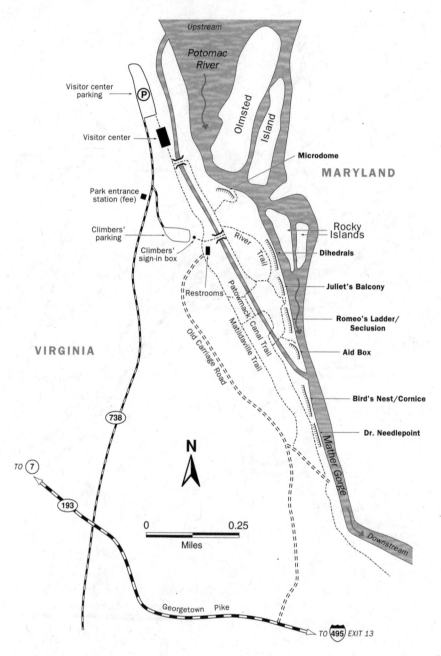

It is important to note that no climbing is allowed around the developed Overlooks, nor in the Patowmack Canal Cut. The Park Service requests that all climbers sign in upon arrival at the park. Sign-in sheets are located in the visitor centers and at the climbers' bulletin board at the lower parking lot.

**Climbing History:** The history of climbing at Great Falls, Virginia, is not well documented, though it is safe to assume that routes here were established by the same individuals who developed Carderock. Certainly in the early years, Carderock was more used than Great Falls due to ease of access and the quaint setting, which was ideal for socializing and meeting climbing partners.

A surge in climbing activity at Great Falls occurred during the 1960s and 1970s as more climbers entered the sport and some individuals sought to escape the crowds at Carderock. The spread-out nature of the climbing areas at Great Falls to this day enables a party of climbers to find their "own" section of rock, particularly when climbing during weekdays or the off-season.

Since the climbing boom of the 1980s and 1990s, Great Falls has become the premier climbing area of the region. Climbing standards were pushed deep into the 5.12 grade by a growing number of local hardmen, who spent many evenings "training" at Great Falls for weekend trips to Seneca Rocks, The Shawangunks, and the New River Gorge. Several of the Great Falls–trained climbers have gone on to climb at a world-class level on crags and mountains around the world.

# TRIP PLANNING INFORMATION

**General description:** High-quality, steep face climbing on the walls of Mather Gorge. Though a few leads are possible, toprope climbing is most popular on the smooth, 30- to 60-foot cliffs.

**Location:** Twenty minutes west of Washington, D.C., in Great Falls National Park.

**Camping:** Lake Fairfax County Park (703–757–9242) is the nearest campground. No camping is allowed in Great Falls Park.

**Climbing season:** Year-round, though climbing on many winter days can be uncomfortable, due to the cliffs' northeast orientation.

**Gear:** A few pieces of long static line or webbing is needed to set up topropes on most routes. A light rack of stoppers and cams may be needed to fortify some anchors.

**Restrictions and access issues:** Climbers are required to sign in at the lower parking lot or visitor center. Climbing is prohibited at overlook areas and the Patowmach Canal Cut.

**Guidebooks:** *Climber's Guide to the Great Falls of the Potomac* by James A. Eakin is the area's only comprehensive guide. A nice "best of" guide to Great Falls has been recently published by Marida Brinkworth.

Nearby mountain shops, guide services, and gyms: Potomac Outdoors (301–320–1544) is located at 7687 MacArthur Boulevard in Cabin John, Maryland, or there are REI stores at Bailey's Crossing, Virginia (703–379–9400) and College Park, Maryland (301–982–9681). For indoor climbing, there are three excellent options: Earth Treks (800–CLIMB–UP) in Columbia, Maryland, or the two SportRock Climbing Centers in Rockville (301–ROCK–111) and Alexandria (703–212–ROCK), Virginia.

Services: All services are available along Georgetown Pike, or nearby off the D.C. Beltway. The nearest gas station is found in the town of Great Falls, just a few miles north of the park, on Georgetown Pike.

Emergency services: Call 911. For a Park Ranger call 703–285–2966. The nearest hospital is INOVA Fairfax Oaks County Hospital (703–391–3600).

Nearby climbing areas: Just across the river there is more good climbing at Carderock and Great Falls, Maryland.

Nearby attractions: That would be Washington, D.C., located about twenty minutes to the southeast.

Finding the crags: Take the D.C. Beltway (I–495) to Georgetown Pike (exit 13). Follow Georgetown Pike about 5 miles north and turn right onto Old Dominion Drive at signs to Great Falls Park. In a little over a mile you'll come to the park entrance station. Continue straight ahead to the large visitor center parking area or make a sharp right and descend into the lower "climbers" parking lot. "Crag approaches" described herein begin from the visitor center parking area—the easiest approach to explain to first-time visitors. Please sign in with the ranger in the visitor center.

# MICRODOME

This small, 40-foot crag is the closest to the parking area. Unfortunately, it offers very little for the beginner or intermediate climber. But if you can climb 5.11, there are several worthwhile routes.

Finding the crag: Five minutes from the visitor center parking area. Take the main trail toward the "Falls Overlooks." Turn left on the path that leads to Overlook 2, then take a quick right on a smaller sandy trail that roughly parallels the river. Follow the sandy path for about 100 yards and locate the second of three faint trails that cut off to the left toward the boulderfield. (If you walk past the faint trails, you'll soon come to a forested area along the sandy trail. Turn around and walk back about 40 yards to find the faint trails.) Follow the faint path through some brush and onto a boulderfield. Angle slightly right as you cross the boulderfield. Look in the distance (toward the river) and spot two large pointed rock formations. Microdome is located directly below the left formation.

MICRODOME

**Descent:** The *Microdome Descent* (3rd Class) is located between the two pointed rock formations. The descent follows a wide crack on the right side of the left rock formation. Diagonal down and left on a series of small ledges. Continue left along the rock face to the base of Microdome.

1.  **MX** (5.11d) Strenuous. Start at the crack system near the bottom, center portion of the bulging wall section. Climb up a few moves, then traverse right on flakes under the roof until you can crank through it and finish up the crack above. Variation: **M-80** (5.10d) Instead of traversing right below the roof, climb up through the roof, then traverse right to the thin crack.

2.  **M-16** (5.11a/b) Begin as in *MX*. Climb up through the roof and continue straight up to the top.

3.  **M-1** (5.10c) Begin on the left side of the overhanging wall and climb flakes up and left to gain lower-angle rock. Wander up a faint seam to the top.

4.  **Vision Route** (5.11d/5.12a) Climb the right side of the overhanging outside corner.

5.  **B-52** (5.9+) Fire up the prominent, overhanging, left-facing corner.

6.  **B-29** (5.6) Climb the large crack on the left side of Microdome.

# DIHEDRALS

One of the more popular areas, Dihedrals is easily identified by the Mather Gorge plaque along the trail at its summit. The climbs here are up to 60 feet high and range in grade from 5.3 to 5.11. There's a little of something for everyone at Dihedrals!

**Finding the crag:** From the visitor center, follow the main trail past the overlook turnoffs and picnic area to the River Trail on your left (watch for wooden marker). Follow the blue-blazed trail through the woods for approximately 250 yards until you come to a small rock outcrop (10 feet high and 25 feet wide) immediately along the right edge of the trail. From this point, continue on the trail for another 100 yards to a rocky clearing and overlook with the Stephen Mather plaque. The plaque is directly above Route 20, *Layback Dihedral*.

**Descent:** You can scramble down on either side of the Dihedrals cliff. Go about 50 yards upstream (to your left when facing river) from the plaque to access the low-angle wall that contains Routes 7–11. The rest of the routes can be accessed via a 3rd-Class break located 25 yards downstream from the plaque.

7. **Skink** (5.8) Begin on a low-angle ramp below an upstream-facing wall with a low overhang. Climb through the right side of the low overhang and continue up a thin seam to the top.

8. **Take Five** (5.5) Begin as in *Skink*. Climb through the notch in the overhang and follow the crack on up.

9. **Overhead Smash** (5.10a) Start below the *Take Five* notch, but traverse left and climb the roof at the crack left of the notch. Finish up left side of face.

10. **The Crypt** (5.3) Start from a sloping ledge at mid-height, then climb the wide, 25-foot-high, right-facing corner.

11. **Stop the Presses, Mr. Eakin** (5.11c) Begin at a left-slanting crack directly below the large, right-facing corner. Climb up the crack, then move right under an overhang and pull it to a large, sloping ledge. Finish up the middle of the left face, between a thin crack and *The Crypt* corner.

12. **Die-Hedral** (5.10c) Climbs the wall about 35 yards upstream from the plaque. Starting on a low platform, scramble up a ramp to the second right-facing corner. Send the dihedral to the top. Using the outside edge makes this route easier.

13. **Executioner's Song** (5.8) Same start as *Die-Hedral*. Climb the ramp for a few moves, then ascend the middle dihedral to a sloping ledge. Move right and up through the left side of an overhang to the top.

DIHEDRALS

14. **R.I.P.** (5.6) Climbs the first dihedral located about 25 yards upstream from the plaque. From a low platform, step up and left to climb the right-facing dihedral to a sloping ledge. Move right to finish up another right-facing dihedral.

15. **Beginner's Chimney** (5.1) Climb the wide crack located about 20 yards upstream from the plaque.

16. **Lichen Wall** (5.4–5.7) Pick your route up the wall left of *Beginner's Chimney.*

17. **Prejudice** (5.5) Beginning just right of a small tree, climb up flakes and a shallow corner to finish about 13 yards upstream of the plaque.

18. **Pride** (5.4) Climb the hand crack and corner located about 10 yards upstream from the plaque.

19. **Ender** (5.11b/c) Located about 5 yards upstream from the plaque and just right of *Layback Dihedral.* Dance up the thin face along a small, left-slanting crack.

20. **Layback Dihedral** (5.4) A popular and quality beginners' route. Climb the prominent, low-angle dihedral located directly below the plaque. Finish right near the top.

21. **The Roll** (5.11d) Start from blocks below a dihedral capped by a large roof. Climb the dihedral, then pull hard moves out the roof along a thin crack and up to the top.

## JULIET'S BALCONY

Named for the prominent ledge at mid-height, this crag is easy to spot, thanks to this feature. A few 25-foot routes start from this "balcony," while several others climb the full length of the wall, beginning from blocks along the river.

**Finding the crag:** From the visitor center follow the Patowmack Canal Trail for eight to ten minutes until the trail splits. Take the left trail down wooden steps (the right trail crosses a small wooden bridge) to an intersection with the River Trail. Go right on the River Trail along an impressive wooden bridge over Dike Creek. Just beyond the bridge, the trail splits in three. While the main trail turns right, you want to continue straight ahead on the middle trail until you reach the clifftop. This puts you over the most upstream of the climbs. Follow the clifftop 15 yards downstream to overlook the middle of Juliet's Balcony.

**Descent:** The bases of *Epigone* and *Sciolist* are just a short scramble down on the upstream side of the cliff. The other routes are most easily reached by rappel or by descending at a 4th-Class break just downstream from the climbs. Hike downstream about 20 yards to a large boulder and descend ledges, or hike another 25 yards to a large gully.

JULIET'S BALCONY

*Lisa Ann Hörst on Left Stuff (5.7), Juliet's Balcony.* PHOTO BY STEWART GREEN

22. **Epigone** (5.6) Start on a sloping shelf below a short upstream-facing wall high above the river. Climb the obvious crack.

23. **Sciolist** (5.10d) Just left of *Epigone,* climb the incipient crack.

24. **Mantlepiece** (5.10d) Around the corner from *Sciolist,* but starting from just above the water, climb up the narrow face between the arête (right) and corner (on your left). The arête and corner are off-route.

25. **Right Stuff** (5.7) Begin on the right side of the large "balcony" ledge. Climb the thin crack and face located on the right side of the upper wall.

26. **Left Stuff** (5.7) A good lead climb or toprope. Starting from the "balcony" ledge, climb the obvious crack up the middle of the upper wall. **Gear:** Stoppers and small-to-medium camming units.

27. **Balcony Corner** (5.5) Climb the left-facing corner located just left of the *Left Stuff* crack.

28. **Backslider** (5.7) On the upstream end of the lower wall, jam the obvious crack up to the "balcony" ledge.

29. **Possibilities** (5.9) Begin just left of *Backslider* and climb the finger crack and shallow, left-facing corner up to The Balcony.

30. **Randomly Vicious** (5.10c) Begin on the left side of the lower wall, then climb the thin face straight up to The Balcony.

31. **Trellis** (5.0) Climb the gully and large, right-facing corner. Often used as a descent route by experienced climbers.

## SECLUSION AND ROMEO'S LADDER

This very popular area has a little of something for everyone. *Juliet's Balcony* (5.1) and *Romeo's Retreat* (5.0) are good beginners' routes, while *Entropy* (5.11b) and *Ergometer* (5.11c/d) are popular with the hard men and women of the region. The climbs here range from 35 to 45 feet in length.

**Finding the crag:** Use the Juliet's Balcony approach. Follow the River Trail beyond Juliet's Balcony. When the trail crosses on wooden planks, hike about 45 yards to an eroded area, and you'll see the low-angle *Seclusion* (5.7) face straight ahead. Follow the trail another 40 yards until the rocks jut out toward the river. This puts you over the middle of the Seclusion area climbs. The Romeo's Ladder routes are just a few paces farther downstream. Continue along the clifftop and you'll soon see a wide upstream-facing rock with cracks—that's *Romeo's Ladder* (5.6). The nice, flat ledge beyond this face is directly above the popular *Entropy* (5.11b) and *Oyster* (5.12a/b) routes.

**Descent:** Routes 32–40 are best reached by zig-zagging down ledges just upstream of the low-angle *Seclusion* route. Routes 41–49 can be easily reached from the downstream side. Follow the River Trail a short way and scramble down (2nd Class) from the point where the trail makes a hard right turn.

ROMEO'S LADDER

32. **Seclusion** (5.7) Begin at a crack in the lower left corner of the face. Climb this feature until it's possible to move right to climb the flaring crack to the top.

33. **Nubbin** (5.1) Climb the low-angle, river-facing wall located around the corner from *Seclusion*.

34. **Zig-Zag Edge** (5.5) Begin below the arête just left of *Nubbin*. Start up a crack until you can move left onto the arête. Trend to the left side of the arête toward the top.

35. **Stan's Lead** (5.5) From below the arête, climb up and left onto a ramp. Continue up into a large corner, which you exit right below the overhang.

36. **Sickle Face** (5.10b/c) About 20 feet left of *Zig-Zag Edge*, boulder up into a short, right-facing corner with a crack. Climb the face right of the crack, moving up and right past a sickle-shaped flake. Mantle up and continue up the face above.

37. **Snowflake** (5.6) A few yards left of *Sickle Face*, climb flakes past a right-facing corner to a finish up the crack in the corner.

38. **Flaky** (5.8) Start below a right-facing corner and flake system. Face climb up the corner and continue up the prominent flake to the top.

39. **Great Beginnings** (5.7) About 10 feet left of *Flaky*, climb pretty much straight up to reach a right-facing corner that begins near mid-height. Follow this to the top.

40. **Nylons** (5.9+) Begin below a small right-facing corner about 10 feet left of *Great Beginnings*. Climb the corner and flakes, then power through a bulge to a low-angle finish.

41. **Original Juliet's Balcony** (5.1) About 50 feet left of *Nylons* and 40 feet right of *Romeo's Ladder*, this route ascends the right side of a large, low-angle wall. Climb up and right past the left side of a small "balcony."

42. **Romeo's Retreat** (5.0) Climb anywhere up the middle of the low-angle wall. The left side of the wall is 4th Class, and is often used as a downclimb.

43. **Romeo's Ladder** (5.6) Popular. This smooth upstream-facing wall is obvious when approaching on the River Trail from the parking lots. The route follows the series of cracks up the smooth face. Climb the "ladder"!

44. **Ergometer** (5.11c/d) Around the arête from *Romeo's Ladder*, climb the thin face, always staying 8 to 10 feet left of the arête.

45. **Lunging Ledges** (5.9) Start below a hanging, right-facing corner and about 10 feet right of *Entropy*. Climb the face to a stance, then up flakes to the corner and the top.

**ROMEO'S LADDER—ENTROPY AREA DETAIL**

46. **Entropy** (5.11b) About 10 feet right of an old bolt ladder, climb the flake to a small overhang. Move left and finish on a large right-facing flake.

47. **The Demon** (5.12d) Possibly the hardest climb at Great Falls. Climb the face between *Entropy* and *Oyster.*

48. **Oyster** (5.12b/c) Climb the face along an old bolt ladder, then finish up the right-facing flake.

49. **Delivery Room** (5.5) Chimney and jam up the crack located about 10 feet left of the old bolt ladder.

## AID BOX

Aid Box is home of some of Great Falls' hardest climbs, as well as one mega-classic crack, *Lost Arrow* (5.10c). While the routes are rather short, they require good technique and lots of power. May the force be with you!

**Finding the crag:** From the visitor center, follow the Patowmack Canal Trail (through right and left bends) for ten to fifteen minutes. Just beyond Lock 1, watch for a trail on your left that crosses the canal on a small foot bridge. Just across the bridge the River Trail bends left (upstream) toward Romeo's Ladder—here you can see Aid Box on your right—scramble through the woods to the base of the crag. To approach from the Seclusion/Romeo's

Ladder area, follow the clifftop (old blue-blaze trail) about 50 yards until you see a beautiful rock "nose" with a sharp, low overhang—that's the P.V. Wall end of Aid Box.

**Descent:** From the upstream end of Aid Box, walk down below the prominent P.V. Wall.

50. **P.V. Wall** (5.12a/b) Start about 10 feet right of the low, arching overhang. Climb up the face, staying right of the overhang and left of the crack in the upper wall.

51. **P.V.O.** (5.12b/c) Stands for Potomac Valley Overhang . . . also stands for "hard route"! Climb the thin crack up to body-wrenching moves under the left side of the overhang. Pull through the left side of the overhang and finish straight up on more reasonable moves.

52. **The Strain** (5.12c) Start up either *P.V.O.* or *Lost Arrow* to access the incipient crack that runs vertically between these routes. Strain up this fine crack.

53. **Lost Arrow** (5.10c) A Great Falls classic! Climb the pin-scared crack and shallow, left-facing corner. Variation: **Terrapin** (5.11c/d) Send the route using only the crack—easier if you have small fingers.

54. **Splinters** (5.7) About 15 feet left of *Lost Arrow* and below a small, low overhang. Climb up to and along the right-facing corner.

55. **The Box** (5.5) Climb the large, right-facing corner located near the middle of the Aid Box wall.

56. **Diagonal** (5.9-) Climb the first 15 feet of *The Box*, then follow the diagonal crack up the left wall.

57. **Monkey Fingers** (5.12a/b) Start about 15 feet left of *The Box* corner and climb the thin, desperate crack.

58. **Dark Corner** (5.6) Climb the obvious corner located about 15 feet left of *Monkey Fingers*.

59. **Skid Row** (5.9) On the upstream-facing wall of *Dark Corner*, climb up about 5 feet left of the corner. Trend left toward the edge and follow the crack and flake.

# BIRD'S NEST AND CANAL CUT (LEFT)

On just about any nice day, you're bound to find a flock of rock climbers perched on the 50- to 60-foot cliffs of the Bird's Nest area—and for a good reason: there are more high-quality climbs here than any other section of Great Falls. Also, detailed below are four routes from the Canal Cut Area just a few paces upstream. Please note that rock climbing is prohibited in the Canal Cut proper.

**Finding the crag:** Take the Patowmack Canal Trail or River Trail to the plaque at Lock 2 (about a fifteen- to eighteen-minute hike). Here, the trail bends to the right away from the canal and goes into the woods. In about 200 yards the trail bends back toward the river and passes over some well-worn rocks. Keep an eye out for the "12" marker stake. Beyond and just left of this marker is a broad "point" of rock, below which are the popular *Bird's Nest* (5.7), *Plumb Line* (5.12b) and *Two-Lane Highway* (5.10a) routes. From here, Routes 60–63 are located about 40 yards upstream on the downstream end of the Canal Cut.

**Descent:** Follow the cliff edge a short way downstream until it's possible to scramble down (in the upstream direction). A sloping ramp will take you down past *Armbuster* and *Z-Slash* to the base of the *Bird's Nest.* During low water, you can scramble farther upstream to the base of *Ain't No Thing.*

60. **Ain't No Thing** (5.9) Begin on the right side of the sloping "boat ramp" ledge. Climb straight up to a cracked section of the overhang. Pull the 'hang and finish up easier rock.

61. **Ain't That Some Shit** (5.10d) This route climbs through three overhangs, beginning from the "boat ramp" below the right side of the low overhang. Crank over the first overhang (horn) and follow a flake to the second 'hang. Move through this on the right and continue up through the third overhang to easier rock.

CANAL CUT—LEFT

62. **Even Stephen** (5.9) Climb the large, right-leaning chimney.

63. **Whatever's Right** (5.11a) Ten feet left of the chimney, climb cracks up to a small ledge below the overhang. Pull through the notch on the overhang and up past the left side of a second 'hang.

64. **Face Flop'n** (5.11d) Climb the right face of the *Eagle's Nest* corner.

65. **Eagle's Nest** (5.9-) Ascend the small, right-facing corner capped by a small roof.

66. **Fair Square** (5.11d/5.12a) Not fair at all—very hard! Climb the arête located just left of the *Eagle's Nest* corner.

67. **Bird's Nest** (5.7) Very popular. Begin below a prominent corner capped by a large, triangular roof. Climb the corner, then exit right around the roof to the top.

68. **Plumb Line** (5.12b) Climb the *Bird's Nest* corner to the base of the large roof. Take a few deep breaths and crank wild moves out the middle of the roof to the top.

69. **Two-Lane Highway** (5.10a) Start on the face immediately left of the *Bird's Nest* corner. Climb the right side of the corner's left face up and around the left side of the roof. Holds in the corner are off-route.

70. **One-Lane Highway** (5.10c) About 20 feet left of the *Bird's Nest* corner and below a crack in the wall above, climb the face to a mantle move,

BIRD'S NEST

*Matt McDonald on Middle of the Road (5.11c).* PHOTO BY ERIC J. HÖRST

then continue up the crack and finish up the slab on *Shoulder of the Road*. Variation: **Middle of the Road** (5.11c) Climb *One-Lane* to the mantle move, then traverse right and climb up the middle portion of the face to finish near the top of *Two-Lane*.

71. **Shoulder of the Road** (5.9) Start just around the corner from *One-Lane Highway*, below a small right-facing corner. Climb the left face of the arête.

72. **The Man's Route** (5.8) Climb the crack up the middle of the face, beginning about 30 feet right of the *Armbuster* corner.

73. **Z-Slash a.k.a. Lightning Bolt** (5.11c/d) A great route, but don't get struck by the vicious move off the horizontal. Ten feet right of *Armbuster*, climb the face, roughly following the lightningbolt-shaped crack system.

74. **Armbuster** (5.9) Very popular and often done as a warm-up for *Z-Slash*. Climb the steep, right-facing corner and crack.

## CORNICE

Just 40 yards downriver from Bird's Nest are a few more good climbs at the Cornice area. The routes here are up to 60 feet high, with the most popular routes in and around the *Cranko* and *Tiparillo* section.

**Finding the crag:** From the #12 stake atop Bird's Nest, follow the River Trail (blue blaze) 30 to 40 yards to an eroded area on the left. From here, scramble right through a few boulders to the top of Cornice.

**Descent:** From the eroded area, continue on the trail another 50 yards downstream. Look for an upstream-facing ramp that leads down to the base of the Cornice climbs.

75. **The Nose** (5.6) Boulder up blocks to the right side of a small overhang. Pull the overhang on the right and follow the crack.

76. **Crank Up** (5.10b) Begin on a ramp below two parallel cracks in the overhanging wall. Scramble up the ramp and climb the right crack.

77. **Cranko** (5.10b) From the ramp, climb the left crack.

78. **Tiparillo** (5.11d) Follow *Cranko* to the obvious horizontal crack. Traverse left along this crack to a small overhang, then climb straight up the face above.

79. **Cornice** (5.7) Begin below the obvious, left-facing corner near the middle of the Cornice wall. Follow this weakness past two overhangs.

80. **Lawrence's Last** (5.1) Ascend the crack and chimney system to a 4th-Class finish.

CORNICE

81. **Darius Green's Flying Machine** (5.10a) Start about 10 feet left of *Lawrence's Last*. Climb on flakes up the bulging wall to a stance. Finish up the wall above.

82. **First Blood** (5.10a/b) Start below and just right of a hanging, left-facing corner. Pull up the bulging face and continue up and slightly right, passing two overhangs.

83. **Conroy Wasn't Here** (5.7) Climb the left side of the wall, using a shallow chimney and the left-facing corner above.

## DR. NEEDLEPOINT

This is the last really good climbing area at the downstream end of Great Falls. There are a few stout 5.11+ testpiece routes to attempt if you visit the Doctor. The climbs here range from 40 to 60 feet in length.

**Finding the crag:** From the top of the Cornice area, follow the trail downstream about 75 yards to the next dramatic cliff dropoff on the left. Spot a prominent, steep, upstream-facing wall—the *Dr. Needlepoint* routes and *Blitzkrieg* climb this face.

**Descent:** Just upstream of *Dr. Needlepoint Corner* there is a 5.0 downclimb that leads to the base of climbs 84–93. Beware: This is a very serious and exposed descent. The downstream routes (beyond Route 93) are easily reached via an easy scramble known as *Poison Ivy Gully*. Follow the trail downstream along the clifftop to a vegetated gully located just beyond the end of the Dr. Needlepoint cliff.

84. **Inclined Plane** (5.7) Start at an overhanging section of rock below a hidden, low-angle corner. Climb up and right to gain the low-angle face. Follow a crack up the face.

85. **A Bridge Too Far** (5.10a) Begin left of *Inclined Plane* and below a high overhang. Climb the corner and ramp to finish up the steep face left of the overhang. Variation: **Overhang Finish** (5.11d) Traverse right below the overhang until you can pull through the right side of the 'hang to finish.

86. **Conroy** (5.7) Start below a triangular overhang formed by two converging cracks. Begin up either crack, then move through the overhang and on up.

87. **Escutcheon** (5.11d) Just a couple of hard moves right off the ground. Begin at a small flake about 10 feet left of *Conroy*, then crank up the steep start and zip up to the top.

88. **Balder** (5.4) Climb the prominent, right-facing crack and corner.

89. **Wall of Da Feet** (5.8–5.9) Climb anywhere up the wall immediately left of *Balder*.

DR. NEEDLEPOINT—RIGHT

DR. NEEDLEPOINT—LEFT

90. **Dr. Needlepoint Descent** (5.0) This route follows a right-facing corner and flakes starting off tiered ledges right of the *Dr. Needlepoint* routes. Exercise extreme caution when descending this route unroped.

91. **Dr. Needlepoint Corner** (5.3) Climb the corner that defines the right side of the *Dr. Needlepoint* face.

92. **Dr. Needlepoint** (5.9) An area classic! Begin on a small ledge left of the corner, then follow the crack system up the center portion of the wall. Variation: **Crewel Work** (5.10a/b) Ascend the face using only the left crack.

93. **Royal Bobbins** (5.11c/d) Climb the face roughly midway between *Dr. Needlepoint* and *Blitzkrieg*.

94. **Blitzkrieg** (5.11d) Fire up the arête that defines the left side of the *Dr. Needlepoint* face.

95. **East Face** (5.7–5.8) Climb anywhere up the face located just right of *Last Exit* and about 50 feet left of *Blitzkrieg*.

96. **Last Exit** (5.6) Start at a left-arching crack located just right of the *Degree 101* buttress. Work up the crack, then continue up the corner and chimney.

97. **Backscratch** (5.10a/b) Begin at the right side of the *Degree 101* buttress and below a hanging, right-facing corner. Climb the steep face up to the right-facing corner and on to the top.

98. **Degree 101** (5.11d) Climb right-facing flakes and incipient cracks up the middle of the overhanging wall.

99. **Corkscrew** (5.4) Last but not least, a very good beginner's route. Starting at the left side of the buttress, wander up a series of left-facing corners.

## BOUCHER ROCKS

This outcrop lies a couple of miles downstream from Great Falls and just a stone's throw west of the I–495 bridge over the Potomac River. Although there are only a half-dozen routes, the approach is short and the rock is pretty good. Climbs are up to 50 feet high, and the area is rarely crowded.

**Finding the rocks:** Exit I–495 at Georgetown Parkway, the first exit south of the Potomac. Turn east on Georgetown Parkway (crossing over I–495) and take the first turn north on Balls Hill Road. Drive 0.4 mile and turn left on Live Oak Drive. You'll cross back over I–495 and go 1.0 mile to a dead end. Park on the right side of the road. From the right side of the turn-around circle, a PATC-maintained trail drops downhill along the highway. Follow the trail along a drainage for 150 yards until it bears left and heads upstream

along the floodplain. Hike about 200 yards, until the trail passes below the 50-foot-high Boucher Rocks crag.

1. **Seeds and Stems** (5.10b/c) Start below the huge ramp and right-facing corner. Climb the thin crack up the corner.

2. **Dancing Climb** (5.8) Scramble up to a small tree at the base of the ramp. Climb the middle of the low-angle ramp.

3. **Long Corner** (5.8) Begin from a ledge about 8 feet above the large, slabby ledge at the base of Boucher Rock. Climb the prominent crack and corner.

4. **Dirty Dancing** (5.10d) Start at a short, right-facing corner, just right of *Long Corner*. Climb the crack and flakes above to the top.

5. **Dirt Wall Direct** (5.10c) Begin 8 feet right of the short corner, then climb up and right on flakes for about 12 feet. Move right, and continue up cracks to a square ledge.

6. **Arch-Sill Start** (5.11c) At a small tree 20 feet right of *Long Corner*, power up the steep face to the ledge.

# HARRISONBURG AREA CRAGS

## OVERVIEW

Over the last twenty years, the small town of Harrisonburg, Virginia, has introduced more than its share of talented rock climbers into the regional scene. This may be partially the result of there being three colleges in Harrisonburg providing a constant stream of active young people into the area. It also helps to have a major East Coast climbing area, Seneca Rocks, close enough for single-day and weekend trips. However, as much as any other factor, the high level of climbing by Harrisonburg locals likely relates to there being four small crags in their home county, allowing quick access to regular, late-day training after school or work. Within twenty minutes of Harrisonburg are the crags of Hidden Rocks, Hone Quarry, Rawley Springs, and Chimney Rock.

The premier Harrisonburg climbing area is Hidden Rocks, located in George Washington National Forest about 12 miles west of town. Here, the 40-foot-high sandstone cliffs are very similar to the rock at the New River Gorge and offer a number of short, but quality leads and dozens of steep, thin, toprope lines. Some of the best routes include *Warmup Crack* (5.5), *Snowblower* (5.9+), *Octave Alteration* (5.10c/d), *Melonhead* (5.11b/c), and the popular leads cracks *Arm and Jammer* (5.7) and *Wham, Jam, Thank You, Ma'am* (5.8).

Just a mile and a half up the road from Hidden Rocks is the Hone Quarry Recreational Area, site of more toproping and bouldering possibilities. The largest outcrop here is Lovers' Leap, with topropes up to 45 feet on rock of varying quality. Hone Quarry also possesses a wealth of bouldering, as well as more traditional recreational activities such as fishing, swimming, and hiking.

Rawley Springs is another good area on national forest land, located just fifteen minutes west of town on US 33. Rawley Springs features dozens of small outcrops on the hillsides along Blacks Run and Gum Run, making this area a particularly popular destination for bouldering. Just a few minutes from the parking area is the Lovers' Wall and Juliet's Tower area with its thin,

# HARRISONBURG AREA CRAGS DETAIL

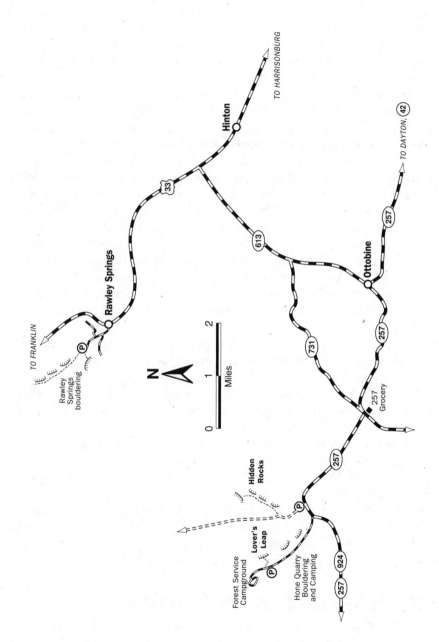

vertical faces and good landings. Still, a toprope might help increase confidence when attempting the 20-foot highball routes up Juliet's Tower.

Chimney Rock is the fourth and oldest Harrisonburg climbing area, with numerous classic climbs up an 80-foot pinnacle. Unfortunately, the crag is on private property and has been closed to climbers since 1994. While this is a significant loss to local climbers, Harrisonburg locals should still feel blessed to have so many other fine climbing areas in the vicinity.

**Climbing history:** Technical climbing began in earnest in the late 1970s and early 1980s when Mike Artz, Kris Kline, and Eddie Begoon were attending college in the Harrisonburg area. A small group of climbers and cavers explored known crags like Chimney Rock and Lovers' Leap, establishing such routes as *Monkey's Swing* (5.7) and *Mike's Prayer* (5.9). Further exploration around the Hone Quarry Recreational Area revealed copious outcrops ideal for bouldering and training, and the area's first 5.11 was soon established.

The major find of the 1980s was a broken cliff hidden on a hillside not more than a mile from Hone Quarry. Naming the area Hidden Rocks, Kline, Artz, and Begoon quickly realized the area's potential and quietly established many of the classic lines, including *Arm and Jammer* (5.7), *Wham, Jam, Thank You, Ma'am* (5.8), and *Intrados* (5.10c). By the late 1980s, Mitch Congdon, Paul Sullivan, and others joined in the new route action by adding worthy lines like *Steamroller* (5.9), *Snowblower* (5.9+), and *Sky's the Limit* (5.10b).

The small outcrops near Rawley Springs also received some action during the 1980s. Long used as a non-climber hangout, the Lovers' Wall and Juliet's Tower area was the first area developed by climbers. Since then, development has been pushed up the hillside across Blacks Run, with numerous excellent problems established by Mitch Congdon, Keith Filter, Gil Smith, and Paul Sullivan.

Over the years Chimney Rock remained a popular climbing destination; however, access problems progressively worsened until a complete closure was imposed in 1994. Since this time, Hidden Rocks has become the undisputed "best" climbing area in the region.

In 1999, longtime activist Lester Zook published *Climbing Rockingham County*. This excellent guide provides information on hundreds of routes and boulder problems in Rockingham County, and will surely help foster the growth of many new generations of Harrisonburg climbers.

# TRIP PLANNING INFORMATION

**General description:** Numerous sandstone crags offering topropes, short leads, and plentiful bouldering.

**Location:** Harrisonburg is in west-central Virginia, roughly midway between Skyline Drive and George Washington National Forest.

**Camping:** Nice, affordable camping is available in Hone Quarry. This national forest campground is self-pay, $4.00 per night.

**Climbing season:** Year-round. West-facing crags at Hidden Rocks can be good on sunny, winter days, while the shaded boulders of Rawley Springs are a cool, summer option.

**Gear:** A standard rack for leads, and a top-anchor rig of long slings and static line for toproping.

**Restrictions and access issues:** Chimney Rock is closed to climbing. The other areas are on national forest land, so all federal regulations apply.

**Guidebooks:** Lester Zook's excellent *Climbing Rockingham County* is the area's only comprehensive guidebook. Jeff Watson's *Virginia Climber's Guide* has a brief section on Hone Quarry that may or may not be of any help at deciphering this area.

**Nearby mountain shops, guide services, and gyms:** The local climbing shop and general climbers' hangout is Wilderness Voyagers (800–220–1878) at 1544 East Market Street. There are no commercial climbing gyms in Harrisonburg.

**Services:** All services are found in Harrisonburg.

**Emergency services:** Call 911 or State Police at 800–553–3144. The nearest hospital is Rockingham Memorial Hospital (540–433–4100) in Harrisonburg.

**Nearby climbing areas:** Old Rag mountain and other areas along Skyline Drive. Franklin, West Virginia, is less than an hour away, with Nelson Rocks and Seneca Rocks not far beyond that.

**Nearby attractions:** Skyline Drive is the ultimate scenic drive, plus there are many excellent trails to hike in Shenandoah National Park and the George Washington National Forest.

**Finding the crags:** All the crags are within 20 miles of downtown Harrisonburg. Driving instructions are provided at the beginning of each section.

# HIDDEN ROCKS

Hidden Rocks is the best climbing area in the Harrisonburg region, with clean, vertical faces not unlike those of the New River Gorge. You'll be sure to enjoy your time at this crag. The climbs do tend to the short side, and some could be done as highball boulder problems, given a crash pad and good spotter. However, most climbers pack a light lead rack or toprope rig and climb the longer crack and roof routes common to this area.

**Finding the rocks:** Take VA 42 South from Harrisonburg about 4 miles and turn onto VA 257 West for another 4.3 miles to Ottobine. Or, from just west of Hinton on US 33, take VA 613 South (Clover Hill Road) for 4.3 miles to Ottobine and VA 257 West. Follow Briery Branch Road (VA 257 West) for 2.8 miles to an intersection with VA 731 at the "257 Grocery" (on left). Turn

# HIDDEN ROCKS

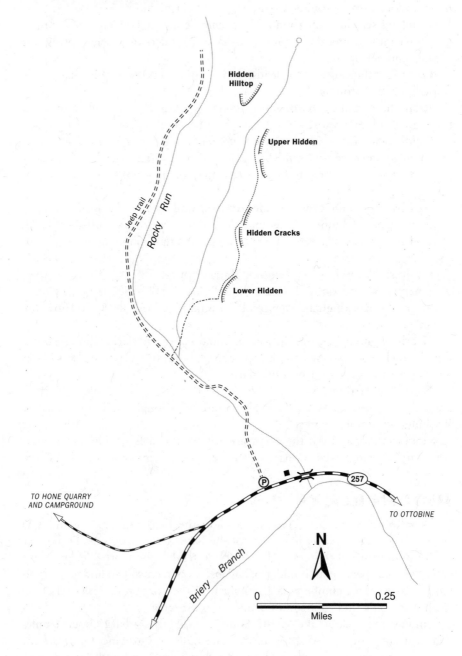

Hidden Hilltop

Upper Hidden

Hidden Cracks

Lower Hidden

Jeep trail

Rocky Run

TO HONE QUARRY
AND CAMPGROUND

P

257

TO OTTOBINE

Briery Branch

N

0          0.25
Miles

right and go 2 miles to a pulloff on the right. Park off the road, and be sure not to block the Dumpster. Be polite to the local residents as you proceed quietly into George Washington National Forest. From the pulloff, follow a trail into the woods and along a small stream. After the trail crosses the stream the third time, follow a right split off the trail and uphill about 125 yards to the Lower Hidden Rocks.

## LOWER HIDDEN ROCKS

1. **Cool Fool** (5.8) Begin from block just right of a tree. Climb the blocky face around the right side of a high overhang.

2. **Sky's the Limit** (5.10b) Start at a good bucket hold and in front of a tree with two trunks just right of *Mike and Eddie's Roof*. Climb the bulging face through a high overhang.

3. **Mike and Eddie's Roof** (5.11b) Good moves on steep rock—recommended as a toprope. Beginning below a bolt, climb through the widest part of the low roof and up to finish through the high overhang on *Sky's the Limit*.

4. **Toprope This!** (5.11b/c) Begin 6 feet right of the prominent chimney and climb through tiered overhangs to an easier finish.

5. **Rainy Day Woman** (5.9+) The *Direct Direct* variation is quite popular. Work up the large chimney to a roof, move right and up a crack and face to the top. Variation: **Rainy Day Woman Direct** (5.10b) Five feet above the roof, move back left and face climb to the top. Variation: **Rainy Day Woman Double Direct** (5.10a) Start up into the chimney, but move right under the first overhang and onto a white face. Crank straight up to finish on the regular route.

6. **Rhodey Corner** (5.8) The *Steamroller* finish is better. Climb the large, often-wet corner through an overhang and straight up. Variation: **Steamroller** (5.9) Just above the overhang, traverse 10 feet left and climb the nice, orange face to the top.

7. **Snowblower** (5.9+) The best route at Lower Hidden. Start below a bolt at the lip of a roof about 5 feet right of a wide crack through the roof. Crank through the low roof and up a left-facing dihedral, passing another bolt, to the top.

8. **Go West, Young Man** (5.11b/V2) Beginning about 25 feet left of *Snowblower*, traverse the cliff base to end at *Cool Fool*.

9. **Undercling Fling** (5.7) Climb a large, left-facing corner, past an overhang about 15 feet up, and finish up a crack.

# LOWER HIDDEN ROCKS

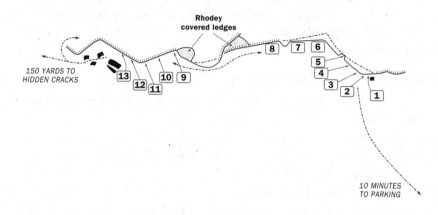

10. **Warmup Crack** (5.5) Very popular. Start up a crack in a short, left-facing corner and move around the left side of a small overhang on your way to the top.

11. **Bucketland** (5.5) Another good warm-up or beginners' route. Just right of a low "nose," commence up green, buckety rock to finish through white bulges.

12. **Lil' Bubba** (5.9) Start just left of low "nose" and work up a short right-facing corner. Continue up a smooth face and crank through blocky bulges (pitons).

13. **Inferno** (5.10b/c) Climb the obvious crack up the middle of the greenish face. Variation: **Mr. Poodlehead** (5.9+) Climb the first few feet of *Inferno* to a stance, then move left and up through an overhang and dirty rock.

## HIDDEN CRACKS—RIGHT SECTOR

14. **Green Cantaloupe Tuesday** (5.11b/c) Start 8 feet right of an obvious corner at a nice slot about 5 feet up. Face climb slots up to finish along thin cracks.

15. **Hungry as a Wolf** (5.9) Beginning 5 feet right of *Green Corner*, work up the smooth face along incipient cracks.

16. **Green Corner** (5.8) Climb the green, right-facing corner. Leadable, if dry.

# HIDDEN CRACKS

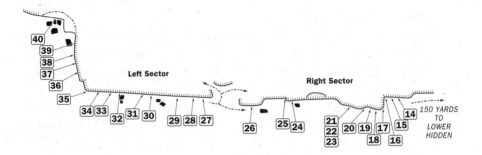

17. **EB Arête** (5.11d) Start under the right side of a low roof immediately left of *Green Corner.* Climb the steep arête.

18. **Genocide** (5.10d) Begin under a break in the low overhang just left of *EB Arête.* Climb through the weakness in the overhang, then work up and right to finish near the arête.

19. **Project X** (5.11d) Beginning a few feet right of *Hairball Jam Crack,* pull through the left side of a low overhang and ascend the smooth face above.

20. **Hairball Jam Crack** (5.7) Climb the prominent, offwidth crack.

21. **Momentary Lapse of Lichen** (5.7) Beginning from a dirty ledge about 6 feet up, climb a smooth, left-facing corner to the top.

22. **Comaraderie** (5.6) Begin as in *Momentary Lapse,* but climb straight up the face, through a concave groove near the top.

23. **Chickadee Corner** (5.4) Starting from the low ledge per *Momentary Lapse,* ascend the left-leaning crack system.

24. **Intrados** (5.10c) Begin below a nice crack up a steep face about 15 feet left of *Momentary Lapse of Lichen.* Climb the crack and overhanging face.

25. **Octave Alteration** (5.10c/d) Start at the left-facing corner just a few feet left of *Intrados.* Climb the corner through a roof and up the face above.

26. **A Bolder Move** (5.10d/V0+) Thirty feet left of *Octave Alteration,* boulder up the short, white face with fine, incipient cracks.

## HIDDEN CRACKS—LEFT SECTOR

27. **Clawin' the Wall** (5.11b/V2) Start 8 feet left of the right end of the cliff and 2 feet right of the thin *Microdigits* crack. Boulder up the incipient microcracks.

28. **Microdigits** (5.10d/V1) Start at a thin crack that makes a sharp bend left about 10 feet up. Send the thin crack to a good horizontal hold. Finish up easier moves to the top, or move left a few feet and downclimb *Doublecrack*.

29. **Doublecrack** (5.5) A popular lead. Jam up the nice, 25-foot-high twin cracks. Variation: **Epileptics Only** (5.6) Climb only using the right crack.

30. **Equilibrium Point** (5.11c) Begin 5 feet left of *Doublecrack,* at two small trees. Climb up and right along a nice crack.

31. **Fallen Boulder** (5.9) Starting just left of *Equilibrium Point,* climb a crack to a mossy ledge. Finish up a left-facing corner.

32. **The Laugh's on Me** (5.9) Beginning from the left side of a boulder, climb face moves to finish up a thin crack.

33. **Arm and Jammer** (5.7) An area classic! Climb the prominent crack that ends at a pine tree 25 feet up.

34. **Wham, Jam, Thank You, Ma'am** (5.8) Climb the left-hand crack to a stance and finish up through a juggy bulge to the top.

35. **Melonhead** (5.11b/c) Start at the left side of a smooth, white arête. Climb the arête, moving around to the right side at mid-height.

36. **Thin Cat** (5.10a) Climb the right crack up a slabby green face, then finish up through the middle of a blocky roof.

37. **Kraken** (5.9) Start at a 5-foot-high triangular flake at the base of a thin crack. Slither up the crack and through the overhang above.

38. **Pegasus** (5.11a) Begin at a thin crack about 3 feet right of a tree. Climb the crack and face to finish up a shallow, right-facing corner.

39. **Welcome to Hidden** (5.10c) Starting at a tree, climb the crack and face through bulges to the top.

40. **Project Roof** (5.12?) Begin on blocks below a huge roof. Start up a crack on the orange wall, then power out the roof . . . if you can.

# HONE QUARRY

Hone Quarry is a popular recreational area just over the hill from Hidden Rocks. Here you'll find a few crags worthy of breaking out the ropes; however, many local climbers visit the area with bouldering on their minds. If this

*Guy deBrun on Arm and Jammer (5.7), Hidden Rocks, Virginia.* PHOTO BY ERIC J. HÖRST

# HONE QUARRY—LOVERS' LEAP

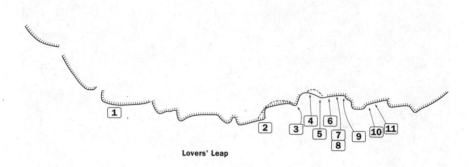

Lovers' Leap

is you, pick up a copy of Lester Zook's *Climbing Rockingham County*, which includes detailed information on bouldering at Hone.

**Finding the crags:** Take VA 42 South from Harrisonburg about 4 miles and turn onto VA 257 West for another 4.3 miles to Ottobine. Or from just west of Hinton on US 33, take VA 613 South (Clover Hill Road) for 4.3 miles to Ottobine and VA 257 West. Follow Briery Branch Road (VA 257 West) for 2.8 miles to an intersection with VA 731 at the "257 Grocery" (on left). Turn right and drive just over 2.0 miles to a sign reading "National Forest Recreational Site: Hone Quarry." Turn right onto a gravel road and go about 1.4 miles to a day-use parking pulloff on the left. Cross the road and follow the national forest trail that leads to Lovers' Leap. It's about fifteen minutes car-to-crag.

## LOVERS' LEAP

1. **Wing Ding** (5.9) On the left side of the wall, locate a large slab with a right-facing corner on its left. Climb the short crack up the middle of the face.

2. **Monkey Swing** (5.7) Beginning at a crooked tree, climb up a right-facing corner, finishing around the left side of an overhang. Variation: **Monkey Swing Roof Traverse** (5.9) Move right through the overhang, along a crack.

3. **Unnamed** (5.6) Climb the face just left of tiered overhangs.

4. **Mike's Prayer** (5.9) Start up a ramp to gain tiered overhangs. Finish out left to a ledge.

5. **Hangover** (5.8) Climb the face right of *Mike's Prayer*, staying right of the overhangs.

6. **Unnamed** (5.9) Begin at a low overhang just right of *Hangover*. Pull through the low 'hang and up easy rock.

7. **Unnamed** (5.8) Ascend along a crack system left of blocky bulges and overhangs.

8. **Unnamed** (5.8+) Climb through the blocky overhangs right of Route 7.

9. **Unnamed** (5.2) Climb easy face to the right of Route 8.

10. **Unnamed** (5.5) Climb the face left of Route 11.

11. **Unnamed** (5.6) Beginning just left of a left-facing corner, work up a few lieback and face moves.

## RAWLEY SPRINGS

Like Hone Quarry, most Harrisonburg-area climbers view Rawley Springs as primarily a bouldering destination. Detailed below is just one of a dozen out-crops in the vicinity of Rawley Springs. However, it is the most popular area and contains the classic, 25-foot Juliet's Tower block. Consider bringing a toprope to work the harder climbs on this block. A spotter will suffice for the rest of the climbs, which average 10 to 15 feet in height.

**Finding the crag:** From Harrisonburg, take US 33 west about 10 miles to Rawley Springs. Turn left onto Rawley Spring Road and drive uphill about 0.5 miles to a Y in the road (note small stone Rawley Springhouse on the left). Bear right onto Upper Rawley Springs Trail and drive another 0.4 mile to a gate and parking on the right. Across from the parking area, follow a trail less than 100 yards uphill to the base of a short, broken cliffband—this is Lovers' Wall. Take the trail right along the cliffbase to *If You Love Me,* which begins at a vertical hairline located just right of a small pine tree

### RUBBLE ROCK

This small boulder is located just downhill from Lover's Wall, along a feeder trail leading to Juliet's Tower.

1. **Rubble** (5.7) Climb up along a broken crack system.

2. **Gravel** (5.6) Climb the corner left of *Rubble.*

### LOVERS' WALL

This cliffband contains boulder problems up to 15 feet in height and of widely varying quality.

3. **If You Love Me . . .** (5.9) Boulder up along a fine crack located just right of a pine tree.

4. **Won't You Please Smile?** (5.8) Climb up past a short, shallow, left-facing corner located about 15 feet right of *If You Love Me* and just left of a pine tree.

5. **Hold Me** (5.9) Send the face roughly midway between *Won't You Please Smile?* and a large, right-facing corner.

# RAWLEY SPRINGS

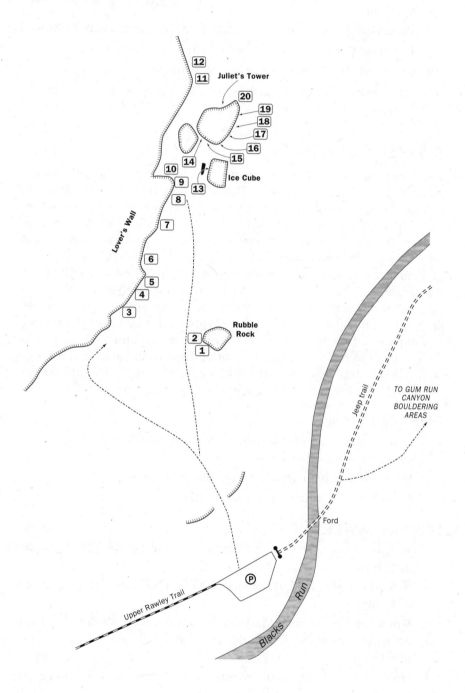

12
11
Juliet's Tower
20
19
18
17
16
15
14
Ice Cube
10
9
13
8
Lover's Wall
7
6
5
4
3

Rubble Rock
2
1

TO GUM RUN CANYON BOULDERING AREAS

Jeep trail

Ford

P

Upper Rawley Trail

Blacks Run

6. **Casual Climbing** (5.8) Boulder up, beginning a couple of paces right of a large, right-facing corner.

7. **Big Bang Theory** (5.10c) Climb up past a tiny overhang about 5 feet off the ground.

8. **I Love Your Face** (5.9) Beginning just right of a dirty gully and left-facing corner, climb up to finish near a large hemlock tree.

9. **Squeeze Me** (5.9) Fire the thin, clean face located left of an arête.

10. **Down At the Corner** (5.8) Climb the right face of the arête.

11. **Dead Zone** (5.9) Hike along the wall, past the Juliet's Tower block, until the cliff and trail bend to the left. Climb up, beginning a few feet right of a dirty, vertical crack.

12. **Mantlepiece** (5.9+) Climb up, beginning a step or two right of *Dead Zone*.

## ICE CUBE
This is a 10-foot boulder immediately adjacent to Juliet's Tower.

13. **Ice Cube Direct** (5.10b) This short problem works up between the left edge of the boulder and a pine tree on the right.

## JULIET'S TOWER
This 25-foot-high block offers the highest quality climbing on this side of Blacks Run. Many of these routes are highball, so consider bringing a short rope and some gear to set up a toprope. All the routes on the clean, steep block are worth doing.

14. **Romeo's Delight** (5.6) A classic, although short, hand crack. Occasionally led by beginners looking to practice jamming and gear placement. Climb the obvious crack up the east face of Juliet's Tower.

15. **Miller Time** (5.12) Climb the desperate face immediately right of *Romeo's Delight.*

16. **Sugaree** (5.10) Boulder up midway between *Miller Time* and the right edge (outside corner) of the east face.

17. **Peace Frog** (5.8) Climb up along the obvious weakness on the left side of the smooth, north face.

18. **Left of Hard** (5.11d) Send the face along a thin, vertical seam.

19. **Hard** (5.12a) Attempt the face just right of *Left of Hard*.

20. **Lunge Cancer** (5.10a) Climb the arête on the right side of the face.

# OTHER VIRGINIA AREAS

There are many smaller, less-developed crags in Virginia, especially along the Blue Ridge Mountains of Skyline Drive, in Jefferson National Forest, and at spots along the Appalachian Trail. Possibly the two best "other areas" are Crescent Rock in Northern Virginia and Iron Gate in the west-central part of the state. While both areas possess only a few dozen routes, the rock is high quality and definitely worth a visit if you live within an hour or two of these crags.

## CRESCENT ROCK

### OVERVIEW

Crescent Rock might be considered a "little, big area" as it packs a lot of great climbing into a cliff not more than 50 feet high and 500 feet wide. Its southwest exposure makes this a popular destination on cold, sunny days from late fall through spring. During the winter, it's quite possible that you'll hike in through a few inches of snow to find T-shirt climbing conditions at the crag.

The rock at Crescent is steep, with mostly small face holds and a few cracks. Protection tends to be sparse and the grades solid—most climbs here are between 5.9 and 5.12—so toproping is the mode of operation for most climbers. On a nice afternoon, you'll likely run into a few other groups of climbers here, so consider sharing your toprope and enjoy a good workout in a pleasant environment. Classic routes include *Crescent Crack* (5.9), *Armed Neutrality* (5.10c), *Green Duchess* (5.11b/c), *3D* (5.8/5.11c), *Crescent Rail* (5.11d), and *Popeye's Last Crank* (5.12a/b).

One minor drawback to the area is the hour-long approach along the Appalachian Trail. While this hike-in acts as a natural defense mechanism against the mass of climbers, those who do make the hike are rewarded with good climbing in a beautiful, natural environment. Similar to the approach to Annapolis Rock in Maryland, the hike-in follows a ridgeline, so there are many more flat sections than hills. Consider it a warm-up, and enjoy the view!

# CRESCENT ROCK

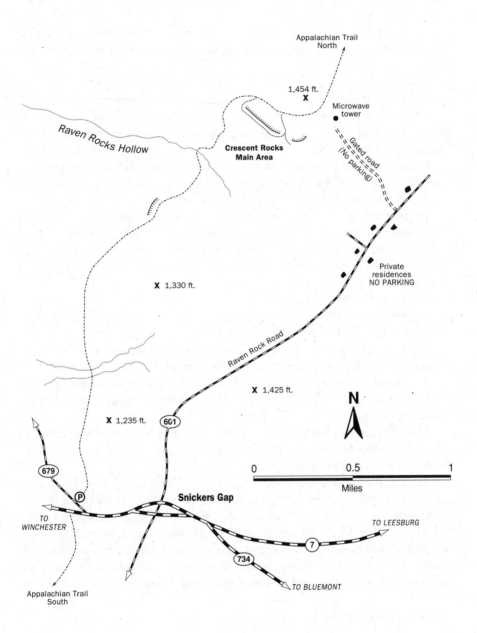

Appalachian Trail North

1,454 ft. X

Microwave tower

Raven Rocks Hollow

Crescent Rocks Main Area

Gated road (No parking)

X 1,330 ft.

Private residences NO PARKING

Raven Rock Road

X 1,425 ft.

N

X 1,235 ft.  601

0        0.5        1
Miles

679

P

Snickers Gap

TO WINCHESTER

TO LEESBURG

7

734

TO BLUEMONT

Appalachian Trail South

# TRIP PLANNING INFORMATION

**General description:** High-quality toproping and a few leads on a steep, southwest-facing, 50-foot crag.

**Location:** The crag is located where the Appalachian Trail crosses from Virginia into West Virginia, roughly midway between Winchester and Leesburg.

**Camping:** Camping is allowed along the Appalachian Trail, and there are several sites on the way in and near the crag.

**Climbing season:** Year-round, although summer afternoons are extremely hot on this west-facing cliff. However, conditions will be perfect on a sunny, winter afternoon!

**Gear:** A standard toprope rig of static line and webbing, as well as a selection of cams are useful in setting up toprope anchors. The lead climbs are mainly cracks that take stoppers and cams to 3 inches.

**Restrictions and access issues:** The only restriction relates to the approach. The "short" fifteen-minute approach from Raven Rock Road is now closed, due to lack of parking around the new private residences that were built during the 1990s. Approach the crag only via the Appalachian Trail—this will take about an hour.

**Guidebooks:** None.

**Nearby mountain shops:** Mountain Trails (540–667–0030) is located about 20 miles west of the crag in Winchester.

**Services:** All services can be found in Leesburg, Virginia (16 miles to the east) or Winchester, Virginia (18 miles to the west).

**Emergency services:** Call 911 or the State Police at 703–771–2533. Loudoun Hospital (703–858–6000) is located twenty minutes to the east in Leesburg.

**Nearby climbing areas:** Maryland Heights and Sugarloaf Mountain are about forty-five minutes to the north, while Carderock and Great Falls are roughly an hour to the southeast.

**Finding the crags:** From Leesburg, take VA 7 west about 18 miles to Bluemont. Here, VA 7 passes over a major ridge (at Snickers Gap). Take the first right turn as VA 7 begins a long, downhill stretch (when going west). There is an Appalachian Trail parking lot on the right side immediately after turning off of VA 7. Park here, and hike the AT about an hour north. Eventually, the trail will lead uphill through a burned section of forest and soon bring you to the top of the cliff. Descend on either side of the crag.

## WASHINGTON WALL

1. **Passage d'Armes** (5.11a/b) Start from the block at the far-left side of the face. Climb up the nose about 12 feet, then move right (below large bucket hold) and finish on the last few moves of *Pyrrhic Victory*.

# WASHINGTON WALL

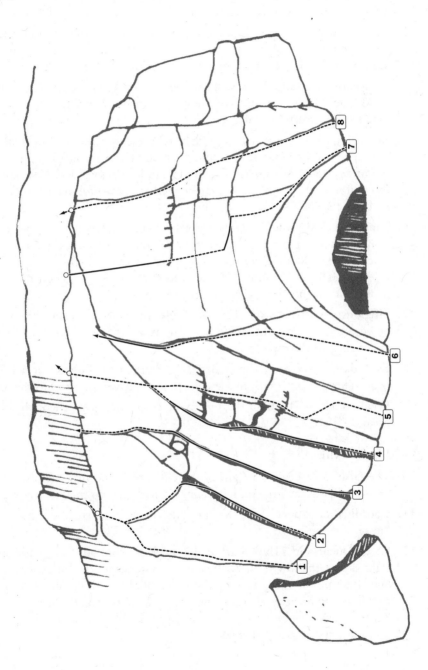

2. **Pyrrhic Victory** (5.11c) Begin partway up on the block and climb a right-slanting crack about 15 feet to a hollow-sounding (tap) flake. Move left a few moves along a faint feature and finish up to notch (20 feet).

3. **Armed Neutrality** (5.10c) Great moves on nice rock. Start about 5 feet left of hand crack at an incipient seam. Climb bouldery moves up the seam to greenish rock, then fire straight up the face to a pine tree.

4. **Crescent Crack** (5.9) An area classic. Jam up the obvious, right-slanting, hand crack. Near the top, you may want to finish straight up toward pine tree (35 feet). Leadable.

5. **Boar Hog** (5.12b) Begin 10 feet right of *Crescent Crack* below a small A-shaped overhang. Start up a thin seam on small, pocket-like openings, but after a few moves reach left to a good, left-facing edge. Now climb difficult moves up past the A-shaped overhang, then follow much better holds to the top.

6. **Popeye's Last Crank** (5.12a/b) Just left of the "crescent cave," begin in a short, shallow, left-facing corner. Climb the corner and right-slanting crack to a left-slanting crack. Finish up past a green patch to easier rock (40 feet). Direct Variation: **What's the Beef** (5.12c) Begin in the left-facing corner and climb straight up past the green patch of rock.

7. **Litigiousness Psychosis** (5.12d) Start just right of "crescent cave" and power up left- and right-facing flakes to an overhang. Move left and up easier rock to the top (45 feet).

8. **Exploding Lawyers** (5.12b/c) Begin 5 feet right of the cave at a briar bush. Thrash up the face to a green crack, which is followed to the top.

9. **Legal Crack** (5.7) Climb the blocky crack located just left of the cliff break (35 feet).

## MAIN WALL

10. **The Dish** (5.8) Begin 15 right of the cliff break and just left of a rock "nose." Climb the broken, left-facing corner, then up the face above.

11. **Coordination Street** (5.10a) Climb the crack just right of the rock "nose" (45 feet).

12. **Green Duchess** (5.11b/c) Start at the block sticking out from under the right side of the low roof. Balance up to a stance on the block, step left and climb up the ramp to a good horizontal crack. Crank up and lunge to the second horizontal crack, then continue to the top (50 feet). Direct Start: **Joker's Gambit** (5.11d) Start right of the block and climb straight up to the first horizontal crack.

CRESCENT ROCK—MAIN WALL

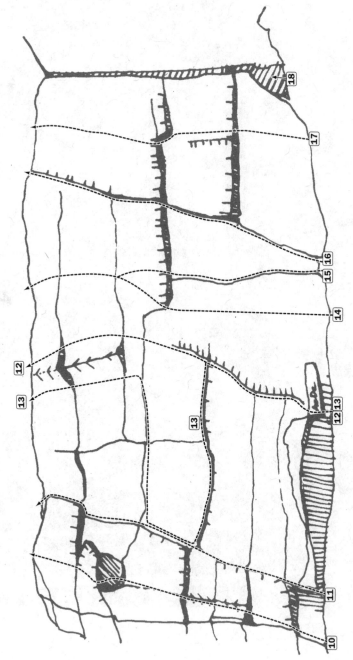

13. **Crescent Rail** (5.11d/5.12a) A real endurance testpiece! Climb *Green Duchess* to the first horizontal crack, then begin traversing left along the horizontal crack to its end. Move up to the second horizontal crack and traverse—hang on—all the way back right. Finish up to top. Consider setting up two topropes near either end of the traverse, or possibly set up a single toprope near the center of the traverses.

14. **Muddy Desperation** (5.9) Look for the dirtiest section of rock and climb it up to and around the left side of the overhang above.

15. **3D** (5.11c) Very popular, especially the left and right variations. Start below the middle of an obvious overhang. Climb straight up through the middle of the overhang to the top (45 feet). **Variation:** Climb around the crux overhang on the left (5.8) or right (5.9).

16. **Notch Johnson** (5.10b/c) Start up through a notch in a low overhang, then continue up through a larger notch to a tree.

17. **Brick in the Wall** (5.12a/b) Near the right end of the Main Wall, begin below the largest roof on the wall. Power through a low overhang (crux) to reach the middle of the second-largest roof. Follow good, horizontal buckets out the roof and then up the face above.

18. **Merde** (5.5) Begin at the base of a large, right-facing corner. Climb up the left side of the left face (40 feet). **Variation:** Climb up the right side of the face (5.2).

## RIGHT SECTOR

19. **Embarrass** (5.8) Begin left of a tree, near the center of the short, low-angle face. Climb the face, angling up and right (30 feet).

20. **Unknown** (5.10a) Start at a crack below a blunt arête and overhang. Ascend the crack in the low-angle face to a ledge. Follow the left crack through the left side of the roof above.

21. **Three Mantles and an Overhang** (5.8) Five feet right of a crack, climb the slabby face to a ledge. Finish up the right crack through the right side of the roof above (50 feet). Variation: **Twitcher's** (5.11b) From the ledge, move right to a bush under a lower roof, and pull the roof.

22. **Unknown** (5.8) Climb a short arête to a ledge, then continue up a flared crack to the top.

23. **Unknown** (5.9) Begin 5 feet right of the blunt arête and climb the face, through a small overhang, to a stance. Move slightly right and crank through the right side of the roof and up the face above.

24. **Psoriasis** (5.9) Start up the greenish face, then follow a flake and crack on up (40 feet).

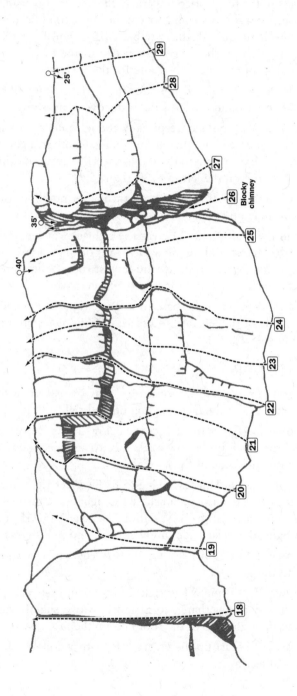

25. **Unknown** (5.9) Begin right of *Psoriasis* and below a slightly concave portion of the face. Climb up through the concave face and finish up a right-facing corner.

26. **Bird Merde** (5.6) Climb the blocky chimney (35 feet).

27. **Rockalicious** (5.10c/d) Just right of the chimney, wander up the steep arête and face to top.

28. **Ganja Piranha** (5.10d) Start below the middle of a mid-height overhang and just right of a tree stump. Boulder up to the 'hang, zig and zag up the short headwall.

29. **The Bitter End** (5.11c/d) About 5 feet right of *Ganja Piranha,* fire up through the right side of the low roof and past thin face moves to the clifftop (25 feet).

# IRON GATE

## OVERVIEW
Iron Gate is a fun little climbing area whose only crime is its close proximity to the world-class climbing areas of West Virginia and North Carolina. Located within an hour or two of Roanoke, Blacksburg, Lynchburg, and Harrisonburg, the area is perfect for a quick weekday afternoon dose of climbing as a tune-up for weekend outings to bigger and better places farther off. However, for the majority of climbers in the Mid-Atlantic region, the closest they'll likely come to this area is about 3 miles, during their drive west on I–64 to the New River Gorge.

Developed during the early and mid-1990s by Dwight Atkinson, Eric Angel, and Marshal Plymale, the hard sandstone at Iron Gate features many Gunks-like horizontal cracks and roofs, but also has the occasional loose hold or dirty bucket. Sport routes are the norm here, with many climbs requiring just a fistful of quickdraws and a 60-meter rope. However, some of the climbs have high first bolts or a few spans of natural protection, so bring some TCUs and small- to medium-sized cams to plug into the plentiful horizontal cracks.

With only thirty routes, Iron Gate is hardly a destination crag for climbers outside the local area. However, if you're passing through this part of the state, consider a short visit to sample a few of the classics such as *Happiness Is Slavery* (5.9+), *Mind Games* (5.10a), the 15-foot *Clown Attack* (5.11d) roof, *A Little Thing* (5.11d/5.12a), and the area testpiece, *Ganja* (5.12b/c).

## TRIP PLANNING INFORMATION
**General description:** Highly fractured, mainly vertical sandstone cliffs with mixed protection and sport climbs up to 90 feet.

# IRON GATE

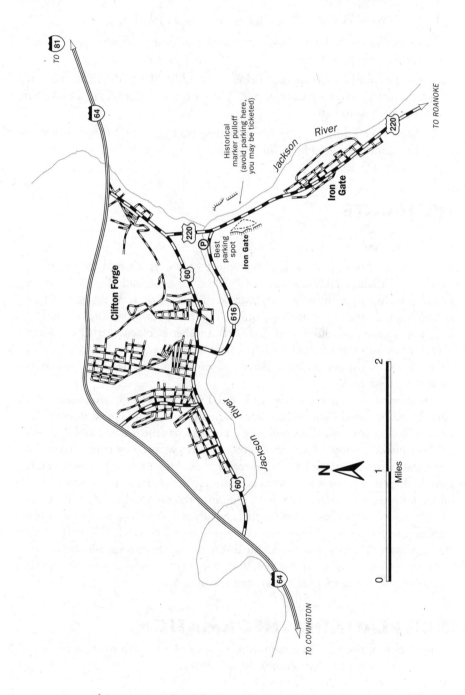

TO 81

64

Historical
marker pulloff
(avoid parking here,
you may be ticketed)

Jackson    River

220

Iron
Gate

TO ROANOKE

220

P
Best
parking
spot
Iron Gate

60

Clifton Forge

616

River

Jackson

60

64

TO COVINGTON

N

0          1          2
         Miles

**Location:** About 3 miles south of exit 27 off I–64 in west-central Virginia, and 1 mile north of the small town of Iron Gate on VA 220.

**Camping:** Ten miles north of Iron Gate along Route 629, there is camping in Douthat State Park.

**Climbing season:** Year-round, although winter can be quite windy and cold.

**Gear:** A dozen quickdraws for sport routes and a supplemental rack of stoppers and cams to 3 inches for the mixed routes.

**Restrictions and access issues:** The crags are on Forest Service land; however, there is no good parking area nearby. There are two small pulloffs along the northbound side of US 220 below the cliffs. Many climbers park in front of the historical furnace, but I've heard of one or two parties being ticketed. The best option is to drive a short distance north of the cliff, turn left onto VA 616, and park off the road immediately on the right. Hike carefully back down the southbound lane of US 220 to the approach trail.

Currently, there is no public access to the cliffs across the river. Please respect this private property by not climbing on the cliffs across from Iron Gate until access is established.

**Guidebooks:** None, other than an Internet mini-guide written by Eric Angel and Dwight Atkinson and posted on The Lynchburg Climbing Club Web site (www.lynchburgclimbingclub.com).

**Nearby mountain shops:** Blue Ridge Outdoors (540–774–4311) has a store about forty-five minutes away in Roanoke, Virginia.

**Services:** Gasoline and food can be found 1 mile south in Iron Gate, and all other services are just a few miles north in Clifton Forge or Covington, Virginia.

**Emergency services:** Call the State Police at 540–863–4416 or 540–863–2513. Stonewall Jackson Hospital (540–462–1200) is located in Lexington, about thirty minutes east on I–64.

**Nearby climbing areas:** The New River Gorge is just over an hour to the west. For some great bouldering, check out McAfee's Knob about forty-five minutes south of Iron Gate and just west of Roanoke on Catawba Mountain.

**Nearby attractions:** There are plenty of hiking, fishing, and camping opportunities in Jefferson National Forest. The beautiful Blue Ridge Parkway is less than an hour east of Iron Gate.

**Finding the crags:** Take US 220 toward the town of Iron Gate. The crags are off the west side of the road, about 1 mile north of Iron Gate and roughly 3 miles south of I–64. There are two small pulloffs directly below the cliffs on the side of US 220's northbound lane. Many climbers park in front of the historical furnace, but it's possible you could be ticketed here. The best option is to drive a few hundred yards north of the cliff, turn left onto VA 616, and park in a pulloff immediately to the right. Hike carefully back down the southbound lane of US 220 to the approach trail (across from the furnace and historical marker). Follow the trail uphill just a few minutes to the base of the cliff near *Mind Games*. A second approach/descent trail is located below *Clown Attack*—this trail is extremely loose and dangerous to both yourself and drivers on the road below. Please use only the trail located near *Mind Games*.

## FETISH WALL

1. **Almond Joy** (5.6) Begin below a gray face with a crack 25 feet right of *Black and Dekker*. Wander up the gray face to a tree. Scramble left across a ledge to anchors on *Black and Dekker*.

2. **Black and Dekker** (5.8) Start at a tree below a left-facing corner, and climb the face past 2 bolts to anchors. A few TCUs might be helpful.

3. **Sterno Inferno** (5.11c) Begin below a crack through an overhang. Climb the blocky face past 2 bolts, then pull through the roof along the cracks and finish up easier rock.

4. **Canned Heat** (5.11c) Begin under the left side of a low overhang. Face climb past a bolt and up a few sporty moves to the next bolt at the roof. Pull the roof and continue up past 4 more bolts to anchors.

5. **Happiness Is Slavery** (5.9+) Great face climbing on the upper wall. Climb blocky horizontal cracks (5.5 with a couple of cam placements) past a small overhang, then dance up the pretty face past 3 bolts to anchors.

6. **Mind Games** (5.10a) Never hard, but very sustained. A classic 5.10a! Start up an easy arête until you can move left and up the face to finish through a small overhang. 9 bolts to cold shut anchors.

7. **Superflake** (5.10a) This route climbs the right-facing flake on the upper wall, just left of *Mind Games*. Climb *Mind Games* to the fifth bolt, then move left to ascend the flake past the overhang (pin) to anchors. The route has also been climbed as an independent line beginning from ledges left of *Mind Games*. Watch out for a bit of loose rock and poor pro up the initial section.

8. **Three-Time Loser** (5.9) Boulder 30 feet up on a ledge below a large, left-facing corner. Climb the crack and corner through a roof to the top.

9. **Pretty Poison** (5.10a) A nice mixed route. Begin at the erosion-control steps and climb the blocky face (bolt) and left side of the prominent arête above. 4 bolts and a few cams to anchors.

10. **Ganja** (5.12b/c) A short, but classic, power face climb. Start just left of a green crack/corner and below a smooth, steep face with bolts. Move up easy rock (bolt) to a ledge, then fire up the white streak past 4 bolts to anchors.

# IRON GATE—RIGHT SECTOR

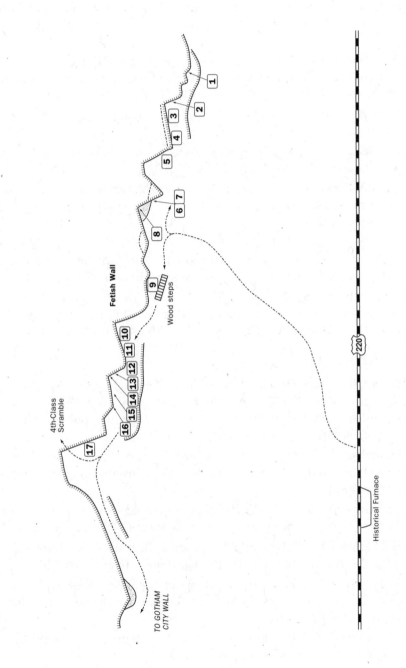

11. **A Little Thing** (5.11d/5.12a) A bouldery crack sequence—quite good! Begin just left of *Ganja* at a vertical fracture below twin cracks. Climb the crack system, staying right of the arête, and move right to anchors on *Ganja*. The toprope grade is 5.11d—it's 5.12a if you place gear on lead.

12. **The Pinch Hitter** (5.9) Begin below a blocky "nose" just right of a left-facing corner. Climb up a short arête and corners past 3 bolts to anchors on *Roasted Dude*.

13. **Roasted Dude** (5.7) Climb the thin face immediately right of the crack. 2 bolts to anchors.

14. **Leather and Latex** (5.6) Climb the obvious, left-facing corner and crack to anchors on *Roasted Dude* (35 feet).

15. **Get the Funk Up** (5.10c) Begin 10 feet left of *Leather and Latex*, and climb the blocky crack to a nice, grooved face. 2 bolts and a couple of TCUs to anchors.

16. **The Catwoman** (5.7) Begin just left of *Get the Funk Up* and climb the right side of the arête until you can move left and finish up a slabby face. 2 bolts and a few trad pieces. Lower from anchors on *Get the Funk Up*.

17. **Whiney Butt** (5.6) What could be more popular than a 5.6 sport route? A good first lead climb. Climb the 30-foot bolted face located just right of the 4th-Class clifftop access. 4 bolts to Metolius anchors.

## GOTHAM WALL

18. **Dead Girls Don't Say No** (5.10a) The farthest-right climb on Gotham Wall, this bolted line is located about 100 yards left of *Whiney Butt*. Climb the face just right of a large, loose-looking roof. 4 bolts to anchors just above an overhang.

19. **Dead and Bloated** (5.10a) Begin on the left side of a low, chossy roof 25 feet left of *Dead Girls*. Climb the nice, gently overhanging face past 4 bolts to anchors.

20. **The Dark Knight** (5.9) Start below a low, rectangular overhang about 12 feet up. Climb the face past 2 bolts to anchors. Bring a few TCUs.

21. **Riddle Me This** (5.10a) Boulder about 20 feet up to a decent belay ledge. Now, climb the nice face through a bulge to anchors. 4 bolts.

22. **Vicki Vail** (5.10c) Begin at a crack system right of a roof 20 feet up. Climb easy crack moves through the roof and up the face to anchors above a small overhang.

23. **The Joker** (5.9) Fifteen feet left of *Vicki Vail*, climb the face on the left side of a roof. 5 bolts to anchors.

# IRON GATE—LEFT SECTOR

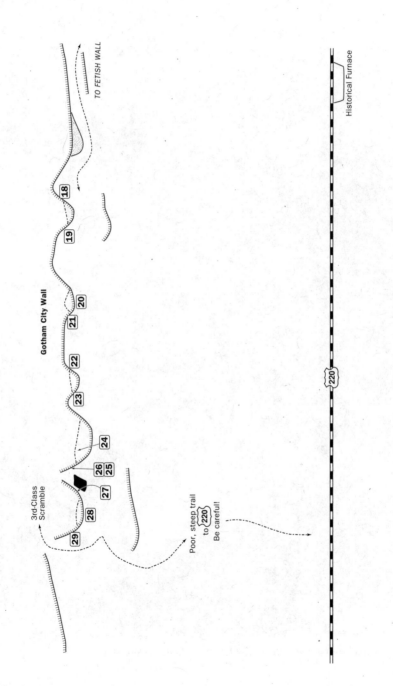

*Eric Angel on Clown Attack (5.11d), Iron Gate.* PHOTO BY ERIC J. HÖRST

24. **Clown Attack** (5.11d) Absolutely classic! The crux reach/lunge to the lip is harder for folks under about 5'10". Climb out the 15-foot roof and up to anchors. 6 bolts.

25. **The Joke's on You** (5.10c) Start up the face left of *Clown Attack,* then traverse right above the roof to climb the arête to the top. 4 bolts.

26. **Big Red** (5.9) Climb straight up the face just left of *Clown Attack.* 4 bolts to anchors.

27. **The Riddler** (5.9-) Beginning from a large block, climb the slabby face past 3 bolts to anchors.

28. **Chopper Chicks** (5.10b) Scramble up to a bolt under the low roof, then continue up a small, right-facing corner to the top. Bring a light rack of stoppers and small cams.

29. **Bip Bap Boom** (5.10b) Short, sustained, and worthwhile. Begin around the left side of a low roof about 40 feet left of *Clown Attack.* Climb the slightly overhanging, 25-foot orange face. 3 bolts to anchors.

# SKYLINE DRIVE

## OVERVIEW

There is a multitude of boulders, small cliffs, and craggy canyons along Skyline Drive in Shenandoah National Park. While these areas have been extensively explored over the last fifty years, none has become a popular climbing destination. This could be due to the $10 entry fee to Skyline Drive, the generally long approaches, or simply because there is better climbing nearby on Old Rag Mountain and Seneca Rocks. Whatever the reason, for the adventurous climber there are miles of canyons and crags to explore in solitude in search for a hidden classic (or enlightenment).

The cliffs at Big Devil's Stairs, Little Stoney Man Mountain, and White Oak Canyon are the tallest and most expansive. Some lead climbs are possible up to 120 feet in height, though toproping is the normal fare in the park. Other, smaller areas with decent toproping and bouldering include Fort Windham Rocks, Compton Peak, Mount Marshall, Little Devil's Stairs, Mary's Rock, Hawksbill Summit, Black Rock, and Split Rock. Be aware that during your travels down Skyline Drive you pass many pulloffs with the names "cliff," "hollow," "rocks," or "canyon" in the name. As a rule, most of these areas are red herrings for a climber driving to the crags described below (though, most offer spectacular scenic views).

While there is clearly a lot of rock in the park and some real potential for further development, don't expect to find large expanses of pristine rock à la Great Falls, Seneca Rocks, or the New River Gorge. Furthermore, many of the

# SKYLINE DRIVE—NORTH AREAS

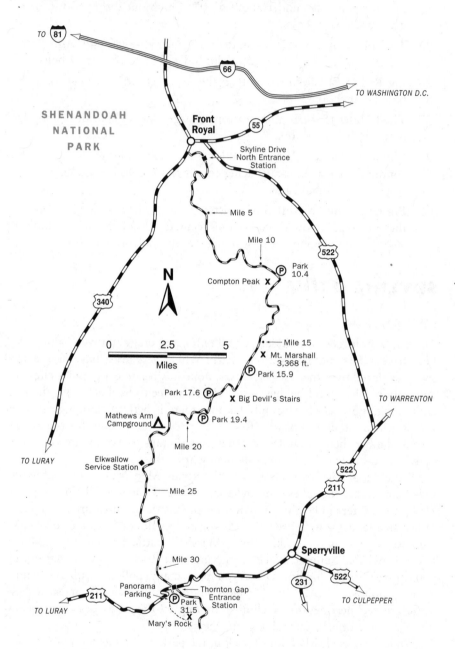

TO **81**

**66**

TO WASHINGTON D.C.

**55**

**Front
Royal**

SHENANDOAH

NATIONAL

PARK

Skyline Drive
North Entrance
Station

Mile 5

Mile 10

**522**

Ⓟ Park
10.4

Compton Peak **X**

**340**

**N**

0          2.5          5

Miles

Mile 15

**X** Mt. Marshall
3,368 ft.

Ⓟ Park 15.9

Park 17.6 Ⓟ

**X** Big Devil's Stairs

TO WARRENTON

Mathews Arm
Campground △

Ⓟ Park 19.4

Mile 20

Elkwallow
Service Station ◆

**522**

**211**

Mile 25

Mile 30

Sperryville

Panorama
Parking

Thornton Gap
Entrance
Station

**211**

Ⓟ Park
31.5

**231**      **522**

TO LURAY

**X**
Mary's Rock

TO CULPEPPER

TO LURAY

# SKYLINE DRIVE—SOUTH AREAS

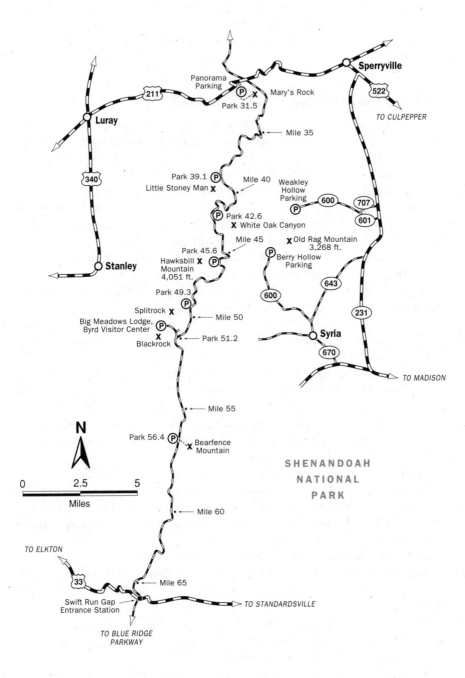

Sperryville

Panorama Parking

211

Mary's Rock

Luray

(P) X
Park 31.5

522

TO CULPEPPER

Mile 35

340

Park 39.1 (P)
Little Stoney Man X

Mile 40

Weakley Hollow Parking

(P) 600 707

Park 42.6 (P)
X White Oak Canyon

601

Mile 45

X Old Rag Mountain
3,268 ft.

Stanley

Park 45.6
Hawksbill X (P)
Mountain
4,051 ft.

(P) Berry Hollow Parking

643

Park 49.3

600

231

(P)

Splitrock X

Mile 50

Big Meadows Lodge,
Byrd Visitor Center (P)
X
Blackrock

Park 51.2

Syria

670

TO MADISON

Mile 55

N

Park 56.4 (P)
x Bearfence
Mountain

0    2.5    5
Miles

SHENANDOAH
NATIONAL
PARK

Mile 60

TO ELKTON

33

Mile 65

Swift Run Gap
Entrance Station

TO STANDARDSVILLE

TO BLUE RIDGE
PARKWAY

crags throughout Shenandoah National Park could be considered adventure climbing areas with the hardships (and rewards) that come with this distinction. Be prepared for long and, at times, steep approaches, wet and/or loose rock, snakes and bears, jungle-like vegetation around the cliffs, and a self-rescue if an accident occurs.

# TRIP PLANNING INFORMATION

**General description:** Relatively undeveloped and "unpopulated" crags from 20 to 120 feet high, scattered along the ridges of the stunning Skyline Drive Scenic Byway.

**Location:** Shenandoah National Park in western Virginia.

**Camping:** There are several NPS campgrounds along Skyline Drive. Mathews Arms (mile 22) is open late May to October, but has no showers. Big Meadows (mile 51) is a full-service visitor center and campground. Lewis Mountain (mile 57) has tent camping, cabins, and a store.

**Climbing season:** Fall is the ideal season to soak up the sights and do a little climbing. Winter is certainly quite cold (remember, these climbing areas are all above 3,000 feet in elevation); however, the lack of foliage is key when trying to explore the many underdeveloped climbing areas.

**Gear:** Bouldering, toproping, and a few traditional lead climbs are all you'll find on the menu along Skyline Drive. Bring a full rack, toprope rigging, and a 60-meter rope.

**Restrictions and access issues:** All NPS regulations apply.

**Guidebooks:** Jeff Watson's *Virginia Climber's Guide* includes a fairly comprehensive section on Skyline Drive. The guide includes numerous cliff topos and route descriptions, though they are at times cryptic and/or incomplete. Proceed with caution when using this information—it seems some of the route information and grades are "guestimates."

**Nearby mountain shops:** Wilderness Voyagers (800–220–1878) in Harrisonburg, Virginia, is the closest climbing shop.

**Services:** On Skyline Drive, the Big Meadows area (mile 51) has all services. Off the drive, head for Front Royal, Luray, Harrisonburg, or Waynesboro for food, gas, and lodging.

**Emergency services:** Contact NPS at 540–999–3500.

**Nearby climbing areas:** Old Rag Mountain features excellent granite climbing in a wilderness setting and is located east of Skyline Drive, near Sperryville.

**Nearby attractions:** What more could you ask? Skyline Drive is the paramount in sight-seeing, whether from your car or while hiking along some of the 500 miles of trails that crisscross the park.

**Finding the crags:** All areas list below are approached from pulloffs along Skyline Drive. See details in each section below.

## COMPTON PEAK AND WINDHAM ROCKS

As the farthest-north crags on Skyline Drive, these two outcrops offer a fairly quick approach from Front Royal. Compton Peak is a small basalt crag with a few topropes up to 40 feet. Windham Rocks, while not spectacular, offers a variety of easy-to-moderate topropes from 15 to 30 feet in height. Both areas require a hike-in of about a mile.

**Finding the rocks:** Park at the Compton Gap pulloff, located at the 10.4 milemark. For Windham Rocks, start up the old road at the far end of the parking area (this is the Appalachian Trail) for 0.2 mile. At the junction, turn left and continue another 0.4 mile to the rocks. For Compton Peak, cross the road and follow the Appalachian Trail for 50 yards, then turn left and hike 0.8 mile to a concrete trail marker. Turn left and continue a few minutes to the rocks.

## MOUNT MARSHALL

Scattered around the summit of Mount Marshall (3,368 feet) are numerous boulders and cliffs, some of which offer decent climbing up to 60 feet. Compared to the other crags along Skyline Drive, Mount Marshall has a short approach—less than fifteen minutes. Climbs are mainly in the moderate range, with a few harder routes through overhangs possible.

**Finding the cliffs:** Park at the 15.9 milemark, and follow the trail toward Mount Marshall. You'll come to the first outcrops on your right in less than a half-mile. More rocks are found farther on toward the summit.

## BIG DEVIL'S STAIRS AND LITTLE DEVIL'S STAIRS

The Big and Little Devil's Stairs are probably the most climbed areas on Skyline Drive—still, don't expect to find a crowd of climbers here. Big Devil's Stairs features a number of leadable routes up to 100 feet in length, located directly below the overlook on the trail. Both areas also have numerous good toprope climbs in the 5.6 to 5.10 range and some good camping spots.

**Finding the rocks:** Approach Big Devil's Stairs from the Gravel Springs Gap parking lot at the 17.6 milemark. From the Gravel Springs Gap Hut, take the Appalachian Trail 150 yards south, then turn left and follow the Bluff Trail for about 1.6 miles to an intersection with Big Devil's Stairs Trail. Continue another 0.5 mile to the overlook. For Little Devil's Stairs, park at the 19.4 milemark and follow a trail to Fourway, then take the Little Devil's Stairs Trail about 2 miles to the crags. The first outcrop in the canyon is located near where the trail crosses the stream.

## MARY'S ROCK

Mary's Rock is a series of small outcrops on the ridge above the Thornton Gap Entrance Station. There are numerous good boulder problems and topropes up to 40 feet. However, you will likely find the hike up more difficult than the climbing since most of the climbs are in the 5.3 to 5.9 range. Fortunately, there's another payoff for completing the 1.7-mile uphill huff—a spectacular 360-degree view!

**Finding the rocks:** Park near the Mary's Rock trailhead, located in the far corner of the Panorama Parking Area (just inside the Thornton Gap Entrance Station near milemark 31.5). Follow the trail 1.7 strenuous miles to the rocks.

## LITTLE STONEY MAN CLIFFS

Like Big Devil's Stairs, the cliff on Stoney Man Mountain offers a variety of climbing on greenstone cliffs up to 100 feet high. A few well-protected lead climbs are possible; however, as usual in the park, toproping is the norm. The hike-in is roughly a half-hour uphill, and the elevations of the rocks are some of the highest in the park (approximately 4,000 feet). It would be wise to pack a raincoat and some warm-weather clothes—as a high-elevation crag, it's usually quite windy.

**Finding the cliffs:** Use the Little Stoney Man Parking Area, located at the 39.1 milemark. Start up the marked trail toward the summit of Stony Man Mountain. In about a half-mile you come to a trail marker—bear right toward Furnace Springs to approach the cliffbase. Otherwise, continue up the main trail another 0.9 mile to the clifftops. From here, it's another 0.4 mile to the summit if you are inclined to bag the peak!

## WHITE OAK CANYON

White Oak Canyon is extremely popular with hikers due to its scenic beauty and six waterfalls. A testament to its appeal is the fact that both White Oak Canyon parking lots—one on Skyline Drive and the other off VA 600 near Old Rag Mountain—are typically packed on weekends. For climbers, the long hike-in will reveal a lot of rock that ranges from piles of choss to some 80-foot, clean sweeps.

Expect to spend some time trying to locate the best rock, especially during the summer when the foliage is rampant. Fall and winter offer the best opportunity to explore the crags of the canyon; however, you can climb just about year-round if you don't mind bushwhacking. Consider picking up a copy of Jeff Watson's *Virginia Climber's Guide,* as it lists a whopping 150 climbs in White Oak Canyon. I cannot vouch for the accuracy and quality of the information, but one would hope it's better than no information at all.

**Finding the canyon:** The White Oak Canyon parking on Skyline Drive is located at the 42.6 milemark. Follow the trail, and you'll find intermittent crags anywhere from 1 to 3 miles down the canyon from the parking lot. You can also approach from the lower trailhead, beginning from the White Oak Canyon parking area located off the left side of VA 600 (this is on the way into the Berry Hollow Parking Area for the climbing on Old Rag Mountain).

## HAWKSBILL MOUNTAIN

Hawksbill Mountain (4,051 feet) is the highest peak in Shenandoah National Park and offers spectacular views of Old Rag Mountain and the piedmont region to the east. The craggy summit area also offers climbers a 70-foot cliff and several smaller satellite boulders and blocks up to 30 feet. Look to set up topropes in the vicinity of the overlook. As a high-point climbing area, expect it to be windy and as much as 25 degrees cooler than in the nearby valley regions.

**Finding the mountain:** Park at the Hawksbill Gap Parking Area (milemark 45.6), and follow the trail 0.8 mile to a junction at the Byrd's Nest Shelter No. 2. Turn right and continue a few hundred yards to the summit. The cliffs are located below the overlook.

## BLACKROCK AND SPLIT ROCK

Blackrock and Split Rock are located along the Appalachian Trail in the vicinity of the large Big Meadows service area, visitor center, and lodge. Blackrock is located but a stone's throw (watch out, this could happen) below the Big Meadows Lodge. Here you find a few dozen moderate toprope lines up to 45 feet. The clifftop also affords a great western view—perfect for watching sunsets.

Split Rock is a smaller outcrop located 1.2 miles north of Blackrock along the Appalachian Trial. The "split rocks" at this area offer a few topropes up to 40 feet at grades from 5.5 to 5.10. A shorter approach to this area is available via the Appalachian Trail from the north (see directions below).

**Finding the rocks:** For Blackrock, exit Skyline Drive at the south entrance to the Big Meadows complex (mile 51.2). Follow signs to the "lodge," past the service center, and eventually bear left at a fork in the road. In about a mile, you arrive at the Big Meadows Lodge. Park to the left of the lodge, and locate a trail leading down to the Appalachian Trail and the cliffs. To approach Split Rock, park at the Fishers Gap Overlook (milemark 49.3). Follow signs to the Appalachian Trail and hike about a quarter-mile south (along white blazes) to the rocks.

## BEARFENCE MOUNTAIN

Bearfence Mountain is best known for its 360-degree view of Shenandoah National Park. The mountain also has scattered outcrops of slippery greenstone that offer climbers some toprope possibilities and bouldering. Despite the *Virginia Climber's Guide* proclamation that this is "the best bouldering area in Virginia," it is hard to find any problems that are even remotely in the same league as the bouldering found at McAfee's Knob, Rawley Springs, or Hone Quarry. Still, there might be enough problems here to keep you busy for an hour or two if you're passing through this section of Skyline Drive.

**Finding the rocks:** Park at the Bearfence Mountain pulloff (milemark 56.4). Cross the road and begin hiking at the sign for the Bearfence Mountain Trail. It's only about 300 yards to the rocks and overlook; the full loop is a half-mile.

# OTHER CRAGS

## MCAFEE'S KNOB

Although there are several small climbing areas in the Roanoke area, such as Tinker Cliffs and the Dragons Tooth, it is McAfee's Knob that stands out as something special. Located less than 10 miles west of town on Catawba Mountain is a myriad of 10- to 30-foot sandstone boulders scattered along the ridge for nearly 3 miles from VA 311 to McAfee's Knob proper.

While it's well over an hour's hike to the summit boulders, you only have to walk about a minute from the parking area to sample the area's unique rock. The gray-and-white boulders stand vertical to severely overhanging, with pockets, incut edges, gritty slopers, and buckets of every shape and size.

Bouldering at McAfee's Knob dates back at least twenty years, with many of the prominent lines established by Roanoke hardmen such as Kenny Parker. As with many climbing areas, new route action comes in waves, and a new generation of young guns is now further exploring the mountain. While there were plenty of hard and serious problems established in the 1980s and 1990s, you have to assume that problems will be going in at V10–V12 and beyond in the near future. Bottomline: If bouldering is your cup of tea, then move to Roanoke and drink at McAfee's Knob. This place *is* the Hueco Tanks of Virginia!

Inquire at Blue Ridge Outdoors (540–774–4311) in Roanoke for more information or to locate a climbing partner—the bouldering on McAfee's Knob is remote, so it would be best not to climb there alone.

**Finding the area:** Take exit 141 off I–81 and follow signs to get onto VA 311 North. Follow VA 311 for 5.5 miles to a large Appalachian Trail parking lot on the left, at the top of the ridge. Walk across the highway and locate the first small outcrop with its overhanging northwest face. If you like, warm up here with a few problems, then begin hiking up the fire road, watching for intermittent boulders, primarily on the right. The full hike to McAfee's Knob proper takes over an hour, even at a brisk pace. But, if you are like most people you may not ever make it there, considering the high-quality blocks you'll find on your way up the fire road. Enjoy your explorations and get pumped!

## LYNCHBURG AREA CRAGS

There are a few small climbing areas of local interest within an hour of Lynchburg, including Raven's Roost, Tunstall's Tooth, and The Trestles areas.

*Taylor Smith bouldering at McAfee's Knob.* PHOTO BY ERIC J. HÖRST

Raven's Roost is the most scenic crag, with its perch along the Blue Ridge Parkway near milemark 11. Here you'll find numerous moderate topropes up to 80 feet, directly below the tourist's overlook. Tunstall's Tooth is an old-timers' area along the north shore of the James River and just west of where the Blue Ridge Parkway crosses the river. There are about twenty routes of so-so quality, ranging in grade from 5.7 to 5.10. The third and, possibly, best area is The Goode Trestles. Built in 1850, these now-abandoned railroad trestles were purchased by the Lynchburg Climbing Club and feature excellent bolted face climbs up to 5.11b. For more information on any of the above areas, visit www.lynchburgclimbingclub.com.

## HIDDEN VALLEY

In extreme southwestern Virginia, near the town of Abingdon, is what may be Virginia's best sport climbing area. Known as Hidden Valley, these pocketed sandstone cliffs have been quietly developed into a small climbing mecca, while the sport climbing hubbub a few hours north at the New River Gorge has garnered all the attention.

This lack of attention doesn't bother the landowner—a climber who bought the cliffs and would like to keep the area low-profile. Strangely, she has put in a climber's parking area and helps subsidize bolting, which has now produced in excess of 200 sport climbs. Of course, these events all but ensure that more climbers will flock to Hidden Valley each season. Bolts are strong "climber magnets," and the cat is out of the bag about this area, both by climber word-of-mouth and through the Internet.

Certainly, the landowner should be credited for securing this wonderful resource and opening it up to climbing. However, we all must hope that she takes a proactive stance in managing the land that will both lower her personal liability and minimize the impact of the ever-increasing number of visitors to the area. Ideally, the landowner will decide to follow the model established by Nelson Rocks Preserve, and transform Hidden Rocks into a nonprofit recreational preserve.

By request of the landowner, directions and route information are not included in this guide.

# CARDEROCK AND GREAT FALLS

(see Washington, D.C., Area Crags Map, page 55)

## OVERVIEW

Carderock is an exceedingly popular climbing area located along the north bank of the Potomac River, just outside Washington, D.C. Featuring cliffs up to 60 feet high and a two-minute car-to-crag approach, the area has long been an after-work favorite of Capital-area climbers. Weekends are likewise busy, as beginner and intermediate climbers infiltrate from other metropolitan areas, such as Baltimore and Philadelphia. Add in "corporate outing" or "climbing school" groups, and you'll understand why this is, per square foot of rock, one of the most highly used areas in the country.

Carderock's cliffs lie in the deciduous woods that line the banks of the Potomac. Providing a sylvan setting for an afternoon of climbing, the trees offer large expanses of shade along the southwest-facing cliffs and plentiful toprope anchors along the clifftop. By late fall, sunshine warms the wall enough for climbing on all but the coldest days. Year-round, Carderock is a great place to climb and bring the family along as well—there are plenty of trails to explore, and this is about as child-friendly as climbing areas come.

With or without the family, be sure to bring your sticky rubber climbing shoes and a carpet swatch. The rock is a slick schist that ranges from slabby to vertical, and the cliffbase consists primarily of lose dirt and sand—erosion is an ongoing problem—so frequent foot wipes are mandatory if you want to keep your shoe soles clean. Some faces are nearly featureless and require superior friction climbing skills on polished rock, while others possess good quartz edges and knobs. Good beginners' face climbs include *Barnacle Face* (5.3), *Beginner's Face* (5.4), *Nubble Face* (5.4), and *Jane's Face* (5.6), while *The Crack* (5.3), *Beginner's Crack* (5.3), and *Easy Layback* (5.4) offer an introduction to crack climbing.

For the more proficient climber, Carderock offers an excellent selection of moderate-to-difficult face climbs that is sure to humble all but the best climbers. With a tradition of hard grades and holds that get smoother every year, Carderock is viewed by many as a sandbag area. A few of the most egregious sandbag ratings have been corrected here (e.g., *Silver Spot,* formerly a 5.10, is more accurately graded 5.12c in this listing); don't be surprised, however, if many climbs still feel up to a full grade harder than in the listing. For a taste of classic Carderock 5.10, try out *Cripple's Crack* (5.10c) and *Leonard's Lunacy* (5.10c/d), and for a 5.11 flashpump get on *The Dream* (5.11c) or *The Rack Direct* (5.11d).

If you arrive at Carderock to find ropes on everything (not uncommon), consider driving just a couple of miles upriver to Great Falls, Maryland. While more spread out then Carderock and of varying quality, the crags on the Maryland side of Great Falls offer a nice getaway from the masses in a more remote setting.

From parking at either the Great Falls Tavern Visitors' Center, or across from the Angler's Inn, a hike along the Billy Goat Trail leads to dozens of small outcrops and a few larger crags up to 60 feet tall. This guide includes just a few of the best areas at Great Falls, Maryland. Approaching from the Angler's Inn, it is just a five-minute walk along the tow path to a couple of excellent topropes on Angler's Inn Rock. From here, turn onto the Billy Goat Trail and hike another ten minutes to Crag X, a small west-facing crag that features numerous moderate topropes ideal for a cool afternoon. Alternatively, begin from the Great Falls Tavern Visitors' Center and make a pleasant ten-minute hike along the tow path to the top of The Bulges area. Here you'll find about a dozen routes from 5.0 to 5.11, including the classic *Super Bulge* (5.11b/c).

**Climbing history:** Carderock is the site of some of the earliest technical climbing in North America, as it's reported that Gus Gambs introduced roped climbing to the area in the late 1920s. In the years that followed, Gambs, along with Paul Brandt, Herb Conn, Don Hubbard, and others established many of the popular lines we know today. It's amazing to consider that possibly the country's first 5.9 moves were free-climbed by Conn in his 1942 ascent of *Herbie's Horror.* This route still feels hard in the year 2001!

After World War II, Carderock became the principal training ground for the growing number of climbers in the Washington, D.C., area. Weekday evenings were spent at Carderock as preparation for weekend trips to Seneca Rocks. Many of the popular moderate climbs of today were established during this period, including *Jan's Face* (5.6), *Triple A* (5.7), and *Biceps* (5.9). Local activists of this era, and equally known for their contributions at Seneca Rocks, include John Christian, Herb and Jan Conn, Jim Shipley, Tony Soler, Richard Leonard, and Arnold Wexler.

From the 1950s though the early 1970s, climbing at Carderock was dominated by members of the Potomac Appalachian Trail Club (PATC). The area's hardest routes were established during this period, including Mike Bank's 1962 ascent of *Silver Spot*—then considered 5.10, and today, minus a few holds, a solid 5.12. Finally, it was John Stannard of Gunks fame that instigated the focus on developing Carderock as a bouldering area, a use that is as popular as ever today. Other climbers making notable contributions or who cut their teeth at Carderock in training for bigger and better things are John Bercaw, Greg Collins, Howard Doyle, Tom Evans, Joe Faint, Charlie Fowler, John Gregory, Greg Hand, Hunt Prothro, Charlie Rollins, Lotus Steele, and Leith Wain.

By the 1980s, the very limited rock had been "climbed out" of new routes. While seemingly infinite variations and "elimination" routes have been created, most Carderock climbers are happy to enjoy the area's natural beauty and climb the many classic moderate routes countless times. However, ever-increasing climber traffic and occasional flooding of the Potomac have resulted in severe erosion along the cliffbase, and some vegetation has been trampled along the clifftop near commonly used toprope anchors. For these reasons, the Park Service was once considering closure of the area to climbers.

Fortunately, a group of concerned climbers formed the Carderock Conservation Committee from members of the American Alpine Club, the Potomac Appalachian Trail Club, and other unaffiliated climbers and hikers. Over the last twenty years, this group has built and rebuilt wooden walkways and constructed several railroad-tie retaining walls. Without these efforts, the river would have surely claimed such fine walls as near *Cripple's Crack* and *Trudie's Terror*, or, worse yet, the area may have been closed to climbing by park managers. Please stay on established trails, and minimize clifftop travel to help prevent further environmental impact.

## TRIP PLANNING INFORMATION

**General description:** Low-angle to vertical cliffs up to 60 feet high and plentiful bouldering with good landings. A few lead climbs are possible; however, these crags were definitely "made" for toproping.

**Location:** Just 2 miles west of the Washington, D.C., Beltway on the Maryland side of the Potomac River.

**Camping:** Lake Fairfax County Park (703–757–9242) is the nearest campground. No camping is allowed at Carderock.

**Climbing season:** This is a year-round crag. Summers are hot, humid, and "greasy"; however, the west-facing crags are ideal for sunny winter afternoon outings.

**Gear:** A few pieces of long static line or webbing are needed to set up topropes on most routes. A light rack of stoppers and cams may be needed to supplement trees atop a few routes.

**Restrictions and access issues:** Stay on established trails, and exit the park by sunset.

**Guidebooks:** The Mountaineering Section of the Potomac Appalachian Trail Club has published *Carderock Past & Present*. This is the area's primary climber's guide and is most notable for its detailed history of climbing at Carderock.

**Nearby mountain shops, guide services, and gyms:** Potomac Outdoors (301–320–1544) is located just up the road, at 7687 MacArthur Boulevard in Cabin John, Maryland. There are also large REI stores at Bailey's Crossing, Virginia (703–379–9400) and College Park, Maryland (301–982–9681). For indoor climbing or guiding, visit Earth Treks (800–CLIMB–UP) in Columbia, Maryland, or the SportRock Climbing Center in Rockville, Maryland (301–ROCK–111).

**Services:** All services are available within 5 miles of Carderock.

**Emergency services:** Call 911 for an ambulance or the police. Chestnut Lodge Hospital (301–424–8300) is in nearby Rockville, Maryland.

**Nearby climbing areas:** The best climbing in the D.C. area is just across the Potomac River at Great Falls Park, Virginia.

**Nearby attractions:** The C&O Canal National Historical Park is facinating to visit, and is located at the parking area for the climbing at Great Falls, Maryland. Of course, there are countless historical sites to visit just thirty minutes away in Washington, D.C.

**Finding the crags:** Take Carderock exit off I–495 and follow Clara Barton Parkway just a short distance to Carderock Entrance. For Great Falls, Maryland, continue a little farther on Clara Barton Parkway until it becomes MacArthur Boulevard, then follow this 2 miles to the entrance for the C&O Canal and Great Falls, Maryland (on left).

# CARDEROCK

**Finding the crag:** Take Carderock exit off I–495 and follow Clara Barton Parkway just a short distance to Carderock Entrance. Park at the farthest lot (upstream) from park entrance. From the rest rooms, follow the wooden walkway to a bulletin board. Continue another 20 yards to the edge of the cliff and the Billy Goat Trail downclimb. This 3rd-Class downclimb is located between the two main cliffs: Jungle Cliff and Hades Heights. Scramble down to the trail below, and turn right to access the Jungle Cliff routes or left for those along Hades Heights. The hike from your car to the far end of either cliff is just five minutes.

## JUNGLE CLIFF

1. **Jam Crack** (5.2) Begin at low-angle detached block located about 100 yards upstream of the 3rd-Class downclimb and 20 feet left of a large,

# CARDEROCK

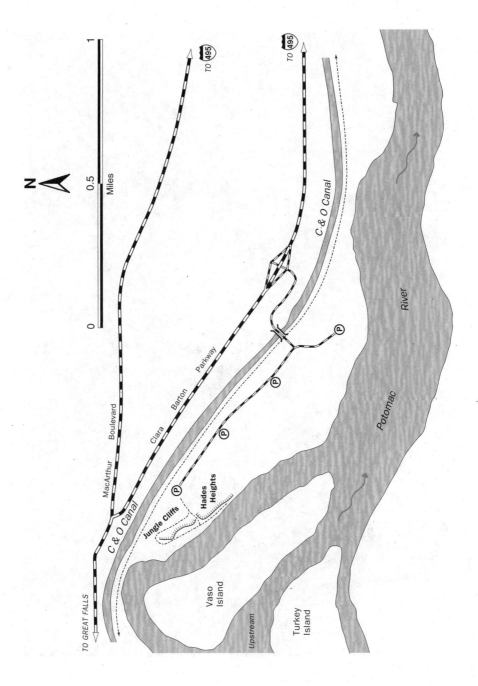

left-facing chimney. Climb the low-angle face to the top of the block and finish up the crack above to the top.

2. **Herbie's Left** (5.6) A good warm-up for *Herbie's Horror.* Start on small blocks just left of a tree and about 10 feet left of *Herbie's Horror.* Climb straight up the face, past two small square-cut overhangs.

3. **Herbie's Horror** (5.9) A fun and technical footwork problem. Begin just right of a small, detached flake in the bottom of *Chockstone Chimney.* Climb small quartz knobs up the center of the face.

4. **Chockstone Chimney** (5.3) Rarely climbed. Scramble up the prominent, left-facing chimney, squeezing behind a chockstone near the top.

5. **Left Edge** (5.3) Climb up the left edge on *Jane's Face,* beginning at a large tree just right of *Chockstone Chimney.*

6. **The Flake** (5.9+) A popular climb, as are all the routes on Jane's Face. Start at the left of three vertical hairline seams about 15 feet right of *Left Edge.* Climb up along the hairline crack to small flakes about 30 feet up. Continue up thin face moves to the top.

7. **Eight Ball** (5.11d) Start just right of *The Flake* and dance up the face between two narrowly spaced hairline seams.

8. **Jane's Face Center** (5.6–5.7) Climb anywhere up the center of the face. Very popular.

9. **Copycat** (5.6) Begin immediately right of a huge tree and wide crack that forms the right side of Jane's Face. Climb the left side of the face without using the edge of the crack. The route is 5.4 if you use the edge of the crack.

10. **Sweethog** (5.6) Start at a small, flaky handhold about 10 feet right of a huge tree and wide crack. Climb straight up the center of the face.

11. **Elsie's Arête** (5.8+) Begin on flaky holds on the right side of a low overhang and arête. Finesse your way up awkward lieback moves and ascend the arête to the top. Good climbing, but much harder for short climbers.

12. **Elsie's Other** (5.7) Climb the grooved, steep face just right of *Elsie's Arête.*

13. **The Dream** (5.11c) Begin below a large, downstream-pointing overhang. Step up on a block to the left side of the overhang. Hand-traverse right along the lip to the center of the 'hang, pull it, and finish straight up easier stone to the top.

14. **The Dream Direct** (5.12a) . . . or is it a nightmare? Start below the middle of the low, protruding roof. Climb hard, bouldery moves through the middle of the roof at a notch.

15. **Vulgarian Wedge** (5.9+) Begin on a small, square-cut ledge just right of *The Dream* roof. Work up the narrow chimney and flake about halfway, until you can move left onto the face and finish straight up to the top. Several variations are possible in the 5.10 and 5.11 range.

16. **The Rack** (5.7) Nice climbing, but a bit more difficult for short climbers. Start below a right-facing "wedge" chimney. Scramble up onto a small blocky stance, then make a few reachy moves up and right over the bulge. Easier moves lead to the top.

17. **The Rack Direct** (5.11d) A great and very powerful sequence up to and past the second overhang. Begin at the base of a sharp arête just right of *The Rack*. Climb the arête past two small overhangs.

18. **Sterling's Crack** (5.7) An area classic. Lieback up the prominent, right-facing corner and crack.

19. **Evan's Bolt Ladder** (5.12d) Desperate. Climb the flaky face between *Sterling's Crack* and the nearly fifty-year-old bolt ladder.

20. **The Nose Direct Direct** (5.11d) Start just right of the old bolt line and climb straight up through the overhang to join the nose about 15 feet up.

21. **Elsie's Nose** (5.10c) From the right side of the overhang, use liebacks to work up and left to join the left-slanting crack. Finish up this to the top.

22. **Elsie's** (5.6–5.8) Climb the grooved wall right of *Elsie's Nose*. The farther left you start, the harder the climbing.

JUNGLE CLIFF

Backside
edge

Vate

23. **The X** (5.7) Begin below a shallow inverted V-shaped overhang 20 yards right of *Elsie's Nose*. Climb up past this feature without using holds in/on the cracks.

24. **Barnacle Face** (5.3) Unique and very popular. Climb wild quartz "barnacles" and flakes, beginning about 10 feet right of *The X*.

25. **Impossible** (5.10a/b) Climb the short, right-facing side of the *Barnacle Face* block.

26. **Buckets of Blood** (5.11d) Climb the overhanging edge just right of *Impossible*.

27. **Swayback Layback** (5.8) Start behind a block and about 3 feet right of a short chimney. Climb straight up to finish in a crack.

28. **Swollen Head** (5.10a) Just right of *Swayback Layback,* start up using a C-shaped handhold. Climb up along a rib and stay right of the crack near the top.

29. **Shipley's** (5.9) Start between the C-shaped handhold and left-facing *Ronnie's Leap* corner. Climb up to an obvious knob about 10 feet up, and continue straight up a groove to the top.

30. **Ronnie's Leap** (5.7) Climb the right face and edge of a small, left-facing corner without using the crack.

31. **The Bump** (5.8) Scum up the often dirty face about 10 feet left of *Beginner's Crack*.

32. **The Diamond** (5.8) Start 3 feet left of *Beginner's Crack* and climb the face straight up to finish around the left side of a small, square-shaped overhang.

33. **Beginner's Crack** (5.3) Classic. It's a rare day that there is not a rope on this route! Lieback the prominent crack.

34. **Beginner's Face** (5.4) Features a nice variety of moves. Start from small boulders just right of *Beginner's Crack,* and climb the center of the face through a small overhang to the top.

35. **Meenehan's Staircase** (5.5) Start right of a large tree and climb the face and ramp up to finish between two blocks. Variation: **Meenehan's Edge** (5.8) Lieback up the edge with your feet on the left face. Avoid using any holds left of the edge.

36. **The Sloth a.k.a. "Back of Meenehan's"** (5.11c/d) Climb the overhanging back side of *Meenehan's Edge* using liebacks, pinches, and heel-and-toe hooks.

· **Note:** The 3rd-Class *Billy Goat Trail Descent* scrambles through the cliff break next to the *Kindergarten* beginner's slab. This short scramble provides quick access to clifftop, rest rooms, and parking lot. Please stay on established trails no matter where you venture at Carderock.

## HADES HEIGHTS

37. **Kindergarten** (5.0) A great beginner's climb—even for grown-ups! Begin at a tree near the base of a low angle wall (on the left as you descend the 3rd-Class downclimb). Climb anywhere up the nice face, using left-facing flakes and buckety holds.

38. **The Nose** (5.3) Climb the prominent "nose" just right of *Kindergarten.*

39. **Spider Walk** (5.7) A nice, but tricky crack sequence. Popular. Ascend the left-angling crack that begins about 10 feet right of *The Nose.*

40. **Silver Spot** (5.12c) The single biggest sandbag in the old, white Carderock guide—hardly 5.10! Begin just right of the *Spider Walk* crack and climb up past the glossy, silver spot on miniscule holds.

41. **Biceps** (5.9) Begin 15 yards downstream of the walkdown below an inverted V-shaped roof. Climb up through the middle of the overhang and finish up and right along a flake to the top. **Variations:** (5.11) Climb through the right or left side of the roof.

42. **Green Bucket** (5.9+) Begin 15 feet right of *Biceps.* Scramble about 20 feet up a slabby face to a thin seam below the left side of the overhang. Climb the seam to the overhang and move slightly right through it to the top.

HADES HEIGHTS

*Kelly Dinneen on Cripple's Crack (5.10c), Carderock.* PHOTO BY ERIC J. HÖRST

43. **Desperation** (5.9+) Start just right of *Green Bucket,* and work up the slab to the right end of the ramp. Move up and right along underclings and pull through the right side of an overhang to good holds.

44. **Golden Staircase** (5.7+) Begin below a prominent crack and large, right-facing corner. Climb on the left side of the crack to gain a sloping stance about 20 feet up. Move left around the outside corner and climb up the nose of rock to the top. Variation: **Face to Right** (5.9) From the sloping stance, continue up the steep rock on the right.

45. **The Crack** (5.3) Begin at the base of a prominent crack and large right-facing corner located about 30 yards right of the 3rd-Class downclimb. Climb the crack and corner.

46. **Nubble Face** (5.0–5.4) Another great Carderock beginner's route. Climb any of the many possible paths up the center portion of the knobby face.

47. **Bulging Crack** (5.6) Start at a small, right-facing flake about 35 feet right of *The Crack.* Climb the crack past the left side of the bulge. Variation: **The Bulge** (5.9+) Climb the corner and directly through the bulge without using the crack or any holds on the right edge.

48. **Friction Layback** (5.6) Start as in *Bulging Crack,* but climb up and right around the right side of the bulge to large, right-facing flakes. Finish up easier rock to the top.

49. **Walk on By** (5.10d) This elimination route climbs the face between *Friction Layback* and *Incipient.* Avoid all the large holds on/near either route.

50. **Incipient** (5.9+) Begin two steps right of *Bulging Crack,* at a thin right-facing flake. Climb up to the overhang and pull it along a tiny vertical seam. Use holds only within 6 inches of the crack.

51. **Chris' Goat** (5.7) Begin as in *Incipient,* but move right beneath the roof to climb the low-angle left face of the arête to the top.

52. **Crippling Paralysis** (5.10d) Dance up the smooth, steep face just left of *Cripple's Crack.* Do not use the crack, nor any holds on *Chris' Goat.*

53. **Cripple's Crack** (5.10c) An awkward, pseudo-crack climb, but nonetheless very classic. Begin at the cracks around the corner from *Nubble Face.* Climb the prominent, left crack past the right side of a small, triangle-shaped roof to a stance on a ramp below a high roof. Finish left along the ramp to the summit slabs.

54. **Cripple's Face** (5.9) Climb the face immediately right of *Cripple's Crack* and finish up and left along the ramp finish of the crack route.

55. **Leonard's Lunacy** (5.10c/d) Begin at a small, left-facing corner 10 feet right of *Cripple's Crack.* Boulder up to a stance on blocks, step left, and

*Kristen Belz on Triple A (5.7), Carderock.* PHOTO BY ERIC J. HÖRST

move up to a stance on a ramp below a roof with crack. Make a reachy move out the roof crack to a good jam, then a better bucket, and much easier moves to the top.

56. **Yellow Jacket** (5.9) Start below an overhanging block 15 feet right of *Cripple's Crack*. Boulder up to a ledge about 25 feet up. Now climb a shallow groove past faint yellow spots to the top.

57. **The Laundry Chute** (5.1) Scramble up the broken, low-angle crack and corner located behind a large tree.

58. **Serenity Syndrome** (5.11b) Climb the extremely thin, flat left face of the obvious, right-facing corner. The left edge is "on," but do not use holds beyond the edge of the arête (i.e., around the outside corner). The next two climbs are other "elimination routes" up this corner.

59. **Flutterby** (5.10c) Climb the right-facing corner using only handholds on the left face, while limiting your feet only to holds on the right face of the corner.

60. **Butterfly** (5.9) Climb the face immediately right of the corner without using any holds in the corner or on the left face.

61. **Merv's Nerve** (5.10d) Only slightly different from *Butterfly*. Climb the face between *Butterfly* and *Easy Layback*—basically, climb a 2-foot-wide path up the center of the face. Crack and face holds on either route are off-route.

62. **Easy Layback** (5.4) A beautiful and super-popular climb. Begin about 15 feet right of *The Laundry Chute* at a right-facing crack that begins behind a large block. Climb the crack.

63. **Eliminates** (5.7) Climb the face just right of the *Easy Layback* crack.

64. **Fingernail** (5.10b) Fingernails might be useful to edge up the thin starting moves. Climb up along the hairline crack located just right of *Easy Layback*. Finish up the corner above to the top.

65. **Zig Zag** (5.12a/b) Zig and zag up the face immediately right of the *Fingernail* seam. Finish up *Triple A*.

66. **Triple A** (5.7) Begin at a 12-foot-high, right-facing flake 15 feet right of *Easy Layback*. Climb the flake and face above to a stance. Finish up through a bulge to the top.

67. **Mad Dog** (5.11a) Begin just right of the *Triple A* flake and below an old sleeve bolt about 8 feet up. Climb straight up the face, roughly midway between *Triple A* and *Trudie's*.

68. **Trudie's Terror** (5.4) Climb the prominent, left-facing corner and crack located just left of where the cliff meets the river.

# GREAT FALLS, MARYLAND

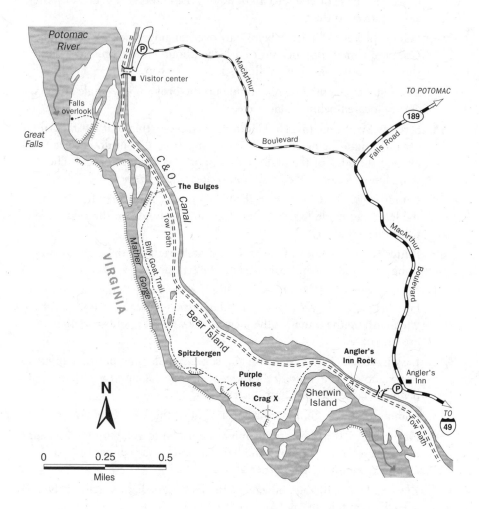

# GREAT FALLS

**Finding the crags:** Take Carderock exit off I–495. Follow Clara Barton Parkway past Carderock. Turn left on MacArthur Boulevard and continue a short distance to the primary climbers' parking area across the road from the Old Angler's Inn (do not park at the Old Angler's Inn). Use this parking area to approach all climbing areas except The Bulges. A much shorter approach to The Bulges is possible from the Great Falls Tavern Visitors Center parking, located 2 miles farther down the road. A $4.00 fee or Golden Eagle pass is required to enter the visitors' center parking area.

## ANGLER'S INN ROCK

This nice, 45-foot buttress lies just five seconds off the tow path! There are two good climbs here—set up a toprope and do both. The car-to-crag approach is less than five minutes from Old Angler's Inn parking area.

**Finding the crag:** From Old Angler's Inn parking area, drop downhill and cross the beautiful footbridge over the canal. Take a right on the tow path and hike about 150 yards until you spot the small outcrop just off the left side of the path. These climbs start from rocks along the water, so you may need to rappel or lower to the bases of the climbs.

1. **Gus' Gambit** (5.9) Climb the obvious crack and corners up the downstream side of the river-facing buttress.

2. **Angler's Inn Overhang** (5.11a) Begin on the right face of a large dihedral just left of *Gus' Gambit*. Climb the face up and slightly right to the first bulge. Over this to a good horizontal crack, then climb up and left through the strenuous overhang.

## CRAG X

This small, west-facing crag is nothing to write home about; however, it is a comfy retreat on cool but sunny winter afternoons. There are several good toprope climbs up to 30 feet.

**Finding the crag:** Park at the Old Angler's Inn lot, drop downhill, and hike the tow path upstream about 500 yards to the Billy Goat Trail on your left. Follow the winding BGT for about ten minutes until you come to a dried-up creekbed/"wash." In another 125 yards you come to a rocky section of trail with a dropoff on your left. Spot a short, upstream-facing cliffband with a large, flat, open "beach area" at its base—this is Crag X. Scramble down over boulders to the cliffbase.

3. **Standard Deviations** (5.8) On the left side of the left outcrop, climb a series of flakes just right of an outside corner.

4. **Under the Big Black Sun** (5.8) Climb the steep face right of *Standard Deviations*.

5. **Ground Zero** (5.9) Climb through the overhangs on the right side of the first outcrop.

6. **More Fun in the New World** (5.6) Scramble up to and climb the obvious crack on the left side of the right outcrop.

7. **Unknown Jugs** (5.4) Start on the boulder near the middle of the right outcrop. Step onto the face and follow jug holds up and right.

8. **Variable** (5.8-) Begin about 8 feet left of an old bolt sleeve, and climb up on blocky holds to a low-angle finish.

9. **Unknown Quantity** (5.9+) A good route with just one hard move right off the ground. Begin below an old sleeve bolt and boulder up to gain a nice lieback crack.

10. **Right of Quantity** (5.7) Just right of *Unknown Quantity*, climb the broken crack to the top.

## PURPLE HORSE

This small outcrop has a beautiful, low-angle face ideal for teaching beginners the basics of footwork and movement. There is also a difficult roof climb that will work the arms quite nicely. Otherwise, the Purple Horse is kind of lame.

**Finding the crag:** From the tow path, take the Billy Goat Trail past Crag X and continue another 400 yards until you cross a small footbridge (pond to the left), then enter a large boulderfield. As the trail nears the river, you'll come to a 25-foot, upstream-facing cliff on your left. *Barn Roof* goes out through the obvious roof, and the *River Wall* is just around on the river-facing side of the outcrop. The approach from parking takes fifteen to twenty minutes.

11. **Barn Roof** (5.9) Climb up to and out the roof on the upstream side of Purple Horse.

12. **River Wall** (5.4–5.8) Climb anywhere up the broad, low-angle face.

## SPITZBERGEN

This 30- to 50-foot cliff has some of the more difficult climbs on the Maryland side of Great Falls. Unfortunately, it also has the longest approach (about twenty-five minutes) of any Maryland-side crag covered in this book.

**Finding the crag:** From the Old Angler's Inn parking lot, follow the tow path upstream to gain the beginning of the Billy Goat Trail. Follow the trail past Crag X and then another 300 yards beyond Purple Horse until you come upon the square-cut-looking cliff along the river on your left.

13. **Soapstone** (5.9) Climb the thin crack up the right side of the downstream-facing wall.

14. **A Winter's Tale** (5.10c) Begin at a small right-facing corner near the middle of the downstream face. Climb the corner, then fire straight up the face above.

15. **Spitzbergen Arête** (5.10d) Starting down near the water, climb up and left through a small overhang on the arête. Now trend up and right to fin-

PURPLE HORSE

ish on the face just left of *A Winter's Tale.*

16. **The AAU Crack** (5.10d) Begin down at the river as in *Spitzbergen Arête,* but traverse left just above the water to gain a hand crack. Jam it up. **Variations:** During the traverse left, you can also climb up either of two weaknesses you pass before gaining the main crack. Both go at around 5.10d or 5.11a.

## THE BULGES

The 60-foot-high Bulges area is readily visible from the downstream crags of Great Falls, Virginia, but still few climbers venture over to check it out. If for no other reason, consider visiting this area once to get on the classic *Super Bulge* (5.11b/c). Climbing here can also be a peaceful getaway from the crowds on the Virginia side.

**Finding the crag:** Park at Great Falls Tavern Visitors Center. From the visitors center, cross the canal and hike downstream along the tow path about one-half mile to the Billy Goat Trail on your right (just before steel bridge over canal). Follow the Billy Goat Trail for 125 yards, then cut off right to the top of Great Falls Bulges.

**Descent:** Facing the river at the top of the main Great Falls Bulges, you find a reasonable 3rd-Class descent located about 40 yards to the right. Beyond (upstream of) the downclimb is the Little Bulges sector. Another

downclimb is located upstream of Little Bulges—use this only to approach Routes 17–19. The base of all other Bulges climbs are best reached via the 3rd-Class descent between the two Bulges sectors.

## LITTLE BULGE

17. **First Lead Corner** (5.0) At the farthest upstream end of the crags, climb the large, somewhat vegetated, broken corner.

18. **Greyish Face** (5.4) Begin just right of the large corner and climb up and right to a stance near the center of the face. Finish straight up around the right side of the bulge.

19. **FUBAR** (5.9) Start on a block below a low roof located about 20 feet right of *First Lead Corner*. Pull the roof and climb up to a stance. Conclude up easier moves on the main nose of the formation.

20. **Orange Groove** (5.9) Begin from blocks below a section of black rock located around the corner and downstream from the *First Lead Corner*. Start up fractured rock a few feet until you can move left to gain an orangish section of rock. Follow this feature to the top.

21. **The Black Bulge** (5.4) Start up fractured rock as in *Orange Grove*, but continue straight up on blocky holds and low-angle stone to the top.

# GREAT FALLS BULGE

22. **Short Line** (5.10d) This 25-foot route is alone on a small, vertical outcrop located right of the Little Bulge and about 25 feet left of *F.M.* Climb a series of cracks up this short, river-facing wall.

23. **F.M.** (5.7) Start at the base of a left-slanting crack/corner system on the left side of the main Great Falls Bulge crag and just right of the 3rd-Class downclimb. Climb the slanting crack and corner up about 20 feet to a stance with short, vertical grooves on the right face. Move up the grooves and climb cracks through the left side of a bulge to the top.

24. **Peg's Progress** (5.4) Begin at the base of a large, left-slanting fracture on the left side of the face. Climb the corner up and right to a sloping ledge. Traverse right about 10 feet and continue up a left-facing corner and flake. Finish on easier moves up and right to the top.

25. **Super Bulge** (5.11b/c) *The* Bulges testpiece route. Just right of *Peg's Progress,* scramble up on a sloping ledge about 10 feet up. Now climb through the bulge at a small corner, then move up through another bulge to a sloping ledge. After a rest, continue straight up through a small, rectangular overhang and a flaky roof to the top. **Variation:** From the sloping ledge below the rectangular overhang, you can move right and finish up much easier terrain on *Peg's Progress.* This bypass around the crux bulges makes the route 5.8.

26. **Narrow Notch** (5.6) Begin at right-slanting cracks near the middle of the face. Follow the cracks to a stance. Continue up and right through a notch to an easy finish.

27. **Wild Thing** (5.10b) Short, but with some good, pumpy moves. Boulder up to a ledge below a pair of cracks out a bulge on the upper right side of the wall. Climb along the cracks, through the bulge to a blocky finish.

# BALTIMORE AREA STATE PARKS

## OVERVIEW

Like Washington, D.C., the Baltimore area possesses a vibrant climbing community that has played a large role in developing Mid-Atlantic climbing over the last thirty years. Local climbers are fortunate to have several small crags within forty-five minutes of Baltimore and one small outcrop that lies less than 5 miles off the Baltimore Beltway! Luckily, the best climbing can be found in Maryland State Parks system, and the land managers continue to view climbers as a legitimate user group. Safe climbing practices and stewardship of the resources will help ensure that these fine training crags remain open for future generations.

Without a doubt, the best climbing is found about forty-five minutes north of Baltimore at the scenic Rocks State Park. It is at this "little, big area" that many young climbers have cut their teeth on the way to becoming nationally recognized climbers. Comprised of a schist similar to the rock of Great Falls and Carderock, Rocks State Park arguably offers more variety with its cracks, corners, knobby faces, overhangs, and steep, bouldery waves of rock. Topropes up to 85 feet are the norm; however, there are a few excellent leads, such as *Vertical* (5.6), *Strawberry Jam* (5.8), *Breakaway* (5.9+), and *Smoke 'N' Ash* (5.10d).

While Rocks State Park is a small area that "climbs big," the outcrops in the long, winding Patapsco Valley State Park truly are small. Located just a few miles west of the Baltimore Beltway, the main crag, often just referred to as "Ilchester," is 35 feet high and not even 100 feet wide. Still, locals have managed to develop and "polish" this gem into a very worthy toproping area, perfectly suited for beginner to intermediate climbers. Popular routes include aptly named *Beginners Slab* (5.4), the prominent corner *Middle Climb* (5.6), and the steep *Blue Rose* (5.8+) finger crack. And, as with most urban climbing areas, there are countless contrived variations and "eliminate" routes that can be created for your climbing pleasure—just tie in and have some fun!

A third park with some quality climbing is Susquehanna State Park, located along the west shore of the Susquehanna River, south of Conowingo.

# BALTIMORE AREA STATE PARKS AND CRAGS

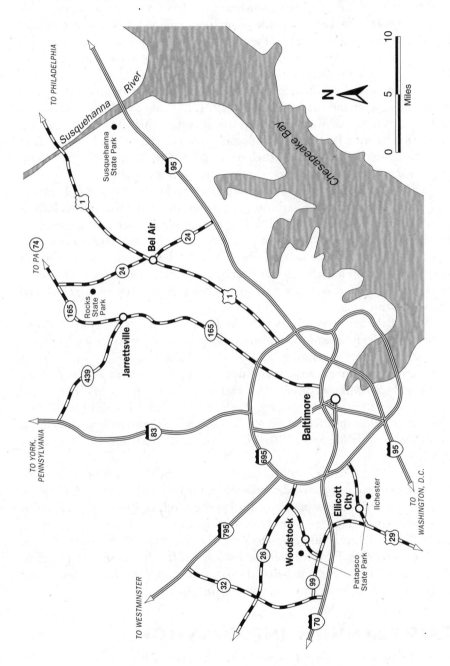

Here, a handful of local hardmen have turned an abandoned granite quarry into a nice little climbing area known as the Mohr Wall. Unfortunately, this state land is land-locked by private properties, making access a real problem. Local activists continue to press the state to provide reasonable access to this public land, but at this time the only legal approach is by boat from Port Deposit. For this reason, no route information is included in this guide.

**Climbing history:** Although recorded climbing history begins with ascents by Mike Endicott and Joe McManus in 1971, it is safe to assume that others, including members of Washington's Potomac Appalachian Trail Club (PATC), visited Rocks State Park in the 1960s and, possibly, the 1950s. It would seem that Rocks' moderate classics, such as *Vertical* (5.6), *Strawberry Jam* (5.8), and *Breakaway* (5.9+) were first climbed during this period.

In 1971 McManus literally uncovered the small Ilchester crag in Patapsco State Park, and along with Endicott put up most of the notable routes, including the classic *Blue Rose* (5.8+). Exploring across the river from Ilchester in 1975, they discovered a small quarry in the woods and climbed *Patapsco Friction Slab* (5.10d). While the friction slab area has been rarely visited in recent years, the outcrop at Ilchester has become extremely popular for after-work workouts—in fact, it is a rare afternoon when there are not topropes draped across this tiny crag.

While Ilchester serves mainly the local climber, the reputation of Rocks State Park quickly spread to climbers in Virginia and Pennsylvania. Weekend climbing has been a mainstay at Rocks since the mid-1970s, and a much larger group of climbers has combined in developing this area. Activists in the 1970s included Mike Endicott, Rick Harward, Sam Spicer, Cliff Stein, Mike Stein, and Milt Strickler; however, it was Endicott and Harward who combined to establish the greatest number of routes. To their credit are hit climbs like *Mike's Finger Buckets* (5.10a), *Biceptennial* (5.10a), and *Golden Arches* (5.11b/c).

During the 1980s and 1990s climbing at Rocks State Park became popular to the point of being crowded on some Saturdays and Sundays. A few new, mainly high-end routes were also added at the hands of Rick Harward, Hugh Herr, and Grant Horner with ascents of *Breakfast of Champions* (5.11c), *Hugh's Face* (5.12c), and *Fever Dream* (5.12a/b), respectively. Meanwhile at the Patapsco crags, local climbers added a few difficult variations and "eliminate routes" at Ilchester, and Rob Savoye and, later, John Kelbel discovered and developed the small crag near Woodstock.

# TRIP PLANNING INFORMATION

**General description:** Toproping and numerous good, one-pitch leads. A few contrived multipitch leads are possible at Rocks State Park.

**Location:** Rocks State Park and Patapsco State Park are both located within thirty minutes of the Baltimore Beltway.

**Camping:** There is no overnight camping in either Rocks or Patapsco State Parks.

**Climbing season:** Year-round.

**Gear:** A standard lead rack of stoppers, TCUs, cams to 4 inches, quick-draws, and runners will suffice for all leads and will aid in setting toprope anchors. Extra webbing and static line are useful for tying off trees.

**Restrictions and access issues:** Maryland State Parks close at sunset—plan to be back to your car before then. An entrance fee is required (most weekends) to park in the lot above the cliffs at Rocks State Park. An annual State Park pass is available for $50 by calling 410–557–7994, though most climbers park for free in the pulloff along Route 24 (below the cliffs).

**Guidebooks:** None, although you can find information on climbing at Rocks State Park and Ilchester on a number of Internet sites.

**Nearby mountain shops, guide services, and gyms:** There is an REI store just north of the Baltimore Beltway in Timonium (410–252–5920). For guide services and indoor climbing, visit Earth Treks Climbing Center in Columbia (800–CLIMB–UP).

**Emergency services:** Dial 911 for police or an ambulance. For state park rangers, call 410–557–7994.

**Nearby climbing areas:** Carderock and Great Falls are about an hour southwest of Baltimore, and the Frederick Area crags described in this book are just over an hour to the west.

**Nearby attractions:** Baltimore's Inner Harbor is a major tourist destination, as is the nation's capital, one hour to the south.

**Finding the crags:** Detailed directions are provided in the respective sections below.

# ROCKS STATE PARK

## OVERVIEW

"Rocks," as it's called by climbers, is the Baltimore area's best crag with its many high-quality topropes and handful of good leads. The schist-type rock climbs similarly to that of Carderock and Great Falls; however, the routes here are as much as twice as high. Consequently, Rocks State Park is a destination area that many climbers drive several hours to visit. Don't miss climbing here in late October or early November, as this wooded climbing area is absolutely gorgeous in the fall. Rocks is also a good winter crag with its many south-facing walls.

**Finding the crag:** From Baltimore, take I–95 north to exit 77 (MD 24). Take MD 24 north, through Bel Air, Rock Spring, and Forest Hill. The park

# ROCKS STATE PARK OVERVIEW

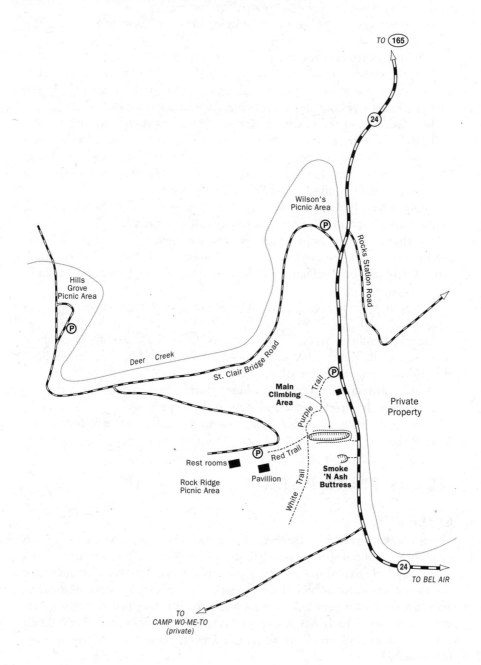

TO (165)

24

Wilson's
Picnic Area

Ⓟ

Rocks Station Road

Hills
Grove
Picnic Area

Ⓟ

Deer    Creek

St. Clair Bridge Road

Ⓟ

**Main
Climbing
Area**

Purple Trail

Private
Property

Rest rooms ■

Red Trail

Ⓟ

**Smoke
'N Ash
Buttress**

Pavillion

White Trail

Rock Ridge
Picnic Area

24

TO BEL AIR

TO
CAMP WO-ME-TO
(private)

# ROCKS STATE PARK DETAIL

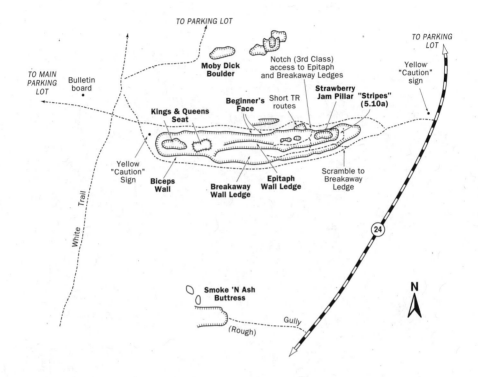

*TO PARKING LOT*

**Moby Dick Boulder**

Notch (3rd Class) access to Epitaph and Breakaway Ledges

*TO PARKING LOT*

Yellow "Caution" sign

*TO MAIN PARKING LOT*

Bulletin board

**Strawberry Jam Pillar**   **"Stripes" (5.10a)**

**Beginner's Face**   Short TR routes

**Kings & Queens Seat**

Yellow "Caution" Sign

**Biceps Wall**

**Breakaway Wall Ledge**

**Epitaph Wall Ledge**

Scramble to Breakaway Ledge

White Trail

24

**Smoke 'N Ash Buttress**

Gully

(Rough)

N

is located on the left about 5 miles north of Forest Hill. There is free parking below the crags, located along MD 24, next to a maintenance building. The park's main parking area (access fee on weekends) is above the cliff, where there is a pavilion and rest rooms. To reach this area, drive a short distance north on MD 24 to a steel bridge and turn left onto St. Clair Bridge Road. Continue 0.8 mile and turn left into the main park entrance. Drive uphill and park in the first lot on the left.

## BICEPS WALL

This popular toprope wall is located just below the King and Queen's Seat area on the uphill, south side of the main rock formation. Topropes are commonly set up by slinging the tall tree growing up along the center of the wall. You can also set directionals or other anchors nearby with natural gear. The routes vary in length from 25 to 50 feet, increasing in height from left to right.

**Finding the wall:** Approach from above the King and Queen's Seat area where the top of the main rock formation meets the hillside. Hike down a short trail along the right (south) side of the cliff, beginning at a yellow caution sign.

# BICEPS WALL

1. **Exhibition** (5.11b/c TR) Start on a green, sloping ledge just right of two small boulders. Climb the left-facing flake and through the overhang at a 3-inch left-facing corner (above the lip of the overhang).

2. **Fever Dream** (5.12b TR) Begin in front of the large tree that's often used as the belay tree for the first four routes on this wall. Climb straight up to the overhang, where you find two tiny undercling holds partway out the overhang. Crank, scrape, and scum past the roof just to the right of a tiny, left-facing corner (see *Exhibition*).

3. **Biceptennial** (5.10a TR) The most popular toprope on this wall. Beginning in front of the large "belay tree," boulder up and mantle onto the sloping ledge. Now follow the line of best holds up and slightly right to

meet the overhang below a large, left-facing corner. Undercling, lieback, and lunge to large holds a few feet above the roof and finish up.

4. **Golden Arches** (5.11b/c TR) Start 6 feet right of *Biceptennial* at side-pull handholds directly below the golden colored, arching right side of the overhang. Climb up to the apex of the "golden arch" overhang, then continue up the middle of the face to the top. **Variation** (5.10) From the arch, climb up much better holds on the right side of the face.

5. **Critter Crack a.k.a. Peanut Brittle and The Flake** (5.5) This route ascends the left-facing crack/flake system located about 20 feet right of the Biceps Wall belay tree. Unlike the other routes on the wall, you can safely lead this route.

6. **The Crux** (5.5) A popular lead. This route begins a few feet right of *Critter Crack* and just below a right-facing corner. Start up, then move right (stance) to a short crack. Continue up past a horizontal crack to another crack, then into a large, right-facing block and on to the top.

## BREAKAWAY WALL

This wall is the heart of climbing at Rocks, and the large ledge at its base can become quite festive on nice weekend afternoons. Two of the area's best leads, *Breakaway* and *Vertical,* are located here; although most often you'll see topropes draping the 80-foot wall. To set up a toprope, 4th-Class up the left side of the notch between the right edge of Breakaway Wall and Strawberry Jam Pillar.

**Finding the wall:** The easiest approach is via a 3rd-Class scramble up the side of the cliff, beginning just above MD 24. If you park up top or are coming in from the King and Queen's Seat area, scramble through the notch formed by the main crag and Strawberry Jam Pillar. Carefully descend a 30-foot, 4th-Class downclimb to gain the right side of the Breakaway Ledge.

7. **Bat** (5.9) Start at the left end of the *Breakaway Wall* ledge at the obvious chimney/crack system. Scramble up the gully, then jam straight out the roof crack and up to a stance. Move right and climb easier rock up to Epitaph Ledge.

8. **Centrifuge** (5.7) Same start as *Bat.* Up the gully to the roof, then move right around this to a nice flake. Lieback the flake to its end, then climb easier face moves to the top.

9. **Centrifuge Direct** (5.8 TR) Start at the base of the gully/chimney but climb the outside corner/arête up past a bulge to the *Centrifuge* flake and then to the top.

10. **Breakaway Left** (5.9-) The classic route at Rocks State Park! Dance up the large, right-facing corner (bolt) to the overhang and move left

# BREAKAWAY WALL

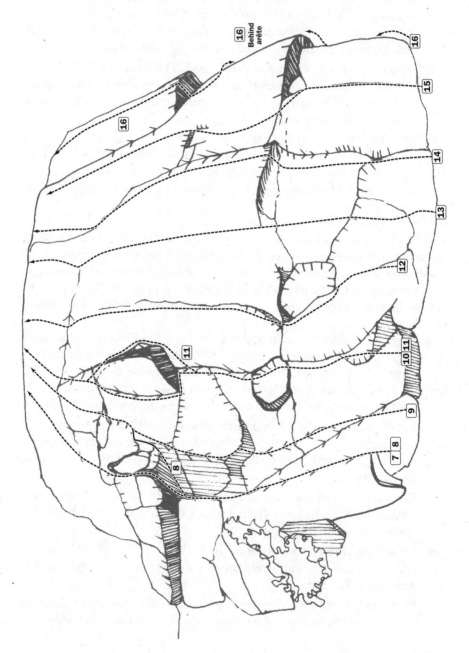

around it and up to a nice rest ledge. Stem up the short corner above (crux) to better holds on greenish rock. Wander up easier rock (5.6 R) to the top. Both *Breakaway* routes are excellent leads if you're solid at the grade.

11. **Breakaway Right** (5.9+) Climb the *Breakaway* corner, but traverse right a few feet below the overhang, then move up to a good lieback crack (pin). Climb the crack to its top (crux), then rejoin the regular route up much easier moves to the top. This variation is more continuous than the regular route, which I think makes this the better way!

12. **Superbulge** (5.12c/d TR) The local testpiece. Some broken holds have made this route even harder over the years. Probably 5.12d (or harder) for shorter climbers. Six feet right of *Breakaway*, climb the left-slanting seam up to a small overhang/flake. Move right, then up the right side of the flake, and where the holds evaporate, power up and slightly left until you reach small, left-facing flakes. Continue straight up to a rest, then climb much easier rock to the top. Variation: **Breakfast of Champions** (5.11d) Climb the first few feet of *Superbulge,* then angle up and right to join *Mike's Finger Buckets* about 30 feet up.

13. **Mike's Finger Buckets** (5.10a TR) Nice climbing, and a good introduction to 5.10. Begin near the center of the *Breakaway Wall* or about 6 feet left of *Vertical*. Follow good holds up a few feet to a flake. Now, grab small flakes/edges and make two hard moves up to a good horizontal crack. Continue up a thin seam, then a blunt arête to the top.

14. **Vertical** (5.6) Very popular as both a toprope and a lead climb. Start about 6 feet right of *Mike's Finger Buckets,* at a vertical crack formed by two nearly touching flakes. Climb up the crack/flakes, then move through the right side of the overhang to a left-slanting crack system. Follow the cracks for about 20 feet, then crank straight up through the bulge on good holds to the ledge.

15. **Bone Jacker** (5.7) Just right of *Vertical,* climb the face to the start of the left-leaning crack. Move right of the overhang and up the steep, rough face to a white headwall. Continue up to *Vertical's* belay ledge.

16. **Piney** (5.10b) At the right end of the *Breakaway* ledge, climb the 12-foot-high, right-facing corner to a bulge. Climb through this on large holds, then up more slabby rock to a roof with an obvious flake. Move out the flake and up to *Vertical's* ledge (with pine tree).

**Note:** Right of *Piney* is a 4th-Class climb up to the base of Strawberry Jam Pillar. From here, you can scramble down to the north face or 4th-Class up to the Epitaph ledge atop the Breakaway Wall.

*Eric McCallister on Vertical (5.6), Rocks, Maryland.* PHOTO BY ERIC J. HÖRST

# EPITAPH WALL

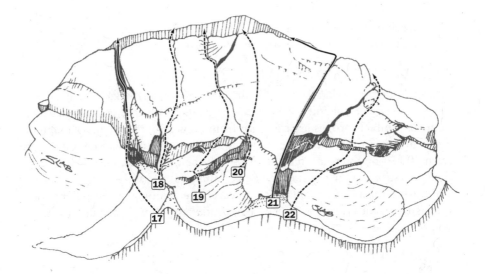

## EPITAPH WALL

Set back above the top of the Breakaway Wall is a 25-foot face with a few good roped climbs and some bouldering. Though one or two of the lines might be worth leading, most parties set up topropes, since there's little room for error when climbing off this elevated ledge.

**Finding the wall:** Locate the notch between the main cliff and Strawberry Jam Pillar, and carefully scramble up 3rd- and 4th-Class moves along the right edge of the main cliff. As you ascend past a pine tree, begin to work left to Epitaph Ledge above the Breakaway Wall.

17. **Epitaph Double Direct** (5.10a) Start at the far end of the ledge and scramble up the painted slab about 10 feet to a large fracture. Climb the flake and short corner to the top.

18. **Epitaph Direct** (5.10a) Six feet left of a low horn, step over a thorny bush and begin on a good horizontal bucket and crack. Climb the center of the wall past two faint, S-shaped grooves.

19. **Epitaph Wall** (5.8) Just left of the low horn, climb up the right-facing flake 15 feet, then go left or right to the top.

20. **Goblin's Eye** (5.8+ TR) Beginning on the low horn, move right onto the face (gray paint) and climb up past a flake, then up and left to the top.

21. **Divirgin Jam** (5.9) In the middle of Epitaph Wall, climb the prominent, right-facing crack to its end (stance on right). Finish up and left to the top.

22. **Breakaway's Escape Hatch** (5.5) Five feet right of *Divirgin Jam,* follow quartz knobs up and right to a ledge. From here, scramble to the top.

## STRAWBERRY JAM PILLAR

This free-standing pillar is the hallmark of climbing at Rocks State Park, and the *Strawberry Jam* hand crack that ascends its south face is the area's most popular climb. Topropes are easily set from bolts atop the pillar, although the 5.4 climb up to the anchors can be quite scary. The climbs range in length from 30 feet on the south face to 45 feet on the north face. On summer days, don't be surprised if the north face is damp, as it readily condenses water vapor from the air on humid days. However, the climbing on the pillar's south face is excellent any time of the year. *Strawberry Jam* is a must-do lead if you're solid at 5.8.

## SOUTH FACE

23. **Rick's Way** (5.4) Start in the notch on the west side of the *Strawberry Jam* pillar. Boulder up a few moves to a small, 6-foot-high crack that leads up to the left side of an overhang/arête. Climb up the crack, step left, and scramble up (pin) easier moves to the top of the pillar and belay bolts (25 feet).

24. **Armless Ambidextrian** (5.10b TR) Just right of *Rick's Way,* climb 12 feet up a thin seam to the overhang, and continue up the arête to the top.

25. **Creakin' Eye Lid** (5.11c/d TR) Begin as in *Armless Ambidextrian* for a few moves, but move right at a good bucket to attain knobby holds on the front face. Now climb a few increasingly difficult moves up the middle of the "knobby" face to finish on the left-slanting top portion of the *Strawberry Jam* crack.

26. **Strawberry Jam** (5.8) An area classic! Begin at the low spot on the blocky ledge directly below the prominent hand crack. Climb the crack and face 20 feet to a bomber flake and undercling. Follow the left-slanting crack to a stance, then boulder up and right to the belay bolts at the top. A well-protected, popular lead.

27. **Strawberry Jam Direct** (5.10a) Climb the regular route to the large undercling, then follow the right-slanting crack to a hollow flake. From

STRAWBERRY JAM
PILLAR—SOUTH FACE

XX Anchors on backside

23

24

25

26

27

28

*Lisa Ann Hörst on Strawberry Jam (5.8).* Photo by Eric J. Hörst

here you can finish up and right on good holds to the top or crank up and slightly left on thin face moves (5.10d) to the bolt anchors on top. The last piece of protection is a bit difficult to place—thus, this route is usually toproped after doing the regular route.

28. **Hugh's Face** (5.12c TR) Powerful! Start on top of the block just right of *Strawberry Jam*. Power up the overhanging face midway between the jamcrack and a shallow, left-facing corner (on your right). Upon reaching "better" holds on the vertical headwall, move slightly right and finish up good knobs on the right side of the face.

## NORTH FACE

29. **First Line** (5.6) Begin from the sloping rock ledge (careful, it can be very slippery) just below prominent twin cracks. Climb the left crack through a bulge and up along a right-facing corner to the slabby finish.

30. **Peanut Butter** (5.5) Same start as the previous route, but climb the right crack straight up through the left side of the overhang. Finish up easy rock to the top of the pillar.

31. **Scared Straight** (5.9) Right of the twin cracks, start up along a thin seam on green rock to a shelf-like stance. Continue straight up through the roof (crux) to the top. To escape the somewhat reachy roof moves, you can move right below the roof to a ledge, then scramble to the top.

## STRIPES WALL

32. **Stripes** (5.10a/b) This lone (but quite good) route is located just below Strawberry Jam Pillar, facing the road. It is most easily reached by hiking down the north side of the rocks about 75 feet past *Peanut Butter*. You may also be able to spot this face from the road and hike straight uphill to it. Either way, scramble to a belay tree at the base of a low-angle slab with a crack that splits a short, vertical wall above it. From here, climb easy slab moves along the crack to reach the "headwall." Now climb the thin crack up past two horizontal cracks (twenty-plus-year-old pins) and finish through a roof to a belay ledge (50 feet). This route is commonly led; however, the aging pitons are questionable . . . consider using a toprope.

## KING'S AND QUEEN'S SEAT AREA

There are several short routes on the north side of the formation that are mainly used for climbing instruction. They are located uphill along the trail that runs from Strawberry Jam Pillar to the King's and Queen's Seat (stacked boulders) area.

STRAWBERRY JAM PILLAR—
NORTH FACE

*Jeff Batzer leading Smoke 'N' Ash (5.10d) (circa 1980).* Photo by Eric J. Hörst

The first two routes are on a 15-foot detached boulder with a large pine tree on top, just right of the notch between the pillar and the main formation. The left route climbs a short lieback seam (5.9), while the right problem ascends a short flake on the arête (5.9-). A toprope can be anchored to the large pine tree above, although some climbers send these routes as highball boulder problems (careful!).

A short distance uphill, there are several popular topropes that begin where the trail passes between the main rock formation (slabby) and some boulders. Three good instructional toprope problems ascent the low-angle face—from left to right, there are a 25-foot, right-facing corner, a 20-foot thin crack, and a 15-foot hand crack—ranging in grade from 5.0 to 5.3.

## SMOKE 'N' ASH BUTTRESS

This small rock formation is known for its classic, 25-foot overhanging hand crack, *Smoke 'N' Ash*. Although many persons toprope this route, it's an excellent, well-protected lead if you've got the guns to hang out and plug the gear!

**Finding the crag:** The best approach is from the road below the rock formation, though you can bushwhack straight through the woods about 200 yards from below Breakaway Wall. From below the main rock formation, walk about 150 yards along the road until you spot a couple of boulders (possibly a cairn) atop the embankment. Bushwhack straight up through the woods, and you'll soon spot the short but impressive hand crack.

33. **Smoke 'N' Ash** (5.10d) A short, sweet lead with great gear. Jam the crack up to the roof and pull through to the top.

34. **Blowin' Smoke** (5.6) Climb the low-angle crack located about 10 feet right of *Smoke 'N' Ash*.

35. **Ash Arête** (5.8) On the arête right of *Smoke 'N' Ash*, climb a thin crack past two pins to the top.

# PATAPSCO VALLEY STATE PARK

Three small cliffs within Patapsco Valley State Park are described below. The Ilchester area is, by far, the best and most popular. The Friction Wall and Woodstock Wall areas are included for informational purposes. These two areas should be of interest only if you live in the immediate area (i.e., they are not very good).

## ILCHESTER CRAG

**Finding the crag:** Exit I–695 at Frederick Road and go west approximately 2 miles to Hilltop Road. Turn left on Hilltop Road and continue through a development and into a forested area. Park in a dirt lot on the left under a

# PATAPSCO VALLEY STATE PARK

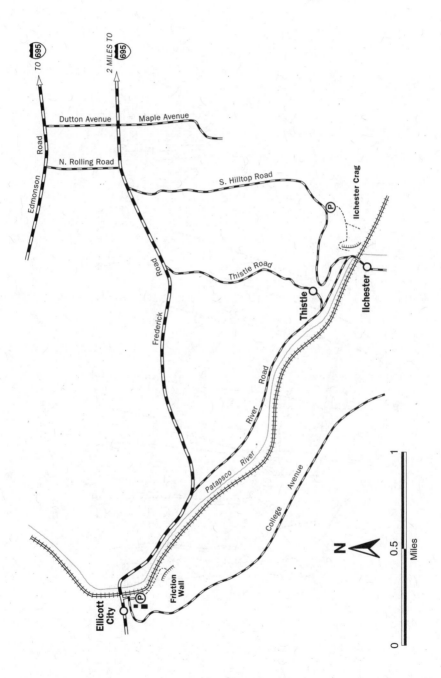

# ILCHESTER CRAG

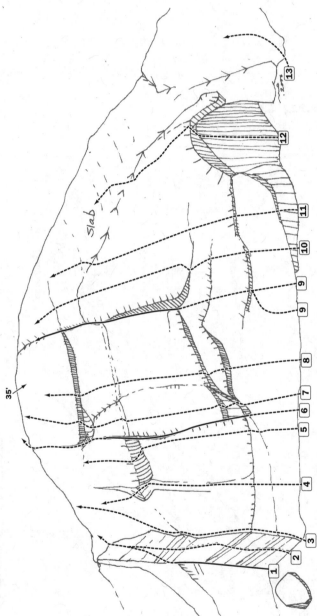

powercut. Hike the trail into the woods—stay right at the split—for about 300 yards to the top of the crag. Descend on either side of the outcrop.

1. **Renaissance** (5.8+) Begin below a dirty corner on the left side of the north-facing wall. Boulder up the corner about 10 feet, then angle up and right across overhanging rock to finish near the center of the face.

2. **Midnight Lightning** (5.10d/5.11a) The hardest moves are right off the ground—bring a crash pad and climb the route as a high-ball boulder problem. Beginning a few feet right of the *Renaissance* corner, power thin moves off the ground and continue up the center of the overhanging face.

3. **Beginner's Corner** (5.5) Climb the left outside corner/arête, starting from a small block at the base of wooden steps.

4. **Ninja** (5.11c/d) Begin halfway between *Beginner's Corner* and the *Blue Rose* crack. Climb through the low roof and up along a thin crack. Continue through a bulge and up to the top.

5. **Captain Crunch** (5.13a) Start just left of *Blue Rose* and climb the face along a black streak and through a bulge. The *Blue Rose* crack is off-route.

6. **Blue Rose** (5.8+) The Ilchester classic. A decent 35-foot lead—bring small to medium stoppers and cams. Jam up the obvious crack. The crux is the start, especially if you're short.

7. **Codie Joe** (5.9) Begin 3 feet right of *Blue Rose*. Pull through a low roof and climb up along a seam, staying roughly 3 feet right of *Blue Rose,* and finish through the left side of a high roof.

8. **High Anxiety Direct** (5.9) Start 6 feet right of the crack. Climb up past two overhangs to a small, right-facing corner. Finish up through the middle of a high overhang.

9. **Middle Climb** (5.6) Begin in front of a tree or, if the rock is wet, a few feet to the left. Climb up to and along the prominent, left-facing, left-leaning corner to the top.

10. **Double O** (5.7) Beginning just right of the tree, climb up along a green streak and past double overhangs. Generally wet, dirty, and . . . green.

11. **Omega** (5.9) Start 10 feet right of the tree and a cool pinch/undercling hold about 6 feet up. Climb straight up through a bulge to a 4th-Class finish. Possible high-ball boulder problem.

12. **Omega Direct** (5.7) Begin below an omega-shaped formation 15 feet right of the tree. Climb up through the middle of the overhang and conclude up 4th-Class rock.

13. **Beginner's Slab** (5.4) Climb anywhere up the 20-foot slab located on the far right end of the outcrop.

# FRICTION WALL

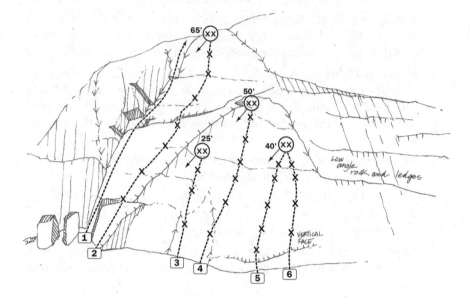

## FRICTION WALL

This wall is worth visiting for just one reason—*Patapsco Slab* (5.10d). Other than this, the area is a nasty, abandoned quarry with a few dirty topropes and four sport routes. Not much is known about the sport routes other than they are likely in the 5.12 range and each possesses a few manufactured holds. I guess they could be fun as project routes if you live near Ellicott City.

**Finding the wall:** From Ilchester, take Frederick Road west to Ellicott City. As you enter town on Main Street, you cross the river and pass under a railroad bridge. Take the first left turn at The Phoenix Emporium and use metered parking located on either side of the lane. Hike away from Main Street along the railroad tracks for roughly 250 meters to a small concrete post on the right. A faint trail leads into the woods about 100 feet to the quarry walls. The routes are located on the left side.

1. **Surrealistic Pillow** (5.10) Recommended only as a toprope. Beginning just left of *Patapsco Slab*, climb up the crack and blocky corners to the top.

2. **Patapsco Slab a.k.a. Friction Slab** (5.10d) A classic friction route! May feel much harder if your friction technique is not up to snuff. Climb the 65-foot slab past 7 bolts to anchors.

3. **40 Weight** (5.11) 3 bolts to anchors.

4. **Unknown** (5.13?) 6 bolts to highest set of anchors.

5. **Unknown** (5.12?) 5 bolts to shared anchors.

6. **Unknown** (5.12?) 4 bolts to shared anchors.

## WOODSTOCK WALL

This wall's only redeeming value is its steepness; otherwise, it's a dirty, damp, 40-foot outcrop that most climbers wouldn't grant a second look. However, local climbers have managed to clean enough holds to establish a dozen toprope routes up through the cliff's blocky overhangs. One can only hope that this crag will improve further with traffic, but for now beware of loose rock and dirt. If you live nearby, it may be worth a visit to get some practice pulling through overhangs, or consider stopping by for a quick bouldering session—the best rock at Woodstock is actually the small bouldering cave located just uphill to the left of the main cliff.

**Finding the wall:** From the Baltimore Beltway get on I-70 West and go about 5 miles to the exit for MD 29N. Take this exit and turn left at the first traffic light onto MD 99. Drive 3.8 miles down MD 99 and turn right onto Woodstock Road. Continue on Woodstock Road for just over a mile and park in a large gravel lot on the left, just before crossing the railroad tracks. Hike down the tracks, away from Ye Old Woodstock Inn, for 200 yards, and you'll spot this small, dirty outcrop on the hillside to the left. Follow a short trail, beginning at a small railroad maintenance shed, up to the cliff.

1. **Quiver** (5.8+) Begin at the base of the prominent outside corner on the right side of the front face. Climb up through a small, arching overhang, then move up along a lieback flake and finish up the right side of the dirty face.

2. **White Stuff** (5.10c) Start 5 feet left of *Quiver*, below a 2- x 3-foot overhang about 10 feet up. Climb up through the right side of this overhang, using a shallow, vertical slot to pull up onto the face above. Finish up easier rock and through ferns to the top (if you choose).

3. **Do or Die** (5.6) Climb the shallow, left-facing, left-leaning corner to a ledge at mid-height. Move right and finish up the face above through ferns.

4. **Imangian** (5.11b/c) Just left of *Do or Die,* climb the more prominent left-facing corner to the base of the obvious, flaring chimney. Make a long reach left to gain holds on the lip of the large overhang to the left. Pull through the right side of this overhang and up to the top.

5. **Orange Juice** (5.6) Start at the small, pyramidal corner and climb up the path of least resistance to gain the flaring chimney. Scum up this to the top.

# WOODSTOCK WALL

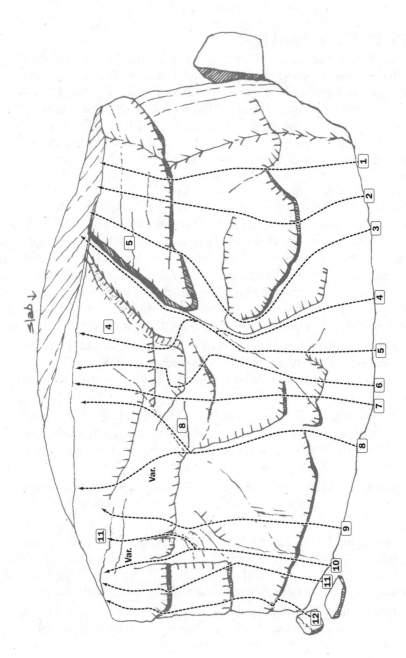

6. **Agitation** (5.11b/c) Begin by pulling through the low overhang just left of the small, pyramidal dihedral. Continue up to a horizontal crack below the first overhang. Hand-traverse left on good holds, then move up and crank back out to the right in an attempt to pull through the middle of the final, rectangular overhang.

7. **Stone** (5.10b/c) Start just left of *Agitation,* and climb straight up the face to pull through the weakness on the left side of the *Agitation* overhang.

8. **Bloody Bucket** (5.9+) Climb the large, left-facing corner to the roof crack. Pull through the roof on the right and follow the right-slanting crack to the top. Variation: **The Wimpy Winner Way** (5.8) Begin as in *Bloody Bucket,* but climb up and left through the roof, following left-slanting features.

9. **Do What!** (5.10c) Start at a 3-foot-high, vertical crack with a large roof about 20 feet above. Work up the discontinuous cracks to the roof. Climb the left-facing handrail out the roof and scum up to the top.

10. **Flying Lessons** (5.10b) Begin just left of *Do What!* and climb up broken rock to below the center of the largest part of the roof above. Stem or chimney out through the middle of the roof and continue up to the top. Variation: **No Fly Zone** (5.10a) From below the large roof, work up through the narrow chimney notch on the left side of the roof.

11. **Mother F** (5.11a) Start on the left side of the front face, below a 3 x 3-foot overhang about 10 feet up. Climb around the right side of this over-hang, step back left, and work up a short crack through another roof to the top.

12. **Dyno Man** (5.8+) Begin from a stance on a small, sloping rock at the left edge of the main crag. Pull up to a bucket on the left side of the 3 x 3-foot overhang, then continue up past some small ledges to finish through another overhang above. Beware of some loose rock.

# FREDERICK AREA CRAGS

## OVERVIEW

Within 20 miles of Frederick, Maryland, and less than ninety minutes from the Baltimore–Washington, D.C., corridor are four areas that offer an alternative to the cliffs of Great Falls and Carderock. Here in the Appalachian foothills is quality climbing in an uncrowded and natural setting. Although you may need to spend a bit more approach time, the investment yields quality rock climbing in a beautiful, mountain environment.

The best of the bunch is Annapolis Rock, located along the Appalachian Trail about 15 miles west of Frederick. The clean, white quartzite and abundant horizontal cracks and overhangs are reminiscent of the Shawangunks in New York. Primarily a toprope area with routes up to 85 feet in height, there are also several wonderful leads, including *Black Crack* (5.9), *The Battlefield* (5.10a), and *Faint's Roof* (5.10a).

Fifteen miles south of Frederick is Sugarloaf Mountain, a privately owned conservation and recreation area with a long history of climbing. The rock here is also a whitish quartzite, but it is much more fractured, and the primary outcrops offer many excellent climbs in the 5.3 to 5.9 range. A satellite crag known as White Rocks possesses a steeper angle, fewer features, and routes up to 5.12a. Toproping is the norm at both areas, but a few quality leads can be done, *Cub Scout Cracks* (5.3), *Seven Wishes* (5.6), and *The Sherpa Connection* (5.8) among them.

Multipitch climbing can be found on the blocky cliffs along the Potomac River, across from Harpers Ferry, West Virginia. Known as Maryland Heights, the cliffs here are the tallest in the area, with a few climbs exceedingly 200 feet. However, the highly fractured, somewhat loose character of the rock makes climbing here a more serious endeavor, despite the moderate grades of many climbs. Primarily an area of local interest, there are two good reasons for non-locals to visit Maryland Heights at least one time: 1) the classic four-pitch *Hard Up* (5.8), which ascends along the left edge of a nineteenth-century sign painted on the cliff; 2) the stunning view of the Potomac River and historic Harpers Ferry available only to climbers perched up on the cliff.

# FREDERICK AREA CRAGS

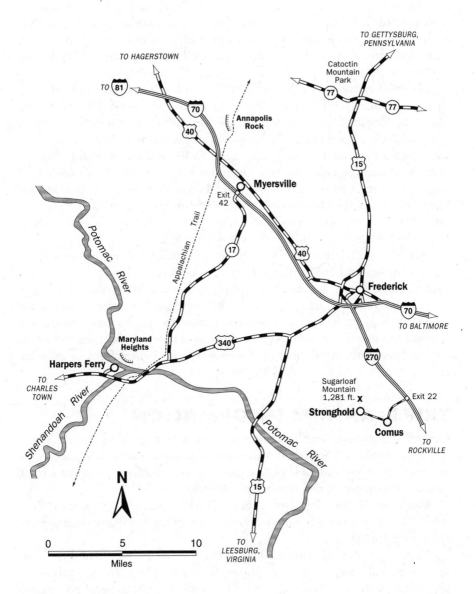

Catoctin Mountain Park, 14 miles north of Frederick, is the final area of note, if only for its small outcrops suitable for bouldering and some elementary toproping. A well-developed trail system leads past such formations as Chimney Rock and Wolf Rock. Both offer a small amount of climbing; however, you must sign in at park headquarters prior to climbing. While you're there, pick up a trail map, and have an enjoyable day hiking and bouldering in this beautiful park.

**Climbing history:** As less noteworthy, off-the-beaten-path crags, the history of technical climbing at Annapolis Rock, Sugarloaf Mountain, and Maryland Heights is largely a mystery. What *is* known is that members of the Washington Rock Climbers' Club and, later, the Potomac Appalachian Trail Club visited these areas as early as the late 1940s and 1950s. In the 1960s, it is reported that Joe Faint climbed Annapolis Rock's *Faint's Roof* (5.10a); the huge roof to its right was aided and named *Nixon's Nose* (A1). At Maryland Heights, many of the first recorded ascents by Rob Savoye and other Baltimore-area climbers took place in the late 1970s and early 1980s. The first party to climb the famous "sign route" is unknown, though.

As with any area that has a long history of climbing but no guidebook, different climbers and even different generations have climbed the same lines, each thinking they had done a first ascent. As a result, some routes have been named and renamed over the years. Whenever original route names are known, this guide has utilized original names. In many cases, though, the route names found in this chapter are those used by climbers of the 1980s and 1990s. The author would be grateful to receive any corrections or information known by long-term patrons of these areas.

# TRIP PLANNING INFORMATION

**General description:** Excellent topropes and a few leads up to 80 feet at Annapolis Rock and Sugarloaf Mountain. Numerous multipitch climbs exist on the cliffs of Maryland Heights. Catoctin Mountain Park possesses a small amount of bouldering and toprope possibilities.

**Location:** All four areas lie within a 20-mile radius of Frederick, Maryland, and between sixty to ninety minutes west of the Baltimore–Washington, D.C., megalopolis.

**Camping:** Camping is allowed along the Appalachian Trail, and there are some especially nice sites atop Annapolis Rock. There are several campgrounds in Catoctin Mountain Park (301–663–9330) and nearby Cunningham Falls State Park (301–271–7574).

**Climbing season:** Climbing is possible year-round, though it can be significantly windier and colder at these mountain locations than in the metropolitan areas to the east. Mild winter days yield good climbing conditions at the west-facing crags of Maryland Heights, Annapolis Rock, and portions of Sugarloaf Mountain.

**Gear:** A full rack of stoppers, cams to 4 inches, several quickdraws and runners, and a 50-meter rope are sufficient for the lead climbs at these areas. Many of the topropes at Annapolis Rock and Sugarloaf Mountain require long webbing or static line runners to reach anchor trees beyond the clifftops.

**Restrictions and access issues:** Sugarloaf Mountain closes at sunset, so be sure to exit the rocks well ahead of time. Catoctin Mountain Park requires all climbers to register (and sign a waiver) at the visitor center. Forest Service and National Park Service regulations apply at Annapolis Rock and Maryland Heights, respectively. Climbers are required to sign in (and sign out) at the ranger station in Harpers Ferry prior to climbing at Maryland Heights. You may be "rescued" and fined if you do not!

**Guidebooks:** None, other than this guide and some text information available on the Internet. See Indy's Underground Guide to Sugarloaf Mountain for more routes on Sugarloaf Mountain as well as at other Maryland crags. Visit this online guidebook at www.bcpl.lib.md.us/~indy/climbing/guide.html.

**Nearby mountain shops and gyms:** The Trail House (301–694–8448) in Frederick is the nearest outdoor shop. For an indoor gym you'll need to drive to Earth Treks (800–CLIMB–UP) in Columbia or Sportrock (301–ROCK–111) in Rockville.

**Services:** All services are available in Frederick, although you'll find gas and fast food along the main highways to and from each crag.

**Emergency services:** Call 911 for police and other emergency services. The nearest hospital is Frederick Memorial Hospital (301–698–3300).

**Nearby climbing areas:** Crescent Rock is less than an hour away on VA 7 west of Leesburg, Virginia. Of course, the crags at Carderock and Great Falls are also just an hour away to the southeast.

**Nearby attractions:** The historic town of Harpers Ferry is highly recommended for a half-day of touring. For a relaxing, nonclimbing day in the mountains, visit Catoctin Mountain Park and Cunningham Falls State Park for scenic hikes and beautiful campgrounds.

**Finding the crags:** All crags are within 20 miles of Frederick, Maryland. Detailed directions are included in each section below.

# ANNAPOLIS ROCK

The clean white faces of Annapolis Rock arguably offer the state's finest climbing opportunities. However, with an hour-long approach along the Appalachian Trail, the crags are visited by more hikers than climbers. The area's west exposure provides a great view of the Potomac River Valley and, quite often, a stunning sunset. Consequently, Annapolis Rock is a popular

# ANNAPOLIS ROCK

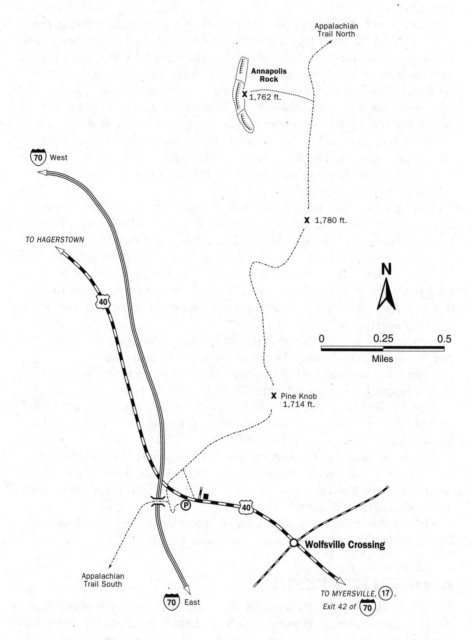

Appalachian
Trail North

Annapolis
Rock
**X** 1,762 ft.

**70** West

TO HAGERSTOWN

**40**

**X** 1,780 ft.

**N**

0      0.25      0.5
Miles

**X** Pine Knob
1,714 ft.

**P**   **40**

◯ **Wolfsville Crossing**

Appalachian
Trail South

**70** East

TO MYERSVILLE, **17**,
Exit 42 of **70**

camping area with AT hikers, and there are numerous sites located near the overlook at the top of the cliff.

**Finding the area:** Take I–70 to exit 42 for Myersville. Turn north toward Myersville and drive a short distance into town—keep a close watch for a right turn onto MD 17 (easy to miss). Take MD 17 about 0.5 mile north to an intersection with US 40. Turn left and take US 40 west for about 2.5 miles to a large Appalachian Trail parking area on the left near the crest of a long hill—park here.

Cross the road and begin hiking up a narrow dirt trail that, for a short time, parallels US 40. Soon the trail bends right and merges with the Appalachian Trail. Follow the AT about 2 miles north to a downhill-sloping, blue-blazed trail that breaks off on the left. There may or may not be a small square sign reading "Annapolis Rock: View and Spring" nailed to a tree at this intersection. Follow the blue-blazed trail (not the AT) about five minutes to the top of the cliffs above *Faint's Roof*. From the overlook, Argo Rock is about 75 yards to the right (north); the South End Area is roughly 100 yards to the left.

## ARGO ROCK

This 40-foot-high, 40-foot-wide rock prow is located at the far north end of the area. From below *Faint's Roof*, hike about 75 yards north along the cliff-base to reach this dramatic outcrop. When approaching from the overlook, follow a trail north along the clifftop for about 75 yards and locate a casual walkdown at the far end of the cliff.

1. **The Battlefield** (5.10a) Great climbing all the way. An excellent lead with an exciting finish! Start near the middle of the clean white face, below a discontinuous, thin seam. Face climb along the thin seam to gain a good horizontal crack below the first overhang. Move a bit left and up through tiered overhangs, passing left of a small, triangular "nose," to a good bucket hold at the lip of the overhang. Mantle past the lip and up easier moves to a good belay ledge (40 feet). **Gear:** Stoppers, camming units to 3 inches and a couple of small TCUs for above the lip (optional). Variation: **Exit Field Right** (5.9) Climb up along the seam to below the first overhang, then angle up and right along a series of good holds to work around the right side of the final roof. Finish just right of a large, protruding flake to the belay ledge (45 feet).

2. **Argonaut** (5.11c) Highly recommended as a toprope. Climb the prominent, southwest-facing arête. There are two possible starts: 1) Climb the first 12 feet of *The Battlefield*, then hand-traverse right to gain the overhanging start of the arête; 2) Start below and right of the arête and climb easy moves up to a stance below the right side of the arête. Either way,

# ANNAPOLIS ROCK—LEFT SECTOR

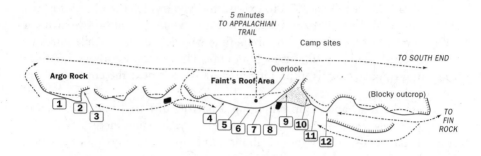

there is 10 feet of desperate climbing past the steep, bottom portion of
the arête, then much easier moves to the top (40 feet).

3.  **Wall of Wander** (5.8) Another really good climb up a wild-looking wall.
    Leadable if you're solid at the great. Start at a crack and short corner
    below the right side of the prominent *Argonaut* arête. Climb up the
    short crack and step left to a stance below a small roof with a thin seam.
    Pull up onto the wild face and climb pretty much straight up staying
    about 5 feet right of the arête. Hidden horizontals make this climb sur-
    prisingly doable and protectable (40 feet). **Variation** (5.6) Start up the
    short crack and corner, but step right onto a low ledge. From here, climb
    up the middle or right side of the face.

## FAINT'S ROOF AREA

This huge, 20-foot tiered roof system is located directly below the Annapolis
Rock Overlook. Descend ledge systems and a few 4th-Class moves, beginning
about 20 yards north of the overlook.

4.  **Cell Phones and Fast Food** (5.9) A great jug-haul through a series of
    small overhangs. Good gear all the way—bring cams up to 3 inches.
    Begin 10 feet left of *Faint's Roof*, at a tree against the cliffbase. Scram-
    ble up small ledges to the first overhang (just right of a wet streak). Fol-
    low good holds through four overhangs to belay at a large boulder on a
    large, vegetated ledge (35 feet).

5.  **Faint's Roof** (5.10a) Annapolis Rock's most intimidating line, and a
    good lead if you are solid on 5.10. Climb easy rock up to the obvious
    weakness through the large roof system. Work out through the tiered
    roof and up a short crack to a mossy ledge (40 feet). Belay here, then
    scramble 4th-Class moves to the Annapolis Rock Overlook area. **Gear:**
    Camming units up to 3 inches. Protection out the roof is good, but dif-
    ficult to place at the lip. If you're solid at the grade, simply run it out
    past the lip; otherwise, set up a toprope.

*Cindy Guthier leading Faint's Roof (5.10a).* PHOTO BY ERIC J. HÖRST

6. **Nixon's Nose** (A1) A popular aid route out the roof crack (old pitons) right of *Faint's Roof*.

7. **Blood and Pus** (5.10d) A good sustained toprope. Start at a black and orange patch of rock 10 feet left of *Ounce of Perception*. Follow streaks up and right to a stance under a 3-foot roof about 35 feet up. Using a small undercling hold, move left through the roof along a left-angling crack to gain flaky jugs and a short, black crack. Pull up onto the face and climb much easier rock to the top (85 feet).

8. **Ounce of Perception** (5.9+) A most popular toprope climb. Start below a low triangular overhang under the far right side of the roof system and at blocks stacked against the wall. Climb through the right side of the low 'hang and up through two more overhangs at a V-notch. Continue up much easier, but nice rock to finish around the left side of a roof at a pointy flake (85 feet).

9. **Pound of Obscure** (5.3) Begin from ledges 10 to 15 feet right of *Ounce of Perception*. Climb juggy rock up and left, then around bulges to an easy finish.

10. **Face the Roof** (5.8+) Begin on blocks near the middle of the northwest-facing wall located opposite *Ounce of Perception*. Start up blocky face moves, then a brief smooth section to a good hold below the middle of the obvious overhang. Reach past the overhang to hidden, but good holds and finish up the face (40 feet).

11. **Face the Notch** (5.4) Start at a large oak tree below a blocky corner. Scramble up easy moves to gain the white face below a notch in the right side of a high overhang. Work up through the notch to the top (55 feet).

12. **In Your Face** (5.3) Beginning at a small oak tree below a high, pointed roof, climb up low-angle rock and pass around the left side of the pointed roof (50 feet).

# FIN ROCK

This 30-foot-high, free-standing block is located about 60 yards south of the *Faint's Roof* area and the overlook. It is easily accessible, either along the cliffbase or from the overlook. Several good toprope routes ascend the steep, west face of this formation. Locate a short, 4th-Class climb on the back of the block to set toprope anchors.

13. **Part Man, Part Monkey** (5.7) Begin at a rhododendron bush about 10 feet left of *Amazon from Ozegna*. Ascend the bulging face, passing a right-pointing flake at mid-height.

14. **Amazon from Ozegna** (5.7) Start below a low overhang with a crack. Follow a broken crack and small corners up and right.

# ANNAPOLIS ROCK—RIGHT SECTOR

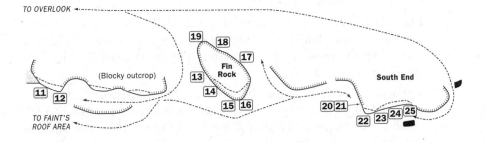

15. **Aqua's Ascent** (5.9) Commence below a large, tiered roof about 10 feet right of *Amazon from Ozegna*. Climb straight up through the left side of the large, tiered roof and up easier rock to the top.

16. **A Call to Arms** (5.9) Beginning just right of *Aqua's Ascent,* climb through the right side of the tiered roof at a square-shaped cut into the lip.

17. **Blondes Just Wanna Have Fin** (5.5) Wander up the middle of the southeast-facing wall, passing a large ledge at mid-height.

18. **End of the Day Wall** (5.8/5.10) Climb the right side of the southeast-facing wall, beginning from roughly midway between a crack on the left and a tree on the right. Grade varies, depending on where you climb up the initial face.

19. **Access Arête** (4th Class) Starting from stacked blocks, boulder up the northeast edge of Fin Rock to set toprope anchors on the summit.

## SOUTH END

At the far south end of Annapolis Rock you'll find a 50-foot-high, white buttress with a number of good topropes and one heck of a great lead climb named *Black Crack*. Approach the area from either above or below—it's easily located about 100 yards south of the overlook and *Faint's Roof* area.

20. **Black Hole Sun** (5.6) Begin on a small ledge below a low, tiered roof about 20 feet left of *White Arête*. Climb up the blocky, left side of the roof system (35 feet).

21. **High Hopes** (5.9) Begin on the small ledge per *Black Hole Sun*. Boulder up to the widest part of the low roof and hand-traverse 5 feet right before continuing up to the top (40 feet).

22. **White Arête** (5.8) Good climbing up the first 20 feet of the arête—the rest is very easy. Climb the prominent, white arête located about 10 feet left of *Black Crack* (50 feet).

23. **Black Crack** (5.9) The best route at Annapolis Rocks. Good holds (and gear) all the way, but steep enough to pump you up! Climb the bulging face along the prominent crack system (50 feet). **Gear:** Stoppers and camming units to 3 inches.

24. **Cynosure** (5.10b/c) Somewhat reachy, but excellent! Commonly toproped after doing *Black Crack*. Beginning 6 feet right of *Black Crack*, climb the bulging face, staying about 6 feet right of the crack throughout. About three-quarters of the way up, exit right around a prominent overhang to finish up on the *Illusion* crack (50 feet). Variation: **Cynosure Direct** (5.11a/b) Three-quarters of the way up, pull through the difficult overhang and finish up the short hand crack at the top of *Black Crack*.

25. **Illusion** (5.8) Start about 12 feet right of *Black Crack,* below a low roof with a triangular feature on the underside. Climb through either side of the low roof and up to a stance below a large overhang with a crack. Continue up through the buckety overhang and notch to the top (50 feet).

# SUGARLOAF MOUNTAIN

Sugarloaf Mountain (1,282 feet) is a beautiful conservation and recreation area with a variety of small crags that have been a popular climbers' playground since the late 1940s. The highly fractured white quartzite on the mountain offers beginner and intermediate climbers plenty of lines on which to practice crack climbing, stemming, face climbing, friction, and pulling overhangs. While a few routes are leadable, toproping is the primary mode of climbing here.

The three most popular outcrops are Middle Earth, The Pillar, and the Boy Scout Ledges. All are located near the summit of the mountain and only a few minutes from each other. A few other smaller crags, such as Devil's Kitchen and Mottled Wall, are located within the park, but not covered here due to their poor quality or limited number of routes. However, there is one excellent satellite crag known as White Rocks, located on the west side of the mountain. This steep, 40-foot cliff possesses the hardest routes at Sugarloaf, and it is the most popular destination for expert climbers visiting Sugarloaf Mountain.

As a final note, this privately owned recreation area is open only from sunrise to sunset. Climbing here is a privilege that we can assume will continue as long as climbers maintain a good safety record and follow all regulations, including exiting the park *before* dark.

# SUGARLOAF MOUNTAIN OVERVIEW

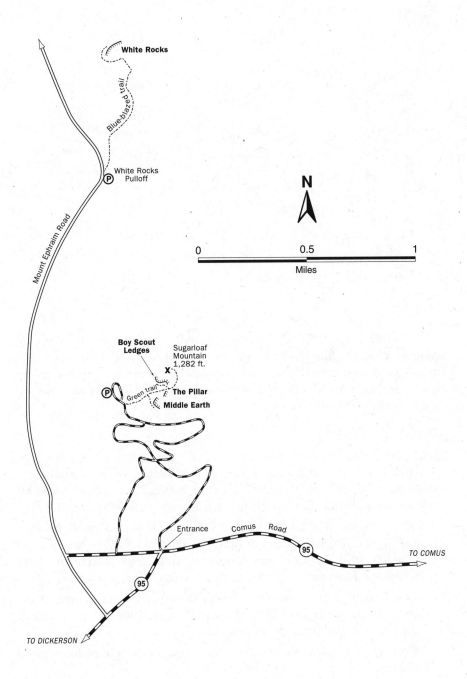

# SUGARLOAF MOUNTAIN DETAIL

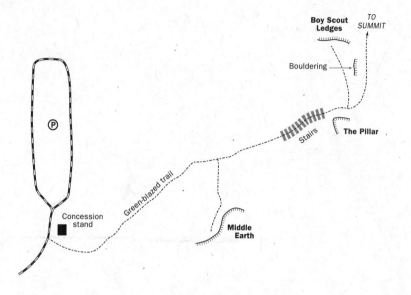

**Finding the area:** Take I–270 to exit 22, and get on MD 109 west toward Comus. Follow this for about 3 miles to an intersection with Comus Road. Turn right onto Comus Road and continue a couple of minutes to the entrance to Sugarloaf Mountain. Take the one-way road up the mountain and park in the large West View lot.

## MIDDLE EARTH

**Finding the rocks:** From the West View lot, take the green trail, which begins just right of the snack shack (seasonal). Follow the beautiful stone-step trail uphill about five minutes to the Middle Earth crag on the right. Scramble through a small boulderfield to the first route on the left side of the outcrop.

1. **White Quartz Wielder** (5.8) Climb the wide crack to a stance below a roof. Pull through the roof just right of a small crack under the roof and continue to the top (35 feet). Variation: **The Lemon Merchant** (5.10) Climb the face just left of the crack and finish through the roof.

2. **Bloodguard** (5.10a) An area classic. Begin below the center of the smooth face just right of *White Quartz Wielder*. Climb up the middle of the face and pull through two overhangs to the top (35 feet).

3. **Cording** (5.3) Climb the obvious crack system just right of *Bloodguard* (30 feet).

MIDDLE EARTH

MIDDLE EARTH

4

5

6

7

Cave route
(4th Class)

8

9

10

11

12

4. **Butterfingers** (5.8) Begin below a blocky crack-and-roof system on the left side of the next buttress right of the *Bloodguard* face. Climb along the crack/weakness through a series of blocky overhangs and staying left of the large roof at mid-height (30 feet).

5. **Rhythm Roof** (5.9) Begin in a slabby corner below a large roof at mid-height. Climb the corner to the roof, move right a few moves under the roof until you can pull through and finish on good holds to the top (35 feet).

6. **Seven Wishes** (5.6) Very popular. Start in the obvious, left-facing corner with a sharp, short arête just to the right. Climb the corner to finish up and slight left along a nice crack (40 feet).

7. **I Am a Cam** (5.7) Climb into the yawning chimney and finish up the face right of *Seven Wishes* (40 feet).

8. **A Flake Called Lee** (5.5) Start just right of a tree at a vertical crack that begins 8 feet above the ground. Climb the crack and right-facing flake above to a slabby finish (40 feet).

9. **For Short People Only** (5.4) Climb the wide, blocky crack just right of *A Flake Called Lee* (35 feet).

10. **Hyper-Gamma-Spaces** (5.12a) Hyper hard! Begin at a left-facing corner below a huge roof. Climb the corner, then take a deep breath and crank out the big roof to finish up an obvious hand crack (35 feet).

11. **In Your Head** (5.7) Start below the center of a low overhang on the right wall below the huge *Hyper-Gamma-Spaces* roof. Climb up through the middle of the low roof and finish in the easier crack and corner above (35 feet). Variation: **Shadow Warrior** (5.9) Start left of the regular route and climb up the main corner to the large roof. Traverse right under the roof to finish up the corner above.

12. **Sugarloaf Arête** (5.7) Climb the bulging arête just right of the *Hyper-Gamma-Spaces* roof (40 feet).

13. **Black Planet** (5.9) Nice face climbing with a number of possible variations. Begin right of *Sugarloaf Arête* and directly below a purple splotch of rock at mid-height. Climb the center of the face, passing just left of the purple splotch (35 feet). Climb the right side for a much easier variation, or send the left side with no arête holds for the full 5.9 effect!

## THE PILLAR

The Pillar is located just a minute or two up the main trail above the Middle Earth area.

14. **Pebbles and Bam-Bam** (5.4) A popular route for beginners, with numerous easier and harder variations. Be creative and have fun! Climb anywhere up the very featured, slabby, front face of The Pillar (40 feet).

15. **Just Another Crack in the Wall** (5.1) Climb the large crack up the very low-angle back side of the outcrop (30 feet). Variation: **Little Herc** (5.9) Begin down and right of the wide crack and just off the rock stair. Climb a short, overhanging crack to gain the main route about 12 feet up.

## BOY SCOUT LEDGES

This crag is the closest to the summit of Sugarloaf Mountain. Follow the green trail past Middle Earth and The Pillar, and you'll come to the Boy Scout Ledges on the left. The car-to-crag approach is about ten minutes.

16. **The Prow Right** (5.10d) Begin below the right side of the obvious roof. Climb easy moves up the right side of the face to the roof. Move up and left to finish up the face on the right side of the prow (30 feet). You may also want to try to climb more directly out the prow—possibly 5.12a?

17. **The Prow Left** (5.7) Start up the left outside corner to the left edge of the roof. Finish up and right on the face above the left side of the prow.

18. **Cub Scout Cracks** (5.3) Extremely popular as an introduction to crack climbing. Begin a few paces left of *The Prow* and climb any of the easy cracks up the low-angle face (35 feet).

19. **Indiana Mark vs. The Weather God** (5.4) Begin below the right side of a low roof that's just left of *Cub Scout Cracks*. Climb the wide crack through the right side of the roof (30 feet).

BOY SCOUT LEDGES

20. **Time of the Prophets** (5.7) Climb the offwidth crack through the next low roof left of *Indiana Mark*.

21. **Wish You Were Here** (5.8) Climb reachy moves out the next roof left of *Time of the Prophets*. Move through the notch and up easier rock to the top (25 feet).

## WHITE ROCKS

Located a mile-and-a-half northwest and 500 feet lower than the summit of Sugarloaf Mountain, White Rocks offers stronger climbers a bit more challenging lines than those at the main crags. Most of the routes here are toprope-only, poorly protected lines; however, there is one notable exception. The 40-foot *Sherpa Connection* crack is an excellent 5.8 lead with adequate gear.

**Finding the rocks:** Take Comus Road to the intersection in Stronghold with the Sugarloaf Mountain entrance on the right. Instead of turning right into the park (as for the main climbing areas), continue straight ahead on Comus Road a short distance to an intersection with Mount Ephraim Road. Turn right and take Mount Ephraim Road about 2 miles to a small pulloff (only holds two cars) on the right, at the trailhead for North Peaks Trail. Follow a blue-blazed trail about fifteen minutes uphill to an overlook (the top of White Rocks) on the left.

# WHITE ROCKS

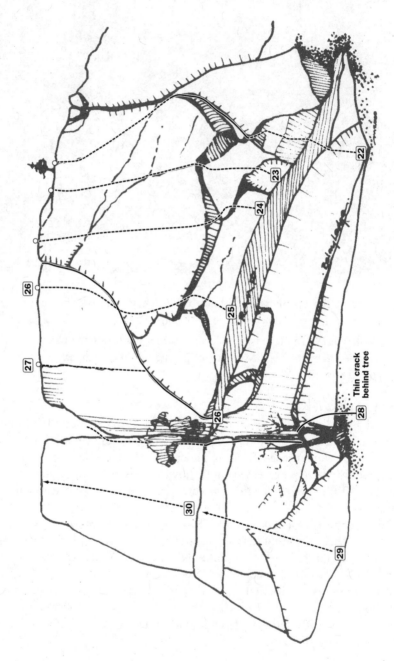

22. **Phasers on Stun** (5.4) Scramble up onto blocks at the base of a left-leaning crack on the right side of the main, vertical White Rocks face (just left of a broken, left-facing corner). Climb the crack to finish just right of a small pine tree.

23. **Dogs of War** (5.12a) Powerful face climbing past two one-finger pockets! Start up on the low-angle ramp at a detached flake and directly below a small pine tree at the top. Fight your way straight up the desperate face to finish near a small pine tree (30 feet from ramp or 50 feet from ground).

24. **Hubble** (5.11c/d) Very sustained. Begin on the ramp below the right side of a small, low overhang. Climb up and slightly left on small flakes to finish a few feet left of the small pine tree (30 feet from ramp).

25. **Force Ten** (5.10c/d) Good moves on good rock, but with a tricky start. Scramble up the ramp to the center of the vertical main face. Climb difficult moves off the ramp, through the left side of the low overhang. Continue up and left to a black spot of rock midway up *The Sherpa Connection* crack. Finish up the crack to the top, or climb the direct finish. Variation: **Direct Finish** (5.11a/b) From the black spot of rock along the crack, climb straight up the thin face above.

26. **The Sherpa Connection** (5.8) *The* White Rocks classic! Start at the large tree on the left end of the ramp and climb the prominent, right-angling crack to the top (30 feet off ramp or 50 feet from ground). This crack is leadable with a light rack of stoppers and small- to medium-sized camming units.

27. **Where Eagles Dare** (5.10d) Begin as in *The Sherpa Connection*. Climb the first 10 to 15 feet of the crack, then fire straight up the wall along a thin seam.

28. **Gap of Rohan** (5.6) Begin behind a tree, at a crack on the right side of *Climber Sensitivity Training Wall*. Climb the nice, 25-foot crack to a stance left of the *Sherpa Connection* tree. Continue straight up past a tree and through the obvious gap on the left side of the vertical main wall (50 feet). Leadable with a selection of gear up to 4 inches.

29. **Climber Sensitivity Training Wall** (5.8) A small, but beautiful wall with a number of good variations. Set up a toprope and "train" a while! Begin at the base of the beautiful, clean, 25-foot wall located just below and left of the main White Rocks face. Climb anywhere up the center of the face. It's possible to contrive sequences up to at least 5.10—use your imagination.

30. **Thumbthing Else** (5.9) Climb the center of the slightly overhanging face directly above *Climber Sensitivity Training Wall*. A toprope can be set

up so that you can climb *Climber Sensitivity Training Wall* and finish on this route (20 feet from ledge or 45 feet from base of CSTW).

# MARYLAND HEIGHTS

Also known as "Harpers Ferry," the cliffs of Maryland Heights are actually located across the river from the historic town of Harpers Ferry, West Virginia. With the highest cliff in the northern Virginia and western Maryland area, you'd think the rock here would be packed with climbers every weekend. Well, it's not—and for good reason. While the cliffs at Maryland Heights are over 200 feet high, they are also quite loose and vegetated. Toproping here can be difficult, and the lead climbs are often scary, so most climbers choose to simply climb elsewhere. However, there are a few good routes to do here if you are adventurous or live in the immediate area. There are certainly many more possible routes beyond what is included in this guide, though the names, amount of protection, and rock quality are big unknowns.

It's important to note that all climbers are required to sign in and out at the National Park Service ranger station in Harpers Ferry. Unregistered climbers will be "rescued" and fined by park rangers—don't laugh; it has happened. Since you need to sign in at Harpers Ferry, many climbers choose to park in town (or at the visitor center and ride the bus into town) and hike across the pedestrian bridge that parallels the railroad tracks to the cliffs. Once you find parking, it's only about five minutes from the ranger station to the cliffs. It is also possible to park below the cliffs, along Sandy Hook Road in Maryland. However, you'll need to hike across the river twice to sign in and out.

**Finding the area:** As explained above, it may be best to approach the cliffs from Harpers Ferry. Harpers Ferry is located along US 340 about 20 miles southwest of Frederick and 6 miles northeast of Charles Town, West Virginia. Whichever way you come, exit US 340 at the Harpers Ferry exit and follow signs to the historic district or the tourist parking area (if you plan to ride the bus in). Either way, you will be charged a $5.00 entrance fee—bring your Golden Eagle pass if you own one. From the Lower Town District, take the pedestrian bridge across the Potomac River to the base of the cliffs.

## MAIN WALL

1. **"A" Route (5.1)** Not a good route. However, local rappel freaks and rescue personnel commonly scramble up the slab to set rappels and practice rescue exercises. Begin at the base of the prominent, low-angle, left-facing corner located about 100 feet right of the sign. **Pitch 1:** Climb the slabby face up to a ledge with a tree (85 feet). **Pitch 2:** Move up the corner into a chimney, then move right and finish up the face to the top (80 feet). **Descent:** Walk off, or arrange two long rappels from trees.

# MARYLAND HEIGHTS

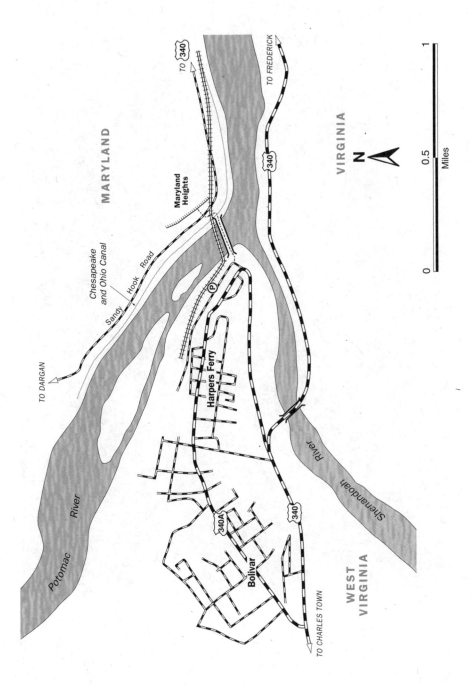

MARYLAND HEIGHTS

*Mark Kochte on Hard Up (5.8), Maryland Heights.* PHOTO BY ERIC J. HÖRST

2. **"C" Route** (5.4) Begin where the approach trail reaches the cliffbase, below and just right of the sign and below the 4th-Class scramble up to the starting ledge for *Hard Up*. **Pitch 1:** Wander up somewhat vegetated rock to gain a grassy ramp. Follow the ramp to its end (110 feet). **Pitch 2:** Climb more or less straight up on blocky rock to the cavelike hollow located right of the sign's top (35 feet). Carefully scramble right along ledges to the walk-off.

3. **Hard Up** (5.8) Great position and challenging moves across a historical landmark make this a regional classic! A nice winter outing (but a summer scorcher), given the black, west-facing rock. The route also offers one of the best views of historic Harpers Ferry. Scramble 25 feet up onto a nice ledge directly below the sign and at the base of a prominent, left-facing corner. **Pitch 1:** Climb the corner to a stance, then move left to a sloping belay ledge with bolts (35 feet). **Pitch 2:** Step left to a short corner and decipher awkward moves up to a ramp. Move up to another short corner with a crack and pull over this to a nice belay ledge (bolts) and the lower left edge of the sign (30 feet). **Pitch 3:** Face climb up the left side of the sign until you can move left and ascend the arête to a large, rocky ledge with tree (50 feet). **Pitch 4:** Climb the blocky chimney up to a large tree (35 feet). **Descent:** Most people do two rappels—80 feet from the tree to the bolt belay at the end of the 2nd pitch, and 60

feet from the bolts to the ground. You could also climb a final pitch up easy, but somewhat loose rock to the summit, then walk off. **Note:** The first two pitches can be climbed as a single pitch, but expect some rope drag.

4. **The Sign Route** (5.10) Climb the first two pitches of *Hard Up* to the belay ledge at the lower left corner of the sign. Now, follow the right-slanting crack across the middle of the sign to a cavelike formation and ledge above and beyond the upper right corner of the sign. Expect some awkward moves and a bit of a challenge placing gear. Exit right across ledges to the walk-off.

5. **Hard On** (5.9) This 35-foot pitch is really a variation to the 4th pitch of *Hard Up*. From the 3rd pitch belay ledge, climb up to the prominent roof crack located on the face right of the chimney. Pull through the roof and up to the rappel tree.

6. **"D" Route** (5.4) A surprisingly popular route, given the significant amount of vegetation along portions of the route. Scramble up to the obvious, left-facing, right-leaning corner located about 25 yards left of the start to *Hard Up*. **Pitch 1:** Climb the left-facing corner all the way up to the large, 3rd pitch belay ledge on *Hard Up*. **Pitch 2:** Climb the left-facing chimney to a large tree. **Descent:** Most people do two rappels— 85 feet from the tree to the bolt belay at the end of the 2nd pitch, and 65 feet from the bolts to the ground. You could also climb a final pitch up easy, but somewhat loose rock to the summit, then walk off.

7. **Dee's Rival** (5.6 R) This route climbs the prominent, left-facing, slabby, gray face located about 100 feet left of the sign. Follow the approach trail that begins about 100 feet left of the white house, and scramble up and right onto a ledge at the base of the slabby face. **Pitch 1:** Beginning from the middle of the ledge, move up and right to ascend the low-angle face along a line about 5 feet left of its right edge. Belay at a small ledge with a crack and small tree (85 feet). **Pitch 2:** Continue up to the over-hang and work right and up, aiming to finish at the trees at the top of the chimney on *"D" Route* and *Hard Up*. **Descent:** Most people do two rappels—85 feet from the tree to the bolt belay at the end of the 2nd pitch, and 65 feet from the bolts to the ground. You could also climb a final pitch up easy, but somewhat loose rock to the summit, then walk off.

## GUESS WALL

These two climbs are short, but quite nice. Unfortunately, it is rather difficult to access the starts of both routes. Guess Wall is a 60-foot-high buttress, facing the river, located midway between the *Dee's Rival* ledge and Frenzy Wall.

**Finding the wall:** Approach on the trail that begins at the "attention climbers" sign about 100 feet left of the white house. Follow the trail uphill to the rock and look for a 60-foot-high buttress with a ledge at mid-height (with a cedar tree). Since the climbs begin from the mid-height ledge, you need to either scramble up 5.0 rock to gain the ledge or hike to the top of the face and rappel from a pine tree.

8. **Yellowjacket** (5.7) Climb the crack up the right side of the face (30 feet).

9. **Good Guess** (5.8+) Climb a left-facing corner and crack through a small roof to a pine tree (30 feet).

## FRENZY WALL

**Finding the wall:** Approach as for Guess Wall, but trend left just before reaching the cliffbase. Look for a 65-foot-high, semi-detached block located about 100 feet left of Guess Wall. *Sunshine Dream* ascends a blocky crack system up the front of the buttress (facing the river), while *Frenzy* is located around to the left on a nice orange wall facing upstream.

10. **Sunshine Dream** (5.3) Climb the blocky crack up the front side of the pillar. Worth doing only if you're climbing *Frenzy* as well.

11. **Frenzy** (5.5 R) Climb the nice, orange-and-black face along a small, right-slanting dihedral and finish through a small overhang along a crack. Usually climbed as a toprope.

# COOPERS ROCK

## OVERVIEW

Stretching along the western flank of the Allegheny Mountains from southwestern Pennsylvania to north-central West Virginia is Chestnut Ridge, named for the trees that once densely forested the region. For climbers, this region is "gritstone central," as there are countless coarse-grained sandstone cliffs scattered along the 75-mile ridge. While many small cliffs and bouldering areas still await to be discovered by climbers, Coopers Rock stands out as the crown jewel of Chestnut Ridge climbing areas with its 450 routes and seemingly limitless number of boulder problems.

Located in beautiful Coopers Rock State Forest, the cliffs of Coopers Rock overlook the 1-mile wide, 1200-foot deep Cheat River Gorge, just 10 miles east of Morgantown, West Virginia. From the main parking area along the rim of the gorge, it's just a short downhill hike to enter the staggering maze of boulders and short cliffs that serve as the most popular climbers' playground in southwestern Pennsylvania and northern West Virginia.

Like the world-famous gritstone of Great Britain, the rock at "Coops" tends toward thin, technical face climbing with less-than-adequate protection. This makes the area an ideal face climbing proving ground where most climbers push their limits with the safety of a toprope belay. Especially popular are Jimi Cliff and Big Blocks of the Roadside Rocks area. Here, you'll find 30- to 50-foot vertical face climbs with easy toprope rigs and a car-to-crag approach of less than five minutes. Jimi Cliff classics include *The Arch* (5.6), *Copenhagen* (5.9), *Crimper* (5.10a), and *Titanium Digits* (5.10d).

Coopers Rock also possesses a handful of bolted face climbs and more than a few nice cracks. At Haystack Block you'll find *Needle on the Haystack* (5.10a/b) and *Rebolting Development* (5.10c/d), two absolutely classic, 50-foot, bolted slab routes that end on a small summit with a dramatic view of the Cheat River. With very few visible handholds, these two climbs will test your "pure friction" skills and certainly feel harder than 5.10 if you're not proficient at this type of climbing. Likewise, numerous finger- to hand-sized cracks scattered around the Roadside Rocks area are perfect for honing your crack climbing skills.

Lest we not forget the myriad pocketed, bulging boulders scattered about the bases of the taller cliffs—Coopers Rock may be the premier bouldering area of the Mid-Atlantic region. Although this guide does not include any of

# COOPERS ROCK OVERVIEW

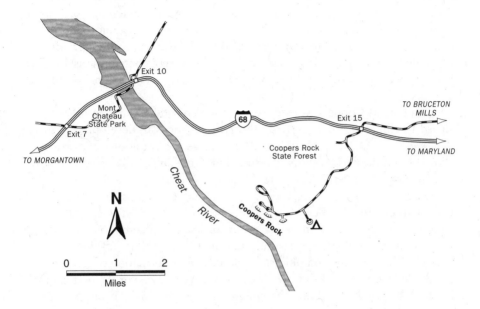

the boulder problems, you will walk by dozens of classic problems on your way to the roped routes described below.

As a final note, it is important to emphasize that rock climbing in Coopers Rock State Forest is a privilege, not a right. The entire area was closed to climbing in 1985, though all but the Overlook Area were reopened a few years later, thanks to the efforts of local activists. In 2000, The Access Fund financed, and local members constructed, a climbers' kiosk at the main parking area. Regardless of where you climb at Coops, please sign in at the kiosk and check for climbing-related announcements.

**Climbing history:** While it is believed that climbers visited Coopers Rock during the 1960s, the first recorded ascents occurred in the 1970s as a small number of climbers explored the crags around the park's overlook. Notable climbs of this era include Bob Value's 1974 ascent of *Needle on the Haystack* (5.10c/d) and Rich Pleiss's 1975 lead of *Rebolting Development* (5.10a/b). These friction climbs up Haystack Block are especially impressive, considering that the hard, non-sticky rubber shoes of that time smeared only slightly better than a of pair of roller skates.

In 1978, Bill Webster published *Gritstone Climbs,* a climber's guide to the rock of the Chestnut Ridge area. The guide included 120 routes at Coopers Rock, and it served to increase climbing activity and discovery of new areas in the years that followed. During the early 1980s, an energetic group of mainly Pittsburgh-area climbers began developing Roadside Rocks. Ed McCarthy, Chris Lea, and Don Wood commenced the action by climbing many of the obvious crack and face lines, and soon the local hardman-of-the-era, Cal Swoger, joined in and introduced the 5.12 grade. Rapid development continued through the 1984 season with significant contributions by Scott Garso, Adam Polinski, Carl Samples, Dave Sippel, Glenn Thomas, and Rick Thompson.

Climbing at Coopers Rock ceased in the mid-1980s as the entire area was closed to climbing. Local activists shifted their focus to developing routes at the then-new hot spot, the New River Gorge. Negotiations between local climbers and the park eventually resulted in reopening of all cliffs except those within view of the tourists' overlook.

Since the reopening, slow development has continued, as Brent Banks, Kurt Byrnes, Joe Hestick, Carl Samples, and others have added worthy climbs. In recent years, an active group of local boulderers has pushed the Coopers Rock bouldering scene into national focus by establishing countless high-quality problems and publishing bouldering information on the Internet.

While Coopers Rock is now a mature area with some of the best climbing in the East, it is still without a comprehensive guidebook. This is expected to change soon with the publication of Rick Thompson's *True Grit*. A longtime local activist and nationally known guidebook author, Thompson will surely provide Coopers Rock climbers with a complete historical overview as well as detailed maps and descriptions to even the most remote gritstone outcrops.

# TRIP PLANNING INFORMATION

**General description:** High-quality gritstone climbs up to 50 feet in height. Although predominantly a vertical toprope area, Coopers Rock does possess everything from bolted slabs to steep finger cracks and a lifetime's worth of boulder problems.

**Location:** Just under 3 miles off exit 15 of I–68, in northern West Virginia.

**Camping:** A beautiful state forest campground is located just 1.3 miles from the main parking area at Roadside Rocks. The campground is open from April 1 to December 15 and costs $16 per night. Call Coopers Rock State Forest campground (304–594–1561) for more information.

**Climbing season:** Spring and fall feature the most consistently good conditions, though locals climb pretty much year-round. Some good winter climbing is possible along the sunny faces of Jimi Cliff, but keep in mind that the access road is gated during the winter months—bring a mountain bike, or else you'll need to hike the 2.5 miles from the gate to the Roadside Rocks area.

**Gear:** A standard toproper's rig of long webbing loops and static anchor lines is needed for many of the toprope setups. A standard rack will be helpful

# COOPERS ROCK DETAIL

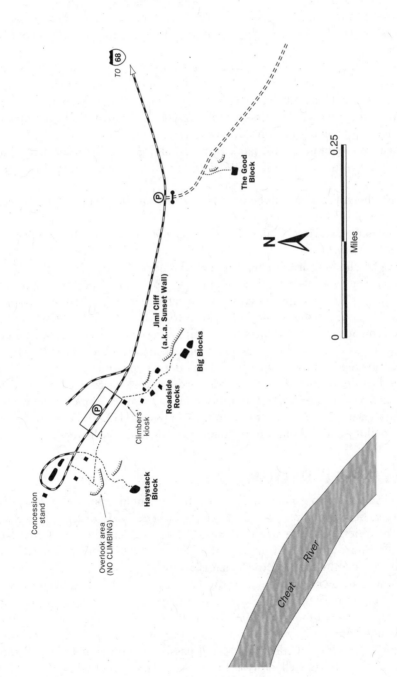

TO 68

The Good Block

N

Miles
0      0.25

Jiml Cliff (a.k.a. Sunset Wall)

Big Blocks

Roadside Rocks

Climbers' kiosk

Concession stand

Overlook area (NO CLIMBING)

Haystack Block

Cheat River

with some toprope riggings and more than enough for the handful of short lead climbs. A 50-meter rope (165 feet) is sufficient for all routes.

**Restrictions and access issues:** No climbing is permitted within sight of the tourists' overlook. The park closes at dark, so be sure to get back to your car by sunset.

**Guidebooks:** Bill Webster's *Gritstone Climbs,* published in 1978, is long out-of-print and a real collector's item. A couple of home-published mini-guides have been circulated in recent years, and some information can be found on the Internet. The first complete guide to the area, Rick Thompson's *True Grit,* is planned for publication in the near future.

**Nearby mountain shops, guide services, and gyms:** The nearest climbing shop is Adventure's Edge (304–296–9007) at 137 Pleasant Street in Morgantown.

**Services:** All services can be found just a few miles west of the area at exits 10, 7, and 4 off I–68.

**Emergency services:** Call 911. Contact Coopers Rock State Forest at 304–594–1561.

**Nearby climbing areas:** There are several other climbing spots within Coopers Rock State Forest—see Rick Thompson's upcoming *True Grit* for details. Countless other gritstone outcrops are located within an hour of Coopers Rock; however, the south rim of the Cheat River Gorge is the closest.

**Nearby attractions:** Coopers Rock State Forest is a great place for hiking, fishing, cross country skiing, or just enjoying nature. The Cheat River is a popular recreational waterway with many options possible.

**Finding the crags:** Take I–68 across northern West Virginia to exit 15. Follow signs to Coopers Rock. From the Interstate it is: 0.3 mile to the gate at the park entrance, 1.6 miles (total) to the campground, 2.4 miles to the Good Block pulloff, and 2.8 miles to the main parking and concession area.

# HAYSTACK BLOCK

This gigantic, 50-foot-high block is located downhill from the park's main overlook, but its summit provides arguably a better view of the Cheat River than the official Coopers Rock Overlook. Two excellent, bolt-protected friction climbs ascend the low-angle, uphill side of the block. These routes can also be toproped from the rappel chains on the summit.

**Finding the block:** Park in the second lot near the pavilions and concession stand. Follow the farthest left of the multiple, signed, overlook trails (with handicap access symbol) to the left of the left-most pavilion. Here the paved trail bends right, and a well-worn dirt trail turns left. Ignore these and walk straight downhill on a faint trail. You'll pass a cave on your right and soon see the "J" crack as well—this is Lizard Wall, and it is *closed* to climbing. From below the "J" crack, the trail diagonals left, and in 25 yards you'll see

HAYSTACK BLOCK

*Lisa Ann Hörst following the classic Needle on the Haystack (5.10a/b), Coopers Rock.*
PHOTO BY ERIC J. HÖRST

Greenback Wall and its obvious lieback crack on your left. Zig-zag downhill another 100 yards to Haystack Boulder—look through the trees for its pointed summit. The full approach is just over five minutes.

1. **Standard Route** (5.2 R/X) The easiest route to the summit of Haystack Block. Commonly soloed to set topropes on the friction slab climbs. Begin below the right line of bolts and traverse up and right along a buckety line of pockets to a stance at the low-angle arête. A 4th-Class scramble up the arête will bring you to the summit and chain anchors (60 feet). Variation: **Standard Direct** (5.8) About 15 right of the regular start, begin from boulders below the arête and jump to the "lip" of the low overhang. Pull up past the right side of the roof and continue up the face and arête to the summit (50 feet).

2. **Needle on the Haystack** (5.10a/b) Classic! Climb easy moves to the first bolt, then friction up past three more bolts to chains on the summit. **Variation** (5.9) A popular toprope with a brief crux sequence. A good warm-up for *Needle on the Haystack*. Begin below the right line of bolts

and move up the right-slanting line of pockets to climb the face midway between the arête and the line of bolts.

3. **Rebolting Development** (5.10c/d) Climb the left line of bolts, beginning at two handhold pockets about 6 feet off the ground. 4 bolts to chain anchors.

4. **Cheat Crack** (5.5/5.7) Walk around to the river side of the block and you'll find a crack up the right side of a wildly sculpted face. Climb the crack (or anywhere up the face) to the slabby finish and anchors (55 feet).

# ROADSIDE ROCKS

This popular area features many good 30- to 40-foot toprope routes, as well as a handful of well-protected leads. The climbs at Roadside Rocks are near-vertical and tend to be fairly technical in nature. Classics include the four climbs through the Sunset Wall Overhang (1–4) and *The Arch* (5.6), *The Icon* (5.5), *Copenhagen* (5.9), *Wayward Penguins* (5.10b), *Organic Matter* (5.5), *Super Alloy* (5.10c), *Titanium Digits* (5.10d), and *Grunge Festivale* (5.6).

Topropes are easily set-up from trees—bring some long loops of webbing or a couple of pieces of static line for rigging. Keep clifftop travel to a minimum, and consider sharing your rope with other climbers to reduce traffic and impact in the forest above. In April 2000, The Access Fund built a climbers' bulletin board at the Roadside Rocks trailhead. Please sign in all members of your climbing party and check the board for any relevant announcements.

**Finding the rocks:** Park in the first lot and hike down the trail that begins behind the green bulletin board. The trail soon turns upstream (away from the overlook) and passes through a beautiful, Fontainebleau-like boulder-field. Numerous 15- to 20-foot topropes are possible here, and there are dozens of established bouldering routes up to V-6. Continue along the flat path just another minute or two and arrive at a 40-foot wall on your left (3-foot overhang near top) and a huge, detached block on your right. This is the Jimi Cliff and Big Blocks area, about a 300-yard hike from the bulletin board and parking.

## JIMI CLIFF (A.K.A. SUNSET WALL)

1. **Arch Roof** (5.9) Begin below a short, left-facing corner near the left end of the wall. Climb up along a black streak just right of the corner and through the roof at an obvious crack.

2. **Wide Point Roof** (5.10a/b) Start in front of a tree and climb through a low roof. Fire straight up the face and out the roof at its widest point.

# JIMI CLIFF (A.K.A. SUNSET WALL)

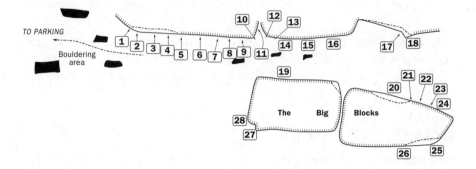

3. **Roof Flake** (5.9) Begin 5 feet right of a tree near the middle of a small, low ledge. Face climb up to and out the roof flake.

4. **Reachy** (5.8) At the right end of a small, low ledge, begin up the face and past the right side of a bulge to finish out the crack in the roof above.

5. **The Arch** (5.6) Climb the obvious, left-leaning corner and finish to the right of the roof (35 feet). A good lead with decent gear.

6. **The Icon a.k.a. Central Face Climb** (5.5) Begin 6 feet right of *The Arch* corner and climb the series of small, left-facing flakes.

7. **Crimper** (5.10a) Start below a short, vertical crack at the upper, right portion of the wall. Climb straight up the blank-looking face to finish in the vertical crack.

8. **Rubbin' the Nubbin'** (5.11a) A technical crux that will test your footwork and problem-solving skills. Begin about 5 feet right of *Crimper* and just left of a large "lip" of rock about 6 feet off the ground. Finesse your way straight up the wall, using tiny, left-facing edges through the mid-height crux.

9. **Absolutely Nubbin' a.k.a. Stop 'N' Go** (5.9) About 6 feet left of the chimney, climb up to and through a series of flakes to easier rock above.

10. **The Alzheimer's Advantage** (5.11a/b) This squeezed-in route is worth doing if you have a toprope on *Absolutely Nubbin'*. Begin on the round arête on the left side of the chimney. Work your way up along a black streak, using no holds on *Stop 'N' Go* until near the top.

*Climber on The Arch (5.6), Jimi Cliff.* PHOTO BY CARL SAMPLES

11. **Into the Sunset** (5.6) Climb the 35-foot, full-body chimney.

12. **Dude Point Direct** (5.12b) Formerly a reasonable 5.11, a broken flake now makes the route a solid 5.12. Begin just inside the chimney and power up the blunt arête on the right. Just wait 'til you feel the tiny, one-finger pocket on the crux move!

13. **Dew Point Arête** (5.10c/d) Another somewhat contrived toprope that you can do after warming up on *Copenhagen.* Begin about 3 feet right of the chimney, at a short left-facing corner just off the ground. Climb straight up, using holds independent of *Copenhagen,* except for a right-hand sloper just above mid-height.

14. **Copenhagen** (5.9) A Jimi Cliff classic! Start 6 or 7 feet right of the chimney and directly below a series of pockets about 20 feet up the wall. Dance your way up the face-and-pocket moves to the top.

15. **Stockholm** (5.7) Begin at right-facing flakes about 12 feet right of *Copenhagen.* Climb up the flakes, then move left a few moves and continue straight up to finish just right of the summit blocks. Variation: **Direct Start** (5.8) Begin 6 feet left of the regular start and climb pretty much straight up the face.

16. **Lacuna** (5.11a/b) Start below a mid-height pocket about 6 feet right of right-facing flakes of *Stockholm.* Boulder past the pocket to the top, or be safe and toprope this 20-foot route.

17. **Tread Lightly** (5.11d) Hard, but very good! From the main Jimi Cliff wall, scramble through a few small boulders about 20 yards to a large, triangle-shaped roof about 12 feet up. This route climbs through the left side of the roof, past a loose flake, and finishes through an overhang at a left-facing corner.

18. **Triangle Roof** (5.8) Hone your roof-pulling and heel-hooking technique on this one. Begin below the triangle roof and pull through the right side to a stance. Finish up easier moves to one more tricky sequence at the top (25 feet).

## THE BIG BLOCKS

19. **Wayward Penguins** (5.10b) This route is located on The Big Blocks opposite the chimney of *Into the Sunset.* Begin 15 feet left of the arête and directly below a vertical "suitcase handle" hold about halfway up the wall. Climb up past the "suitcase handle" and use flakes to work slightly right to a small ledge near the top. A more difficult finish can be climbed straight up without the use of the small ledge.

BIG BLOCKS—LEFT

Var.

24a
24
23
22

20. **Zig-Zag Wanderer** (5.8-) Hike about 30 yards to the middle of the left Big Block. Scramble up on low ledges to reach a nice, right-slanting, finger crack. Climb the short crack, then out the flake in the roof above (40 feet). Leadable.

21. **Full Moon Afternoon** (5.5) Toprope the face midway between the *Zig-Zag Wanderer* finger crack and the left-facing *Organic Matter* flake.

22. **Organic Matter** (5.5) Climb the obvious, left-facing flake (40 feet). Leadable.

23. **Super Alloy** (5.10c) This difficult route ascends the thin face immediately left of *Organic Matter*. Climb about 4 feet left of the flake and do not use any holds on the flake. **Variation** (5.9) The easiest path up this part of the wall. Climb to just past mid-height, then move left past a pocket to finish *Titanium Digits*.

24. **Titanium Digits** (5.10d) This and the previous two routes are popular face climbs on good rock. Left of *Super Alloy*, climb near the middle of the face, following a faint white streak. Variation: **Schoonerete** (5.6) Climb the juggy flake and arête to the left.

25. **White Wall Overhang** (5.9) Around on the river side of the rock, you'll find a short, white face capped by a 2-foot overhang. Start on the left or right side of the white face and work up under the overhang, then up the cracks above to the top. A decent 40-foot lead.

26. **Grunge Festivale** (5.6) A popular lead with lots of good gear. Begin just left of the white face, at a low, right-arching, shallow overhang. Climb the convoluted crack and knobby face to the top (35 feet).

27. **Access Crack** (5.2) This 20-foot, left-facing corner is located on the far-left end of the river-facing side of the Big Blocks wall, and it is commonly soloed to set up topropes on other Big Blocks routes.

28. **Affinity Triangle** (5.11a) Though short, this nice arête is worth the small effort it takes to set a toprope on it. Climb the slightly overhanging arête just left of *Access Crack*.

## THE GOOD BLOCK

The Good Block offers a few mixed routes on its downstream-facing, 35-foot face. The two middle routes are the best, and can be easily toproped from chain anchors on the summit. These routes can also be led, but in addition to the few bolts, you'll want a few small- to medium-sized camming units.

Finding the block: Park in a small, roadside lot located 2.5 miles (on the right) from the park entrance, or just 0.3 mile and on the left when coming from the Sunset Wall and main parking area. Cross the road and step around a metal gate. Follow a mainly level, grassy path for about 180 yards to the beginning of a slight uphill grade. Here you descend diagonally downhill on

THE GOOD BLOCK

a faint trail. Just 50 yards downhill, you pass along the base of the nice, 25-foot Squirrel Soup block with a couple of possible topropes. From here, The Good Block is just another 50 yards down the trail—look for the mossy, uphill side of the block with a rhododendron bush on top. Scramble around the left side of the block to the much nicer, downstream-facing side.

1. **Stud** (5.6) Step up onto a small, low ledge and climb up the low-angle arête and face (bolt) to the summit. Most often climbed to set topropes on the more difficult face routes to the left.

2. **A Very Good Climb** (5.9) A popular route on good rock. Beginning at a low, right-facing corner, climb straight up past a horizontal crack (need 0.5-inch–1-inch cams) and 3 bolts to chain anchors on the summit.

3. **A Good Climb** (5.7) This route also starts in the low, right-facing corner, but it moves left along the first horizontal crack to climb easier face moves to a bolt. Finish up an easy, left-facing flake to the summit anchors. Variation: **Direct Start** (5.12b/c) About 8 feet left of the regular start, power through the low roof to reach the normal route about 15 feet up. Good luck!

4. **Wimp** (5.9-) This route begins from a boulder at the left end of the face. Pull a strenuous move through the low roof and past a pair of pockets to the lower-angle face above. Continue up and right to finish just left of Route 3.

5. **Blockage** (5.13+?) This long-standing project is located on the river side of The Good Block. Locate chains atop the block above this beautiful, steep, and extremely reachy project. Bring your stilts.

# SENECA ROCKS

## OVERVIEW

Rising 960 feet above the North Fork of the South Branch of the Potomac River, Seneca Rocks has no peer in the Eastern U.S. with regard to its awesome position and unique, knife-blade character. Seneca Rocks is also the most intimidating and serious climbing area in the Mid-Atlantic region: It is the scene of eleven deaths over the last thirty years.

Once the premier climbing area in the region—a distinction now held by the New River Gorge—Seneca Rocks remains the only true, multipitch climbing destination between the Shawangunks and Stone Mountain. It also differs from the New in its abundance of moderate (5.5 to 5.9) classic lines. As a bastion of ground-up ethics and natural protection, Seneca requires competent gear-placing and routefinding skills. Few climbs at Seneca are defined by a line of bolts—instead cracks and corner systems, and long, wandering face climbs are the norm. And despite the 1990s upgrading of many popular lines, younger climbers may still find that many routes feel undergraded. The bottomline: Seneca Rocks in not a place to thoughtlessly push your limits.

Seneca Rocks also offers the summit experience gained by climbing to the top of the South Peak. It is reputed to be the highest summit east of Devils Tower that only can be accessed via 5th-Class climbing. While you're up there, sign the summit register and enjoy the hundreds of feet of exposure on both sides of the 15-foot-wide fin!

**Climbing history:** The area's first climbers were undoubtedly the Seneca Indians, who inhabited the Mouth of Seneca for many centuries. The first ascent of the South Peak seems to date back to a 1908 visit by a government surveyor named Donald Bittinger. It is believed that he inscribed the petroglyph reading D.B. SEPT 16 08, still faintly visible today on the summit of the South Peak. The likely path of his ascent is *Old Man's Route* (5.2), the easiest path to the South Peak summit.

The pioneers of technical climbing were Paul Brandt, Don Hubbard, and Sam Moore. Equipped with a rope and three carabiners, they made a bold ascent of the South Peak in 1939. Their route, *Skyline Traverse* (5.3), remains one of the area's most popular routes, and its airy second pitch traverse is absolutely classic! The other important ascent of this era was the

# SENECA ROCKS OVERVIEW

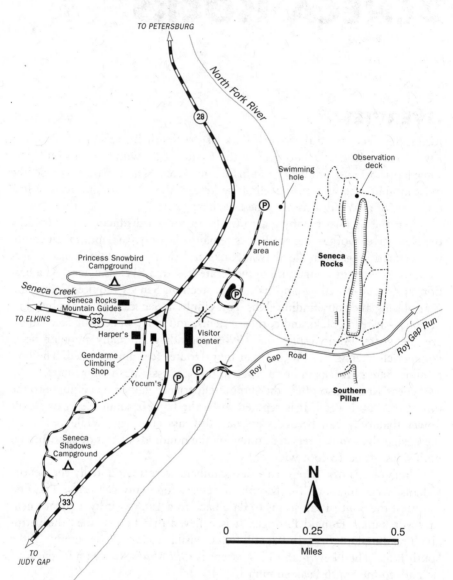

TO PETERSBURG

North Fork River

28

Observation deck

Swimming hole

Picnic area

Seneca Rocks

Princess Snowbird Campground

Seneca Creek

Seneca Rocks Mountain Guides

TO ELKINS

33

Harper's

Visitor center

Gendarme Climbing Shop

Yocum's

Roy Gap Road

Roy Gap Run

Southern Pillar

Seneca Shadows Campground

33

TO JUDY GAP

N

0          0.25          0.5
Miles

# SENECA ROCKS DETAIL

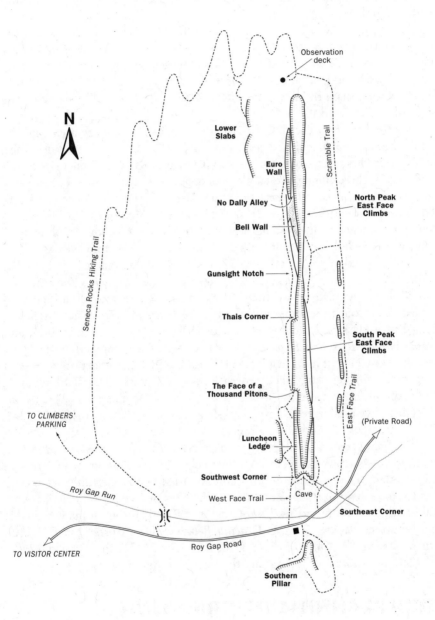

Observation deck

Lower Slabs

Euro Wall

No Dally Alley

Bell Wall

Gunsight Notch

Thais Corner

The Face of a Thousand Pitons

Luncheon Ledge

Southwest Corner

West Face Trail

Cave

Scramble Trail

North Peak East Face Climbs

South Peak East Face Climbs

East Face Trail

(Private Road)

Southeast Corner

Seneca Rocks Hiking Trail

TO CLIMBERS' PARKING

Roy Gap Run

TO VISITOR CENTER

Roy Gap Road

Southern Pillar

N

1940 climb up the now-fallen Gendarme. This 30-foot-high, free-standing pinnacle in the middle of the Gunsight Notch was the area's trademark climb until it toppled in 1987.

During World War II, the U.S. Army's 10th Mountain Division did extensive training at Seneca Rocks. Their legacy is two popular routes, *Conn's East* (5.5) and *Conn's West* (5.4), and countless soft iron pitons left *in situ*. Though only a few of the relic pitons remain today, the volume of iron banged into cracks during these training camps led one section of cliff to be named "The Face of A Thousand Pitons."

For the next two decades, activists were mainly Pittsburgh-area climbers and Potomac Appalachian Trail Club (PATC) members who refined their skills on the thin faces of Carderock and Great Falls. With limited gear and lots of guts, these climbers freed many of Seneca's most imposing and obvious lines, including *Pleasant Overhang* (5.7), *Green Wall* (5.7), *Soler* (5.7+), *Ye Gods and Little Fishes* (5.8-), *Triple S* (5.8+), and *Marshall's Madness* (5.9). Some of the legends involved in these first ascents are the likes of John Christian, Jan and Herb Conn, Jim Shipley, Tony Soler, and Arnold Wexler.

A new group of young, talented climbers pushed the standards even higher in the late 1960s and 1970s. George Livingstone freed *Madmen Only* (5.10a), Pat Milligan jammed up *Castor* (5.10a) and *Pollux* (5.10a), John Stannard pulled out through the large roof of *Totem* (5.11a), and Herb Laeger ticked a long list of classics, including *High Test* (5.9+), *Nip and Tuck* (5.10c), and *Terra Firma Homesick Blues* (5.11c R). Others, including Jeff Burns, Jack Beatty, Matt Hale, Hunt Prothro, Ray Snead, and Cal Swoger all pioneered routes that further established Seneca Rocks as a world-class climbing area. However, no one was more prolific than Howard Doyle and Eric Janoscrat. Together, they established over seventy-five routes, including *Ambush* (5.11a), *Sidewinder* (5.11a), and *Drop Zone* (5.11b).

The final stage of development took place from about 1985 to 1995 as a handful of well-traveled, mainly Virginian climbers focused on the poorly protected, blank faces and the South End cave area. Utilizing mainly ground-up tactics and a load of testicular fortitude, the likes of Pete Absolon, Mike Artz, Eddie Begoon, John Bercaw, Tom Cecil, and Rod Hanson all made valuable contributions. Routes such as *Dracula Beach* (5.11c), *Mister Jones* (5.11c), *Put a Wiggle In Your Stride* (5.11d), *The Threat* (5.12b), *Psycho Driller* (5.12c), and *Cannibals* (5.13a) are the legacy of this latest era.

# TRIP PLANNING INFORMATION

**General description:** High-quality, multipitch climbing on gem-hard Tuscarora Sandstone.

**Location:** The rocks tower over the Village of Seneca Rocks at the intersection of West Virginia 55, 33, and 28. The nearest larger towns are Petersburg (23 miles north) and Elkins (32 miles west).

**Camping:** There are two campgrounds near the cliffs. Seneca Shadows, operated by the Forest Service, is the nicer campground. It is also quite pricey at $8.00 for a walk-in and $12.00 for a drive-in site. For reservations, call 800-280-2267. Princess Snowbird Campground is located directly across from the rocks, with the affordable rate of $5.00 per night. Register at Yocum's store across the road.

**Climbing season:** As with every crag in this guide, fall is the best season. Winter and early spring tends to be quite windy and cold. It also rains frequently during the spring and summer months. Summer is persistently humid; however, the area's many classic moderates are very climbable, even on the most tropical July days.

**Gear:** Bring a full rack, including micro nuts, wired stoppers, TCUs, and four-cam units up to 4 inches. A dozen quickdraws, at least six slings, and extra 'biners are needed to clip fixed protection and tie off trees. A single 165-foot (50 meter) rope will work for most routes; however, many climbers use double-rope technique on the more serious face routes. A 200-foot (60 meter) rope is needed on some sport routes and to descend from some of the anchors recently added atop popular traditional lines. Most Seneca Rocks climbers consider a helmet *mandatory,* due to the occasionally loose character of the rock.

**Restrictions and access issues:** Seneca Rocks lies within Monongahela National Forest and all federal regulations apply. Park only in designated areas, stay on established trails, bury human waste, and pack out all your trash. Keep Seneca Rocks beautiful!

**Guidebooks:** Bill Webster and Rich Pleiss published the first major guide to the area in 1975. Over the next fifteen years, Webster went on to write five more editions before passing the torch to local guide/activist Tony Barnes. In 1995, Barnes published the extremely comprehensive *Seneca: The Climber's Guide.* A revised edition of Barnes's guide should be out in 2001—pick up a copy!

**Nearby mountain shops, guide services, and gyms:** John Markwell's The Gendarme (304–567–2600) climbing shop is located behind Harper's General Store. With no bar in town, its front porch is *the* hangout for drinking, route beta, and finding partners. The Gendarme is also home of Seneca Rocks Climbing School. Across the street from Harper's Store is Seneca Rocks Mountain Guides and Outfitters (304–567–2115 or 800–451–5108). Run by long-time activist Tom Cecil, Seneca Rocks Mountain Guides and Outfitters offers the area's only climbing wall.

**Services:** Two general stores are located at the main intersection in the Village of Seneca Rocks. Both stores have dining areas, and Harper's Front Porch

(upstairs) is especially popular for its good pizza and unparalleled scenic dining. For an affordable breakfast, Hendrick's 4-U Diner is the long-standing
tradition. The 4-U Diner and Motel are located just a few miles south of town
on Route 33. Motel rooms and cabins are available at Hendrick's 4-U
(304–567–2111) and at Yocum's (304–567–2351), respectively. Another
option is Nelson Rocks Mountain Cabins (304–567–3169), located just 10
miles south of Seneca Rocks.

**Emergency services:** A rescue cache is located on the front porch of The
Gendarme. Call 304–567–2412 for an ambulance or rescue services. The closest hospital is Grant Memorial (304–257–1026) in Petersburg.

**Nearby climbing areas:** Seneca Rocks has several sister crags, including
Champe, Judy Gap Spires, and Nelson Rocks. There is also climbing near
Smoke Hole Caverns and along North Fork Mountain—inquire at the local
climbing shops for details.

**Nearby attractions:** The Seneca Rocks Discovery Center is a must-do for
all first-time visitors to the area. Also nearby are Seneca Caverns and Smoke
Hole Caverns. Forty-five minutes away is Canaan Valley ski area, which offers
year-round recreation, including mountain biking, hiking, and fishing.

**Finding the crags:** Drive to the Village of Seneca Rocks on WV 28, US 33,
or WV 55, and you can't miss the rocks! Most climbers use the Picnic Area
parking lot (site of the old Visitor Center) located just 200 yards north of the
main intersection. Parking at the Seneca Rocks Discovery Center is another
option.

# SOUTHERN PILLAR

**Finding the pillar:** Walk up Roy Gap Road to a boulder (with plaque) on the
right. Take the trail that begins just beyond the boulder and follow it up to
the base of the pillar near the start of *Gephardt-Dufty*. The other routes
described here are located immediately to the right.

**Descent:** The hike off the top of Southern Pillar is pretty nasty. Consequently, most of the routes described below are equipped with rappel anchors
(usually coldshuts) at the end of the best climbing. If you do top out, descend
via the steep, east side trail. Use extreme caution not to trundle any rock as
you top out and exit onto the trail.

1. **Gephardt-Dufty** (5.7+) Stunning and airy, but watch out for a bit of
   loose rock. Climb carefully and enjoy! Start at the base of the main fin.
   **Pitch 1:** Climb straight up the front edge of the fin to a good belay (120
   feet). **Pitch 2:** Continue up the fin about another 120 feet to its top. **Pitch
   3:** Scramble across an obvious chimney to finish up a neighboring buttress (60 feet). **Descent:** Hike off.

SOUTHERN PILLAR

2. **Slipstream** (5.10a) Begin as in *Daytripper* and climb up about 20 feet to a stance. Traverse left 10 feet and follow thin cracks to a short, left-facing corner with a widening crack. Finish up along a flake to anchors above (75 feet).

3. **Daytripper** (5.10a) Start at a small pine tree 20 feet left of *Right Tope* and below a shallow, right-facing corner about 25 feet up. Climb up to and along the corner to its end. Now traverse up and left toward the main fin and belay at anchors above *Slipstream* (80 feet).

4. **Right Tope** (5.9) Begin at a short left-facing corner near two tall pine trees about 20 feet left of *Roy Gap Chimneys*. Climb corners up and right, then back left to a small overhang. Pass this on the right and continue up the face to anchors at an overhang (90 feet). **Descent:** Continue up to finish on *Gephardt-Dufty,* or use a 60-meter rope to rap from the anchors.

5. **Climbin' Punishment** (5.8) Begin at a left-facing corner just left of *Roy Gap Chimney*. **Pitch 1:** Climb the crack and corner to a small ledge on the left. Continue up another corner, past a couple of small overhangs to lower-angle rock and a belay below a roof (110 feet). **Pitch 2:** Climb past the roof on the left and finish up steep moves to anchors on the left wall (60 feet). **Descent:** From these anchors, a 165-foot rappel will just get you to the ground. However, since rope snag has been a problem on the "pull," consider doing three short rappels. Begin with a 50-foot rappel to anchors just right of *Roy Gap Chimney* (at a stance below an obvious roof), then do another rappel to a tree with slings, and from there rap to the ground.

6. **Roy Gap Chimneys** (5.6) Two-hundred feet of chimney-climbing madness. Start below the towering chimney on the right side of the main Southern Pillar fin. **Pitch 1:** Climb blocky moves to gain the obvious chimney above, then work up this to a belay on the right wall (90 feet). **Pitch 2:** Continue up another 80 feet or so to a nice belay on the right. **Pitch 3:** Start up the chimney a short way, then move right to climb a short corner on the buttress and continue to the top (45 feet). **Descent:** Rap off after the second pitch or finish the route and hike off.

7. **Ambush** (5.11a) Begin about 5 feet right of a 20-foot-high, capped chimney and 10 feet left of *Block Party*. Fire up the blocky crack through a bulge to shared anchors.

8. **Block Party** (5.8) Popular as a warm-up for (or to set up a toprope on) the neighboring *Ambush*. Start at a left-facing corner about 15 feet right of a 20-foot-high, capped chimney. Climb up the blocky corner and crack to a ledge with anchors (40 feet).

# SENECA SOUTH END—ECSTASY BUTTRESS AND CAVE AREAS

**Finding the area:** Walk up Roy Gap Road until you see the first buttress of rock on your left. Follow a blue-blazed trail that begins at a small stone wall just across Roy Gap Run. Hike uphill a short way until the trail splits near the base of the buttress. The routes described below are along the right-hand trail, which leads along the South End of the cliff. The left branch of the trail continues uphill along the Southwest Corner and West Face.

9. **Ecstasy** (5.7) Absolutely classic! Begin at the left side of the South End, at the base of a blocky, low-angle buttress. **Pitch 1:** Climb easy rock to a ledge about 25 feet up (optional belay here). Follow cracks up the white face to a stance beneath an overhang (100 feet). **Pitch 2:** Start up the large crack on the right for about 15 feet, then begin the exciting traverse right and upward across the very exposed, orangish face to right-leaning cracks and an airy belay stance below a bulge (70 feet). **Pitch 3:** Move right a few feet to a steep crack and climb up past a bulge. Wander up the face above to finish left of the trees above (50 feet). **Descent:** Scramble north over Luncheon Ledge and hike down the switchbacks on the West Face Trail. **Variation: Southwest Buttress** (5.5) Begin the second pitch, but where the regular route traverses right, continue straight up large cracks (some loose rock) to a good ledge (50 feet). Rappel from a tree 100 feet down the west side of the buttress or finish up *Ecstasy Junior* (see Southwest Corner section).

10. **Muscle Beach** (5.11b) A classic Ray Snead route and another former "Seneca 5.10." Pump up one, two, or all three pitches. Rap anchors allow an easy descent from either of the belays. Start left of the huge cave, near a few trees below a square-cut overhang. **Pitch 1:** Climb up and left to the corner and crack on the left side of the square-cut overhang. Move left around the 'hang and crank up to anchors above (50 feet). **Pitch 2:** Move up and right to a stance, then continue up over a bulge and along a pair of cracks. When the cracks end, move left and fire up steep rock to anchors on the left side of the *Simple J. Malarkey* ledge (90 feet). **Pitch 3:** Start up the white corner, but after a few moves step right and crank through the roof to the top (40 feet). **Descent:** Rappel from anchors at the end of either Pitch 1 or Pitch 2, or top out and hike down the West Face Trail from Luncheon Ledge.

11. **Dracula Beach** (5.11c) Sport route. The first 50 feet is quite popular. Begin left of the cave and about 20 feet right of *Muscle Beach*. Climb easy rock up to a line of 3 bolts that lead out left above a large, square-shaped roof. Finish left to the anchors on *Muscle Beach* (50 feet). **Descent:** Rappel off. **Variation: Direct Finish** (5.12a) Continue straight up past 5 more bolts (110 feet).

ECSTACY BUTTRESS

*Barb Hansen on the second pitch of Ecstacy (5.7), a true Seneca classic.* PHOTO BY HARRISON SHULL

12. **The Threat** (5.12b) Sport route. Steep and pumpy. One of the many fine routes established by local climbing guide Tom Cecil. Begin on a black, sloping ledge just inside the cave on the left wall. Climb blocky rock up to a smooth, orange-and-white bulge, then up steep, white rock to anchors. 7 bolts.

13. **Fine Young Cannibals** (5.12c/5.13a) Sport route. This is Seneca Rocks' first 5.12 and first 5.13—freed to the first set on anchors (5.12c) in 1981 by Cal Swoger, then to the top (5.13a) by John Bercaw in 1988. On the left wall of the cave, climb up along a thin crack and short, shallow, right-facing corner past 3 bolts (and old pins) to coldshuts (5.12c to this point). Continue up and left past 3 more bolts to anchors above the lip of the cave.

14. **Predator** (5.12a) Sport route. Beginning 10 feet right of *Fine Young Cannibals,* climb the overhanging, flaky face past a bulge to anchors. 4 bolts.

15. **SJM Cave Start** (5.8) A short, but popular rain-day route. On the right side of the cave, climb through blocky overhangs to anchors about 30 feet up.

16. **Simple J. Malarkey** (5.7) Airy and committing—a "must-do" if you are solid at the grade. Start at a section of black rock on the face just right of the cave opening. **Pitch 1:** Climb the black face to a ledge (35 feet). **Pitch 2:** Move left and climb a low-angle ramp past a short break to the ramp's end (75 feet). **Pitch 3:** Climb the steep wall up and right to an easy finish (50 feet) or better yet, step left and climb the last pitch of *Muscle Beach* up the steep corner and through the roof (5.8, 40 feet). **Descent:** Scramble north over Luncheon Ledge and hike down the switchbacks on the West Face Trail.

# SENECA SOUTH END—TOTEM AND SKYLINE BUTTRESSES

These routes ascend the tall buttresses on the east side of the South End. They are easily reached from the Ecstasy Buttress and Cave Area or by hiking up Roy Gap Road to near the Southeast Corner and taking a blue-blazed trail on the left. Follow the trail up the hill and take the left split to the base of Totem Buttress.

17. **Totem** (5.11a) A John Stannard classic, established in 1971. The second pitch contains the famous crux roof, while the third pitch is a wonderful 5.8 romp up the top half of the buttress. Begin at the base of the tall, sloping buttress, which rises to meet a prominent roof. **Pitch 1:** Climb the buttress to a belay at anchors under the right side of the roof (85 feet). **Pitch 2:** Crank out the roof along fixed pins and pull up to a small

belay stance at anchors (25 feet). **Pitch 3:** Continue up along an inside corner, through an overhang, and up to a belay stance (120 feet). **Pitch 4:** Finish up the corner to the walk-off (40 feet). **Descent:** Scramble up and left to Luncheon Ledge and the West Face Trail.

18. **Ye Gods and Little Fishes** (5.8) A well-protected and "light" 5.8. Many parties just climb the first pitch and then rappel from anchors. Begin just right of a square, cavelike opening at the base of a huge, left-facing corner. **Pitch 1:** Climb the crack and corner to a ledge and anchors on the right (90 feet). **Pitch 2:** Climb a flake on the left wall, past an overhang, and finish up the second and third pitches of *Skyline Traverse*. **Descent:** Rappel from the anchors (need 60-meter rope!) at the end of the first pitch, or follow *Skyline Traverse*.

19. **Drop Zone** (5.11b) Commonly toproped after climbing the first pitch of *Ye Gods*. Quality all the way! Beginning right of *Ye Gods*, climb the smooth, steep face along many discontinuous cracks (pin) to finish a few feet left of the outside corner (90 feet). **Descent:** Rappel from anchors shared with *Ye Gods* and *Candy Corner*—need 60-meter rope!

20. **Candy Corner** (5.5) Start at the base of a tall right-facing, left-slanting corner system 25 feet right of *Ye Gods*. Ascend the corner to reach anchors on the *Drop Zone* ledge (95 feet). **Descent:** Use a 60-meter rope to rappel from anchors or continue up 30 feet of easy rock to the first belay on *Skyline Traverse*.

21. **Spinnaker** (5.10c) Spectacular position; well-protected, and very much worth doing. However, it takes a bit of work and some "traffic dodging" to gain this clip-up on the obvious fin high above *Ye Gods and Little Fishes*. **Pitch 1:** Climb the first pitch of *Skyline Traverse* to the nice, but often-crowded belay ledge. **Pitch 2:** Do the airy 5.3 traverse left, and work a few moves up the broad chimney and face to gain the first bolt on the right wall. From here, follow the bolt line up the steep face and arête to anchors. 8 bolts.

## SOUTHEAST CORNER

**Finding the area:** Hike up Roy Gap Road past the Ecstasy and Totem Buttresses to the blue-blazed Southeast Corner Trail on the left. Follow the trail uphill along the beginning of the east face and scramble over a few dirty ledges to the base of the right-facing *Skyline Traverse* chimney.

22. **Skyline Traverse** (5.3) Known for the exposed, second-pitch traverse, the route is never hard and always well-protected. Very popular. Scramble up a few 4th-Class moves to gain a nice belay ledge at the base of the prominent, right-facing chimney. **Pitch 1:** Climb the juggy chimney to a

ledge, step right, and continue up a left-facing corner about 20 feet to a belay ledge on the left (90 feet). **Pitch 2:** Make the exciting traverse left to gain a low-angle face inside a wide chimney. Follow the easy face up and left to gain a sloping ledge with a belay tree (75 feet). **Pitch 3:** Continue up nice cracks in the chimney to finish on a somewhat loose 4th-Class move to trees. You can avoid loose rock at the end of the pitch by exiting right near the top (50 feet). Either way, exercise extreme caution not to knock loose rock down the chimney—a few of Seneca's most popular routes are located directly below in the *Ye Gods* corner. **Descent:** Locate a vertical slot above and left of the third pitch belay. Either squeeze through the slot to a dirty chimney or, better yet, climb juggy, 4th-Class moves up the short face to the right of the slot. From here, follow ledges northward to reach Luncheon Ledge and the West Side Trail.

## SOUTH PEAK—EAST FACE

The East Face of the South Peak possesses some of Seneca's highest quality rock and most classic lines. Except for *Orangeaid* and *Alcoa Presents,* the routes described below all begin off Upper Broadway Ledge.

**Finding the face:** The full Broadway Ledge system stretches from the top of the South End to just left of the Gunsight Notch. Unfortunately, a short section of 5.0 climbing divides the ledge into two sections—Lower Broadway and Upper Broadway—so accessing climbs on the South Peak East Face is not always straightforward. Depending on your game plan, you may want to access Upper Broadway via the East Side Trail or by doing a short roped pitch up some 5.0 rock from Lower Broadway.

Hike Roy Gap Road past the Southeast Corner to the blue-blazed East Face Trail on the left. Follow this trail uphill (passing along the right side of a small rock fin that parallels the East Face) for about ten minutes to a point just above the Gunsight Notch. Here, cut left on a blue-blazed feeder trail toward the Gunsight Notch. In about 80 yards you come to a 10-foot-high outcrop—carefully boulder up a few slippery 5.0 moves to a good ledge. Take the trail that splits left along a dirty ledge, then up and left through some 3rd-Class moves (watch for blue markers) along a series of small, rising ledges to gain Upper Broadway Ledge at the bases of *Castor* and *Pollux.*

You can also access Upper Broadway Ledge by climbing a South End or Southeast Corner route to gain Lower Broadway Ledge. Walk northward along Lower Broadway, past a short chimney with a chockstone, until you come to another steep section of rock. Move around to the right and ascend an exposed 5.0 section of rock (please rope up!), then scramble up over tree-covered ledges to the base of the East Face near *Dirty Old Man.*

**Descents:** Since most climbers leave their packs on the ledge, it's most

# SOUTH PEAK—EAST FACE

common to rappel back down to Upper Broadway (see route descriptions for rappel details). If you're climbing with all your gear, there are two possible ways to descend to the base of the West Face. Experienced climbers sometimes downclimb the *Old Ladies' Route* (5.2) to Luncheon Ledge; however the preferred path is to squeeze through the *Traffic Jam* chimney and do two or three rappels to the ground.

23. **Dirty Old Man** (5.6) Locate an obvious, left-facing corner that begins near the left end of Upper Broadway Ledge. **Pitch 1:** Climb the face and flake just left of the corner, then move up and way right to a good ledge (60 feet). **Pitch 2:** Climb up to and follow a steep, right-facing corner to Summit Ledge (70 feet). **Descent:** Rappel 75 feet from the large tree on Summit Ledge down to anchors at the top of the first pitch of *Frosted Flake*. From here, rappel 50 feet to Upper Broadway Ledge.

24. **Put a Wiggle In Your Stride** (5.11d) Sport route. Recommended as a toprope after climbing *Frosted Flake*. Starting on ledges just left of *Frosted Flake*, climb the smooth face past 4 bolts (45 feet). **Descent:** Rappel from anchors on *Frosted Flake*.

25. **Frosted Flake** (5.9-) A high-quality, popular, and "light" 5.9. Certainly easier than *Triple S* (5.8+)—go figure! Begin below a right-facing flake that begins at a small tree about 15 feet up. **Pitch 1:** Scramble up over a ledge and block to the tree and the beginning of the flake. Send the beautiful flake and crack system, passing right around an overhang, then back left to a small ledge with anchors (50 feet). Many parties rappel from here. **Pitch 2:** Work up and right into a corner. Follow this a few moves, then move left onto the face and climb past bulges to Summit Ledge (75 feet). **Descent:** Use the large tree on Summit Ledge to rappel back to the anchors at the top of the first pitch. From here, rappel 50 feet to Upper Broadway Ledge.

26. **T.R. Rap and Tap** (5.11d) Sport route. Start climbing from a block leaning against the wall about 20 feet right of *Frosted Flake*. Fire up the face along an orange streak and small right-facing corner to rappel anchors (70 feet). 6 bolts.

27. **Mister Jones** (5.11c) Sport route. Begin on a sloping ledge about 30 feet left of *Soler* and 10 feet right of a small pine. Start up green rock, then work up the thin, white face above to rappel anchors (80 feet). 6 bolts.

28. **Soler** (5.7+) An area classic with a spectacular second pitch. The first pitch is a bit run-out, although not hard, along a section of 6-inch crack. No doubt, a stout 1951 first ascent by Tony Soler. Begin at a prominent, left-facing flake system that slants up and right. **Pitch 1:** This long, rising pitch climbs the flake until it curves right to form a ledge. Belay below an orange ramp (135 feet). **Pitch 2:** Climb the broken ramp to an overhang with a small, left-facing corner. Pull through this and follow cracks up the face until they end. Continue on face holds to a ledge, then finish up and right on a crack to the South Peak summit (140 feet). **Descent:** Scramble north from the South Peak and follow the *Conn's East* descent path.

# SOUTH PEAK—EAST FACE

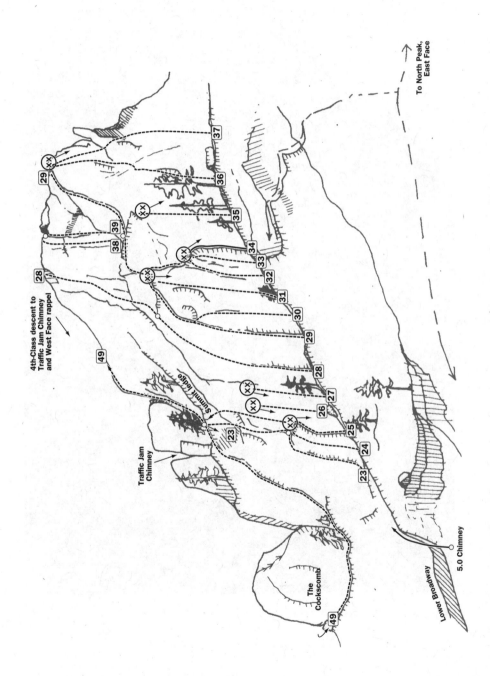

4th Class

4th Class from
East Face Trail

# SOUTH PEAK—EAST FACE

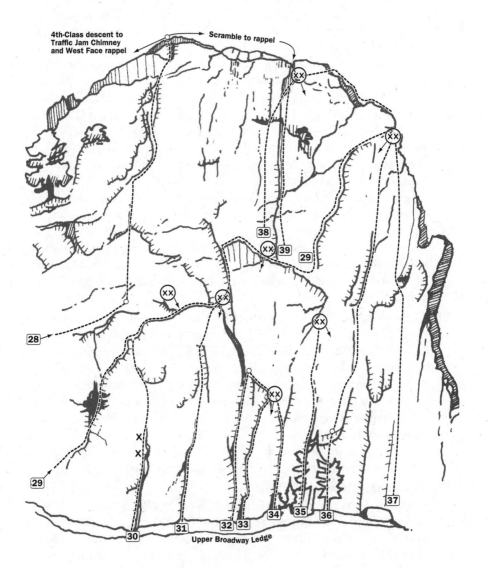

4th-Class descent to
Traffic Jam Chimney
and West Face rappel

Scramble to rappel

38

39

29

28

29

30

31

32 33

34

35

36

37

Upper Broadway Ledge

29. **Conn's East** (5.5) This long, wandering route (established in 1944) follows the "easiest" path up the middle of the steep East Face of the South Peak. Care must be taken to stay on route, as the route crosses over many other climbs along the way. Start at a left-facing corner located about 20 feet right of Soler. **Pitch 1:** Climb the corner up and right to a chockstone in the main flake. Continue up and right along a huge flake and chimney to its top. Move right to a belay at coldshuts (130 feet). **Pitch 2:** Move off the right end of the ledge (exposed) and climb up and right through a bulge to good holds. Traverse right about 20 feet to belay anchors at the base of *Orangeaid* and *Alcoa Presents* (50 feet). **Pitch 3:** Scramble right to an arching, left-facing crack, and climb this to the base of a chimney. Move past a chockstone and ascend a gully to a large ledge (80 feet). **Pitch 4:** Step right and climb up along the summit ridge. **Descent:** Locate a small keyhole notch with fixed slings atop *Alcoa Presents*—from here it's 180 feet down to Upper Broadway, so you'll need to do three rappels. The first is an 80-foot shot down to the ledge and anchors at the start of *Alcoa Presents*. Next, rappel 60 feet to a ledge and anchors midway up *Conn's East Direct Start* and just right of the top of *Pollux*. Conclude with a 40-foot rappel to Upper Broadway Ledge.

30. **The Changeling** (5.11c) A great 5.11 face climb with a well-protected crux. Start below a shallow, right-facing flake about 35 feet right of *Conn's East*. **Pitch 1:** Climb the flake to its end, then continue up the face past 2 bolts (strenuous clips) and along a crack to an overhang. Move left around the overhang and continue to the belay at anchors on *Conn's East* (90 feet). **Pitch 2:** Finish up *Conn's East* or climb one of the other, harder routes on the upper headwall. **Descent:** Rappel 100 feet from anchors at the end of the first pitch, or climb the second pitch of *Conn's East* to the anchors at the base of *Alcoa Presents*. From here you can do two shorter rappels back down to Upper Broadway Ledge.

31. **Terra Firma Homesick Blues** (5.11c R) Some of the best climbing at Seneca, but a very serious lead, with difficult-to-place small gear. Highly recommended as a toprope. Begin left of *Castor,* at a short, right-facing corner. Climb the corner and thinning crack system into a 20-foot stretch of consistently thin face climbing. Push ahead to reach a thank-god horn, then finish up an easier crack system to anchors (100 feet). **Gear:** Bring RPs, wired stoppers, and TCUs, as well as some other cams up to 3.5 inches for the start and finish. Also, a 60-meter rope is required to rappel from the anchors. **Descent:** Rappel 100 feet from anchors, or climb the second pitch of *Conn's East* to the anchors at the base of *Alcoa Presents*. From here you can do two half-rope rappels back down to Upper Broadway Ledge, or climb either *Alcoa Presents* or *Orangeaid*.

32. **Castor** (5.10a) A very popular crack climb with the hardest moves right off the ground. Start on small blocks 10 feet right of a nice pine tree, and send it! **Descent:** Most people do a 40-foot rappel from anchors located just to the right, at a stance partway up *Conn's East Direct Start*. You can also ascend the left-slanting ramp about 60 feet to anchors atop *Terra Firm Homesick Blues*. Set up a toprope (need 60-meter rope) on *Terra Firma* or proceed up the second pitch of *Conn's East* to a ledge and the beginning of *Orangeaid* and *Alcoa Presents*.

33. **Pollux** (5.10a) More sustained than *Castor,* but every bit as popular. For many years both routes were considered "solid Seneca 5.9"—now upgraded to 5.10a, they are surely many climbers' first 5.10 leads. Climb the crack located just a few yards right of *Castor*. **Descent:** Same as *Castor*.

34. **Conn's East Direct Start** (5.8) Begin 8 feet right of *Pollux,* at two shallow, right-facing corners leading to a chockstone flake about 12 feet up. Climb tricky moves up to the shallow corners, then continue along an easier, widening crack to a ledge and anchors at the base of a prominent, left-slanting ramp. Move right and climb a short corner and right-slanting ramp way up to another ledge. Now traverse back left to the ledge and anchors below *Orangeaid* and *Alcoa Presents* (110 feet). **Note:** Some parties just climb the first 40 feet (includes the crux right off the ground) and rappel from the first set of anchors. This is also popular as a lead-in route to the similarly graded *Alcoa Presents*.

35. **Spock's Brain** (5.11a) A good introduction to Seneca Rocks 5.11. Decent protection if you bring plenty of small stoppers and TCUs. Start 20 feet right of *Conn's East Direct Start* at a short, right-facing corner. Climb the corner and small cracks through a bulge and work up and slightly left to finish at anchors (90 feet).

36. **High Test** (5.9+) With three good cruxes, this route is at the far end of 5.9+. A great lead if you're solid at the grade. Begin at a tall pine tree about 40 feet right of *Conn's East Direct Start* and below a small ledge about 25 feet up. Climb up to the ledge (optional belay). Step right and climb a left-facing corner until you can move right to gain discontinuous cracks. Work up the cracks and thin face above to an overhang, then continue up the obvious, right-facing corner and crack system to anchors (130 feet). **Gear:** Bring a full rack and take care to protect the middle section well. Consider using double ropes to decrease rope drag, or break the climb into two pitches. **Descent:** Rappel 110 feet from anchors, or scramble up to the notch in the South Peak (above *Alcoa Presents*) and do three rappels per *Conn's East* descent instructions.

37. **Nip and Tuck** (5.10c) A long, exciting pitch. Start from a large block on the far-north end of Broadway Ledge. Climb thin cracks up and left to

an overhang about 100 feet up. Follow the cracks through the overhang and up to anchors (120 feet). Descent: Rappel 110 feet from anchors, or scramble up to the notch in the South Peak (above *Alcoa Presents*) and do three rappels per *Conn's East* descent instructions.

38. **Orangeaid** (5.10b) Definitely "magazine material," this route was featured on the cover of *Rock & Ice* in 1998. Start by climbing one of the previous routes to gain the ledge and anchors at the end of the second pitch of *Conn's East*. Beginning left of the belay anchors, jam the beautiful cracks up the orange wall to a roof. Pull this and continue up easier rock above to the top (100 feet). Descent: Same as *Conn's East*.

39. **Alcoa Presents** (5.8) Very popular. Just right of anchors at *Conn's East* second pitch belay ledge, climb the crack and shallow, right-facing corner to a notch in the summit ridge (80 feet). Descent: In the notch, rappel from a rock horn with slings 180 feet (need two 60-meter ropes) to Upper Broadway Ledge, or do three shorter rappels—the first, an 80-foot rappel down to the anchors at the start of *Alcoa Presents*, then rap 60 feet to a set of anchors just down and right from the top of *Pollux*, and conclude with a 40-foot rappel to Upper Broadway Ledge.

# NORTH PEAK—EAST FACE

**Finding the face:** Hike Roy Gap Road past the Southeast Corner to the blue-blazed East Face Trail on the left. Follow this trail uphill (passing along the right side of a short rock fin that parallels the East Face) for about ten minutes to a point just above the Gunsight Notch. Here, cut left on a blue-blazed feeder trail toward the Gunsight Notch. In about 80 yards you come to a 10-foot high outcrop—carefully boulder up a few slippery 5.0 moves to good ledge. Take the right trail and scramble uphill about 30 yards to the base of *Lichen or Leave It* and *Roux*.

**Descent:** Tree rappels are available on most routes. If you top out on a route, scramble north along the summit toward the tourists' observation deck. From here you can descend on the East Face Trail (if you want to do another route) or hike the tourists' trail down the west side to the parking lot.

40. **Lichen or Leave It** (5.8 R) Rope up at a short face about 20 feet below the prominent, left-facing *Roux* corner. Boulder up to a large ledge, then climb up and left past black streaks (5.6 R) toward a pine tree. Now climb the nice crack above to a good ledge and rappel tree (90 feet).

41. **Helter Skelter** (5.10c) Some great finger jamming! Climb two-thirds of the way up the *Roux* corner until you can traverse left to ascend a thin and sustained crack to a ledge and tree (90 feet). Descent: Rappel from tree.

# NORTH PEAK—EAST FACE

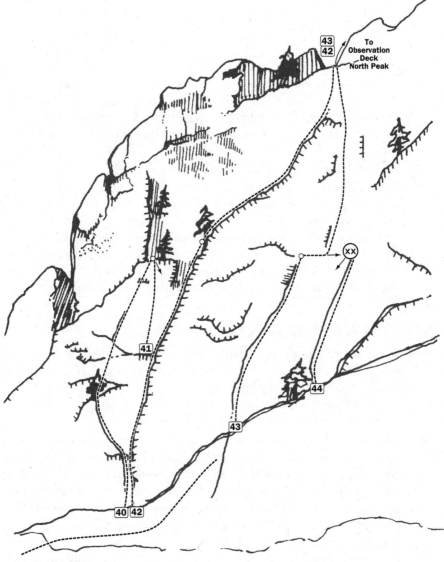

To
Observation
Deck
North Peak

From East Face Trail

42. **Roux** (5.3) Begin at the base of a short face about 20 feet below a prominent, left-facing corner. **Pitch 1:** Climb the corner, using holds mainly on the right wall, up to a tree and ledge (90 feet). **Pitch 2:** Diagonal up and right on easy terrain to the summit (60 feet). **Descent:** Hike north along the summit ridge to the tourists' deck and descend on either the east side or tourists' trail.

43. **Unrelenting Verticality** (5.9 R) The start is sporty, but if you're solid at 5.9, it's a great pitch. Start about 40 feet right of *Roux*, at obvious diagonal cracks up a smooth face. **Pitch 1:** Climb the steep cracks to a ledge with pine tree (55 feet). **Pitch 2:** Escape right to anchors on *Rox Salt* or traverse right to gain a flaky crack system. Work up this to near the top, then wander up and left on easy ground to the top (90 feet). **Descent:** Rappel after the first pitch, or summit and hike off.

44. **Rox Salt** (5.7) A popular first pitch—short, but quite nice. Locate another right-leaning crack about 15 feet right of the *Unrelenting Verticality* cracks. **Pitch 1:** Climb the crack up and right to an anchor (40 feet). **Pitch 2:** Rappel from the anchors or move up and finish up the crack on Pitch 2 of *Unrelenting Verticality* (90 feet). **Descent:** Rappel after the first pitch, or summit and hike down along the tourists' trail (on west side) or along the East Side Trail (if you plan to do another route).

## SOUTHWEST CORNER

**Finding the area:** Walk up Roy Gap Road until you see the first buttress of rock on your left. Follow a blue-blazed trail that begins at a small stone wall just across Roy Gap Run. Hike uphill a short way until the trail splits near the base of the buttress. Follow the trail up the slope to an impressive set of wooden steps at the base of the Southwest Corner.

45. **The Burn** (5.8) One of the best 5.8 pitches at Seneca. Begin on a block at a tree directly above the top of the wooden steps. Climb the juggy corner and cracks to a stance below a small overhang about 60 feet up (optional belay). Pull through the overhang and climb the beautiful finger cracks to a large ledge (95 feet). **Descent:** Rappel from tree or anchors above—use a 60-meter, or two shorter ropes.

46. **Sunshine** (5.10a R) Recommended as a toprope. Begin just left of *The Burn* and beneath a bolt about halfway up the pitch. Climb small edges and cracks to the bolt. Continue past a bulge and onto a white face, then move up and left to finish on the *Ecstasy Junior* crack (95 feet). **Gear:** Bring RPs; small, wired stoppers; TCUs; and a medium-sized piece for the finish. **Descent:** Rappel from a tree or anchors above—use a 60-meter, or two shorter ropes.

# WEST FACE OVERVIEW

North Peak

South Peak

Cockscomb

Humphrey's Head

Bell Wall

Gunsight Notch

Euro Wall

Face of a Thousand Pitons

Luncheon Ledge

Southwest Corner

Trail

47. **Ecstasy Junior** (5.4) Scramble about 150 feet uphill from the Southwest Corner proper and boulder up to a ledge with a large pine tree. **Pitch 1:** Begin at the tree and traverse right about 10 feet to gain a vertical crack. Follow this up through a bulge to the large ledge with trees above (65 feet). **Pitch 2:** Climb the large, right-facing corner to an overhang. Pull around this and continue up the crack and face to a ledge (70 feet). **Descent:** Do two rappels from trees back down the route—use a 60-meter, or two shorter ropes for the second rappel.

## COCKSCOMB, HUMPHREY'S HEAD, AND THE FACE OF A THOUSAND PITONS

**Finding the area:** Walk up Roy Gap Road until you see the first buttress of rock on your left. Take a blue-blazed trail that begins at an obvious set of stone steps just across Roy Gap Run. Hike uphill a short way and stay left as the trail splits near the cliffbase. Continue up wooden steps and a series of switchbacks to gain a plateau with numerous hemlocks. Here, the trail bends right through a brief talus field and then ascends a few 3rd-Class moves to a split in the trail. Take the right split to access Luncheon Ledge and routes on Humphrey's Head and Cockscomb. The left trail leads directly to The Face of a Thousand Pitons.

48. **Humphrey's Head** (5.2–5.4) This small pinnacle, located on the far right skyline, is popular with beginning climbers. It's not uncommon for Luncheon Ledge to be clogged with climbing school students psyching up for their first rock climb. Begin from Luncheon Ledge and climb anywhere up the west face to the top of the pinnacle (40 feet). **Descent:** Rappel or lower from anchors, or downclimb (5.0) along the north ridge until you can scramble down to Luncheon Ledge.

49. **Old Ladies' Route** (5.2) Typically crowded on weekends, this climb is the easiest path to the South Peak summit. Experienced climbers sometimes descend on *Old Ladies'* after doing other climbs on the South Peak. Start from Luncheon Ledge, at a point below the notch between Humphrey's Head and Cockscomb. **Pitch 1:** Cimb up through the notch and belay on a flat ledge with a nice view to the east (100 feet). **Pitch 2:** Move right and down onto a ledge on the East Face and traverse right to several large trees (75 feet). **Pitch 3:** Climb up and right to the end of the ledge, then ascend a sloping flake and chimney (100 feet). **Pitch 4:** Scramble about 100 feet right to the summit ridge, or climb more directly up exposed 4th-Class moves to the summit. **Descent:** Reverse the route, preferably with a belay on all four pitches, or use the *Old Man's/Neck Press* rappel route (see South Peak—West Face section).

COCKSCOMB AND
THE FACE OF A
THOUSAND PITONS

50. **Broken Neck a.k.a. Breakneck Direct** (5.10b R) Begin on a ledge at a small tree (tie in) directly below a crack that begins above a small overhang about 15 feet up. Climb carefully up awkward moves (poor protection) and through a small overhang to gain the crack. Continue up the crack and right-facing flakes to a ledge and rappel anchors (80 feet). **Note:** Some parties begin farther left and climb easier moves up and right to gain the crack.

51. **Breakneck** (5.6) A popular route to the top of Cockscomb, but you'll need to do some extra climbing up onto the South Peak to rappel off. Begin below a prominent, left-facing corner near the center of Cockscomb's west face. **Pitch 1:** Climb up to a small tree, then traverse right until below a huge, left-facing flake (30 feet). **Pitch 2:** Climb along the flake and up to a good ledge (45 feet). **Pitch 3:** Move up and right to gain a crack system, then follow the crack up to a ledge (45 feet). **Pitch 4:** Continue to the top of Cockscomb (20 feet). **Note:** While climbing the route in four short pitches reduces rope drag, many persons combine Pitches 1 and 2, and Pitches 3 and 4. Keep in mind that the descent requires some additional roped climbing (5.4), so allow enough time for this. **Descent:** Downclimb along the north ridge to a ledge in Windy Notch (just above *Triple S*). Now climb up the east face of the notch along cracks and through an overhang (5.4) to the South Peak summit ledges (40 feet). Pass through the Traffic Jam Chimney and descend via the *Old Man's Route* rappel route (see *Old Man's Route* for details).

52. **Triple S** (5.8+) Maybe the best pitch at Seneca, and, no doubt, a solid 5.9 anywhere else in the country! Established in 1960 by Jim Shipley and Joe Faint. Climb the crack and corner that defines the right side of The Face of a Thousand Pitons (90 feet). **Descent:** Rappel from anchors on the right wall—you'll need a 60-meter rope!

53. **Marshall's Madness** (5.9) A great route, especially the first two pitches. Tom Marshall must have been a bit mad to send this route in 1955! If 5.10a is your grade, then the *Crack of Dawn* variation is a must-do. Begin on a nice belay ledge below the crack system that splits the left side of The Face of a Thousand Pitons. **Pitch 1:** Crack-climb past a small overhang to a stance with anchors (40 feet). **Pitch 2:** Continue up the crack and chimney system about 60 feet, until it's possible to trend left across easy rock to a belay with anchors on the outside corner (75 feet). **Pitch 3:** Move back right and run up the top portion of the crack/chimney system to anchors at the top (50 feet). **Descent:** You can bail off the route from anchors at all three belays, or from the South Peak summit descent via *Old Ladies' Route*, or use the West Face rappel over *Old Man's Route*. **Variation: Crack of Dawn** (5.10a) Climb the crack/chimney system of *Marshall's* second pitch for about 40 feet, until you can

THE FACE OF A THOUSAND PITONS

move right to a small overhang split by a stunning crack above. Jam up the beautiful crack to anchors (120 feet). **Descent:** Use two 165-foot ropes for a single rappel back to the base, or continue to the South Peak summit descent via *Old Ladies' Route,* or use the West Face rappel over *Old Man's Route.*

## SOUTH PEAK—WEST FACE

**Finding the face:** Walk up Roy Gap Road until you see the first buttress of rock on your left. Take a blue-blazed trail that begins at an obvious set of stone step just across Roy Gap Run. Hike uphill a short way and stay left as the trail splits near the cliffbase. Continue up wooden steps and a series of switchbacks to gain a plateau with numerous hemlocks. Here, the trail bends right through a brief talus field, then ascends a few 3rd-Class moves to a split in the trail. Follow the left trail a short distance to meet the West Face below The Face of a Thousand Pitons. The West Face Trail continues along the cliffbase (follow blue blazes) past Thaïs Face and below the Gunsight Notch to the North Peak West Face.

**Descents:** South Peak, West Face routes are all descended via rappel. A single 60-meter (200-foot) rope is ideal, although you can safely rappel most routes with a 50-meter (165-foot) cord.

The standard rappel route begins at the base of the *Traffic Jam* chimney atop *Old Man's Route.* From the South Peak summit, scramble southward along the summit ledges to an obvious chimney/notch. Squeeze through the chimney to a pine tree and a set of rappel anchors. A 50-foot rappel will place you on the south end of the broad *Old Man's* traverse ledge. From here it's about 140 feet to the ground, so if you have two ropes you can make it in one go. Otherwise, you'll need to do two more rappels: the first, a 70-foot run to anchors at the top of *Neck Press's* first pitch, and then another 70 feet to the ground.

As an alternative to the second and third rappels (in case of a "traffic jam" on *Neck Press*), walk carefully northward and down to a large pine tree near the middle of the *Old Man's* traverse ledge. Rappel 70 feet and swing about 20 feet left to reach another tree on the *Le Gourmet* traverse ledge. From here, one final 80-foot rap puts you on the ground.

54. **Cottonmouth** (5.10a) If the first pitch doesn't pump you up, give the excellent second pitch variation a run. Begin just left of the outside corner that defines the left edge of The Face of a Thousand Pitons. **Pitch 1:** Start up shallow, right-facing corners, then move left and ascend jagged right-facing corners and flakes to a ledge with anchors (90 feet). **Descent:** Use a 60-meter rope to rappel from the anchors, or climb the

SOUTH PEAK—WEST FACE

excellent 5.10 variation to finish on the South Peak summit. Variation: **Venom** (5.10b) **Pitch 2:** From the belay ledge, step left and climb a right-facing flake and corner up to anchors at the *Marshall's Madness* belay on the outside corner (60 feet). **Pitch 3:** Traverse left onto the West Face to gain a thin crack that splits the wall and climb it to the top (65 feet). **Descent:** Use the *Old Man's Route* rappel route.

55. **Sidewinder** (5.11a) One of many hard, classic routes put up by Howard Doyle and Eric Janoscrat. Begin about 8 feet left of *Cottonmouth*, at a right-facing corner capped by a small overhang. **Pitch 1:** Climb the corner, then straight through the overhang and up along a thin, vertical crack until you can traverse left to anchors at the *Neck Press* belay ledge (65 feet). **Pitch 2:** From the right side of the ledge, work up through a small roof and follow a small, diagonal crack to a left-facing corner. Continue to a belay tree. **Descent:** Use the *Old Man's Route* rappel route.

56. **Neck Press** (5.7) A popular, moderate path to the South Peak summit. Start 25 feet left of the large outside corner, at a white-and-green, right-facing corner. **Pitch 1:** Climb the corner and press on through a few steep moves to a ledge with anchors (60 feet). **Pitch 2:** Move left and climb the corner and wide crack to the right end of the *Old Man's* traverse ledge (65 feet). **Pitch 3:** Climb the crack and corner system located to the right of the easier last pitch of *Old Man's Route* (60 feet). **Descent:** Easy—do three rappels from fixed anchors on *Neck Press* belay ledges.

57. **Le Gourmet Direct** (5.6) Begin at the base of the blocky, south-facing wall located 40 feet left of The Face of a Thousand Pitons. **Pitch 1:** Wander up and right, then back left to finish along the arête to a belay on the *Old Man's* traverse ledge (110 feet). **Descent:** Rappel from anchors, or climb to the summit via the last pitch of *Neck Press*, *Old Man's Route*, or the *Traffic Jam* variation.

58. **Le Gourmet** (5.4) Start around the outside corner to the left of *Le Gourmet Direct*, at a short right-facing corner with a tree at its base. **Pitch 1:** Climb the corner about 15 feet to its end, then move left along the ledge for 20 feet to gain another right-facing corner. Follow this up to a tree and ledge (70 feet). **Pitch 2:** Traverse about 30 feet right and climb up to the outside corner of the south-facing *Le Gourmet Direct* wall to a belay ledge (90 feet). **Pitch 3:** Scramble up and left (3rd Class) to the base of the south-facing chimneys at the left side of a clean face (40 feet). **Pitch 4:** Finish up the right-hand chimney and crack system (75 feet). **Descent:** Use the *Old Man's Route* rappel route.

59. **Prune** (5.7) Locate a left-facing flake about 6 feet off the ground and about 30 yards left of *Le Gourmet*. **Pitch 1:** Climb up along the flake and low-angle face to a stance. Step left and continue up a clean section of rock with a short crack to a small belay ledge (85 feet). **Pitch 2:** Continue straight up along cracks and blocks to a narrow stance. Follow a left-leaning finger crack along a clean section of wall to a ledge with a tree (85 feet). **Pitch 3:** Climb a right-facing flake until forced left, then work up and back right past some small cracks to a good belay (70 feet). **Pitch 4:** Finish up a left-facing corner and flake (50 feet). **Descent:** Use the *Old Man's Route* rappel route.

60. **Old Man's Route** (5.2) The original trade route up the tall West Face of the South Peak. Start on a dirty ledge directly below the prominent *Thaïs* corner. **Pitch 1:** Move up and right over easy ledges to a short, left-facing corner and crack. Follow the crack and continue scrambling along the weakness to the base of a chimney (150 feet). **Pitch 2:** Climb the chimney (30 feet). **Pitch 3:** Move right across a long ledge with trees and set up a belay near the right (south) end (100 feet). **Pitch 4:** Scramble up and right along a corner and past a chockstone to the next belay at a tree and anchor bolts (40 feet). **Pitch 5:** Pass through the *Traffic Jam* chimney to the Summit Ledge, and scramble northward along the rising ledges to the South Peak summit. **Descent:** Reverse the last pitch to the west side of the *Traffic Jam* chimney and the first set of rappel anchors. A 50-foot rappel places you on the south end of the broad *Old Man's* traverse ledge. From here it's about 140 feet to the ground, so if you have two ropes, you can make it in one go. Otherwise, you'll need to do two more rappels: the first, a 70-foot run to anchors at the top of *Neck Press's* first pitch, and then another 70 feet to the ground. As an alternative to the second and third rappels (in case of a "traffic jam" on *Neck Press*), walk carefully northward and down to a large pine tree near the middle of the *Old Man's* traverse ledge. Rappel 70 feet and swing about 20 feet left to reach another tree on the *Le Gourmet* traverse ledge. From here, one final 80-foot rap puts you on the ground.

61. **Traffic Jam** (5.7) A mini-classic. This short crack is on the white, south-facing wall that forms one side of the chimney near the top of *Old Man's Route*. You also pass it when descending from the South Peak to the beginning of the *Old Man's/Neck Press* rappel route. Climb the clean crack up the wall of the chimney (40 feet). **Descent:** Scramble back down to the chimney, and use the *Old Man's Route* rappel route.

SOUTH PEAK—WEST FACE

62. **West Pole** (5.7+) A fine climb—more intimidating than it is hard. Climb the first pitch of *Old Man's Route* until you can move left to a large ledge with a pine tree (about 75 feet above the ground). Set up a belay at a tree just left of twin cracks. **Pitch 1:** Crack-climb to a stance below a large double overhang (70 feet). **Pitch 2:** Follow the cracks through the overhangs and head up a left-facing corner to a stance. Finish up and right to a pine tree on a large ledge (65 feet). **Descent:** Use the *Old Man's Route* rappel route.

63. **Thaïs** (5.5) Begin at the base of the huge left-facing corner near the right side of the north-facing wall. **Pitch 1:** Climb the face straight up to a belay at the base of a deep chimney (75 feet). **Pitch 2:** Work up the chimney and crack above, then angle slightly right to a belay ledge just left of a crack (110 feet). **Pitch 3:** Diagonal up and right to gain a sloping belay on the outside corner of the face (60 feet). **Pitch 4:** Move back left to the inside corner and climb directly up to a loose gully and ledge below the South Peak summit (60 feet). **Pitch 5:** Finish up 4th-Class terrain to the summit (50 feet). **Descent:** Use the *Old Man's Route* rappel route.

64. **Pleasant Overhangs** (5.7) The second pitch is classic—and if you like exposure, the tiny belay ledge at its end will be very pleasant! From below a huge roof that slants left from the *Thaïs* corner, scramble up along easy ledges to a belay stance at a tree at the base of a blocky, left-facing, right-slanting corner (about 100 feet left of the *Thaïs* corner). **Pitch 1:** Traverse up and right to a corner/chimney with a chockstone and move up to a stance. Continue up along several easy overhanging corners, always trending up and right toward the intersection of the roof and *Thaïs* corner. Belay at a small ledge (100 feet). **Pitch 2:** Execute the exciting traverse left under the huge roof and, at its end, pull up through a small overhang to a small, airy belay (60 feet). **Pitch 3:** Climb the left-facing corner up increasingly easy moves to the next belay (60 feet). **Pitch 4:** Scramble to the summit (30 feet). **Descent:** Walk south along the summit ridge until you can scramble down onto the summit ledges on the east side. Continue southward and pass through the *Traffic Jam* chimney to the *Old Man's Route* rappel route.

65. **Green Wall** (5.7) A "light" 5.7—very classic! Begin at two left-facing corners (and a large flake on the left) below the right side of the Gunsight Notch and down and left of the huge, green-and-white wall. **Pitch 1:** Climb the easiest path up the corners to gain a large ledge (35 feet). **Pitch 2:** Walk right across the ledge and set up a belay at a small tree

*Kyle Hörst following Green Wall (5.7), Seneca Rocks.* PHOTO BY ERIC J. HÖRST

below the prominent, left-facing corner (40 feet). **Pitch 3:** Climb the beautiful corner past a small overhang and up easier moves to a ledge (100 feet). **Pitch 4:** Scramble up and right to the South Peak and summit register (50 feet). **Descent:** Walk south along the summit ridge until you can scramble down (4th Class) onto the summit ledges. Continue south along the east side ledges and pass through the *Traffic Jam* chimney to the *Old Man's Route* rappel route.

66. **Tomato** (5.8) Features a really great second pitch. Begin as for *Green Wall,* below a large flake and two left-facing corners. **Pitch 1:** Climb the flake to a ledge with trees (35 feet). **Pitch 2:** Move right a few feet and ascend a long, left-facing corner. Continue up the dihedral to finish up easier rock to the summit ridge (120 feet). You can now walk or crawl along the summit ridge to the register. **Descent:** Walk south along the summit ridge until you can scramble down onto the summit ledges on the east side. Continue south a short way and pass through the *Traffic Jam* chimney to the *Old Man's Route* rappel route.

## NORTH PEAK—WEST FACE (THE BELL WALL)

**Finding the crag:** Take the West Face Trail per the approach to the South Peak West Face. From below The Face of a Thousand Pitons, follow the blue-

THE BELL WALL

*Kurt Byrnes on Madmen Only (5.10a).* Photo by Carl Samples

blazed trail as it climbs up and left along a series of dirty ledges to a high point below the Gunsight Notch. Walk another 30 yards through some bushes to a blocky, right-facing corner. Climb a few 5.0 moves to gain a ledge system that ramps up and far left. Follow this all the way to the mouth of the huge No Dally Alley chimney. Now, scramble back to the right and up to the base of the Bell Wall.

Descent: All routes described end at anchors; however, a 60-meter (200-foot) rope (or two shorter ropes) is required to reach the ledge.

67. **Madmen Only** (5.10a) Another classic! Begin at the obvious, right-facing corner and crack located just left of the Gunsight Notch. Climb up into the corner and continue until it's possible to move right into a wide crack. Continue up to anchors (85 feet). Variation: **Psycho Killer** (5.11b) Where the regular route moves right, continue up and left to gain a shallow, right-facing corner. Crank through a bulge and climb up and left to anchors atop *Psycho Driller* (95 feet). **Descent:** Rappel off.

68. **Psycho Driller** (5.12c) Sport route. Insanely difficult—free-climbed by Jim Woodruff. Begin on top of a block about 30 feet left of *Madmen Only*. Climb the steep face past 6 bolts to anchors (90 feet). **Descent:** Rappel off.

69. **Malevolence** (5.10c) Start along the right side of a boulder located about 60 feet left of the *Madmen Only* start. Climb a crack and face above to a right-facing corner. Work up the corner and crack to its end. Traverse right to gain another corner, then head straight up to the top (95 feet). Variation: **Direct Finish** (5.12b) Instead of moving right at the top of the corner, crank straight up past 3 bolts. **Descent:** Rappel off.

70. **Bonsai** (5.12b) Sport route. Begin below a small pine tree left of *Malevolence*. Face climb past 8 bolts to anchors (90 feet). **Descent:** Rappel off.

# NELSON ROCKS

## OVERVIEW

Climbers in the densely populated Mid-Atlantic region have no choice but to accept that climbing resources are extremely limited compared to other parts of the country. Harder to accept, though, is the trend of climbing areas being closed or access being limited by private landowners. Fortunately, a break in this trend has occurred in Pendleton County, West Virginia, where a nonprofit recreation preserve has purchased one of the region's most prominent and unique rock formations.

Established in 1998 by Stuart, LaVonne, and Grace Hammett, the Nelson Rocks Preserve (NRP) features two quarter-mile-long parallel rock fins—think Seneca Rocks times two!—with steep routes ranging from 40-foot clip-ups to three-pitch traditional lines. Nelson also possesses West Virginia's longest climb, *Millennium* (5.7), a nine-pitch, 1,000-foot, rising traverse of the East Face of the West Fin. NRP charges a modest $5.00 day-use fee to all recreational users.

Located 10 miles south of Seneca Rocks, Nelson is comprised of the same Tuscarora Sandstone as Seneca and Champe. However, the double-fin rock formation and more-fractured character yield a very different climbing experience. Whereas Seneca Rocks offers a multitude of well-protected, moderate corner-and-crack routes like *Green Wall, Le Gourmet,* and *Triple S,* Nelson has but a handful of such routes. Instead, Nelson has been blessed with steep faces, featuring a diverse array of some of the coolest holds you'll ever lock your fingers onto. The climbing surface ranges from smooth to washboard to blocky and is loaded with a cornucopia of small finger pockets, crimpers, knobs, and full-hand wrapper jugs. No doubt, these fins were made for climbing!

One feature common to Seneca Rocks and Nelson is the tendency to loose rock and dicey protection on some routes. While a few well-protected, traditional lines have emerged—*The Laeger Route* (5.8) and the classic *Crescendo* (5.10a) are good examples—mixed routes and sport climbs are the norm at Nelson. Many climbs require a rack of stoppers, TCUs, and cams up to 3 inches, plus a handful of quickdraws to clip bolts through blank sections of rock. A number of all-bolt routes have recently been established—this is where Nelson really outshines nearby Seneca Rocks—with high-quality clip-

# NELSON ROCKS PRESERVE

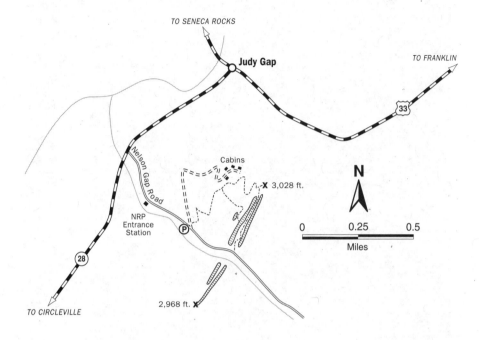

ups like *Sticky Fingers* (5.7), *Sorry Howard* (5.9), *Lifers* (5.10a), *The Foundation* (5.10d), *Written In Stone* (5.11c), and *Excalibur* (5.12a).

Beyond climbing, Nelson Rocks Preserve is a great place for hiking, picnicking, or just relaxing on the porch of a rustic mountain cabin. The NRP features several miles of beautiful trails leading to a summit overlook with a spectacular 360-degree view of the North Fork and Germany valleys and Spruce Knob. Newly established as a recreation preserve, you can expect additional trails and many more rock climbs to be added in the years to come.

In the long run, Nelson Rocks Preserve may be more than just a climbing area, as it offers a new paradigm through which access for climbers can be permanently secured through private ownership of a not-for-profit preserve. While some may dislike the "pay to climb" formula, the revenue generated by climbers supports the access and material improvements that the Hammetts' vision and commitment to stewardship have brought. I say "kudos" to the Hammetts for securing the area's accessibility for future generations of climbers and other outdoor enthusiasts.

**Climbing history:** Prior to the creation of the Nelson Rocks Preserve in 1998, climbing at Nelson could have been viewed as trespassing. Nelson's previous owners did not encourage nor obstruct climbing, and the handful of

*Dan Miller airing it out on the exposed Nelson Rocks classic The Diamond (5.11b).*
PHOTO BY HARRISON SHULL

climbers frequenting the area did not publicize their activities or keep formal route information beyond a new-route notebook at The Gendarme climbing shop. Much historical information has been forgotten or remains to be rediscovered—but here's what we know so far.

The first technical climbers at Nelson were U.S. Army mountain troops who trained here during World War II. One guidebook author has estimated that 75,000 soft-iron pitons were driven into the crags at Champe, Nelson, and Seneca Rocks, and some are still extant at Nelson (please leave them undisturbed as historical relics). It is likely that members of the Potomac Appalachian Trail Club (PATC) who climbed at Seneca during the 1950s and 1960s visited Nelson as well. The first recorded ascents came in the 1970s when Howard Doyle, Herb Laeger, Hunt Prothro, and others free-climbed obvious lines, such as *The Laeger Route* (5.8), *Crescendo* (5.10a), and *Stone Gallows* (5.10b). Howard Doyle went on to climb most of the natural lines on The Pillar's South Face and did a nine-pitch traverse route on the West Fin, East Face known today as *Millennium* (5.7).

From the mid-1980s to the mid-1990s, slow development continued through the efforts of Seneca Rocks activists such as Eddie Begoon, Mike Artz, Tom Cecil, Tony Barnes, Darell Hensley, and Howard Clark. The difficult face climbs established during this period often incorporated fixed protection to bridge long gaps between natural gear placements. However, the routes established were mainly ground-up and remain bold ascents to this day. A few of the better routes put up during this period are *Fist Chicken* (5.8), *Iroquois League* (5.10a), *Runaway Truck Ramp* (5.10d), *Scimitar* (5.10c), *Merlin* (5.11a/b), *The Diamond* (5.11b), *Porcelain Pump* (5.11c), *Written in Stone* (5.11c), and the routes on the so-called Sport Wall.

Since the creation of the Nelson Rocks Preserve, route development has accelerated, with the number of routes at Nelson nearly doubling over three seasons from 1998 to 2001. While some natural lines are still emerging in unexplored areas, bolt-protected face climbs (mixed and sport) are most common today. And, in contrast to sport climbs at Seneca Rocks or the New River Gorge that come in at "5.12 something," the majority of Nelson sport routes at present are in the 5.7 to 5.11 range.

As in the pre-NRP days, new route development is at the hands of a small group of locals, which includes Eric Anderson, Tom Cecil, Chris Clark, Sandy Fleming, Dave Martin, and Matt Murray. Recently established classics include the first pitch of *Diamonds Are Forever* (5.6), *Mike's Hike* (5.6), the 14-bolt *Sorry Howard* (5.9), *34D* (5.10b), an overhanging jugfest named *The Foundation* (5.10d), and the exposed *Notch Up Another One* (5.11a). Nice areas for beginner-level toprope climbs are the short Area 51 Wall and the left side of The Pillar South Face.

All new routes must be approved by NRP management and in accordance with NRP use guidelines, which are available at www.nelsonrocks.org.

# TRIP PLANNING INFORMATION

**General description:** Approximately 100 routes on Seneca Rocks–like Tuscarora Sandstone, with traditional routes up to three pitches in length and many one-pitch sport climbs.

**Location:** One mile south of Judy Gap and 10 miles south of Seneca Rocks, West Virginia.

**Camping:** There is no camping at Nelson Rocks Preserve; however, the Nelson Rocks Mountain Cabins are within walking distance of the cliffs. For more information, call 301–627–5301 or visit www.nelsonrocks.org. The two closest campgrounds are at Seneca Rocks. Seneca Shadows, operated by the Forest Service, is $8.00 for a walk-in and $12.00 for a drive-in site. For reservations, call 800–280–2267. Princess Snowbird Campground is located directly across from the Seneca Rocks Picnic Area and costs $5.00 per night. Register at Yocum's Store across the road.

**Climbing season:** Late March through early November offers the greatest number of good climbing days, although the summer months are rather humid. A few mild stretches occur each winter, though rainy, windy periods are more common in the mountains of West Virginia.

**Gear:** For the traditional and mixed routes, bring a full rack of wired stoppers, TCUs, four-cam units, a dozen extra 'biners and a handful of slings. A 200-foot (60-meter) rope is recommended, though not needed for every route. A few climbs require two ropes to rappel from anchors. For sport climbing, bring up to sixteen quickdraws and a 60-meter rope. A helmet and a conservative approach to pushing your limits would be prudent for many routes.

**Restrictions and access issues:** A $5.00 day-use fee is required to climb or hike at NRP and can be purchased at the entrance station on Nelson Gap Road. An annual pass is available for $30 via mail or the NRP Web site. Recreation fees are used to build trails, maintain vault toilets, and replace aging fixed anchors. Other restrictions include: no dogs, no radios, and no placement of fixed protection without permission of NRP management.

**Guidebooks:** This guide is the first printed matter on climbing at Nelson Rocks. Hopefully it will serve as a foundation on which a comprehensive guide will be built in the future. Meanwhile, current new route information is available at the NRP Web site.

**Nearby mountain shops, guide services, and gyms:** Seneca Rocks Mountain Guides and Outfitters provides the only guide services available at NRP. Located across the street from Harper's Store at Seneca Rocks, the shop also offers supplies, the latest Nelson beta, and the area's only climbing wall. For more information, contact Tom Cecil at 304–567–2115 or 800–451–5108. Also in the town of Seneca Rocks is the historic Gendarme climbing shop (304–567–2600), located behind Harper's Store.

**Services:** The nearest gasoline and food are found in Riverton, just 3 miles north of Nelson. Two fully stocked general stores and restaurants are located

# NELSON ROCKS PRESERVE CLIMBING AREAS

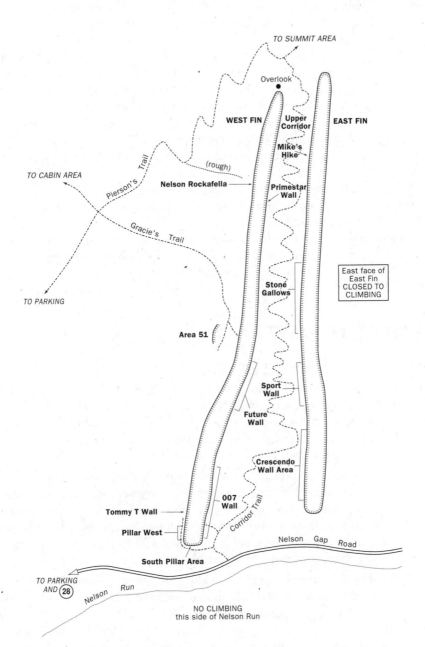

TO SUMMIT AREA

Overlook

WEST FIN    Upper Corridor    EAST FIN

Mike's Hike

TO CABIN AREA

Pierson's Trail

(rough)

Nelson Rockafella

Primestar Wall

Gracie's Trail

East face of East Fin CLOSED TO CLIMBING

TO PARKING

Stone Gallows

Area 51

Sport Wall

Future Wall

Crescendo Wall Area

007 Wall

Tommy T Wall

Corridor Trail

Pillar West

Nelson Gap Road

South Pillar Area

TO PARKING AND (28)

Nelson Run

NO CLIMBING
this side of Nelson Run

at the main intersection in the Village of Seneca Rocks. Popular breakfast spots are Valley View (5 miles north of Nelson) and Hendrick's 4-U located just 8 miles north of Nelson. Motel rooms are also available at Hendrick's 4-U (304–567–2111).

**Emergency services:** Call 304–567–2412 for an ambulance or the police. The closest hospital is Grant Memorial (304–257–1026), an hour away at Petersburg. Considering that this is so far away, and that there are no local rescue organizations, it would be prudent to climb well within your abilities and be prepared for the unexpected.

**Nearby climbing areas:** Other than Seneca Rocks (fifteen minutes north of Nelson), the closest cragging area is Franklin, located thirty minutes to the east.

**Nearby attractions:** Spruce Knob, West Virginia's highest point, is just across the valley from Nelson and well worth the visit. Seneca Caverns is just minutes away in Riverton.

**Finding the crags:** Locate the intersection of WV 28 and US 33 in eastern West Virginia—this intersection is the booming metropolis of Judy Gap. Just a half-mile south of Judy Gap you'll find Nelson Gap Road. Follow this gravel road a few hundred yards to the Nelson Rocks Preserve Entrance Station.

# WEST FIN, WEST FACE

## NELSON ROCKAFELLA WALL

**Finding the wall:** Take Pierson's Trail to a point about a 0.25 mile beyond the cabins, where the trail turns sharply left up a steep, rocky slope (just before the trail narrows) and where the top of West Fin is first visible. At this point, cut directly across toward the fin (some bushwhacking) and walk down the talus slope until you spot the bolted lines on the left.

1. **Free Nelson** (5.11c) Currently the farthest-left route on the wall. Climb easy rock past a bolt to a ledge (medium stopper). Continue up a steep, discontinuous crack system past four bolts to a horizontal crack (optional medium stopper between third and fourth bolt). Traverse right and finish up a short crack to anchors (70 feet). **Gear:** A couple of medium stoppers and a blue Camalot.

2. **Nelson Rockafella** (5.11b) A high-quality mixed route. Beginning 30 feet right of *Free Nelson*, climb moderate rock (need gear) up to ledge. Now follow a left-leaning crack past 6 bolts (75 feet). Belay at a large tree with an excellent view of the main Nelson corridor or move left and use the anchors atop *Free Nelson*. **Gear:** A few medium-to-large stoppers and a gold Camalot for the start.

3. **Half Nelson** (5.10d) Commence 25 feet right of *Nelson Rockafella*. Climb past three bolts to a right-trending ramp. Work up the ramp (gear), then follow a left-leaning crack past 4 more bolts. Belay from the large tree atop *Nelson Rockafella* (85 feet). **Gear:** A few medium stoppers and cams to one inch.

4. **Full Nelson** (5.10c) Starting 20 feet right of *Half Nelson*, climb along a line of 9 bolts to a belay tree (110 feet). Rappel from tree atop *Nelson Rockafella*. **Gear:** A 1.5-inch cam for between the second and third bolts.

## AREA 51 WALL

Area 51 is a secluded, 45-foot-high toproping wall located midway up the West Fin. Two sets of fixed anchors can be threaded from the top, and there is a large pine tree just uphill that serves as the anchor for *Jet Propulsion Lab*.

**Finding the wall:** While you could make the long uphill hike from The Pillar area, it's much easier to hike in from the cabins via Gracie's Trail. Where the trail turns downhill at the rocks (below a prominent chimney), follow the west face of the fin down a wooded gully to gain the top of the west-facing Area 51 Wall (on your right).

5. **Jet Propulsion Laboratory** (5.5) Loose, but better than it looks from below. Start in the corner just left of a large arête. Follow the corner and flakes, trending left to finish up the face to the large belay tree.

6. **Intruder Alert** (5.10) Start 10 feet right of a large corner and chimney, and directly below the left set of toprope anchors. Face climb through a tricky overlap, then finish up a beautiful, knobby face. **Variation** (5.7) Begin on *Alien Autopsy;* once past the right edge of the overlap, move left to finish on the face.

7. **Alien Autopsy** (5.7) Begin about 25 feet right of the chimney and below the right end of an overlap. Climb the face and a right-facing corner to the toprope anchors.

8. **Black Bag Job** (5.7) Twenty feet right of *Alien Autopsy*, climb up to and along a shallow, right-facing corner. Trend left to anchors at the top of *Alien Autopsy*.

## PILLAR NOTCH AREA AND LOWER WEST FACE

The Pillar is the southernmost end of the West Fin, just above Nelson Gap Road, separated from the main fin by a notch accessible by scrambling from the west, or by climbing the first pitch of *E-Z Wider* on the 007 Wall.

**Finding the area:** From the top of the Corridor Trail stairs, walk left around the South Face of The Pillar. Hike uphill a short way to The Pillar Notch on your right.

9. **Tommy T** (5.6) Climb the 6-bolt line located about 50 feet uphill (left) of The Pillar Notch on the west face of the main fin. May feel 5.7 or 5.8 if you climb a "tight" line along the bolts.

10. **Notch Up Another One** (5.10d/5.11a) What a great route! Sustained, steep face climbing up the prominent, slightly overhanging face above The Pillar Notch. Some loose rock will clean up in time, but beware. Scramble up into The Pillar Notch and belay below the line of bolts up the steep, south-facing edge of West Fin. Climb up and right along the 8-bolt line to anchors.

11. **Millennium** (5.7) Possibly West Virginia's longest climb! This 9-pitch route begins at The Pillar Notch and climbs a rising traverse along the East Face of the West Fin. The route ends above the right side of The Future Wall. Start behind a small tree on the north side of the notch, climbing up and right onto the east face to the belay anchors atop *E-Z Wider*. Alternatively, climb *E-Z Wider* to attain the first set of anchors, or climb the first two pitches of *Diamonds Are Forever* to gain the second set of belay anchors. Carry a light rack of stoppers and cams, as well as a handful of quickdraws for the occasional bolt. There are two-bolt anchors located at each belay station. With nearly 1,000 feet of climbing, plan to spend the day! **Descent:** You can get to the ground in two rappels using a 60-meter rope. Begin with a rappel down and somewhat left to gain the stance and anchors atop *Oz* (approximately 40 feet below the 8th belay station). From here, it's another 80 feet to the ground. Three rappels are necessary if you're using a 50-meter rope. Start by rappelling the last pitch of the route back to the Pitch 8 anchors. From here, rap to the *Oz* anchors, then to the ground. **Note:** Visit www.nelsonrocks.org to download a phototopo of this 9-pitch route.

12. **Pillar Summit Route** (5.4) Scramble up to the notch and the base of The Pillar's north face. Climb the face behind a large tree, trend right behind a huge flake, and move up to the large summit platform with bolt anchors (70 feet). To descend, it's best to either downclimb the route, or rappel to anchors on the narrow ledge atop *Solar Plexus*. From here you can toprope the flake routes or rappel 70 feet to the ground.

The following routes are located on either side of a large detached flake on the west face of The Pillar. Beware of loose rock—belay away from the fall line or consider climbing *Pillar Summit Route* and setting up a toprope.

13. **Solar Plexus** (5.6) Begin below the left side of the detached flake. Scramble up easy rock to the left-facing corner and climb this to a ledge with anchors (70 feet).

14. **Polar Sexes** (5.7) From below the pillar, scramble up and right onto a broken ledge/flake. Climb the right side of the detached flake to shared anchors (70 feet).

THE PILLAR

19

20

21

23

20 21

22

Not all bolts shown

# THE PILLAR—SOUTH FACE

**Finding the face:** Climb the beautiful wooden stair leading up from Nelson Gap Road to the base of the West Fin. The South Face routes face the road immediately to your left.

15. **Mountain Dew** (5.2) Begin on the left (west) side of The Pillar's south face. Climb a short, right-facing corner and low-angle face to a tree.

16. **Mountain Don't** (5.4) Start 10 feet right of the short corner and just right of a tree. Climb up a small nose and low-angle rock to anchors.

17. **Sidwell** (5.6) Begin at triple right-facing corners about 20 feet right of *Mountain Dew*. Climb up along the middle corner to anchors; many variations possible.

18. **Pillar Direct** (5.10c/d) Start at the anchors above the top of *Sidwell*. Climb the upper portion of the south face to The Pillar's summit.

19. **Dominion** (5.10b) Good, steep climbing. Start 10 feet left of a small, cavelike roof. Climb the broken, left-facing corner past 8 bolts to anchors (80 feet).

20. **Ed's Fudge Shop** (5.10a/b) A harder version of Seneca's *Triple S* corner—really fun stemming and plentiful gear. Begin about 15 feet right of the small, cavelike roof at the right side of a triangle-shaped slab. Climb up the slab to gain the large corner and crack. Climb the crack to anchors on the right (75 feet).

21. **The Wax Museum** (5.11a) Sustained and technical. Begin below the right side of the large, triangle-shaped slab. Work up on the slab to mid-height, then fire up a system of convoluted cracks to anchors (70 feet).

22. **The Petting Zoo** (5.10d) Begin 15 feet left of the outside corner that marks the right edge of the South Face. Start by bouldering up and left, then climb straight up the middle of the face (65 feet).

23. **Blue Ridge Magazine Trash** (5.8) Climb the left side of the large, blocky, outside corner (50 feet).

# WEST FIN—EAST FACE

## 007 WALL

**Finding the wall:** From the wooden stairs, follow the Corridor Trail a few paces uphill to a short 007 Wall feeder trail on your left. Climbs start below the large pine on the ledge below The Pillar Notch.

24. **E-Z Wider** (5.6+) The first pitch is popular by itself, or you can combine both pitches into an enjoyable long pitch. **Pitch 1:** Climb an awkward, wide crack and chimney past 5 bolts to a ledge with a large pine

OO7 WALL

Not all bolts shown

(*5.5, 50 feet*). **Pitch 2:** From the pine, climb the corner to the right, past 7 bolts to anchors (*5.6, 70 feet*). Most parties skip the last clip and move left to the corner, finishing on the first pitch of *Millennium*. **Gear:** Supplement bolts with a few stoppers and cams up to 2 inches. **Descent:** Two rappels to the ground.

25. **Shaken, Not Stirred** (5.8) From the *E-Z Wider* pine tree, move 15 feet up the ledge toward the notch. Climb a crack through a bulge; continue on *Millennium* past a bolt at another bulge to anchors atop E-Z *Wider*.

26. **License to Drill** (5.8–5.10a) Start 5 feet right of *E-Z Wider*, at a bulging, left-facing corner. Climb along a line of 5 bolts to anchors (*5.8, 40 feet*). From the anchors you can step left to a ledge and access other routes above, lower off, *or* continue up the arête above past 3 more bolts to a second set of anchors (*5.10a, 35 feet*)

27. **Never Say Never** (5.8–5.10c) Awkward 5.8 climbing leads to absolutely fabulous 5.10 face climbing up the headwall. Start just right of *License to Drill*. Climb up the blocky, left-facing corner to a bulge, move right around this and up to anchors (*5.8, 40 feet*). Lower off, or continue climbing up the steep, sustained face above to anchors (*5.10c, 35 feet*). 9 bolts to the second set of anchors.

28. **Mr. Bigglesworth a.k.a. Disney Channel** (5.4) Not recommended, except as a means to set up topropes on the two previous routes. Begin 30 feet right of the *E-Z Wider* crack, below a section of lower-angle rock. Climb up and left past two bolts to access the low set of anchors on either *Never Say Never* or *License to Drill*.

29. **Diamonds Are Forever** (5.6–5.8). Start 15 feet uphill from *Mr. Bigglesworth* and just right of a large tree. **Pitch 1:** Climb along the line of 7 bolts to a crack (bring a few large stoppers) and trend right to finish on a small ledge with chains (5.6). This pitch is a full 85 feet, so a 60-meter rope is needed to safely rappel from the anchors. **Pitch 2:** Climb a blocky corner past the *Millennium* ledge to anchors on a higher ledge (end of the second pitch of *Millennium*)(5.4). **Pitch 3:** Climb the crack to the top of the fin, just right of a large, teetering block. **Note:** No fixed anchors (5.8). The first pitch is a fine, easy sport route—sustained but never hard. The third pitch is not recommended for 5.8 leaders.

30. **Snake Oil** (5.7) Start below a left-facing flake and corner 40 feet uphill of *Diamonds Are Forever*. Climb the corner (need 2- to 3-inch cam) to the first bolt, then up blocky face moves and past a bulge. Move way

right after the third bolt to join *Sticky Fingers* at the last bolt. Lower from shared anchors.

31. **Sticky Fingers** (5.7) Well-protected and much better than the previous route. A good first 5.7 lead with only one or two crux moves. Begin at a tree and shallow right-facing corner about 20 feet right of *Snake Oil*. Climb the line of 7 closely spaced bolts to anchors.

## THE FUTURE WALL

**Finding the wall:** Exit the Corridor Trail about 50 feet downhill of The Sport Wall and cross talus to the base of the bulging white wall.

32. **Paradigm Shift** (5.12b) A difficult Eddie Begoon and Mike Artz route. Climb the line of bolts located about 60 feet left of *One World* (glue-in bolt line). 8 bolts to anchors.

33. **Lifers** (5.10a) Local hardmen Tom Cecil and Tony Barnes teamed up to establish this classic sport route. Climb the line of bolts, beginning 30 feet uphill of *Paradigm Shift*. 9 bolts to anchors.

34. **One World** (5.10d) Climb the prominent line of glue-in bolts up the steep, orange-and-white face. Finish up and right to anchors on *The Foundation*.

35. **The Foundation** (5.10d) One of the best sport climbs at Nelson, this route ascends good holds up a steep wall and concludes through a tricky bulge to anchors. 8 bolts.

36. **Project** (bolts with no hangers)

37. **New Beginning** (5.11a/b) Begin at a left-facing flake with an obvious undercling overhang about 12 feet up. Climb the flake past the overhang (gear) to a high first bolt. Continue up steep, left-facing corners past 3 more bolts to a stance above an overhang. Fixed stoppers at anchor.

38. **The One Tree** (5.12a/b) Begin just left of a large, loose-looking, left-facing corner at a low overhang. Start up through a bulge (missing bolt hanger) and climb the thin moves along many left-facing flakes and through a roof to anchors. 7 bolts.

39. **Shorty** (5.11b) Size doesn't matter here—this is a great climb! Begin at a short, left-facing corner and boulder up and left to gain a right-facing flake. Continue up flakes above to a stance with anchors. 3 bolts.

40. **Oz** (5.7+) Another good Nelson 5.7 sport climb. Begin at a shallow, right-facing corner and tree about 25 feet uphill of *Shorty*. Climb up and trend slightly left to finish at the low set of *Millennium* rappel anchors. 8 bolts.

# THE FUTURE WALL

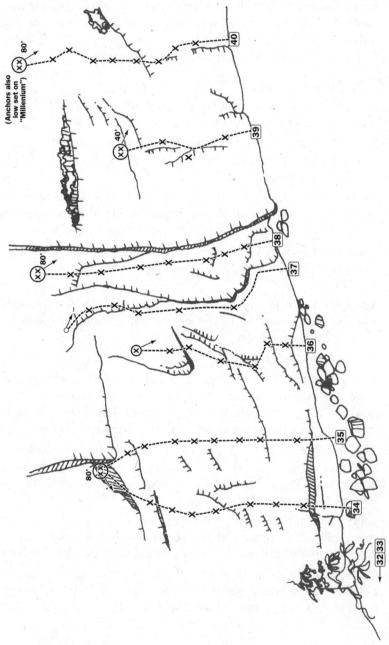

## UPPER CORRIDOR WEST

**Finding the area:** Located near the top of the West Fin, you can approach on the Corridor Trail from below, from above via Pierson's Trail, or rap in from above by scrambling or climbing a route on the Upper West Side.

41. **The Trip** (5.7) Hike the Corridor Trail to the second switchback that almost touches the East Fin. **Pitch 1:** Begin at a bolt 12 feet up, placing a #1 Camalot first. Climb right of the first two trees, left of a third to shuts (80 feet). **Pitch 2:** Climb up, angling right then left to shuts right of a prominent pine (70 feet). **Pitch 3:** Scramble along a ledge up to the base of a large, dying pine, then diagonal right to the top (60 feet) **Gear:** Full rack. **Descent:** Rappel from shuts on the East Face beyond the second pine over *Annihilator.* Double-60-meter rap to the ground. Dirty in spots. Most loose rock has been cleaned, but caution is advised.

42. **Annihilator** (5.10d) Hard work from the first move; lots of crimps and precise footwork required. The belayer must be extra sharp due to ground fall potential until past the fourth bolt. Stick-clip the first bolt or use your shortest quickdraw. Located on a clean orange wall at the very top of the fin. Climb *The Trip* and scramble down the ledge after the second shuts to the base, or rap/toprope from the third shuts (50 feet). Six bolts.

43. **Sorry Howard** (5.9) A stellar moderate sport route—don't let the ugly start deter you. At the second switchback above *Written in Stone,* locate a large tree with a big, rotting log next to it. Climb an easy, mungy, loose face, then up through a series of pumpy bulges. Shift gears for some delicate face climbing on fantastic white-and-orange rock, and finish up a short crack to anchors (14 bolts, 165 feet). Carry some medium cams or nuts for the top. Avoiding the crux, overhanging bulge by moving right makes the route about 5.8. **Descent:** Two ropes, or walk off uphill to Pierson's Trail.

44. **Primestar** (5.10) Trad route through satellite dish–type depression.

## EAST FIN, WEST FACE

## UPPER CORRIDOR EAST

Few established routes exist high on the East Fin, but much potential exists.

**Finding the area:** It's a hike either way—from the top or the bottom of the Corridor Trail. If you approach from the top via Pierson's Trail, hike downhill to the West Fin overlook. From the point where you step down into the corridor at the large sign, five switchbacks will take you to the first route

45. **Hemlock Roof** (5.9 TR) On the east side, at a huge hemlock tree and

wooden steps, there is an arching roof above. Climb cracks to the roof, then pull through to an easy finish on good, knobby rock. Scramble up from the next higher switchback to set up a toprope from the large pine above.

46. **Mike's Hike** (5.6) A fun climb, and worth the hike. One switchback below the previous climb find a landscaping tie set up as a belay bench. Climb the de-lichened path up a slabby face to anchors (80 feet). 7 bolts.

## STONE GALLOWS WALL

**Finding the wall:** Hike the Corridor Trail ten to fifteen minutes until you spot the prominent, right-facing Stone Gallows corner slanting up and right along the West Face of the East Fin.

47. **You Are What You Is** (5.11) Start on a sloping block 20 feet left of a large, right-facing corner. Climb the gray face past 4 bolts to a bushy ledge with anchors. **Note:** There are a couple of routes up the cracks and chimney in the large, right-facing corner. Beware of loose rock.

48. **Written in Stone** (5.11c) Classic! Begin at a right-facing flake on the right wall of a large, right-facing corner and chimney system. Climb up and right to the first bolt, then fire straight up the beautiful orange face to shared anchors. 8 bolts. **Gear:** Some people like to carry a small TCU or Tricam for the top.

49. **The Jellyfish Route** (5.12b/c) Start 15 feet right of the large corner below jellyfish-shaped cracks with fixed pins. Climb past the fixed pitons, a bolt, and another pin. Move right onto a slabby ramp and follow this past a couple of bolts to anchors.

50. **Tentacle** (5.12d) Begin at a tree just right of *The Jellyfish Route.* Solve the desperate sequence past 3 bolts, then move right and finish up the slabby ramp to anchors.

51. **Runaway Truck Ramp** (5.10d–5.11a) Begin at a white section of rock below a low, arching overhang. Work up and right to the first bolt (stick-clip), then climb the textured, left-ramping face to anchors. 8 bolts.

52. **The Laeger Route a.k.a. I Left My Nuts at the Hardware Store** (5.8) A good climb, but watch for a bit of loose rock. **Pitch 1:** Climb a right-facing corner to a ledge and anchors (50 feet). **Pitch 2:** Continue up an obvious, left-facing corner to a second set of belay anchors (60 feet). **Pitch 3:** Follow the crack system up to another set of anchors near the top of the fin (70 feet). Descend via three rappels.

53. **Fist Chicken** (5.8) Beginning 8 feet right of *The Laeger Route,* boulder up the face to a low bolt. Continue up a small, right-facing corner, then face climb up and left to the ledge and anchors on *The Laeger Route.*

STONE GALLOWS

54. **Scimitar** (5.10c) Begin at a large tree 15 right of *The Laeger Route*. Face climb past 3 bolts to a stance. Continue up lower-angle rock to a steep, orange-and-white face. Follow bolts along a left-facing flake to anchors below a roof. 6 bolts. **Gear:** Bring a few medium-sized stoppers and cams.

55. **Porcelain Pump** (5.11) One hundred feet of climbing that just gets better and better all the way to the anchors. Begin on a rising ledge with trees and ascend easy rock (gear) past a small overhang and bolt to a stance. Now climb the stunning, bulging face past 8 bolts to finish in a short, right-facing corner high on the wall. **Gear:** A few cams for the start and a 60-meter rope to rappel from coldshut anchors. TCUs or Tricams (first three sizes) help at the top.

56. **The Diamond** (5.11b) Start at the farthest-right pine tree on the rising ledge. Begin up broken rock (gear) and through a small overhang about 20 feet up. Continue up the steeper orange face above, pulling through two overhangs to gain a stance with anchors. 8 bolts.

57. **Stone Gallows** (5.10b) The most natural and intimidating line at Nelson. A worthwhile classic if you're solid at the grade. Beware of some loose rock. **Pitch 1:** Start as for *The Diamond,* but climb up and right through a few dicey moves to gain the prominent, right-facing corner. Work up the corner to a belay (fixed pins) below a roof (100 feet). **Pitch 2:** Move right around the roof and up the corner to a set of anchors on the right face near the top of the corner (100 feet). **Gear:** Stoppers, and a full set of cams to 4 inches. **Note:** Need two 60-meter ropes to make one long rappel to the ground.

**Note:** The following three routes ascend the full height of the huge wall right (downhill) of *Stone Gallows.* These are mixed routes, requiring a rack; two ropes recommended.

58. **Monkey Head** (5.10d) Two to three pitches to shared anchors at the top of *Stone Gallows.*

59. **UFB a.k.a. UFBL—Un-Freaking Believably Loose** (5.10d). Located about 200 feet downhill of *The Laeger Route* and 150 feet uphill of the detached flake that marks the left side of The Sport Wall. Face climb past a few widely spaced bolts with intermittent gear placements. Two pitches. Anchors at top of first pitch; second pitch shares anchors with *Iroquois League.*

60. **Iroquois League** (5.10a) Begin at a right-facing corner about 50 feet left of an obvious, 60-foot-high detached flake. **Pitch 1:** Climb the corner on gear, then slightly left past a few well-spaced bolts to a set of anchors (130 feet). **Pitch 2:** Continue up the face past a couple more bolts to anchors just below the top of the fin (110 feet). **Gear:** Stoppers and a full

set of cams to 4 inches. **Note:** Need two 60-meter ropes to make one long rappel to the ground.

61. **House of Cards** (5.7) Begin at a short crack just left of the tall, detached flake. Jam up to a low ledge and the first bolt on right. Face climb past 4 more bolts and a runout to anchors.

62. **Spirit Team** (5.9) This route begins in the notch directly above the tall, narrow, detached flake and climbs the south-facing edge of the fin to anchors. A mixed route with some loose rock. Climb *House of Cards* to gain the notch and the start of the route.

## THE SPORT WALL

**Finding the wall:** Hike the Corridor Trail about ten minutes until the trail ascends a series of landscaping ties along the base of the East Fin.

63. **Franklin's Tower** (5.7) Climb the right side of the prominent, 60-foot-high, detached flake. Gear can be placed in cracks on the narrow left face, and there is a bolt at the crux. Finish right to anchors on *Bitchin Squaw.*

64. **Bitchin Squaw** (5.11a) Technical, sustained, and very good! Begin 6 feet right of the detached flake and ascend the face past 6 bolts to anchors.

65. **Rampage** (5.10d) Start at a shallow, right-facing corner leading up to a high first bolt. Continue up past two more bolts to a stance, then up a short, white face past another bolt to a tree with rap slings. 4 bolts.

66. **Red Man** (5.10c) Begin 6 feet right of *Rampage* and climb up and right to the first bolt and small left-facing flakes. Work up the flakes and face above to a stance, then step left a few feet and continue past the last bolt on *Rampage* to the rappel tree. 5 bolts.

67. **Warpaint** (5.11a) The hardest and most "sporty" route on the wall. Recommended as a toprope. Climb tiny, right-facing flakes past 2 bolts to a stance below an overhang. Work up a short crack and move around the left side of the overhang (bolt) to anchors above. **Gear:** Bring HBs and other small nuts (crucial placement under the overhang), TCUs and Tricams. Stick-clip first bolt.

68. **Stone Boy** (5.10b) Begin at a small, left-leaning, right-facing corner. Climb up the ramping corner to a high first bolt (hard to see), then up flaky holds to anchors above a small overhang. 5 bolts.

69. **Chortle Head** (5.11a) Enjoyable, sustained climbing, but often damp. Start at the base of the long, shallow, right-facing ramp. Climb straight up the face, staying mainly right of the bolt line, to anchors. 5 bolts.

# THE SPORT WALL

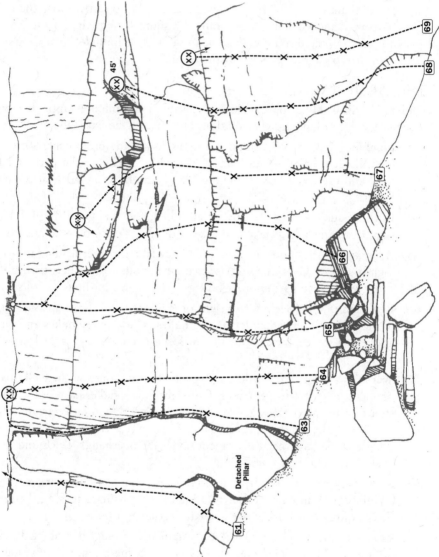

**Note:** The next two routes are located just downhill (right) of The Sport Wall and begin up on a ledge with hemlock trees.

70. **Unnamed** (5.11b) Reportedly a quality face climb. Send the line of 7 or 8 bolts to anchors.

71. **Child of Stone** (5.10c) This mixed route is also supposed to be quite good. Beginning right of the previous route, climb a weakness past 4 or 5 bolts to end at shared anchors. **Gear:** Bring a light rack of small-to-medium stoppers and cams.

# CRESCENDO WALL AREA

## LOWER CRESCENDO WALL

**Finding the wall:** Hike the Corridor Trail just over five minutes, until a large switchback meets the base of the East Fin. Two routes begin where the Corridor Trail turns back away from the fin (uphill of the Crescendo Wall proper). A third route, *Bottom Line,* is located far downhill of the switchback and the base of the East Fin. Scramble downhill along the side of the fin to approach the start of this climb.

72. **Unnamed** (5.11a) Begin just right of a hemlock tree where the trail switchback turns away from the Crescendo Wall Area. Begin up moderate moves past a slot (need TCUs), then up to a high first bolt. Continue up past 2 more bolts to shared anchors.

73. **Unnamed** (5.12a) Start below a low roof with right-facing flakes and bucket holds. Stick-clip the first bolt and crank through the roof on sloping holds (hard!), then continue up sustained moves past 4 more bolts to shared anchors.

74. **Bottom Line** (5.5) This route begins far downhill of the previous routes, at two left-facing corners near the bottom of the East Fin. **Pitch 1:** Climb licheny, low-angle rock to a large ledge. Move right to belay at a boulder—bring long slings to tie off (5.0, 40 feet). **Pitch 2:** Move back left and climb a short face into a lower-angled corner. Climb the corner to a spacious ledge with gear belay (5.5, 80 feet). **Pitch 3:** Scramble up blocks and broken rock to gain the large, tree-covered ledge below Crescendo Wall (5.0, 30 feet). Walk off to left.

## UPPER CRESCENDO WALL

**Finding the wall:** Follow the Corridor Trail past a couple of short switchbacks, until it finally meets the East Fin. Scramble up right then back left (a few 4th-Class moves) onto a large, tree-covered ledge.

*Eric Hörst on Crescendo (5.10a), Nelson Rocks.* PHOTO BY STEWART GREEN

34D Wall

UPPER CRESCENDO AREA

75

76

77

77

78

P

80

79 80

81

Access from trail

75. **Presto** (5.10d TR) Twenty feet left of anchors on the ledge atop the first pitch of *Crescendo*. Toprope the discontinuous crack and thin face.

76. **Allegro** (5.10c R) Start at anchors atop Pitch 1 of *Crescendo*. Follow line to left of *Crescendo,* up small, right-facing corner to anchors at top of *Crescendo*.

77. **Crescendo** (5.10a) Nelson's most classic route, established in the mid-1970s. The first pitch is a good 5.9-climb by itself. The second pitch is a classic finger crack à la Seneca's *Castor* and *Pollux*. Begin on the tree-covered ledge, at a nice right-facing corner and directly below a beautiful crack in the headwall above. **Pitch 1:** Climb the right-facing corner and face on the left to a belay stance and anchors (5.9, 45 feet). **Pitch 2:** Move up and right to gain the finger crack and jam it up to the belay ledge with anchors (5.10a, 70 feet) **Descent:** Do two rappels or, better yet, climb a route on 34D Wall above.

78. **Moderato** (5.5) Used as a quick approach to 34D Wall, or as part of a nice, moderate outing in combination with *Bottom Line* and *The Buttpucker Traverse*. **Pitch 1:** Begin at a small tree in a large, right-facing corner to the right of *Crescendo*. Climb the corner to bolt anchors on a ledge (5.5, watch out for fragile flakes). **Pitch 2:** Continue left and up along the ledge to a tree and anchors below 34D Wall (4th Class). Descend per 34D Wall.

79. **Merlin** (5.11a/b) An excellent mixed-gear route. Begin right of *Crescendo*, at a right-facing corner and flakes leading up to a prominent arête. Work up and left (gear) to gain the bolted arête. Climb the face and arête past a pin and 4 bolts, then move left (need 1.5-inch cam) to anchors atop *Crescendo*.

80. **Kamikaze** (5.10 R) Begin as for *Merlin,* but climb the scary-looking offwidth crack and corner right of the *Merlin* arête. **Gear:** Big Bros helpful.

81. **Excalibur** (5.12a) A sustained and very thin face climb. Send the line of 6 bolts located right of *Kamikaze*.

82. **Morning Glory** (5.10) Discontinuous crack up the center of the wall. Gear and quality unknown . . .

83. **Unknown** (5.9) Scramble right and slightly down from the base of *Crescendo*. Climb cracks to a ledge with a tree. Belay, or continue through the wide crack above. **Variation:** After the belay ledge with tree, climb cracks to the right of the wide crack. Belay in the notch above and rappel from mank.

84. **Tom and His Hero** (5.10d R) Route up south face of fin, through a roof.

34D WALL

85

86

87

88

90

91

92

93

94
XX

89

XX

XX

XX

Not all bolts shown

## 34D WALL

This wall is located above Upper Crescendo Wall. You'll need to climb *Moderato* or some other Crescendo Wall route to gain the narrow ledge below 34D Wall.

**Finding the wall:** Climb *Moderato*. The first few routes begin near the tree on the left side of the ledge, while the others begin at anchors behind a large block. *Cop a Feel* begins on the far-right end of the ledge, just right of the *Crescendo* anchors. Descend via two rappels from anchors on the spacious ledge under the left side of the wall, or from the anchors at the top of *Crescendo*.

85. **Piton Crack** (5.8) Begin on the upper left end of the ledge and climb the obvious crack past a pin to anchors.

86. **Prime Directive** (5.9+) Climb a right-facing flake and crack to a sling anchor atop the fin.

87. **Shape Shifter** (5.10c) This is a toprope climb up the face just left of *34D*. Lead *34D*, then set the toprope.

88. **34D** (5.10b) Begin at the double-bolt anchor near the middle of 34D Wall; climb along the left line of bolts to a high set of anchors.

89. **The Buttpucker Traverse** (5.2) From anchors next to a tree at the right side of the large ledge below the wall, hand-traverse right along a horizontal flake out to anchors atop *Crescendo*. Clip the lower bolts on the sport routes above where possible. Flipping the rope behind the flake to protect the leader and second is a good idea. Looks casual at first, but the exposure gets intense! **Descent:** Rappel down *Crescendo*.

90. **Missing Ramsey** (5.11a/b) 8 bolts to shared anchors.

91. **Lyons Share** (5.10d) 8 bolts to shared anchors.

92. **Barnyard Taboo** (5.11a) 8 bolts to shared anchors.

93. **Heavy Petting** (5.8) 8 bolts to shared anchors.

94. **Cop a Feel** (5.6) Beginning on the right end of the ledge, climb the right-facing, left-leaning corner up to anchors above *Heavy Petting*. This route is loose and not recommended.

# SUMMERSVILLE LAKE

## OVERVIEW

The cliffs surrounding Summersville Lake would be the Mid-Atlantic region's premier sport climbing area if it were not for the New River Gorge just 20 miles to the south. Still, Summersville (as it's called by climbers) is an exceedingly popular area known for its unique lakeside cragging and diverse array of classic clip-ups that range from slabby 5.8 faces to seriously overhanging 5.13 testpieces.

Summersville Lake is the result of a dam built along the Gauley River in the 1970s and managed by the U.S. Army Corps of Engineers ever since. The lake immediately became a major hit with boaters and waterskiers, but it wasn't until the New River Gorge boom days of the late 1980s that climbers gave the cliffs around the lake's edge a look. What they found was more great rock—clean, featured Nuttall Sandstone just like at the New—but with a very obvious barrier to developing the area. The initial forays were made by boat, and soon a section of cliff along the north shore was discovered to have dry ground at the cliffbase. This half-mile section of wall is now the heart of Summerville climbing and includes areas such as The Coliseum, The Gun Wall, The Mega Boulder, The Excellent Buttress, and The Orange Oswald Area. The approach is a pleasant fifteen-minute hike ending at a ladder downclimb to the cliffbase.

The cliffs surrounding the rest of the lake have seen some development, though mainly during the winter when the lake is drained. From October to March you can explore the rest of the cliffs by foot; otherwise you'll need to rent a boat. The Pirate's Cove is especially popular for "water bouldering" in the summer and roped climbing in the winter. Don't miss *Mutiny* (5.11c/d), a sharp overhanging arête that's extremely popular during low-water season.

However, the vast majority of climbers visiting Summersville stick to climbing from dry ground. The seventy-two routes covered in this guide are accessible year-round (i.e., without a boat!), and are all sport climbs. While there are a few traditional lines in the area, it's the sport climbs that make Summersville such a popular destination with climbers of all ability levels.

# SUMMERSVILLE LAKE

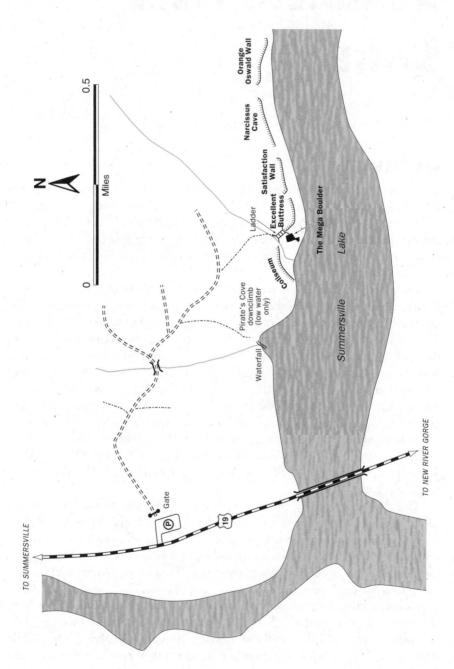

Orange Oswald Wall

Narcissus Cave

Satisfaction Wall

Excellent Buttress

Ladder

Coliseum

The Mega Boulder

Pirate's Cove downclimb (low water only)

Waterfall

Summersville Lake

Summersville

N

Miles

0          0.5

Gate

P

19

TO SUMMERSVILLE

TO NEW RIVER GORGE

The Gun Wall and Orange Oswald areas are most popular due to their high concentration of clip-ups in the 5.8 to 5.11a range. Unlike nearby New River Gorge, Summersville possesses many good sport climbs below the 5.11 level, and there are more than a dozen 5.8 and 5.9 sport climbs. Some of the classic moderates include *Hippie Dreams* (5.8), *Jeff's Bunny Hop* (5.8), *Sniff the Drill* (5.8), *Menace Alert* (5.9), *Trigger Happy* (5.9+), *Orange Oswald* (5.10a), *Strong Arming the Little Guy* (5.10b), *Baby Has a Bolt Gun* (5.10b), *Stick 'em Up* (5.10b), *Flight Path* (5.10c), and *In the Line of Fire* (5.10d).

Summersville also offers a tick list of classic 5.11s and 5.12s that are every bit as good as their peers at the New. Don't-miss routes include the sustained *Satisfaction Guaranteed* (5.11c), the stunning *Under the Milky Way* (5.11d) arête, and the pumpy *Narcissus* (5.12a), but it's the trilogy of 5.13s out the unrelentingly steep Coliseum that have garnered Summersville national recognition. Permanently equipped with quickdraws and awaiting your best efforts are *Apollo Reed* (5.13a), *Mercy Seat* (5.13a/b), and *the Pod* (5.13b). Get busy!

**Climbing history:** Climbing at Summersville Lake began in the late 1980s when Rick Thompson and a few other Pittsburgh-area climbers decided to take a rest day from new-route development at New River Gorge. From western Pennsylvania, they had driven by Summersville Lake countless times on their way down US 19 to climb at the New. On this day, they rented a boat and put up the first routes at what would soon become another major West Virginia climbing area.

With no delay, Thompson reported his findings to other activists at the New River Gorge, but most were just too busy for such a novelty as climbing from a boat. In summer 1991, Doug Cosby and a couple of other Washington, D.C., climbers took the initiative and returned to Summersville Lake to follow up on Thompson's lead. Again by boat, they explored the seemingly endless rock walls that retain the lake's clear, blue waters. To their surprise, they found an extended stretch of quality rock that did, if fact, have dry land at the base. Cosby quickly determined a "boatless" access to these areas and, almost single-handedly, drilled and climbed the first routes at The Gun Wall, The Mega Boulder, and The Excellent Buttress.

By fall 1991, a few other climbers had joined Cosby; in particular, Steve Zich and Gary Beil put in a lot of hard first-ascent work. Some of the classics established include Thompson's *She Got the Bosch, I Got Drilled* (5.10a), Steve Zich's *Stick 'em Up* (5.10b), Doug Cosby's *Process of Elimination* (5.11a) and *Satisfaction Guaranteed* (5.11c), Brian Kelleher's *Under the Milky Way* (5.11d), Eric Hörst's *Animal Logic* (5.12a/b), and Cosby's *Angle of Attack* (5.12c).

The real breakthrough year was 1992, as Porter Jarrard shifted his focus from New River Gorge to Summersville long enough to forge three incredible lines up the outrageously overhanging wall of the Coliseum. Most famous is

*Apollo Reed* (5.13a), maybe the most attempted 5.13 in the eastern United States.

Slower, "fill-in" development continued from 1993 to 1998 as both ends of the grade spectrum were expanded. Some of the more popular moderates put in are Chris Petty's *Hippie Dreams* (5.8), Jeff Smith's *Jeff's Bunny Hop* (5.8), Shane Smith's *Baby Has a Bolt Gun* (5.10b), and Gary Beil's *Trigger Happy* (5.9+) and *Moon Pie Deluxe* (5.11a). Higher-end routes established during this period include Howie Feinsilber's *Narcissus* (5.12a) and Brian McCray's *Suicide Blonde* (5.13a), both at the Narcissus Cave Area.

At present, slow development continues along the Summersville lakeshore. Some excellent new routes have gone in at a variety of smaller "satellite areas", however, the sections covered in this guide remain the primary destination for most climbers. Inquire at Blue Ridge Outdoors in Fayetteville for access information and the route beta if you're interested in exploring some of the new areas.

# TRIP PLANNING INFORMATION

**General description:** Marbled Nuttall Sandstone cliffs surrounding the clear, cool waters of Summersville Lake. Primarily a sport climbing area, the crags range from 30 to 90 feet in height, with grades from 5.8 to 5.13.

**Location:** South-central West Virginia, near the town of Summersville and about 20 miles north of New River Gorge.

**Camping:** There are two campgrounds at Summersville Lake. Mountain Lake Campground (304–872–4220) costs $7.00 per night and is located on Airport Road. From the climbers' parking lot take US 19 North for 0.9 mile, turn left on Airport Road, and go 1.7 miles to the campground. For Battle Run Campground, take US 19 South for 3.6 miles, then turn right onto WV 129 and follow signs to Summersville Dam. In about 3 miles you'll cross the dam, then go another half-mile to Battle Run on the right. There are also two full-service campgrounds near New River Gorge. Mountain State Campground (304–574–0947) is located on Ames Heights Road, and Chestnut Creek Campground (304–574–3136) is along Lansing Road. A final option is Roger's Rocky Top Retreat atop the Kaymoor climbing area. Roger's has no showers; however, this is the cheapest camping area and a good spot to locate a climbing partner.

**Climbing season:** It is possible to climb at Summersville year-round, but fall is by far the best season. From October to March the lake is drained, so you can climb at many other areas, including The Pirate's Cove, without a boat. Summer is, of course, hot and humid—but the lake offers the opportunity to take a dip in the cool water between routes.

**Gear:** A dozen quickdraws and a 50-meter rope are all you need for most routes. A 60-meter rope is needed for a few of the longer climbs.

**Restrictions and access issues:** Summersville Lake is managed by the U.S. Army Corps of Engineers, which is, fortunately, open-minded about climbing activities and further route development. However, much of the surrounding land is private property, and, with some real-estate development underway, there have been a few changes in the parking and access. In 1999, the U.S. Army Corps of Engineers created a large new parking area for climbers, and clifftop access seems secure for the long term.

**Guidebooks:** The primary guide to the area is Steve Cater's *New River Gorge Rock Climbers' Guide,* which includes a chapter on Summersville. Unfortunately, this guide contains some incorrect route information. You may also be able to find a copy of Roxanna Brock's and Brian McCray's *The Best Sport Climbs of the New River Gorge,* which also includes a brief section on Summersville.

**Nearby mountain shops, guide services, and gyms:** Blue Ridge Outdoors (304–574–2425) is *the* place for climbing and camping gear, clothing, and beta on all the latest climbs and areas. It is located in Fayetteville, at the corner of Wiseman and Court. Guiding is available through Hard Rock (304–574–3092) and New River Mountain Guides (304–574–3872).

**Services:** All services are available in Summersville, just a couple of miles north of the lake on US 19.

**Emergency services:** Call 911. The nearest hospital is Summersville Memorial Hospital (304–872–2891).

**Nearby climbing areas:** Well, there's an area called New River Gorge just 20 miles to the south!

**Nearby attractions:** The Gauley River is perhaps the East Coast's premier Class V whitewater run. Of course, there is also the New River, located 20 miles to the south. These rivers offer world-class whitewater rafting and kayaking. Visit Starrk Moon Kayaks (304–574–2550) on Court Street in Fayetteville for more information on the local whitewater.

**Finding the crags:** The climbing at Summersville is located near the US 19 bridge over Summersville Lake. Park in the dirt lot off the northbound side of the road, just north of the bridge. Follow a dirt road up the grassy hill then back downhill about 400 yards to a wooden bridge across a stream. Cross the wooden bridge and take the first right turn onto another dirt road. Continue another 100 yards to a fork in the road—take the right-hand trail. In about 50 yards, you'll see a faint trail off to the right—this trail leads to The Pirate's Cove downclimb (only usable during low water). Stay on the main road and continue roughly another 250 yards to a well-worn trail off to the right. Take this trail downhill and cross a small stream to a ladder. Descend the ladder and follow the trail a few paces to The Mega Boulder. The full approach takes about fifteen to twenty minutes.

# SUMMERSVILLE—LEFT SECTOR

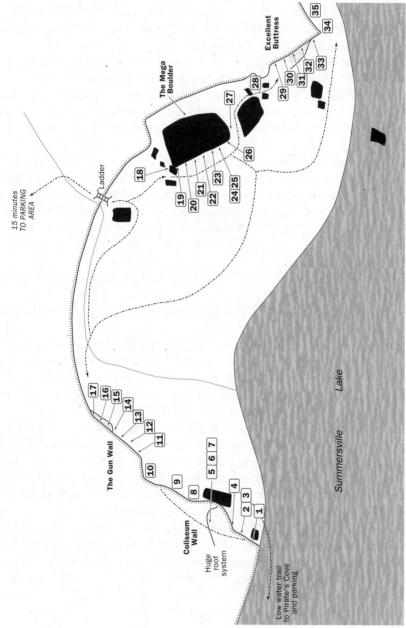

THE COLISEUM

Bad block

1

2 3

4

5

6

7

5 6 7

# THE COLISEUM

One of the steepest walls in the country and without question the most impressive wall at Summersville. Bring a 60-meter rope and fully loaded guns, and climb fast!

**Finding the area:** From The Mega Boulder area, backtrack to the down-climb ladder and follow the trail along a small stream to The Gun Wall. Beyond this, you can't miss the massive, tiered roof systems of The Coliseum. From October to March, you can also approach from The Pirate's Cove via the low-water trail.

1. **Reckless Abandon** (5.12b/c) Start on the left side of a ledge at an 8-foot-high, right-facing corner. Boulder up to a stance, then race up the white face through three roofs. 8 bolts to anchors.

2. **Surfer Rosa** (5.12d) Begin 10 feet right of *Reckless Abandon* and 10 feet left of a huge chimney. Climb up stacked blocks to a roof and continue straight up through four more roofs. 8 bolts to anchors.

3. **Lobbying in the Crumble** (5.12b) Begin as in *Surfer Rosa,* but move right at the third bolt and climb the right side of the white face. 8 bolts to anchors.

4. **Tobacco Road** (5.12a/b) Beginning just right of a huge chimney, boulder up and right to the first bolt at the roof. Traverse right 15 feet, then crank through a big ceiling and up to anchors. 8 bolts.

5. **Mercy Seat** (5.13a/b) Another Porter Jarrard classic. Start on *Apollo Reed,* but move left after the third bolt (and trend carefully left around a loose block) along a handrail out a roof. Continue the pumpfest up to the last bolt—from here most people lower to the ground. 10 bolts.

6. **Apollo Reed** (5.13a) *The* Summerville classic! Considered a "light 5.13a," this route has been many East Coast climbers' first 5.13. Begin in front of the huge "belay-slave" block and directly below a loose-looking, rectangular block about 30 feet up. Power up past the difficult knee-bar moves, then go right at the third bolt (and right of the loose block) and crank up increasingly difficult moves toward the top. Most people lower from the last fixed draw. 10 bolts.

7. **Project**—Start up *Apollo Reed,* then move right after the fifth bolt and continue up and right to finish in the prominent, right-facing dihedral near the top.

8. **B.C.** (5.13b/c) Begin 15 feet left of *The Pod,* at a small, left-facing flake about 8 feet up. Pump straight up past ten roofs to a cruxy finish. 11 bolts to anchors.

*David Blocher on the most excellent Apollo Reed (5.13a), Summersville Lake.* PHOTO BY STEWART GREEN

THE COLISEUM

STILL LIFE

10

9. **The Pod** (5.13a/b) Starts on the right side of the wall, at small, right-facing flakes below a low roof. Send the line of 9 bolts out tiered roofs to anchors. **Direct Finish Project:** From the anchors, continue up to a second set of anchors.

10. **Still Life** (5.13d) This long-standing project was finally freed by Joel Brady in 1999. It is currently the hardest route at Summersville Lake. Locate the line of 8 bolts up the steep face between The Coliseum and The Gun Wall.

# THE GUN WALL

Also known as The Perot Wall, this short, wildly-featured face offers several fun 3- to 4-bolt climbs. When dry, there always seems to be climbers here. Unfortunately, it can remain wet for days or weeks during a damp weather pattern.

**Finding the area:** From the bottom of the downclimb ladder, follow the trail west (back toward US 19) along a small stream to gain the base of The Gun Wall.

11.  **Do It** (5.11a) This is the left-most line on The Gun Wall. Start at a tiny ledge about 3 feet off the ground, and climb up and left past a couple of bolts. With just 2 bolts in 40 feet, it's not the rave route of The Gun Wall.

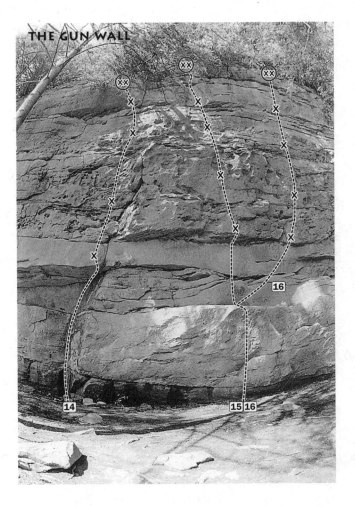

THE GUN WALL

12. **Trigger Happy** (5.9+) Popular. Climb the right-facing flake system and face past 4 bolts to anchors.

13. **Stick 'em Up** (5.10b) Possibly the best route on the wall. Begin at the right-facing flake of *Trigger Happy*, but move right to follow the right line of 4 bolts to anchors.

14. **Gun Lust** (5.10c) Sporty to the first bolt, but quite good after that. Boulder up a left-facing corner to a high first bolt, then continue up steep moves past 3 more bolts to anchors.

15. **Armed and Dangerous** (5.10b/c) Start on the low ledge and climb the left line of bolts to anchors. 4 bolts.

16. **Gunned, but Not Forgotten** (5.10b) From the low ledge, climb on huecos past 4 bolts to anchors.

17. **In the Line of Fire** (5.10d) Beginning on the ledge, climb the right line of 4 bolts to anchors.

# THE MEGA BOULDER
# A.K.A. D.C. MEMORIAL BOULDER

A power climber's dream crag. Barely 30 feet high, this huge boulder has a severely overhanging west face with numerous 3- to 5-bolt routes.

**Finding the boulder:** From the base of the downclimb ladder, follow the trail pretty much straight ahead toward the lake. You soon pass along the right side of this mega-sized boulder.

18. **Spider Needs a Thesaurus** (5.11d) Start on a flat boulder and climb the dirty face just left of the overhanging arête. 5 bolts to anchors.

THE MEGA BOULDER

19. **Angle of Attack** (5.12c) Start on the flat boulder at the left edge of The Mega Boulder. Climb juggy holds up the overhanging arête. 4 bolts to anchors.

20. **Animal Logic** (5.12b) Extremely popular. Begin 15 feet right of *Angle of Attack* and climb the short but powerful line past 3 bolts to a concluding lunge and anchors.

21. **Project**—1 bolt.

22. **Skinny Legs** (5.13b) Start 20 feet right of *Animal Logic*. If you can, climb the thin, strenuous face past 4 bolt to anchors.

23. **Pro-Vision** (5.13a/b) Begin 10 feet right of *Skinny Legs* and just left of a short, right-facing corner. Send the steep, 4-bolt line to anchors.

THE MEGA BOULDER

24. **Straight Up and Narrow** (5.12a/b) Commence in a right-facing corner and climb up and right to the first bolt. Now, fire straight up through the bulge to anchors. 3 bolts.

25. **Process of Elimination** (5.11b) Begin on *Straight Up*, but move right after the first bolt and climb a right-facing flake to independent anchors. 3 bolts.

26. **The Route of All Evil** (5.11c) Start at knobby holds about 10 feet from the right edge of the face. Climb up to and along the right-facing flake past 3 bolts to anchors.

# SUMMERSVILLE—MIDDLE SECTOR

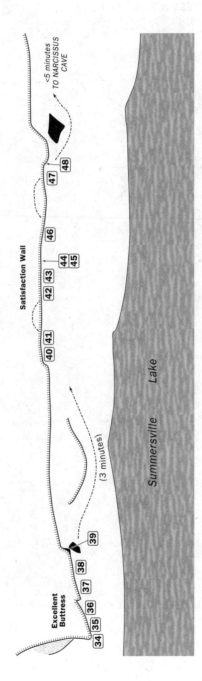

EXCELLENT BUTTRESS A.K.A. LONG WALL

27. **Psycho Babble** (5.12a) Start right of the arête and face climb up to anchors. 5 bolts.

## EXCELLENT BUTTRESS (A.K.A. LONG WALL)

Home of Summersville's first climbs, Excellent Buttress offers high-quality face climbs from 40 to 70 feet in length.

**Finding the wall:** Beginning from the right side of The Mega Boulder, follow a trail east (away from US 19) a short distance until you have to scramble up over a series of blocks and across a slabby ledge. As you descend from the blocks, you'll see Excellent Buttress straight ahead and on your left.

28. **Ingrate** (5.9) This short arête climb is located left of where the approach trail scrambles down blocks. 3 bolts.

29. **Chewy** (5.10b) Climb the 4-bolt line on the left side of the wall.

30. **Menace Alert** (5.9) Begin at a 10-foot-high, left-facing flake and climb past 4 bolts to anchors.

31. **Go Ballistic** (5.10c) Good, steep 5.10 face climbing. Begin 6 feet right of *Menace Alert* and fire up past 5 bolts to anchors.

32. **Flight Path** (5.10c) Climb a right-facing flake to reach a high first bolt, then continue up past 3 more bolts to anchors.

33. **Six Dollars** (5.11d) Begin on the right side of a blocky ledge and climb up and right on good holds to gain the first bolt. Now work straight up the left side of the arête to anchors. 6 bolts.

34. **Under the Milky Way** (5.11d) Great arête climbing, and one of the better routes at Summerville. Boulder through the starting roof and hike the arête past 7 bolts to anchors.

35. **Flirting with E** (5.11d/5.12a) "E" as in empty. Speed up the first line of bolts, beginning 20 feet right of the *Under the Milky Way* arête. 6 bolts to anchors.

36. **Maximum Overdrive** (5.11c) Crank a bouldery move to a bucket, then climb mid-range 5.11 to the top. 7 bolts to anchors.

37. **Spice** (5.11b/c) Begin at a left-facing flake about 25 feet right of a prominent crack. Climb the flake up through a roof and finish up a slabby face. 5 bolts to anchors.

38. **Gimme Some Tongue** (5.11a/b) Start 5 feet right of *Spice* and climb flaky holds through a roof. 5 bolts to anchors.

39. **No Way, José** (5.11a) Begin atop a 15-foot-high block and climb the arête and face past 4 bolts to anchors.

# EXCELLENT BUTTRESS

# SATISFACTION AREA

Named for the brilliant *Satisfaction Guaranteed,* this area also possesses a few really unsatisfactory "dogs."

**Finding the area:** From the middle of Excellent Buttress, follow the trail less than five minutes beyond the *Under the Milky Way* arête to locate the first route in the Satisfaction Area.

40. **BSIAGE** (5.10b) Start 20 feet left of a low roof and climb up along a waterstreak. Six bolts to anchors.

41. **Bored Spitless** (5.10b/c) Begin 10 feet left of a low roof and work up through licheny moves to a stance. Finish up better closing moves. 6 bolts to anchors.

42. **Tequila Maria** (5.10b/c) Fifteen feet right of the low roof, start up mossy rock to engage the nicer face above. 6 bolts to anchors.

43. **Lichen8er** (5.10b/c) Not pretty! Begin at a short groove with tons of lichen about 10 feet right of *Tequila Maria.* 6 bolts.

44. **Two-Finger Limit** (5.8) Start on *Make Way for Dyklings,* but move left to gain a high first bolt. Continue up past 5 more bolts to anchors.

45. **Make Way for Dyklings** (5.10a) Worthwhile. Start at a nice pocket handhold about 10 feet left of a tree. Climb straight up the clean streak. 6 bolts to anchors.

46. **Short Pirouette** (5.10d) Begin at small vertical grooves on a clean face 30 feet right of *Dyklings.* Climb the short line of 3 bolts to anchors about 35 feet off the deck.

47. **Satisfaction Guaranteed** (5.11b) This route has it all—a Summerville Lake classic! Begin at a 15-foot-high vertical seam below the right side of a high roof. Boulder up through a low roof, then straight up the seam to a few slab moves. Pull the high roof at right-facing flakes and finish up thin face moves to anchors. 8 bolts.

48. **No Refund** (5.10b) Start 10 feet right of *Satisfaction Guaranteed* and just left of a green crack. Climb the face and corner to a ledge, then run up a slab to a steeper finish. 7 bolts to anchors.

# NARCISSUS CAVE

Not exactly a cave, but this 50-foot roof does provide a rainy-day refuge. Narcissus is the most popular rainy-day route, and *Suicide Blonde* is the project route of choice.

**Finding the area:** From the Satisfaction Area, follow the trail away from the cliff and continue a few minutes until the trail bends back to the cliffbase near the beginning of the Narcissus Cave area.

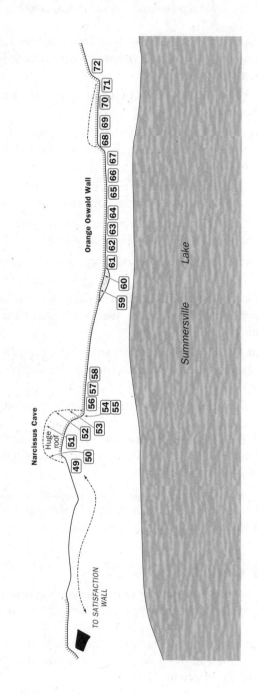

49. **Smilin' Jack** (5.11c) Begin at a right-slanting crack 10 feet left of Narcissus Cave. Climb the line of 6 bolts to anchors.

50. **Narcissus** (5.12a) Pumpy and very classic! Climb the obvious line out the left side of the cave roof. 6 bolts to anchors. Variation: **Direct Start** (5.12d) Begin left of the normal start and climb difficult moves up to join the regular route. 6 bolts.

51. **Project**—Crack out huge roof. 10 bolts.

52. **Long Dong Silver** (5.12d) Begin in the back of the cave and climb out the line of 8 bolts to anchors. To avoid severe rope drag, use two ropes and drop one midway out.

53. **Deep Throat** (5.13c) Start on a boulder along the right side of the cave. Crank straight out the white, flaky ceilings. 7 bolts to anchors.

54. **Suicide Blonde** (5.13b) Start on the right side of the arête that forms the right margin of Narcissus Cave. Work up the arête to the first bolt, then move left and hike the steep wall past 5 more bolts to anchors.

55. **Simple Minds** (5.12a) Same start as *Suicide Blonde*. Climb the vertical right side of the arête. 4 bolts to anchors.

56. **Jeff's Bunny Hop** (5.8) Maybe the best, most popular 5.8 at Summerville Lake. Starting just right of Narcissus Cave, climb the wildly featured face past 6 bolts to anchors.

57. **Sniff the Drill** (5.8) Begin at trees right of *Jeff's Bunny Hop* and send the line of 6 bolts to anchors.

58. **That Eight** (5.7) Beginning just right of the trees, stroll up the face past 5 bolts to anchors.

## ORANGE OSWALD WALL

Per lineal foot, maybe the most popular climbing wall in West Virginia. Inviting orange rock and plenty of great handholds make this rock home to some of the best moderate sport climbing anywhere in the region.

**Finding the wall:** Continue just a short distance beyond the Narcissus Cave area until the trail descends a slight hill along the base of an orange wall near the lake shore.

59. **Fabulous Groupies** (5.9) Locate a 5-bolt line just left of a left-facing, low corner (trad route). Climb the convoluted face to anchors.

60. **Hippie Dreams** (5.8) Begin on the right side of a low ledge about 10 feet right of *Fabulous Groupies*. Climb up and right past 7 bolts to anchors.

61. **Souled Out** (5.9) Start on the left side of a face below 2 bolts leading to a ledge about 25 feet up. Climb to the low ledge, then up the face above past 4 more bolts to anchors.

62. **Chunko Goes Bowling** (5.9) Begin at a left-facing flake just right of *Souled Out*. Roll up past 7 bolts to anchors.

63. **Voodoo Surfing** (5.10b) Start 10 feet right of *Chunko Goes Bowling* and climb along the line of 7 bolts to anchors. Hang 10b!

64. **Orange Oswald** (5.10a) Super popular! Begin in a small, left-facing corner and fire straight up past 7 bolts to anchors.

65. **Strong Arming the Little Guy** (5.10b) Another good one. About 20 feet right of *Orange Oswald*, pull your way up the middle of the orange wall. 6 bolts to anchors.

66. **Baby Has a Bolt Gun** (5.10c) Good, well-protected climbing on what was once a traditionally protected line. Begin 15 feet right of the previous route and fire up the juggy face through overhangs. 8 bolts to anchors.

67. **She Got the Bosch, I Got Drilled** (5.10a) A classic Rick Thompson route and route name! Start just left of a large, right-facing corner, and crank to a bucketfest past 8 bolts to anchors.

68. **Moon Pie Deluxe** (5.10d) Begin around the corner to the right of *She Got the Bosch*. Scramble up ledges to a high first bolt, then blast up through a couple of 'hangs and 6 more bolts to anchors.

69. **Barfing Butterflies** (5.11b) Start at the base of a prominent, right-facing corner. Climb straight up the white face and through a roof to anchors. 7 bolts.

70. **Scoot Your Muffin** (5.10d) Begin at a tree 20 feet right of the right-facing corner. Climb the nice face through tiered roofs. Six bolts to anchors.

71. **Thou Shall Not Chum** (5.11a) Beginning 5 feet left of the outside corner, work up the face and through the right side of bulges to anchors. 6 bolts.

72. **Unnamed** (5.11b) A few yards around the corner from *Thou Shall Not Chum*, climb the short, bulging face past 3 bolts.

# NEW RIVER GORGE

## OVERVIEW

Over the last fifteen years, New River Gorge has gone from an unknown climbing area to the premier cragging destination in the Eastern United States. Previously, the Shawangunks or, arguably, Seneca Rocks held this distinction, but today it's hard to name any crag in the country, let alone the world, that matches New River Gorge in quality, quantity, and diversity of climbing.

The New (as locals affectionately call it) is located in the rolling hills of southern West Virginia, far from any major metropolitan areas. Here, the mighty New River cut a 1,000-foot-deep gorge, the rim of which is lined with 50- to 150-foot cliffs for miles and miles. One cliff, Endless Wall, runs unbroken for almost 4 miles along the north rim of the gorge. In all, there are about 15 miles of rock at The New.

The rock at The New is Nuttall Sandstone. Harder than many types of granite, the rock is surprisingly user-friendly, as it has good frictional properties for smearing, yet a fine-enough texture that you can climb for days without shredding your fingertips. But if the quality and quantity of rock at The New isn't enough to impress you, the shear diversity of climbing types encountered during a short stroll along the cliffbase will blow your mind. From textbook finger and hand cracks to perfectly cleaved dihedrals and arêtes to pocketed faces and massive, tiered roof systems, The New has it all!

For example, consider Diamond Point, a tiny fraction of the appropriately named Endless Wall. In less that 100 yards of cliff, you find a handful of classic cracks like *Remission* (5.10b), *Can I Do It 'Til I Need Glasses* (5.10c), and *Raging Waters* (5.11a), as well as a broad selection of bolt-protected face climbs like *Strike a Scowl* (5.10b), *Homer Erectus* (5.11b), and *The Glass Onion* (5.10b). However, a pair of Diamond Point classics located side by side can sum up The New's unmatched something-for-everyone character. *Leave It to Jesus* (5.11d) is possibly the best finger crack in the gorge and just 20 feet to its left is *The Gift of Grace* (5.12b), a four-star sport climb up a stunning arête.

And, the parade goes on. . . . Just five minutes upstream from Diamond Point is the Honeymooners' Ladder area with more than a dozen hyperclassic sport routes like *Jesus and Tequila* (5.12b) and *Quinsana Plus* (5.13a). Or how about a fifteen-minute hike downstream to Fern Point, where you'll find a perfect blend of classic traditional and sport lines side by side. Then

# NEW RIVER GORGE OVERVIEW

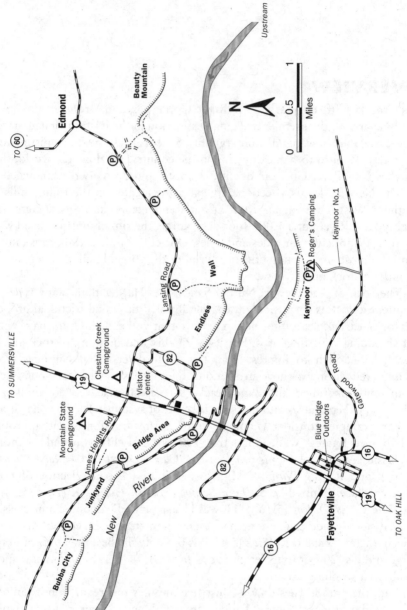

*Bill Chouinard counts his blessings on Sanctified (5.13a), Kaymoor Crag, New River Gorge.* PHOTO BY HARRISON SHULL

there is the other 90 percent of the New River Gorge to explore—the beauti-ful orange, pink, and white Nuttall Sandstone just never seems to end.

With nearly 2,000 routes in the New River Gorge, it's a tough job decid-ing on a "select" 15 percent of the routes to include in this guide. In addition to covering many of the popular areas like Diamond Point, Fern Point, Junk-yard, Bridge Buttress, and Butcher Branch, I've also included a variety of less-crowded areas, such as Fern Buttress, Beauty Mountain, and parts of Bubba City. If you plan to spend more than a few days at The New, I suggest you pick up a copy of Rick Thompson's *New River Rock*. This book provides the most comprehensive coverage of the area, and Rico's cliff topos and area his-tory are second to none.

**Climbing history:** Although technical climbing began in the Mid-Atlantic region as early as the 1920s, the New River Gorge saw virtually no action until the mid-1970s. In 1975, Rick Skidmore of nearby Charleston captured the first known lead at The New with the now-classic *Zag* (5.8) on Bridge Buttress. Soon a handful of other local climbers, including Nick Brash, Bruce Burgin, Steve Erskine, and Hobart Parks joined Skidmore, opening up the Junkyard and Beauty Mountain areas with ascents of classic cracks like *New Yosemite* (5.9) and *Supercrack* (5.9+). Meanwhile, Seneca Rocks was in its heyday of development, and word of the miles of high-quality sandstone just a couple of hours south fell on deaf ears. Seneca Rocks was to remain king of the Mountain State for the rest of the decade.

The 1980s began with the first infusion of outside talent and energy in the form of Mike Artz, Tom Howard, Rich Pleiss, Doug Reed, and Cal Swoger. Endless Wall was discovered in 1981, but the talent pool remained small. Consequently, development progressed slowly, mainly along the better-known crags of the Bridge Area, Beauty Mountain, and Junkyard. Classics estab-lished in the early 1980s include *Brain Teasers* (5.10a), *Rod Serling Crack* (10b), *Underfling* (10b), and The New's first 5.11, *Englishman's Crack* (5.11a).

In 1983 the next wave of would-be activists arrived from the surrounding states of North Carolina, Virginia, and Pennsylvania. The rate of new-route development and the standard of climbing increased steadily over the next three years, as the likes of Andrew Barry, Rick Fairtrace, Kris Kline, Ed McCarthy, Carl Samples, Rick Thompson, and Phil Wilt began making regu-lar weekend trips to the area. During this period the 5.11 grade became firmly established as the new-route emphasis focused on The New's many stunning cracks. Notable ascents include *Remission* (5.10b), *Burning Calves* (5.10b), *Wham, Bam, Thanks for the Jam* (5.10b), *Rapscallion's Blues* (5.10c), *Linear Encounters* (5.11a), *High Times* (5.11a), *Chasin' the Wind* (5.11b), *Mari-onette* (5.11c), *Right Son of Thunder* (5.11c), and *Leave It to Jesus* (5.11d).

The 1987 season began with the publication of Rick Thompson's *New*

*River Rock*. The guidebook contained over 450 routes and dozens of mouth-watering photographs. Finally, the secret was out, and new climbers from up and down the East Coast were rolling into the gorge every weekend. One of those new arrivals was Kenny Parker, who quickly uncovered Bubba City as a crag climber's paradise. In a few short months, Parker, John Regelbrugge, and friends established a tick list of Bubba City classics, including *Basic Bubba Crack* (5.9), *The Raging Tiger* (5.10d), and *Face It, Bubba* (5.11a).

The focus of new-route activity quickly shifted to Bubba City just as two new "rope guns" arrived on the scene in the form of Eddie Begoon and Eric Hörst. Along with Artz and Thompson, this small crew attacked the seemingly blank faces at Bubba City. Using minimal fixed protection, the standards were pushed well into the 5.12 range. For a short time, a minimalist approach was utilized as serious "mixed" lines went in, like Begoon's *Whamarete* (5.11d R) and Hörst's *Innocence Mission* (5.12c R). However, power drills and "Euro-tactics" were quickly adopted by local activists, and the sport climbing era arrived at The New, punctuated with the area's first 5.13, *Diamond Life,* in October 1987.

Over the next four seasons, over 500 sport routes would be established by a small band of energetic locals. Leading the way were Mike Artz, Eddie Begoon, Eric Hörst, Rick Thompson, and new arrival Porter Jarrard. But no one was more prolific than the tall southerner, Doug Reed. New 5.12 routes were going in weekly, including classics such as *Freaky Stylee* (5.12a), *Dead Painters' Society* (5.12a), *Michelin Man* (5.12a), *Hell-Bound for Glory* (5.12a), *Bubbacide* (5.12b), *Sacrilege* (5.12b), *Jesus and Tequila* (5.12b), *The Gift of Grace* (5.12b), *Pudd's Pretty Dress* (5.12c), *Green Envy* (5.12c), and *Stealth 'n' Magic* (5.12d). Some world-class routes also fell at the 5.13 grade, such as *Welcome to Conditioning* (5.12d/5.13a), *Libertine* (5.13a), *Locked on Target* (5.13a), *Dissonance* (5.13a), *Stabat Mater* (5.13b), *Sweetest Taboo* (5.13b), and *The Racist* (5.13c).

By spring 1991, the New River Gorge had become world famous and the most important climbing area in the eastern United States. And, just when you thought the marquee couldn't get any brighter, Doug Reed discovered the massive tiered roofs of the Kaymoor "Hole."

Many climbers had gazed across the gorge from Endless Wall to the rock at Kaymoor, but only Rick Fairtrace had visited the area and quietly climbed a few crack routes back in the late 1980s. Reed's rediscovery of Kaymoor shifted the new-route focus to the shaded walls along the south rim of the gorge. In an amazing seven-month effort, Doug Reed, Porter Jarrard, and Doug Cosby developed nearly the whole area! Added to the long list of New River Gorge classics were *Flight of the Gumbie* (5.9), *The Rico Suavé Arête* (5.10a), *Sancho Belige* (5.11c), *Magnitude* (5.11d), *Dining at the Alter* (5.12a), *Thunderstruck* (5.12b), *Lactic Acid Bath* (5.12d), *Burning Cross* (5.13a), and *Blood Raid* (5.13a).

Development slowed from 1992 to 1996, as there seemed to be no new cliffs to discover in the New River Gorge proper. However, two areas north of the gorge were gathering attention: The Meadow and Summersville Lake. Back at The New, all the "easy" lines had been established, but the remaining smooth, steep faces yielded a few noteworthy lines. New high-end routes to go included Thompson's *The Weatherman's Thumb* (5.12d/5.13a), Reed's *Dial 911* (5.13a), and *The Pocket Route* (5.13a), Hörst's *Just Send It* (5.13a/b), Cosby's *White Lightning* (5.13b), and Harrison Dekker's testpiece, *The Travesty* (5.13d).

The last round of intense development before the National Park Service ban of power drills occurred at The Cirque of Upper Endless Wall. Opened by Reed back in 1989, the area was primarily developed by Roxanna Brock and Brian McCray. During 1996 and 1997, the pair drilled, prepped, and sent nearly twenty 5.12 and 5.13 lines, as well as The New's first 5.14, *Proper Soul* (5.14a). Other popular Cirque routes include *New Life* (5.11b), *Power Lung* (5.11c), *Finders Keepers* (5.12b/c), *New Testament* (5.12d), *Ride the Lightning* (5.13b), and *Losers Weepers* (5.13b/c).

# TRIP PLANNING INFORMATION

**General description:** Excellent one-pitch face and crack routes on impeccable Nuttall Sandstone. Unquestionably, possesses the Eastern United States' highest concentration of sport climbing.

**Location:** South-central West Virginia, about 25 miles north of Beckley and an hour east of West Virginia's capital, Charleston.

**Camping:** Two full-service campgrounds are located just off US 19, north of the bridge. Mountain State Campground (304–574–0947) is located on Ames Heights Road, and Chestnut Creek Campground (304–574–3136) is found along Lansing Road. Roger's Rocky Top Retreat is the popular, low-budget, no-frills camping area located atop the Kaymoor climbing area. While there are no showers, this is the best place to stay if you're looking for a climbing partner.

**Climbing season:** When it comes to year-round weather quality, this is no Boulder, Colorado. The one well-publicized downside to the New River Gorge is indeed the weather. Spring is the season of clouds and showers in the mountains of West Virginia, and three dry days in a row is a rarity. From May through August, high humidity is a major drawback. As with most Eastern climbing areas, September and October are prime months: The days are consistently mild and dry, the nights are cool and crisp, and the changing leaves are heavenly. Late November through February can be cold and snowy, although a few warm stretches each month allow good winter climbing. Keep an eye on the forecast.

**Gear:** Bring a 200-foot (60 meter) rope and fifteen quickdraws if you plan on sport climbing. Traditional routes require a standard rack of wired stoppers, cams to 4 inches, and at least a half-dozen flexible-stem TCUs and small Friends (or other four-cam units) for the common New River Gorge "letter slots." A 165-foot (50-meter) rope will suffice for traditional routes, although some climbers employ doubled thin (9 mm) ropes on the more technical face routes.

**Restrictions and access issues:** Most of the climbing in The New is on National Park Service land. Therefore, all NPS regulations apply, including no use of power drills, and no unleashed pets at any time.

**Guidebooks:** Several New River Gorge guides have been published, but none with the authority, clarity, and back-of-hand area knowledge of Rick Thompson's *New River Rock*. The other popular guide is Steve Cater's *New River Gorge Climbers' Guidebook*, which includes numerous cool, 3-D cliff topos.

**Nearby mountain shops, guide services, and gyms:** Blue Ridge Outdoors (304–574–2425) is *the* place for climbing and camping gear, clothing, and beta on all the latest climbs and areas. It is located in Fayetteville at the corner of Wiseman and Court. Guiding is available through Hard Rock Climbing Services (304–574–3092) located at 131 South Court Street and through New River Mountain Guides (304–574–3872).

**Services:** All services are found in Fayetteville and Oak Hill. For good coffee and breakfast, check out Cathedral Café on Court Street in Fayetteville. Sedona Grill, just over a mile east of Fayetteville on WV 16, is a good place for dinner. All types of fast food can be found just down the road in Oak Hill. For lodging, there's a Comfort Inn (304–574–3443) just south of the US 19 bridge. The off-season rates are especially affordable.

**Emergency services:** Call 911 for an ambulance or the police. Contact the National Park Service at 304–465–0508.

**Nearby climbing areas:** The extremely popular Summersville Lake area is located just thirty minutes north along US 19. Other nearby areas include The Meadow and Bozoo. Inquire at the local climbing shop for more information on other local climbing spots.

**Nearby attractions:** The New and Gauley Rivers are West Virginia's top "amusement park rides." These rivers offer world-class whitewater rafting and kayaking. Visit Starrk Moon Kayaks (304–574–2550) on Court Street in Fayetteville for more information on the local whitewater. Excellent mountain biking, hiking, and trail running are found throughout the park. Check out Ridge Rider Mountain Bikers (304–574–BIKE) in Fayetteville. Finally, there is the New River Gorge Visitor Center just off US 19 on the north side of the bridge. Next rainy day, visit the center and learn about the fascinating history of the gorge and the building of the world's longest span bridge.

Finding the crags: The heart of New River Gorge climbing lies just a mile north of Fayetteville where the amazing US 19 span bridge crosses the gorge. Detailed directions to each crag are found below.

# BUBBA CITY

Bubba City is a great "little" climbing area. The ten crags that comprise Bubba City stretch out for over a mile and by themselves would be considered a major East Coast climbing area. In the context of The New, Bubba is just "another" great crag.

Bubba City is popular for a number of reasons: The approach is short, the 30- to 70-foot height and the mainly vertical nature of the routes make the climbs less intimidating than the typical route at Endless Wall or Kaymoor, and the south-facing walls make for comfortable climbing conditions on cooler days. These attributes make Bubba City a route-bagger's dream.

Described below are forty-six climbs at the four most accessible Bubba City crags. All but a few are clip-ups, so you may want to lighten your pack to include just a rope and a fistful of quickdraws. Get ready to bag a bunch of routes and have a ton o' fun. Keep an eye out for Bubba!

Finding the crags: Just north of the US 19 bridge, take Ames Heights Road for 1.3 miles to a pulloff and dirt road on your left (park within view of the main road). Hike the dirt road 300 yards to a trail that cuts off to the left. Follow this trail another 200 yards to the cliff break between Bubba Buttress and Central Bubba. As you descend the break (facing the river), Bubba Buttress (and Route 9) is just 50 yards to your left, and the first route at Central Bubba is just around the corner to your right. The car-to-crag approach time is less than ten minutes.

## BUBBA BUTTRESS

1. **Reason Over Might** (5.12a) Begin 12 feet right of twin cracks and climb the face past five bolts to coldshuts.

2. **Truth or Contra-Expenses** (5.12a) Start at twin cracks and follow the line of five bolts to anchors shared with the previous route.

3. **Dumbolt County** (5.10b) Start at the nice arête just left of twin cracks. Dance up the right side of the arête—watch for a pin on the left side (50 feet).

4. **Immaculate Combustion** (5.10d) Start at a short, right-facing corner 8 feet left of a crack. Climb up and left to a bolt. Continue on a diagonal path up and left (bolt on left) to a ledge, then straight up the white face past another bolt and pin to the top. Variation: **Fierce Face** (5.11a) From the first bolt, climb straight up past two bolts and a pin to the top. **Gear:** Both routes require a light rack of stoppers and small cams.

# BUBBA CITY, JUNKYARD, AND BRIDGE BUTTRESS AREA

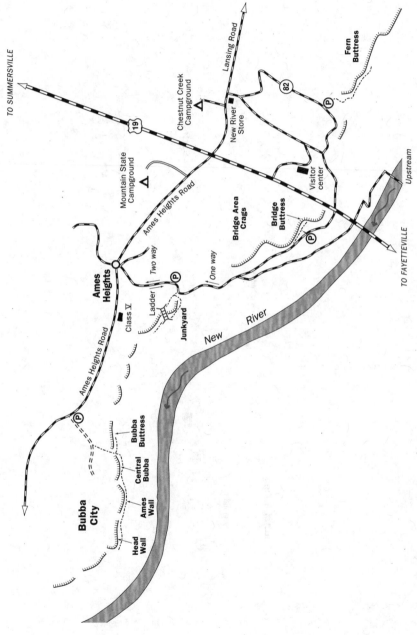

TO SUMMERSVILLE

Lansing Road

Fern Buttress

Chestnut Creek Campground

New River Store

19

82

Mountain State Campground

Ames Heights Road

Visitor center

Bridge Area Crags

Bridge Buttress

Two way

One way

Ames Heights

Ladder

Class V

Junkyard

New River

Ames Heights Road

Bubba Buttress

Central Bubba

Bubba City

Ames Wall

Head Wall

Upstream

TO FAYETTEVILLE

# BUBBA CITY—RIGHT SECTOR

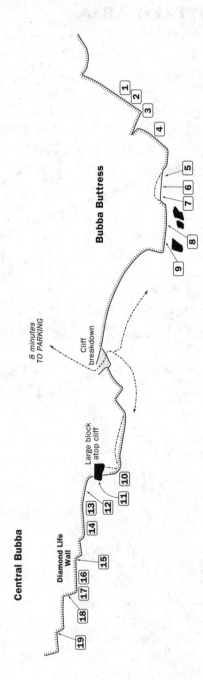

Bubba Buttress

Central Bubba

Diamond Life Wall

8 minutes
TO PARKING

Cliff breakdown

Large block atop cliff

5. **Flexible Strategies** (5.12b). Begin at a line of bolts 5 feet right of a crack and 40 feet left of *Immaculate Combustion*. Climb the crack a couple of moves until you can move right to the first bolt. Now, fire straight up the line of bolts to the top. This route has two cruxes—12b (low) and 12a (high)—with a good rest in between.

6. **Bubbarete** (5.10b) Start at a finger crack leading to a low roof and just left of the bolts on *Flexible Strategies*. Climb the crack up to a roof, then traverse right 15 feet to a flake and finish up the white arête (70 feet).

7. **Basic Bubba Crack** (5.9) Begin in a right-facing corner below a roof. Jam the crack to the top (70 feet).

8. **Face It, Bubba** (5.11a) Bubba City's first route, established by Kenny Parker and John Regelbrugge in February 1987. Jam the prominent finger crack through a small roof, then face climb up and right to a bolt. Conclude up a shallow corner past a pin (65 feet).

9. **Harmonic Jello** (5.12a) Begin 12 feet left of the *Face It, Bubba* finger crack, and climb bouldery face moves through a bulge to a stance. Continue up past another crux to anchors. 5 bolts.

## CENTRAL BUBBA

10. **The Cutting Edge** (5.12a/b) Technical and quite good. Start at a small dihedral and a good horizontal crack located about 15 feet right of a large, left-facing corner. Move up the short corner and hand-traverse out the horizontal crack to climb up the blunt, white arête. 8 bolts.

11. **The Raging Tiger** (5.10d). A great mixed route up beautiful rock. Just right of the large, left-facing corner, climb a flake system up to a stance. Continue up the tiger-striped wall (bolt) to coldshut anchors under the large roof.

12. **The Golden Escalator** (5.11a) Popular. Start on a block about 15 feet left of the large, left-facing corner. Climb the pocketed, edgy face past 3 bolts to anchors.

13. **Brown Out** (5.11d) Beginning 10 feet left of *Golden Escalator,* climb the thin, brown face past 4 bolts to anchors.

14. **Hydroman** (5.11c) About 30 feet left of the large, left-facing corner, locate a line of bolts leading to a roof near mid-height. Climb up through the roof and continue up and left to anchors. 6 bolts.

15. **Sheer Energy** (5.11b) Right of *Diamond Life,* climb the hanging, left-facing corner through a bulge to anchors. 6 bolts.

16. **Diamond Life** (5.13a) West Virginia's first 5.13, established in 1987 by Eric Hörst. Begin 20 feet left of *Sheer Energy* and boulder up easy rock

# BUBBA CITY—MIDDLE SECTOR

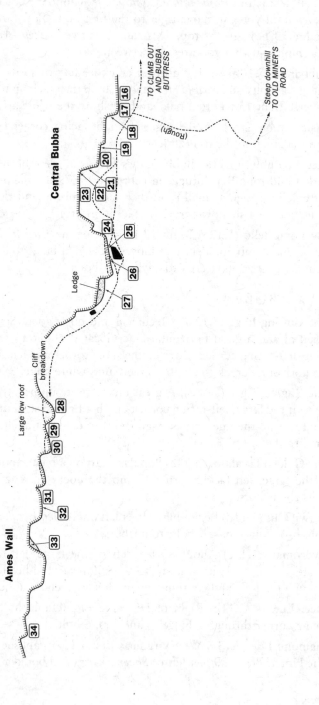

to a pin, then crank small edges and shallow pockets up the vertical, gray face to anchors. 4 bolts.

17. **Bubbacide** (5.12b) This four-bolt arête route packs a lot of great climbing and two really hard moves. Begin up the right side of the arête to a small roof. Move left around this, then immediately back right to finish past a crux bulge to coldshuts. Variation: **Lean Production** (5.12c) From the left side of the low roof, continue up the more difficult left side of the arête all the way to the top.

18. **Into the Fire** (5.12b) Fifteen feet left of the *Bubbacide* arête, climb the center of the face past a small overhang to slings in a tree. 5 bolts.

19. **Shear Strength** (5.11b) A beautiful dihedral! Climb the nice, left-facing corner past two pins to a bolt anchor (45 feet). **Gear:** Quickdraws, TCUs, and wired stoppers.

20. **Stop the Presses, Rico Suavé** (5.12c) Just left of the *Shear Strength* dihedral, levitate up the line of five bolts to coldshuts.

21. **Desperate but Not Serious** (5.12b) The name says it all. Start a few paces right of a large, left-facing corner. Power up past two bolts to a stance at the base of shallow corners. Continue up past two more bolts to coldshuts.

22. **Axis Bold As Bubba** (5.9) Climb the prominent, left-facing corner to a sometimes-dirty mantle finish (40 feet).

23. **The Raptilian** (5.10c/d) A popular warm-up route. Slither up the center of this gray face, past four bolts to anchors.

24. **Whamarete** (5.11d R) Climb up this steep, clean arête past a single pin. Great climbing, but marginal pro—an ideal toprope. A typically gutsy route by Eddie Begoon and Mike Artz.

25. **Arapiles Please** (5.12b) Climbs the beautiful face about 15 feet left of a sharp arête. Begin up past a bolt and pin, then hang on through increasingly difficult moves past three more bolts to anchors.

26. **Look Who's Pulling** (5.11a/b) Juggy climbing through tiered roofs makes this quite popular. Start just left of large blocks in a small, left-facing corner near the center of the wall. Move up the corner a few feet, then follow a line of four bolts straight up through tiered roofs to coldshuts.

27. **Insistent Irony** (5.10b) Start just left of a wide crack in a left-facing corner. Climb the thin, less-than-vertical face past three bolts to anchors. Lower off, or climb one of the 5.12 clip-ups on the upper wall.

# BUBBA CITY—LEFT SECTOR

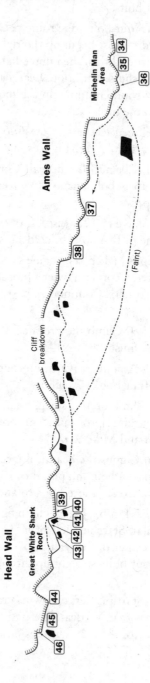

## AMES WALL

Beyond *Insistent Irony*, the downstream trail turns right as the cliffband bends back into the hillside. Hike about 100 yards past a brief cliff break, to the beginning of Ames Wall.

28. **Darwin's Dangle** (5.11d) Rope up where the trail passes under a huge roof. Climb easy moves up to the roof, crank out past two bolts, and turn the lip. Continue up the face past a bolt to anchors.

29. **Tongulation** (5.11d) Start up the left-facing corner on the right side of the orange *Likmé* wall. Continue up past three bolts, pull the roof on the right (bolt), and continue to the top.

30. **Likmé** (5.12a) One of the few rainy-day routes at Bubba City. Begin below the left side of a colorful wall about 20 yards beyond the large *Darwin's Dangle* roof. Wander up the line of five bolts on the left side of the orange-and-black-striped wall. Rappel from anchors under the large roof.

31. **Boschtardized** (5.11c) Start about 15 feet left of a short, V-shaped dihedral. Follow nice face moves past two bolts to a stance (pin). Move right, then continue up past two more bolts to the top. Rappel from a nearby tree, or walk off upstream and descend the break between Ames Wall and Central Bubba.

32. **Fingers in Da Dyke** (5.11b) Climb the line of 4 bolts just left of *Boschtardized*. A good route, but there are no anchors.

33. **Tasty Flake** (5.8) A nice trad route in the midst of sport climbing heaven. Climb a left-facing flake up a huge, right-facing corner located about 50 feet left of *Boschtardized*.

34. **The Attacktician** (5.11a) Technical and very good! Begin 10 feet right of a blunt arête and climb the nice face past 4 bolts to anchors.

35. **Radial Rimmed** (5.10c) Another enjoyable 5.10 clip-up. Climb the face just right of an obvious offwidth crack. 6 bolts to anchors.

36. **Michelin Man** (5.12a) One of the many great 5.12s in the gorge! Just left of a large offwidth, follow a line of bolts up bulging waves of beautiful white sandstone. 8 bolts to anchors.

37. **A-Pocket-Leaps Now** (5.13a) Start in a short, left-facing corner capped by a low roof located about 100 yards downstream from *Michelin Man*. Stick-clip the first bolt, then power and lunge up the steep white face. Two other sport routes finish at these anchors and can be toproped or led for an extra pump. The left route is 5.12c, and the right route is 5.12a.

38. **Keine Kraft** (5.11d) Beautiful climbing. Follow the trail about 30 yards past *A-Pocket-Leaps Now* to the "can't miss it" orange face. Begin up a crack and corner, past a bolt and tiered roofs (two more bolts), to a

lieback crack and easier face above (55 feet). **Gear:** Quickdraws, TCUs, and small-to-medium stoppers.

## HEAD WALL

From the orange *Keine Kraft* face, walk about 300 yards downstream and past a cliff break. As the next cliff begins, you pass among some large boulders and soon arrive at the base of the prominent, white *Incredarete*.

39. **Reaches from Hell** (5.11c/d) A bit reachy, but still devilishly good fun! If you're short (and even if you're not), consider doing the *Skinhead Grin* variation—it's also quite good. About 20 feet right of *Incredarete*, start below a crack through a roof about 20 feet up. Climb blocky moves to the first bolt below a small roof. Follow the bolted line up to a short crack, then continue up and left (pin) to a hanging, left-facing corner. Finish up the corner and face above to anchors. Variation: **Skinhead Grin** (5.11b) Climb *Reaches* to the third bolt, then follow bolts up and right through a juggy roof to coldshuts.

40. **Critical Path** (5.12a) Begin on blocks below the right side of the prominent white arête. Start up through a low roof, then find the "critical path" up the right side of the arête. 5 bolts to anchors.

41. **Incredarete** (5.12c) Start on a blocky ledge on the left side of the arête. Climb easy moves to a fixed piton. The "business" now begins, as you fight up the center of the face left of the arête. 4 bolts to shared anchors.

42. **Masterpiece Theater** (5.12d/5.13a) Steep climbing on positive holds. Just left of a large offwidth crack, send the line of five bolts out the overhanging orange wall to a stance. Dance up the headwall (more hard moves) past two more bolts.

43. **The Great White Shark** (5.12c) Bubba City's *Foops!* Climb through the obvious roof just left of *Masterpiece Theater*. From a flaky ledge, follow a line of four bolts up to and out the right side of the 12-foot roof. You'll find a stance and coldshuts just above the lip (25 feet).

44. **Dreams of White Hörsts** (5.13a) Powerful moves on pristine rock. Begins about 50 yards downstream from *The Great White Shark* roof. Climb the right side of the bright white arête past three bolts to a stance. After a well-deserved rest, climb less-difficult but nice moves up the second half of the arête (past bolt and pin) to coldshuts.

45. **Little Creatures** (5.10d) Begin below a left-facing crack through a roof near the center of the face. Climb this weakness to the top (55 feet).

46. **Two Orgasaminimum** (5.10c) Start a short way up the obvious chimney until you can move out onto the right wall (bolt). Continue up and right to a good stance, then on up the prow to a short crack and the top (70 feet).

# JUNKYARD

Junkyard was one of the first areas developed in The New, and it continues to be an extremely popular area to this date. It's not hard to understand why: The approach is short; there are a number of good, moderate face and crack climbs; and unlike most crags at The New, topropes are easy to rig. Bring a modest rack of stoppers and camming units if you plan to lead-climb, since most of the routes require traditional gear. There is also a popular bouldering area located in a "cave" near the descent ladder. Described below are eleven of the 100+ routes available for your climbing pleasure.

**Finding the crag:** From US 19 on the north side of the bridge, turn onto Ames Heights Road and go 0.5 mile to a left bend in the road. Here, turn left (not the sharpest left) and descend about 0.2 mile to two parking pulloffs on the left side of the road just before the road becomes one-way. Hike across and down the road just a few paces to the right side of the hairpin turn, where two trails begin. The left trail descends to the downstream end of the Junkyard crag—the first route described below is just two or three minutes down the trail. The right trail provides clifftop access to the popular New River Gunks section of Junkyard and, beyond that, the downclimb ladder. It's just over a five-minute hike to the ladder.

From the Bridge Buttress Area, you'll need to use a different approach (since WV 82 is now one-way below the bridge). Follow the one-way road downhill and turn right at the first hairpin turn. This one-way road leads back uphill and eventually intersects with Ames Heights Road above the Junkyard crags. Driving uphill, you'll find the two parking pulloffs on the right side of the road just after a sharp right bend.

1. **Rapscallion's Blues** (5.10c) Junkyard begins with this classic, located about 75 yards beyond the upstream descent. Climb the prominent, right-facing dihedral through double overhangs near the top (55 feet).

2. **Four Sheets to the Wind** (5.9+) Another great route. Start at a left-facing corner 30 feet left of *Rapscallion's Blues*. Ascend the crack and left-facing corner through roofs to an alcove on the left. Finish straight up (60 feet).

3. **New Yosemite** (5.9) About 40 feet left of *Four Sheets*, you'll find a sweet, 35-foot splitter hand crack. Send it!

4. **New River Gunks** (5.7) An excellent, moderate face climb—these days it's a popular beginners' route! Start up the right side of a low-angle face to a good horizontal crack. Traverse right about 8 feet, then up a thin crack to a right-facing corner. Finish through the roof above at a wide crack (65 feet).

5. **Team Jesus** (5.10a/b) Begin at a prominent, thin crack up the middle of the face, about 15 feet left of *New River Gunks*. Work up along the

# JUNKYARD

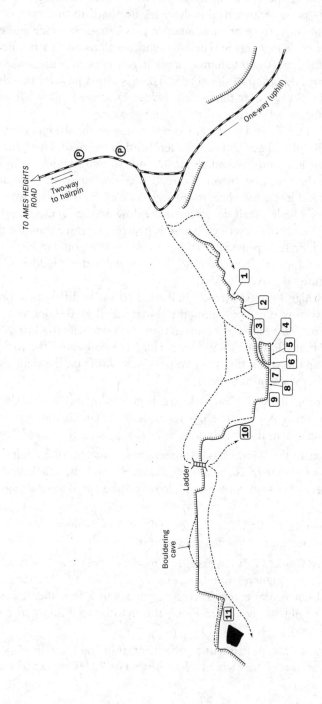

crack and face to a ledge. Move right, then up a right-facing flake and through the middle of an overhang to the top (60 feet).

6. **The Distortionist** (5.6) Start just right of a chimney, squirm up a short, 5-inch crack to lower-angle rock. Finish up the slabby arête (50 feet).

7. **Reachers of Habit** (5.11a) A nice sport route. Begin in front of a tall tree just left of a chimney. Climb the face and a seam to a small, right-facing corner and a stance with anchors. Two pitons and 2 bolts.

8. **Mystery Dance** (5.12b) Begin 15 feet left of *Reachers of Habit* and climb the steep face past a pin and 4 bolts to anchors.

9. **The Entertainer** (5.9+) Classic! Start at a beautiful hand crack 10 feet right of an outside corner. Climb the narrowing crack about 30 feet to a horizontal crack. Move left a few feet and continue up a crack and flake (65 feet). Variation: **Realignment** (5.10d) At the horizontal crack 30 feet up, climb the thin seam up and right to the top.

10. **Stuck in Another Dimension** (5.11a) Climb the wide crack through the large roof located on the downstream-facing wall about 50 feet left of *The Entertainer* (70 feet).

11. **Zealous** (5.11a) Climb the beautiful finger crack above a low roof located about 75 yards downstream of the ladder (60 feet).

## BRIDGE BUTTRESS

Bridge Buttress is many climbers' first stop upon arriving at The New, probably because of its location directly below the visitor center and the US 19 bridge. While there are some excellent routes here, don't spend too much time at this crag, as there are many bigger, better things to be found in the gorge.

**Finding the crag:** From the visitor center, follow the narrow WV 82 downhill past two sharp right turns. Soon you'll pass under the huge US 19 span bridge. Park in one of the pulloffs on the left. The climbs are immediately across the road.

1. **Let the Wind Blow** (5.12a) Start 6 feet right of the *High Times* crack and climb the crimpy, three-bolt face to anchors. Popular as a rainy-day route.

2. **High Times** (5.10c) A nice crack that's quite popular on rainy days. Most often climbed to anchors below the roof (30 feet).

3. **West Virginia Highway a.k.a. Coal Miner's Daughter** (5.12b) Left of *High Times,* follow a line of 9 bolts up the face and through the roof to anchors. Stays dry on rainy days.

# BRIDGE BUTTRESS

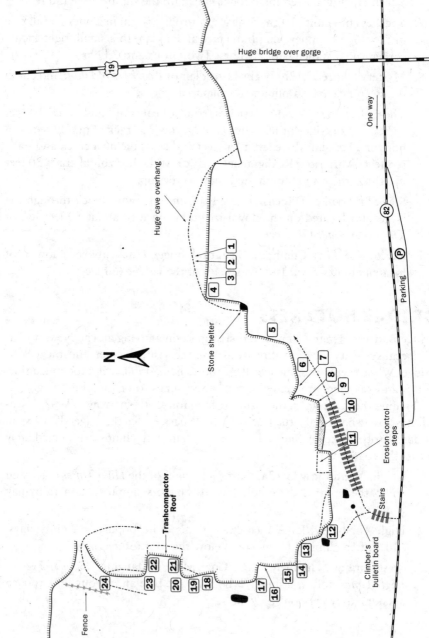

Huge bridge over gorge

19

One way

82

P

Parking

Huge cave overhang

Stone shelter

N

1
2
3
4
5
6
7
8
9
10
11
12
13
14
15
16
17
18
19
20
21
22
23
24

Erosion control steps

Stairs

Climber's bulletin board

Trashcompactor Roof

Fence

4. **Labor Day** (5.10c) Begin 30 feet right of a small stone shelter and climb the large, right-facing flake to the roof. Move left and continue up to a pine tree (50 feet). Often climbed to the roof on rainy days.

5. **The Stratagem** (5.11d/5.12a) Good, pumpy sport climbing; unfortunately it can be a bit dirty near the top. It's the line of bolts starting about 20 feet left of a large, right-facing corner.

6. **The Layback a.k.a. Zig** (5.9) Begin 40 feet right of *Angel's Arête* and climb the nice, right-facing flake (50 feet).

7. **Blunder and Frightening** (5.10b) Begin below a thin crack located about 15 feet right of a large, left-facing corner. Climb the face, then jam a curving crack to its end. Head up and a bit left to the top (45 feet).

8. **Mega Magic** (5.12b/c) A thin, technical face climbing testpiece that's often toproped. Climb the line of bolts on the face just right of *Angel's Arête*.

9. **Angel's Arête** (5.10a/b) Airy, a bit scary, but wonderful! Start on the right side of the arête located at the top of the erosion-control steps. Climb up past a pin until you can move around to the left side of the arête. Finish up easier moves to the top (60 feet).

10. **Zag** (5.8) Popular as both a toprope and lead. Beginning from a ledge, climb the obvious splitter hand crack (55 feet).

11. **Handsome and Well Hung** (5.11a) This stunning, right-facing corner is located directly behind the climbers' bulletin board. Begin on the left end of the *Zag* ledge and climb the corner to anchors (40 feet).

12. **Englishman's Crack** (5.11b) The New's first 5.11—put up by none other than Doug Reed in 1983. This route follows a wide crack through a roof and up a short corner to a stance (old bolt). Finish up the *Easily Flakey* ramp and flake (70 feet).

13. **Easily Flakey** (5.7 R) A popular toprope with several more-direct variations. Start up a large corner to a tree, then traverse right 15 feet to an old bolt. Now climb the prominent flake and dihedral to the top (85 feet).

14. **Team Machine** (5.12a) A classic Bridge Buttress face climb. Start directly below a nice horizontal slot on the left side of a low outside corner. Boulder up to the slot and first bolt above. Continue up the blunt arête and face to anchors. 5 bolts and optional TCU between first and second bolt.

15. **Stretch Armstrong a.k.a Ruptured** (5.11c) Just left of *Team Machine*, climb the face past 5 bolts to anchors.

16. **Jaws** (5.9) Popular, but consider taping to avoid the "bite." Jam the crack up a right-facing corner and past a tree near the top (55 feet).

17. **Are You Experienced?** (5.12c) Climbs the arête left of *Jaws*. Beginning left of the arête, climb the crack and move right (bolt) to finish on the right side of the arête (65 feet).

18. **Tree Route** (5.10a) The tree is history, so begin in a left-facing corner with a stump! Climb the crack and flaring chimney (65 feet).

19. **Marionette** (5.11c) Classic and very memorable. Begin at a small, left-facing corner located about 10 feet left of *Tree Route*. Climb the crack and corner to a small roof. Now, hang in there all the way up the long, discontinuous crack system to the top (70 feet).

20. **Dresden Corner** (5.11d R) Recommended as a toprope. Start below a nice, hanging dihedral about 15 feet up and just left of a large, triangular roof. Climb up the corner, past a bolt at mid-height, to the top. **Gear:** Bring brass nuts (both kinds!), ball nuts, and small TCUs. Variation: **A Touch of Tango** (5.11b/c) From about 15 feet up *Dresden Corner*, traverse right to the arête. Climb the arête and right face to the top (75 feet). A better lead.

21. **Chockstone** (5.9) Start on the right wall below the "trash compactor" roof and climb the left-slanting crack and corner to a tree (60 feet).

22. **Underfling** (5.10b) Climb up to the left side of the "trash compactor" roof. Undercling out the roof, then up a dihedral to the top (60 feet). Often wet.

23. **Locked on Target** (5.13a) A John Bercaw testpiece. Starting a few paces left of *Underfling*, climb up to and through a roof at a bolt. Continue up the strenuous face past two more bolts to an easy, low-angle finish.

24. **Butterbeans** (5.10a) About 40 feet left of the "trash compactor" roof and adjacent to the downclimb gulley is an impressive, 4-inch crack. Climb the 45 feet of offwidth madness.

# ENDLESS WALL

## FERN BUTTRESS

As one of The New's more low-profile areas, Fern Buttress is (for those in the know) a favorite "get-away" crag on busy weekends. Here you'll find a high concentration of sport routes from 5.10a to 5.13b. The twenty-three routes described below are all within a fifteen-minute walk of the parking area.

**Finding the area:** From US 19 North, turn onto Lansing Road and go just 0.4 mile to Fayette Station Road (WV 82). Turn right (stay left at split) and travel 0.7 mile to a pulloff on the left. Park here and hike just over five minutes to the first routes on Fern Buttress. From the pulloff, hike down a short,

# ENDLESS WALL/BEAUTY MOUNTAIN OVERVIEW

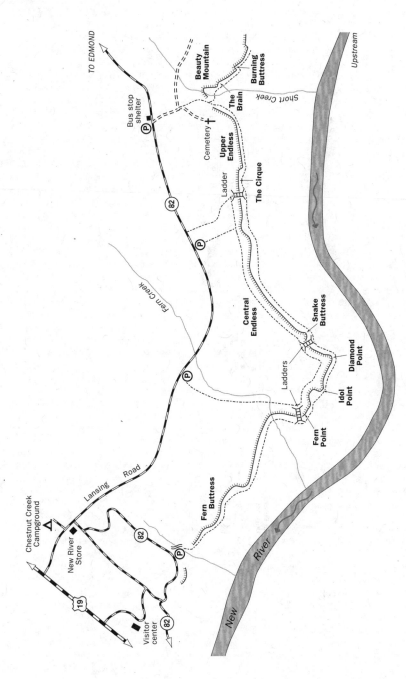

# FERN BUTTRESS—LEFT SECTOR

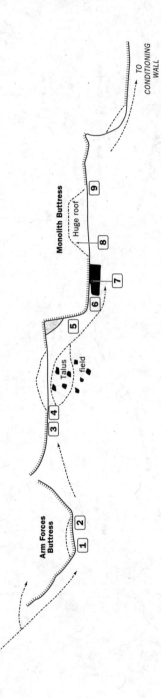

steep hill and continue across the top of a waterfall. Turn right (downhill) and follow a left-curving trail (stay left at split) about 200 yards to the beginning of the nearly 4-mile-long Endless Wall.

## ARM FORCES AREA

1. **Ron Kauk Gets a Perm** (5.11d) Begin at a short, vertical crack 15 feet right of a large tree. Climb the line of 5 bolts along an orange crack and around the left side of an overhang to anchors.

2. **Arm Forces** (5.11c) Starting 15 feet right of *Ron Kauk,* crank up past 4 bolts to anchors.

3. **The Mega Jug** (5.11b) Follow the trail about 60 yards to the next short wall. Begin at a tree below a short, right-facing flake. Climb the left line of 4 bolts (past the "mega jug") to anchors.

4. **October Surprise** (5.10d) Begin 6 feet right of *The Mega Jug.* Clip up the right line of 4 bolts to anchors.

## MONOLITH BUTTRESS AREA

Follow the trail about 80 yards to the next buttress.

5. **Teleconnections** (5.11c/d) Climb the bolted fracture to its end (about 30 feet up), then traverse right a few moves and finish up the steep face to the anchors. 6 bolts. Direct Start: **Powertalk** (5.12b) Just right of the crack is another line of bolts. Send this to join *Teleconnections* at the fifth bolt. Finish up easier moves to the anchors.

6. **First Person** (5.10c) Begin just left of a large block on the left front side of the buttress. Climb a shallow, left-facing corner past 4 bolts to anchors about 40 feet up.

7. **Close to the Edge** (5.12b) Begin on top of the large block and climb the smooth face past 5 bolts to anchors.

8. **My Stinking Brain** (5.13a) A short distance down the trail you come to a huge amphitheater known as The Monolith. Locate the Kaymoor "Hole" lookalike route out the left side of the roof. 7 bolts to anchors. Another Doug Reed prototype 5.13 route.

9. **Over the Edge** (5.11c) Begin on the face just right of the arête that marks the right edge of The Monolith. Start up juggy holds and follow the left-angling line of 6 bolts to anchors. Direct Start: **Air Apparent** (5.12b) Start below a large crack inside the right side of the cave. Climb buckets up and right to the first bolt, then power up past 2 more bolts to join the regular route at its third bolt.

## BOSNIAN BUTTRESS

Continue on the upstream trail a short distance as it curls around the next buttress. These two routes are located on the upstream-facing wall.

10. **Bosnian Vacation** (5.12d) About 100 yards beyond The Monolith, you'll find an impressive orange arête with a line of 10 bolts up the right-hand face. A Kenny Parker testpiece technical face climb.

11. **Workman's Comp** (5.10d) A popular route with a bouldery start. Begin 10 feet left of a large inside corner and an equal distance right of a crack. Climb through a bulge and up the nice face to anchors. 5 bolts.

## CONDITIONING WALL

Follow the trail about 30 yards to the base of an impressive, white-and-orange wall.

12. **Just Send It** (5.13b) The best 5.13 on this end of Endless Wall. Start below an obvious bucket hold 10 feet off the ground and 10 feet left of a short crack. Boulder up and left past the first bolt (stick-clip) to gain a thin crack. Follow this up along the overhanging, right-facing corner to anchors. A classic Hörst route up great rock. Do as the name says!

13. **Welcome to Conditioning** (5.12d/5.13a) No doubt, a good workout! Use the same start as *Just Send It*—jump up to the bucket, but continue straight up to a small, right-facing flake and the first bolt. Move up to a pocket and lunge left (very hard if you're under 5 feet 8 inches or so) to a good slot. Power up to a horizontal crack and move back right and over a bulge to anchors above.

14. **Stab Me; I Don't Matter** (5.13a) Short, but very bouldery. Start at a short crack just right of *Conditioning*. Begin up and right on jugs to the first bolt. Now, take a stab at climbing the smooth wall and seam to a stance. 4 bolts to anchors.

## GONAD WALL

About 60 yards beyond Conditioning Wall the trail passes an arête and some blocks on the trail. This is the beginning of Gonad Wall.

15. **Muscle Belly** (5.11c) Climb the right side of the arête past 5 bolts to anchors.

16. **Wild Seed** (5.11a) Juggy fun. Start on blocks just right of *Muscle Belly*. Climb the blocky crack, then up the right face and through tiered roofs. 6 bolts to anchors.

17. **Sportin' Fool** (5.11d) Begin at a small tree 15 feet right of a right-facing corner. Climb thin moves past 4 bolts to anchors. This route has been

# FERN BUTTRESS—RIGHT SECTOR

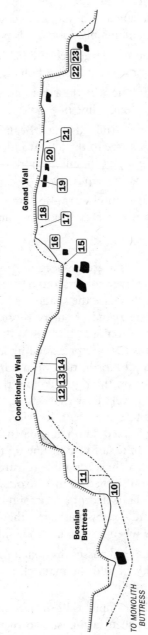

mistakenly identified as *Gonad the Bavarian* in previous guidebooks. *Gonad* climbs the thin crack just to the left.

18. **Foutre à la Doigt** (5.12a) Don't translate this one. Just right of *Sportin' Fool* is another line of 4 bolts up a thin, pocketed face.

19. **Chameleon** (5.10c) Commence from blocks and next to a tree near the middle of the wall. Climb on mainly good holds past 4 bolts to anchors.

20. **Fly Girls** (5.12a) Begin left of a large tree and below the middle of a low roof. Dance and dyno up the steep face. 5 bolts to anchors.

21. **Doer, Not a Critic** (5.11c) Start at the right end of a low roof 15 feet right of *Fly Girls.* Climb along a line of 6 bolts to anchors.

22. **Arbor Day** (5.12a) A popular mixed route. Begin 60 yards right of *Fly Girls,* at a nice arête with a tree to the left. Wander up the smooth right face of the arête, past a bolt, a pin, and 2 more bolts. Bring a selection of stoppers and small cams to keep it safe.

23. **Fragile Egosystem** (5.10a) A good warm-up route. Climb the low-angle, 50-foot face just right of *Arbor Day.* 5 bolts to anchors.

## FERN POINT

This exceedingly popular area has a great selection of sport and trad routes from 5.9 to 5.13. With its many large corners and buttresses, Fern Point is one of the areas where you can easily chase the shade (or sunshine) by just walking a few paces around the corner. And, if one of those all-too-familiar West Virginia showers moves in while you're at Endless Wall, Fern Point possesses about ten good rainy-day routes that are protected by large overhangs.

**Finding the area:** From US 19 North, turn onto Lansing Road and drive 1.4 miles to a large parking lot on the right. Follow the trail on a pleasant, fifteen-minute hike along Fern Creek. Bear right at the "Climber access only" sign and walk about 75 yards to the descent "crevice." Drop down through boulders and a chimney, using a fixed, knotted rope and ladder. You arrive at the base of the sharp *Whip It* arête, a five-bolt line up the edge of the gigantic, detached Fern Point block. A short scramble (upstream) through a large, chimney-like corridor brings you to the rest of the routes, beginning with the fabulous *New Age Equippers.* Four decent sport routes climb the constantly shaded walls of the corridor and nearby boulders—they are all 5.12s and are probably best saved for a time when it's too hot to climb other routes.

24. **Whip It** (5.12b) Where the trail passes through a tall chimney formed by the massive Fern Point block and the main cliff, climb the sharp arête past 5 bolts to anchors.

25. **New Age Equippers** (5.11c) Popular. Begin next to a tree at the corridor's exit. Climb the sustained face past two overhangs to anchors. 6 bolts.

# FERN POINT AREA

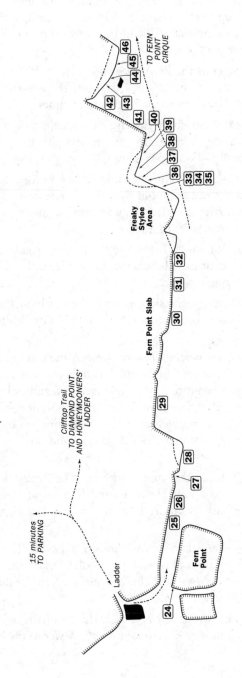

26. **Dangerous Liaisons** (5.12a) Twenty feet downhill from the corridor exit, ascend the thin, gray face along a left-curving line of bolts to anchors.

27. **Linear Encounters** (5.11a) A Fern Point classic. Start in a left-facing corner and jam the crack up past a roof to its end. Continue up a thin, left-angling seam, which is somewhat difficult to protect. Bring small TCUs and wires for the latter part of the route.

28. **Le Futuriste** (5.12b) Start at the left side of a low roof 20 feet right of *Linear Encounters*. Boulder up to the first bolt, then move right to ascend the left side of the white arête. 7 bolts to anchors.

29. **Is It Safe** (5.11d/5.12a) Near the right end of a small, low overhang, climb up on a right-facing flake, and continue straight up to finish at anchors atop a headwall. 8 bolts to coldshuts.

30. **Dead Painters' Society** (5.12a) Thin, technical, and well-protected—a Rick Thompson classic! Located about 40 yards upstream of *Is It Safe* and 20 feet right of a dirty, vegetated crack system. Beginning just right of a tree, send the line of 8 bolts to anchors.

31. **The Magnificent Puddcasso** (5.12a) About 25 feet right of *Dead Painters'* and 10 feet left of the *Mellifluous* crack, climb the slab along a left-angling line of 9 bolts to anchors.

32. **Mellifluous** (5.11a) On the right side of Fern Point, climb the classic hand-and-finger crack to a right-facing flake. Continue up this to a roof and exit left (85 feet).

33. **The Prowesse** (5.9 R) Start where a low roof meets the ground. Step up and traverse left 15 feet to a good horizontal crack. Continue left around the arête and climb up a beautiful, low-angle face to a stance left of the *Stim-O-Stam* anchors. Belay here (or use the *Stim-O-Stam* anchors), or continue up the face above in one long pitch. Protection on the second half of the route is barely adequate, but if you're solid on 5.9, this is a great climb!

34. **Stim-O-Stam** (5.11c) Start at the same spot as in *The Prowesse*. Climb easy moves up and left to a bolt above a good horizontal crack. Continue up the thin face past five more bolts to anchors just right of the arête.

35. **Freaky Stylee** (5.12a) One of the most-climbed 5.12s at The New—maybe it's the exciting moves above the last bolt? Relax and style it! Begin just right of *Stim-O-Stam* and climb straight up the center of the face. 5 bolts to anchors.

36. **Techman** (5.12c) Begin just right of *Freaky Stylee* at small, right-facing flakes. Climb the bright orange face to join *Freaky Stylee* at the last bolt. 7 bolts.

37. **Stealth 'n' Magic** (5.12c/d) This and adjacent routes stay dry on the all-too-common New River rain days. Start just left of the *Biohazard* crack/corner and climb past 7 bolts to anchors.

38. **Biohazard** (5.10a) Climb the cracks and corner to slings under the roof. Lower 50 feet, or escape to the right until it's possible to continue to the top (100 feet).

39. **Fascist Architecture** (5.12c) Begin 15 feet right of *Biohazard*. Climb the right-facing flake and crack to a bulging crux sequence. 5 bolts to anchors.

40. **Party 'Til Yer Blind** (5.10b) Beginning 15 feet right of *Fascist Architecture*, climb the left side of the arête past a bolt at mid-height. Good climbing and decent gear (look on both sides of the arête) make this one of the more popular trad routes in the Fern Point area (90 feet).

41. **Party in My Mind** (5.10b) An Endless Wall classic! Begin at left-facing flakes about 15 feet right of the arête. Climb up and slightly left to follow fantastic holds up the wall (about 10 feet right of the arête) to a small ledge, then along the right side of the arête (90 feet).

42. **Smooth Operator** (5.9+) A great fist-and-hand crack located immediately left of the offwidth corner. Jam the crack and finish along a left-angling corner (85 feet).

43. **Modern Primitive** (5.12b/c) Rope up 25 feet right of the prominent, offwidth crack and corner. Fire the line of 4 bolts to anchors below a roof. Good rainy day route.

44. **Plyometrics** (5.12d) Starting 12 feet right of the previous route, power up a series of flakes and huecos past four bolts to a slot (place TCUs here). Head left to *Modern Primitive* anchors.

45. **Harbinger Scarab** (5.12c) For a preview, check out the *New River Rock* cover photo of Doug Reed on the first ascent. Begin below a prominent, left-facing flake leading to a huge roof. Ascend the flake to the first bolt. Now, follow the line of 9 more bolts through the huge roof and bulging headwall (100 feet). Bring TCUs or wires for the start, and consider using two ropes to reduce rope drag. No anchors.

46. **The Sweetest Taboo** (5.13b) Start below a low roof 10 feet right of a right-facing corner. Climb easy moves up past a bolt and out the roof past another bolt—only 5.10 to this point. The business starts above the lip, as you encounter a powerful sequence past four more bolts to anchors. Stays dry in a light rain.

47. **Pocket Pussy** (5.12b) A short, four-bolt route up a white face. Start in the left-facing dihedral left of the bolt line and climb to a small ledge 10

feet up. Traverse right onto the bolted face, and power up past the four bolts to anchors. Stick-clip first bolt.

48. **Autumn Fire** (5.10b) Climb the obvious crack and corner to the top (70 feet).

## EXODUSTER AREA

49. **Exoduster** (5.10b) By the looks of it, this may be the most-climbed 40 feet of rock in the gorge. Start at a well-chalked, left-facing flake and climb past a series of pockets and slots to anchors below the roof. 4 bolts. Stays day in the rain. Variation Finish: **Eat My Dust** (5.11b) Move left around the roof and up the face to a high set of anchors.

50. **Pre-Marital Bliss** (5.9) Climb cracks in the large, left-facing corner for about 70 feet until you can move right to chains.

51. **Mental Wings** (5.12c) If you got 'em, use 'em! Start in a shallow, right-facing corner about 10 feet right of *Pre-Marital Bliss*. Climb increasingly difficult moves up and right to the arête, then straight up to a ledge. Finish up more-moderate arête moves to anchors near the top.

52. **Smore Energy** (5.11b) A popular route with three cruxes. Start on the face just left of a right-facing corner. Climb into an orange corner, then move right and over a bulge to a good ledge. After a rest and/or picnic, move left and up through another bulge to a thin conclusion. 8 bolts to anchors. Variation: **Chouinard-Steck Variation** (5.11d) Climb *Smore Energy* to the third bolt, then move left past a bolt to finish up the top half of the *Mental Wings* arête.

53. **Hooked on Bionics** (5.11d) Bionics might help on this short, action-packed line. Start at a small left-facing flake 50 feet right of *Smore Energy*. Power up the steep, orange face to anchors above a small overhang (30 feet).

## IDOL POINT AND KAYMOOR SLAB AREAS

Between Fern Point and Diamond Point is about a 0.25 mile of cliff, including the Idol Point and Kaymoor Slab sections of Endless Wall. Although these areas possess dozens of quality routes, I've selected just a handful of popular climbs to check out as you hike the cliffbase between Fern Point and Diamond Point.

**Finding the area:** From the second-to-last route described at Fern Point (*Smore Energy*), follow a trail into the woods and about 150 yards through talus to reach *Idol Point Arête*. Or, from the first route at Diamond Point (*This Sport Needs an Enema*) you only need to hike about 50 yards to reach *Euro-Nation*.

# EXODUSTER AREA, FERN POINT CIRQUE, IDOL POINT, AND KAYMOOR SLAB

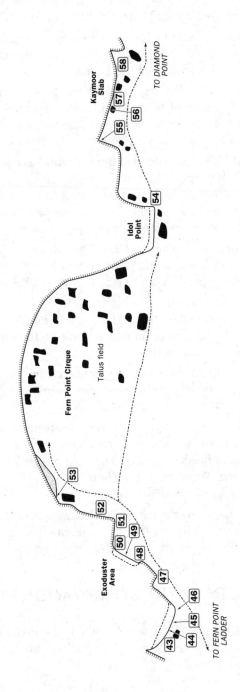

Kaymoor Slab

TO DIAMOND POINT

Idol Point

Fern Point Cirque

Talus field

Exoduster Area

TO FERN POINT LADDER

54. **Idol Point Arête** (5.12a) A stunning, airy line. Start at a wide crack on the right side of the arête and climb past 8 bolts to anchors.

55. **Meniscus Burning** (5.11c) Beginning 10 feet left of a large, right-facing corner, climb the orange face past 4 bolts to anchors.

56. **What Will People Think?** (5.12c) Very sustained. Start on a detached, 6-foot-high flake located about 40 feet right of a large, right-facing corner. Climb the steep face past 8 bolts to anchors.

57. **Fool Effect** (5.9) The ultimate "slabbathon." Begin at a low ledge with a pine tree 30 feet right of *What Will People Think?* Climb the 120-foot, 13-bolt line to the top. No anchors. From the top, it's a double-rope rappel, or you can hike to either the Fern Point or Honeymooners' Ladder.

58. **The Upheaval** (5.9) Very popular, but unfortunately the site of several accidents while lowering. Begin from a ledge just left of a vegetated, left-facing corner. Climb the nice face past 8 bolts to anchors (85 feet). Belay from the ledge, and be very careful when lowering with a 50-meter (165-foot) rope. Be safe and use a 60-meter rope.

59. **Little Help from My Friends** (5.10a) Begin about 50 feet right of *The Upheaval* and just left of a tall, skinny tree. Climb the smooth face to a stance. Continue up a low-angle face to anchors below a pine tree. 8 bolts.

60. **Pudd's Pretty Dress** (5.12c/d) Sustained and quite classic! Start just left of an obvious chimney and climb the left line of 10 bolts up the beautiful, overhanging, orange wall.

61. **Total-E-Clips** (5.8) About 40 yards upstream from *Pudd's Pretty Dress* is another slab route notable mainly for its distinction as Endless Wall's easiest sport route. 5 bolts to anchors.

62. **Flash Point** (5.11d/5.12a) Follow the trail upstream about 75 yards to a polished-looking, orange wall with two lines of bolts. The left line (up the seam) is an unfinished project. The right line of 12 bolts is the fantastic *Flash Point*. **Warning:** The anchors are about 95 feet off the deck, so a 60-meter rope is mandatory to lower off.

63. **Euro-Nation** (5.11c) At the left end of ledge located around the corner from *Flash Point* is a line of 8 bolts beginning from in front of a tree. **Variation** (5.10b) Bypass the crux move off the ground by stemming off the tree.

## DIAMOND POINT AND HONEYMOONERS' LADDER AREA

In the mid-1980s, Diamond Point was known as the home of classic crack climbs such as *Leave It to Jesus, Raging Waters,* and *Remission.* These days the area is better known for its world-class sport climbs like *Homer Erectus,* *Strike a Scowl,* and *Gift of Grace.* Whatever your preference, you'll surely find this to be one of the best crags anywhere!

Just a few minutes upstream from Diamond Point is the Honeymooners' Ladder area, a major hub of sport climbing along Central Endless Wall. There are more than a handful of classics here including *Quinsana Plus, Jesus and Tequila, The Racist, Bullet the New Sky,* and *The Legacy,* to name a few. Bring your big guns!

**Finding the area:** Park at the Fern Creek lot located on Lansing Road about 1.4 miles east of US 19 North. Hike fifteen minutes to the clifftop at Fern Point, bear left, and follow the clifftop trail for another fifteen minutes to the Honeymooners' Ladder descent. Here, facing the crag, you will find *Bonemaster Gear Fling* just to your left and *Muckraker* on your right. Hiking downstream (left) to the Diamond Point crack routes is just a five- to ten-minute trek. The routes described at Fern Point are roughly fifteen minutes farther downstream.

If you are approaching along the cliffbase from Fern Point, Idol Point, or Kaymoor Slab, the first route described below is only about 100 yards beyond *Euro-Nation.* Follow the trail upstream around a pillar (The Finial) then scramble up a short slope onto a broad ledge at the base of a streaked, white-and-orange wall. The first three routes ascend this wall.

64. **This Sport Needs an Enema** (5.12b) Start up a slabby face past two bolts to a stance. Climb past four more bolts up a slightly overhanging orange wall and along left-facing flakes to anchors below a roof.

65. **Homer Erectus** (5.11b) Very popular. Start 5 feet right of a large corner-and-chimney system and climb the face past 9 bolts to anchors.

66. **The Weatherman's Thumb** (5.12d/5.13a) Just right of *Homer* is a difficult, 11-bolt face. Slightly "easier" for tall climbers.

67. **Remission** (5.10b) Classic! Begin at a 12-foot-high, flaring, wide crack with a beautiful hand-and-finger crack above. Climb the leftward-angling crack system (80 feet).

68. **Can I Do It 'Til I Need Glasses** (5.10b/c) Climb the first 12 feet of *Remission,* then hand-traverse right to a right-facing flake and crack. Climb the crack about 30 feet until it's possible to traverse right to the base of a right-facing corner. Set up a hanging belay, or continue up the corner to the top (95 feet). Variation: **Straight Up and Stiff** (5.10d) This direct finish skips the second traverse and continues straight up the crack and left-facing corner to the top (85 feet).

69. **Fine Motor Control** (5.12a) Beginning 8 feet left of the *Raging Waters* flake, climb the steep face past 7 bolts to anchors.

# DIAMOND POINT AREA

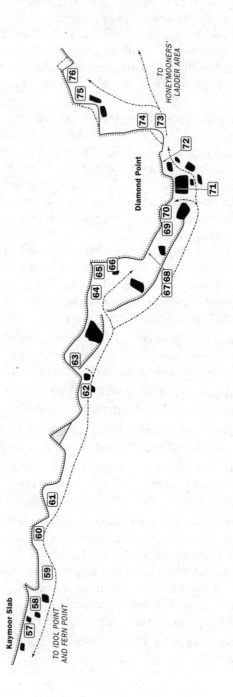

*Rick Thompson on The Weatherman's Thumb (5.12d/5.13a).* PHOTO BY CARL SAMPLES

70. **Raging Waters** (5.11a) Start at a 12-foot-high, left-facing flake at a pine tree. Climb the prominent flake (85 feet).

71. **Strike a Scowl** (5.10b) A delicate and popular face climb. From *Raging Waters,* the upstream trail passes between huge blocks. This route begins from the top of the largest detached block. Boulder 25 feet up onto the nice ledge and set up camp. Now, clip up the edgy, 7-bolt face route to anchors.

72. **How Hard Is that Thing** (5.12b/c) Where the trail curls around the large block and passes back between the cliff and boulders, locate a line of bolts that begins near a left-facing flake about 12 feet right of a wide crack. Power up past a bulge and five bolts to a stance. Catch a rest, then move left and climb the steep, white arête past five more bolts to anchors.

73. **The Gift of Grace** (5.12b) A classic arête. If 5.12b is your grade, this is a must-do route! Stick-clip the first bolt, then jug out left along the lip of a low roof. Now, ascend the right side of the arête to anchors. 8 bolts.

74. **Leave It to Jesus** (5.11d) The best finger crack on Endless Wall. Climb the beautiful splitter crack to its end and traverse left to a ledge on the arête. From here you have three options: lower from *The Gift of Grace* anchors (most popular), climb the left side of the arête to the top (5.9), or move back right and climb a direct finish (5.11b) up a right-facing corner.

75. **Hell-Bound for Glory** (5.12a) Start at a wide crack under a low roof located on the next upstream-facing wall right of *The Gift of Grace.* Move up to the roof, step left, and climb the line of bolts up the steep face (stay right at the third bolt) to anchors. Variation: **Clean Sweep** (5.12c) Move left at the third bolt and struggle up even harder terrain past six more bolts.

76. **The Glass Onion** (5.10b) Start just left of a wide crack/chimney located to the right of *Hell-Bound for Glory.* Climb the face past 5 bolts to anchors.

77. **Harlequin** (5.12b) Begin in front of a tree and near the left end of a couple of long boulders lying along the cliffbase. Clip up a line of bolts and pins to coldshut anchors.

78. **Libertine** (5.13a) On this one, power and endurance will set you free! Start at a small, left-facing flake. Stick-clip the first bolt, then commence along the flake and up through a small overhang. Continue straight up the desperate face to anchors. 7 bolts. Variation: **Oblivion** (5.12d) Move left after third bolt to ascend a separate line of 5 bolts. Prototype Porter Jarrard face routes—stout!

# HONEYMOONERS' LADDER AREA

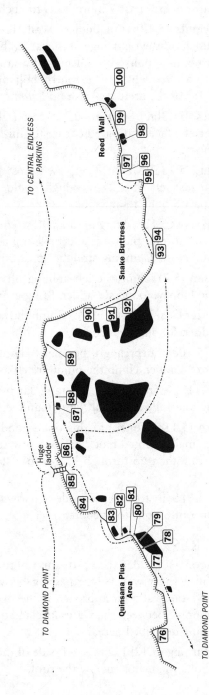

79. **Sacrilege** (5.12b) What a great route! Begin on top of the large "belay block" (stick-clip the first bolt) and grab flaky, slanting holds. Climb the beautiful, featured face past 8 more bolts to anchors.

80. **Jesus and Tequila** (5.12b) An Endless Wall classic! Stick-clip the first bolt, then launch off the right edge of the large "belay block." Climb the curving arête past 9 bolts to coldshuts. Variation: **Get Behind Thee Satan** (5.13a) Move right at the fourth bolt and crank up the very exposed far side of the arête to finish on *Satanic Verses*.

81. **Satanic Verses** (5.13b/c) Start about 15 feet right of the large "belay block." Climb the face and flared corner to finish on the high arête. 11 bolts to anchors.

82. **Quinsana Plus** (5.13a) Maybe The New's most popular 5.13a. Hyper-classic! Begin just left of a 25-foot-high boulder. Climb the beautiful orange wall past 8 bolts to anchors.

83. **Rainy Day Route** (5.12b) Start up a shallow corner to the roof, move about 6 feet left to pull the roof, and finish up a few more hard moves to the anchors. **Note:** Climbing straight up through the roof is 5.12d.

84. **Crescent Moon** (5.7) Climb the left-arching offwidth crack located 30 feet left of the Honeymooners' Ladder. Bring gear to 6 inches.

85. **The Bonemaster Gear Fling** (5.11b/c) Climb the face and small arête just left of the ladder. 8 bolts to anchors.

86. **Muckraker** (5.10d) Surprisingly popular. About 20 feet right of the Honeymooners' Ladder, climb the blunt arête past 8 bolts.

87. **Free Flow** (5.11b) Start on a flat, rectangular block below a low roof. Pull the 'hang and follow the bolt line up and left to anchors. 7 bolts.

88. **Channel Zero** (5.11c) Tune into this one—good climbing all the way. Begin from a small, pointed block below a low roof. Climb flaky holds to a small 'hang, then up through bulges to a slabby finish. 6 bolts to anchors.

89. **Double Flat** (5.9) Start from the left side of a low ledge and climb up and left along a line of 6 bolts to anchors.

## SNAKE BUTTRESS

From the Honeymooners' Ladder, the upstream trail turns away from the cliff and drops downhill a short way before passing between a couple of large boulders. The next large wall you approach is the overhanging, left side of Snake Buttress. Scramble between the white face and a huge block at its base to reach the first route described here.

90. **Mississippi Burning** (5.12b) On the left side of the wall, climb the sharp arête past 7 bolts to anchors below the roof.

91. **Dial 911** (5.13a) Oh, what an awesome route! Dial-in the technical sequence up the left side of the overhanging, white face. 8 bolts to anchors.

92. **The Racist** (5.13b) A Doug Reed testpiece. Starting on the block near the middle of the wall, power up the overhanging, white face past 9 bolts to anchors.

93. **Discombobulated** (5.11a/b) This popular route climbs the left line of bolts up the front of Snake Buttress. Begin 10 feet left of the large tree and climb the face, corner, and high roof to anchors. 8 bolts.

94. **The Legacy** (5.11b) Classic. Start behind the large tree and face climb up to the bolted crack/corner. Continue up the crack and through a roof, then work slightly right to anchors. **Variation** (5.11d) Above the roof, traverse left and finish up a more difficult sequence to a separate set of anchors. **Warning:** A 60-meter rope is required to lower from either set of anchors.

95. **Bullet the New Sky** (5.12a/b) Another stunning New River arête. Fire the arête on the right side of Snake Face. 8 bolts to anchors.

96. **Bloodshot** (5.13a) Begin 12 feet right of a wide crack and large corner. Climb the technical, bulging face past 7 bolts to anchors.

97. **The Pocket Route** (5.13a) Quite good. Locate the second line of bolts right of the wide crack and right-facing corner. Climb the smooth, orange face up and right to a weakness through a roof. 9 bolts to anchors.

98. **Vulcan Block** (5.12c) Start on a small boulder about 40 feet right of the large, inside corner and just right of a tree. Boulder up and right past 2 bolts, then aim straight up the face and finish through a high overhang. 9 bolts to anchors.

99. **Dissonance** (5.13a) Killer. Start at a crack through a low roof about 15 feet left of an arête. Climb the steep face past 9 bolts and a pin to anchors.

100. **New World Order** (5.12b) A popular 5.12b "project route." Start on a block and at the lip of a low roof on the right side of the arête. Climb the sustained face just left of the arête. 7 bolts to anchors.

## THE CIRQUE

If you climb solid 5.13 or want to work The New's only 5.14, then The Cirque of upper Endless Wall is the place for you. There is very little here for the "average climber," though, as nearly all the routes are between 5.12b and 5.14a. **Gear:** You'll need a 60-meter rope and as many as sixteen quickdraws.

# THE CIRQUE

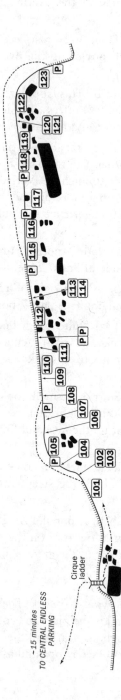

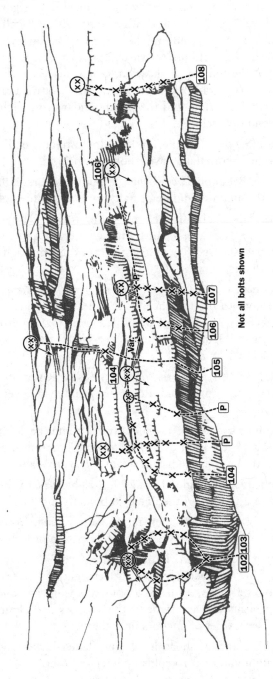

**Finding The Cirque:** Park at a pulloff along Lansing Road about 1.9 miles east of US 19. Follow an often-muddy trail about six to eight minutes to the clifftop trail above Central Endless Wall. Turn left and walk upstream just over five minutes to a downclimb ladder in a large chimney. Scramble down through boulders and continue 60 yards upstream to the beginning of The Cirque. **Note:** At the time of publication, a new, more direct trail was going in to The Cirque. This trail begins 50 yards farther down Lansing Road and roughly follows a powerline and the parkboundary to the clifftop near The Cirque ladder and downclimb.

101. **Hourglass (5.12a/b)** At the far left (downstream) end of The Cirque, climb a right-facing flake past 7 bolts to anchors.

102. **Nag (5.11b)** Begin on *The Warm-Up,* but at the first bolt move left and crank up through the middle of flaky roofs to anchors. 4 bolts.

103. **The Warm-Up (5.11a)** The easiest route in The Cirque begins 20 feet right of *Hourglass,* at a small right-facing crack and corner. Climb up and right past the first few bolts, then crank left through a juggy roof to anchors. 6 bolts.

104. **Old Testament (5.11b)** Start 20 feet right of *The Warm-Up.* The original route goes to the fourth bolt, then traverses right past three more bolts to anchors. Variation: **Satanic Traverses (5.12c)** From the anchors, move down and right to continue traversing for the full length of the low roof to anchors. 19 bolts.

105. **Proper Soul (5.14a)** The first 5.14 at the New River Gorge. This amazing route climbs up to and along the prominent, overhanging, right-facing corner.

106. **New Testament (5.12d)** Another traverse route. Begin at a small right-facing flake 15 feet right of *Proper Souls.* Climb up three bolts and get traversing to the right. Finish at *Satanic Traverses* anchors. 10 bolts.

107. **Norse Code (5.12d)** Begin about 20 feet right of *New Testament* and 10 feet right of a tree. Send the line of 6 bolts to anchors.

108. **Graffiti (5.12a/b)** Start at a left-facing, left-arching, 25-foot-high corner. Climb straight up over the flake to anchors. 5 bolts.

109. **Superstition (5.12d)** Two hard pitches, if you're up to it! Begin at a small, shallow, left-facing corner 25 feet right of *Graffiti.* Start beneath a low roof and follow a line of 5 bolts to a ledge and anchors. The second pitch begins 20 feet right of the anchors and climbs past 6 more bolts to a second set of anchors near the top.

110. **Sloth (5.12c)** Start at short, left-facing flakes 40 feet right of *Superstition.* Climb up and left to coldshut anchors. 6 bolts.

111. **Xanth (5.13b)** Engage 20 feet right of *Sloth* at a nice fingerslot about 8 feet up. Power up past 8 bolts to open coldshuts.

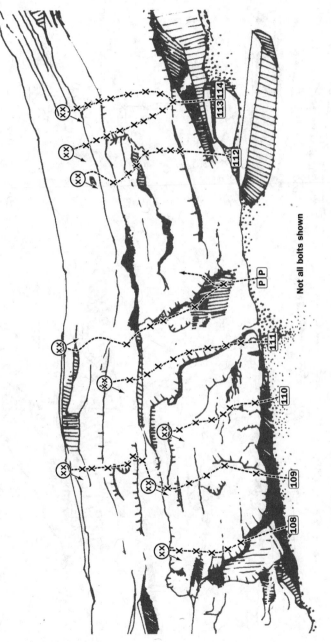

Not all bolts shown

# THE CIRQUE

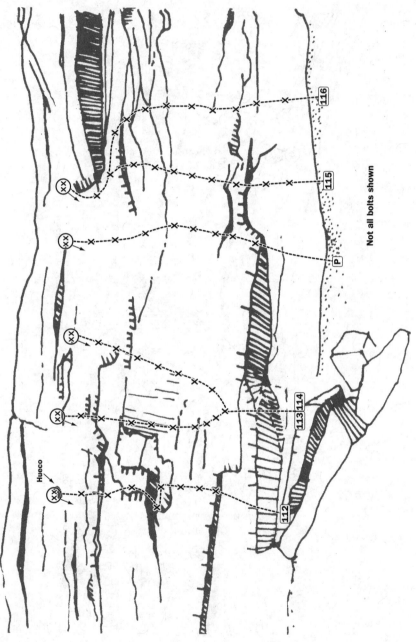

Not all bolts shown

116

115

P

113 114

112

Hueco

112. **High Yeller** (5.13a) Begin on stacked boulders below a 30-foot-wide, horizontal overhang about 10 feet up. Climb along the line of 8 bolts through tiered overhangs to anchors at a large hueco.

113. **Finders Keepers** (5.12b/c) Popular. Begin on boulders at the left end of a low roof and below numerous small, right-facing flakes. Crank up the left-hand line of bolts, using right-facing flakes to reach the anchors. 9 bolts.

114. **Losers Weepers** (5.13b/c) Climb *Finders Keepers* to the first bolt, then move right and up past 7 more bolts to anchors. 8 bolts.

115. **Ride the Lightning** (5.13b) This desperate route starts below an arch in the low roof. Climb along the bolt line to finish around the left side of a hanging, left-facing corner. 10 bolts.

116. **Ragnarock** (5.13b) Begin 25 feet right of *Ride the Lightning*. Follow bolts up and left to finish in the hanging, left-facing corner of *Ride the Lightning*. 10 bolts.

117. **Mr. McGoo** (5.12c) Start on a block about 20 feet right of a small tree. Climb the line of 7 bolts to finish through a roof.

118. **Brian's House of Cards** (5.13c/d) Another McCray desperate. Start at rust-colored rock 20 feet left of left-facing flakes. Power up a steep face to finish in a high right-facing dihedral.

119. **Hasta la Vista** (5.12c) Starting at short, left-facing flakes, work up and slightly left to anchors above a roof. 8 bolts.

120. **New Life** (5.11b/c) A good, long run! Start up right-facing flakes into a nicer, right-facing corner. Continue up and finish left, around possible wet rock, to anchors. 9 bolts.

121. **Live and Let Live** (5.12b) Climb *New Life* to its first bolt, then move right to climb an independent line of 8 bolts through double overhangs. Sometimes wet.

122. **Holier Than Thou** (5.12c/d) Begin from a vegetated stance below a left-arching flake. Escape the vines and climb along a 9-bolt line through a roof to anchors.

123. **The Blacklist** (5.12c/d) Start at a small, left-facing corner a few yards right of a large chimney. Climb the bolted line through roofs to anchors below a high roof. 10 bolts.

# BEAUTY MOUNTAIN

By itself, Beauty Mountain would be a major climbing area anywhere in the country. Simply put, it's got everything: classic cracks, killer sport routes, and good bouldering. Still, this area is overlooked by many visiting climbers

# THE CIRQUE

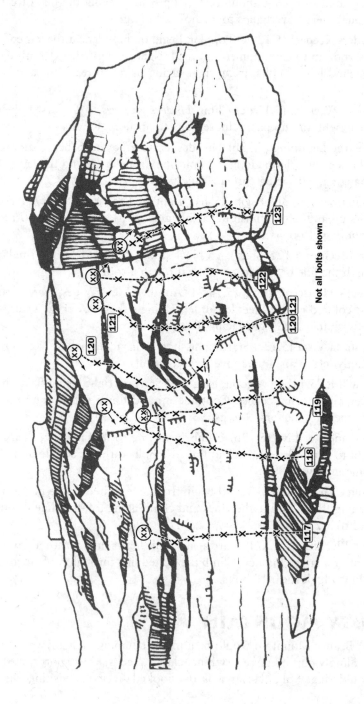

Not all bolts shown

# BEAUTY MOUNTAIN—LEFT SECTOR

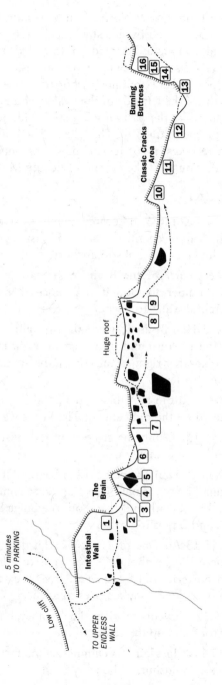

enamored of Endless Wall or Kaymoor. Make a break for Beauty; you won't be disappointed!

**Finding the crag:** From US 19 North, turn onto Lansing Road and travel 2.6 miles to a pulloff on the left (with a small, white schoolbus shelter). Cross Lansing Road and hike along a dirt road for 150 yards to a three-way split. Follow the middle lane back past two private homes, and continue along a faint trail below a power cut. Continue a short distance down a rocky trail and watch for a path off the left side of the trail as you pass a 20-foot, white outcrop on the right. Take the path down a steep hill, across a stream, and another 150 yards to The Brain Wall. The hike to The Brain Wall and the first climbs described here takes about ten minutes—it's only another fifteen to twenty minutes to the routes at the far end of Beauty Mountain.

## THE BRAIN WALL

1. **You Want It, You Got It** (5.9) Located on the left side of The Brain Wall, near where the trail meets the cliffbase and just right of two trees. This casual route climbs past 5 bolts to anchors.

2. **Journey to the Center of the Brain** (5.7) Start just left of the *Brain Teasers* crack. Boulder up and left to a stance, then wander up the center of the "cerebral wall" to anchors (55 feet).

3. **Brian Teasers** (5.10a) Begin at a prominent, right-leaning, finger crack. Climb along the fracture and into a small, right-facing corner. Move right (pin) into another right-facing corner, then climb up past two more pins to anchors (55 feet).

4. **Brain Tweezers** (5.10b) Enjoyable, and a good warm-up. Climb the line of 5 bolts located on the right side of The Brain Wall.

5. **M.E.N.S.A.** (5.11d) Climb the steep gray face just right of the large, dirty corner. 4 bolts to anchors.

6. **Chunky Monkey** (5.12b) The best 5.12 at Beauty Mountain. Start below a white, bulging "belly" about 30 feet up. Face climb up and right to a stance, then take a breath and crank out the bulge and roof to a tricky finish. 6 bolts and 2 pins to anchors.

7. **The Travisty** (5.13c/d) One of The New's hardest routes—a Harrison Dekker testpiece. Begin about 50 feet right of *Chunky Monkey* and climb up to a powerful bulge sequence. If you survive this, move right and finish up some lower-angle moves to anchors. 7 bolts.

8. **Green Envy** (5.12c) Twenty feet left of a chimney, climb through the left side of a low roof and up the center of the face. 7 bolts to anchors.

9. **Disturbance** (5.11d) Just left of a chimney, climb through a low roof and up a thin crack to coldshuts. 7 bolts.

# BURNING BUTTRESS AREA

10. **Happy Hands** (5.9) Begin at a flaring crack 30 feet right of a large, right-facing corner. Jam 70 feet to slings in a tree. Lower off.

11. **Spider Wand** (5.10b) Locate the left-facing dihedral about 40 feet right of *Happy Hands*. Fist-jam the dihedral, pass a roof on the right, then up a crack to the top (70 feet). Variation: **Wham, Bam, Thanks for the Jam** (5.10b) Climb first 25 feet of *Spider Wand*. Now, move right around the corner and jam the beautiful, 30-foot, hand crack that rejoins the regular route near the top.

12. **Burning Calves** (5.10b) A Beauty Mountain classic! Begin at a tall tree about 40 feet right of *Spider Wand* and jam the thin crack to the top (70 feet).

13. **Sportster** (5.13b) Start your engines at a 6-foot-high, right-facing corner below a pretty, orange-and-white wall. Race up this desperate line of 8 bolts.

14. **Grace Note** (5.12b) Ten feet left of *Rod Serling Crack,* you'll find *Grace*. She's got 7 bolts to clip, plus coldshuts.

15. **Rod Serling Crack** (5.10b) Climb the left-facing dihedral and crack through a small roof and up a finger crack to the top. Lower from slings in a tree (75 feet).

16. **Dark Shadows** (5.12a) Send the line of 6 bolts 10 feet right of *Rod Serling Crack*. Coldshut anchors.

## THUNDER BUTTRESS AREA

From Burning Buttress, hike about 200 yards through some boulders to the base of the highest section of Beauty Mountain. Watch for the *Chasin' the Wind* ledge about 30 feet up, below the stunning finger crack on the headwall.

17. **Fat Man's Folly** (5.9) Begin just left of the *Chasin'* ledge at a right-facing corner below a squeeze chimney and crack. Climb the dihedral to the roof, move left, and follow a narrowing crack (80 feet).

18. **Chasin' the Wind** (5.11b) The classic, splitter crack on the second pitch is worth the twenty-five-minute approach. The first pitch begins on a 12-foot high block just right of *Fat Man's Folly*. **Pitch 1:** Climb up and right past a bolt to a nice belay ledge (30 feet). **Pitch 2:** Climb the crack to its end and lower from anchors (65 feet).

19. **Gun Club** (5.12c) Line of 9 bolts just left of *Super Crack*. Free-soloed in 1991 by the late Dan Osman. Note: Take a 60-meter rope.

20. **Super Crack** (5.9+) Mega-classic! Climb the left-facing crack and corner (95 feet).

# BEAUTY MOUNTAIN—RIGHT SECTOR

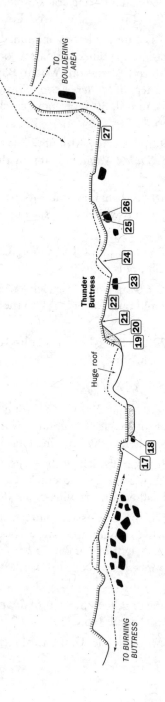

21. **Transcendence** (5.11c) Send the line of bolts up a colorful face just left of a large, right-facing crack and corner (75 feet).

22. **Right Son of Thunder** (5.11c) One of many great trad lines established by 1980s hardman Cal Swoger. Start 40 feet right of *Transcendence* and 12 feet left of an offwidth crack. Begin up a crack, then right past a bolt to a horizontal crack. Traverse left a few moves, then continue up the face to a ledge below a clifftop roof (80 feet).

23. **Concretina** (5.12a) Start on a block about 15 feet right of an offwidth crack. Climb the face past 6 bolts to coldshuts.

24. **Stabat Mater** (5.13b) Notable for its eyebolts, hanging belay, and difficulty! **Pitch 1:** Start on the block and climb past five bolts to hanging belay (5.13b, 35 feet). **Pitch 2:** Fire up past another 8 bolts to the top (5.12b, 60 feet). Established in 1988 by visiting Frenchman, Pierre Deliage.

25. **Loud Noise** (5.12b) Beginning from a block, climb the 95-foot line of 8 bolts to anchors. **Note:** Bring a 60-meter rope.

26. **Let's Make a Deal** (5.11c) Start on right side of the block and climb the face past 6 bolts to coldshuts.

27. **Welcome to Beauty** (5.11b) An area classic. Climb twin hand cracks to a roof, then up a finger crack to the top (90 feet).

# KAYMOOR

This north-facing area is extraordinarily popular with sport climbers, especially during hot weather. Best known for "The Hole" and its difficult routes through a huge, tiered roof system, there is also an excellent selection of more moderate routes at the Butcher Branch area. Bottomline: if you like clipping bolts, Kaymoor has something for everyone!

**Finding the crag:** Take the Fayetteville exit off US 19 and follow WV 16 East through this booming metropolis. Your next turn is a left onto Gatewood Road when you spot Sherry's Beer Store on the right. Take Gatewood Road for 1.9 miles, then turn left at the sign to "Kaymoor #1." The Kaymoor parking area is located one mile down this potholed road, just beyond Roger's Rocky Top Retreat. A second parking lot is located 100 yards farther down the gravel road.

Two trails provide access to Kaymoor. From the first parking area, the Kaymoor Miner's Trail drops quickly downhill to a set of steps located between The Hole and First Buttress areas. This approach takes less than ten minutes. A second trail offers a fifteen-minute clifftop approach to the far end of Kaymoor. Park in the far lot and follow the Butcher Branch/Long Point Trail for ten to fifteen minutes until you can descend a series of switchbacks

# FAYETTEVILLE AND KAYMOOR AREA

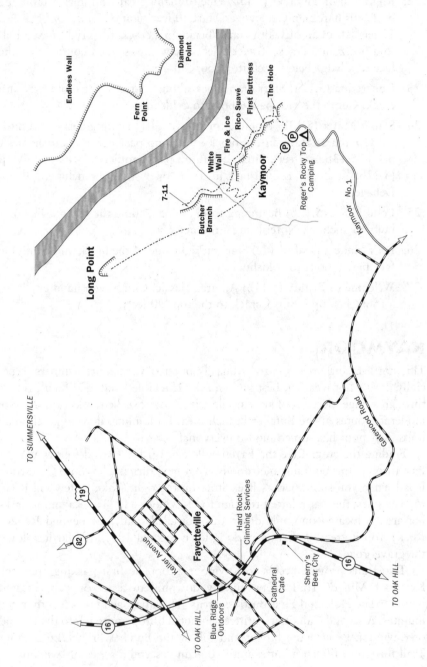

THE HOLE

through the cliff break between White Wall and Butcher Branch. Upon reaching the bottom, turn left and hike about 200 yards to the beginning of Butcher Branch, or turn right and hike an equal distance to White Wall.

## THE HOLE

1. **Project** (5.??) Farthest left line of bolts through the roof. Begin up blocky rock as for *Mojo Hand,* but follow the left line of bolts.

2. **Mojo Hand** (5.12d) Boulder up blocky rock to the first clip, then crank up and right past 5 more bolts to anchors.

3. **Lactic Acid Bath** (5.12d) The route that started it all at Kaymoor. A hyper-classic established by Doug Reed in April 1991. The *Devil Doll* variation is also quite good. Beginning near the center of the huge roof system, start up poor rock past a bolt, then fire out the tiered roofs past eight more bolts to anchors. Don't miss the no-hands rest! Variation 1: **Devil Doll** (5.12d) At the fifth bolt, diverge left past a couple of bolts to finish on the last portion of *Mojo Hand.* Variation 2: **In the Flat Field** (5.13b/c) At the seventh bolt, move left past three more bolts to anchors. Variation 3: **Massacre** (5.13a) From the last bolt, move left and climb by another bolt to independent anchors.

4. **Blood Raid** (5.13a) Begin up a poor-quality, right-facing flake system, then take a breath and power out through a pair of overhangs (Velcro clip on second roof). Finish right to anchors on *Skull Poke.*

5. **Skull Poke** (5.12b/c) Starting up a right-facing flake (bolt), crank out the tiered roofs past 6 bolts. The route is 5.12b if you move right around the last bolt, or 5.12c if you climb straight up.

6. **Burning Cross** (5.13a) Start up the prominent, right-facing corner and fire straight up through the roofs to the highest set of anchors. Variation: **Yowsah** (5.12a) A super-popular link-up established by Mike Freeman. Climb *Burning Cross* to the sixth bolt, then move left to finish past one more bolt to the anchors on *Skull Poke.*

7. **Scar Lover** (5.12c) Climb the *Burning Cross* corner past two bolts, then move right and pull through roofs past 5 more bolts to anchors.

8. **Final Exit** (5.12b/c) Locate the farthest right line of bolts in The Hole area. Face climb past 3 bolts, then up through double roofs and past 4 more bolts to anchors.

## FIRST BUTTRESS

After descending the wooden steps, bear left and follow the Kaymoor Miner's Trail about 50 yards to a faint path leading to the beginning of First Buttress.

# KAYMOOR—LEFT SECTOR

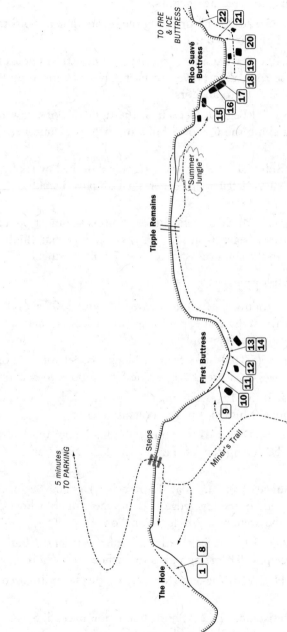

9. **World's Hardest** (5.12a) The first route (from left to right) is an 8-bolt line through multiple overhangs, moving right at the fourth bolt. Variation: **Haulage** (5.12c/d) From the fourth bolt, move left and crank past four more clips to separate anchors.

10. **The Tantrum** (5.12d) Climb up along the second line of bolts through a flaky roof. 7 bolts to anchors.

11. **Sanctified** (5.13a) Start at a flake running out near the middle of the low roof. Send the roof, then power up past 7 bolts to finish up the arête, passing 3 more bolts to anchors.

12. **Tarbaby** (5.12a/b) Begin 6 feet left of the right end of a low roof. Pull the roof and climb the line of 5 bolts to anchors at mid-height on the cliff.

13. **Oh, It's You Bob** (5.11b) Start at the right end of the low roof. Climb up and left to a short, left-facing corner, then up past 3 small overhangs to anchors.

14. **Magnitude** (5.11c/d) This vertical face climb is the most popular route on First Buttress. Begin as in for *Oh, It's You Bob,* but climb the right line of bolts up the smooth, vertical face. 7 bolts to anchors.

## RICO SUAVÉ BUTTRESS

From First Buttress, follow the trail downstream about 250 yards to the popular Rico Suavé Buttress. En route, you'll pass a few less-popular sport routes and the remains of the mining tipple.

15. **Totally Tammy** (5.10a) Start from a block just left of the corner and climb nice moves up a pretty, low-angle face. 5 bolts to anchors.

16. **Grit and Bear It** (5.11a) Beginning off the large, ledgy block, climb the middle of a nice, white face past 5 bolts to anchors.

17. **Not on the First Date** (5.11c) Start on ledge below the left side of a broad arête. Dance up the left face of the *Rico Suavé* arête. 4 bolts to anchors.

18. **The Rico Suavé Arête** (5.10a) Extremely popular. Begin from the extreme right end of the low ledge, or from the ground below. Climb the right side of the arête past 7 bolts to anchors.

19. **Out of the Bag** (5.11c/d) Sustained and quite excellent! Climb the middle of the face past left-facing flakes to anchors below a roof. 8 bolts.

20. **Preparation H** (5.11d) Zig-zag your way up this beautiful arête. 6 bolts to anchors.

21. **Pockets of Resistance** (5.12a) Short, but action packed! Starting 10 feet right of the outside corner, climb past four bolts to anchors.

22. **Nude Brute** (5.13a) Climb the steep, clean face located right of *Pockets of Resistance*. 7 bolts to anchors.

## FIRE AND ICE BUTTRESS

About 200 yards downstream of the Rico Suavé area is the Fire and Ice Buttress. The access trail becomes quite vegetated during the summer months. It's passable, but a bit jungle-ish.

23. **SLAP** (5.12a) Climb the short arête located left of the large, prominent hueco. 4 bolts to anchors.

24. **Carolina Crocker and the Tipple of Doom** (5.12a) Classic. On the front of the buttress, begin under small, tiered overhangs and follow the line of 10 bolts to anchors. Six feet right is the equally classic *Raiders of the Lost Crag* (5.10b) crack system.

25. **White Lightning** (5.13b) Begin at a short, left-facing corner just right of a low roof. Climb the clean, white, slightly overhanging face. 9 bolts to anchors.

26. **Thunder Struck** (5.12b) A Doug Cosby classic. Start on a tall, detached flake and carefully climb up to the bulging, sustained finish up the headwall.

27. **Almost Heaven** (5.10b) A short but popular climb up the face right of *Thunder Struck*. 4 bolts to anchors.

## WHITE WALL

From Fire and Ice Buttress, continue downstream until the trail curls around another buttress. The smooth, downstream-facing side of the buttress is White Wall.

28. **Moon Child Posse** (5.11c) Begin left of a low roof and climb the steep face to a lower-angle conclusion. 8 bolts to anchors.

29. **I Smell A-rête** (5.11c) The left-hand route up White Wall is a 7-bolt romp up the arête.

30. **Dining at the Alter** (5.12a) A popular feast! Start up just left of a vertical seam and past a detached flake to the first bolt. Continue past 6 more bolts to anchors.

## BUTCHER BRANCH

Butcher Branch is Kaymoor's most popular area, probably because of its high concentration of 5.10 and 5.11 sport climbs. The crags here face primarily north, so they remain relatively cool on hot summer days. However, some of the routes can remain damp for a long time after a heavy rain—Endless Wall might be a better choice on such days.

# KAYMOOR—MIDDLE SECTOR

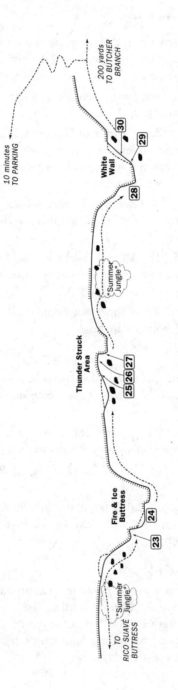

# KAYMOOR—RIGHT SECTOR

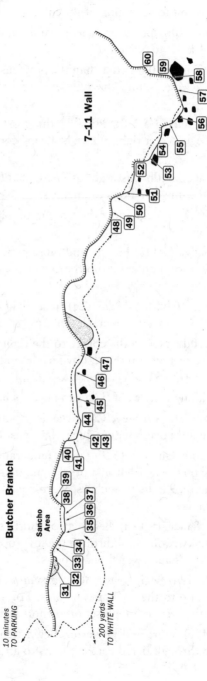

**Finding the area:** The best approach is via the Butcher Branch/Long Point Trail, which begins from the far end of the second Kaymoor parking area. The hike takes about fifteen minutes. From White Wall, you can hike the cliffbase about 400 yards to the beginning of Butcher Branch.

31. **Arpeggio** (5.10d) Begin on a ledge and climb the left line of bolts to anchors. 4 bolts to anchors.

32. **Play It by Ear** (5.10a) Better than the previous route. From the right side of the low ledge, climb the right line of bolts to anchors. 6 bolts to anchors.

33. **The Green Piece** (5.10b) Possibly the most popular 5.10 at Butcher Branch. Begin 6 feet right of a right-facing corner and climb past 6 bolts to anchors.

34. **Low Voltage** (5.10b) Just right of *The Green Piece,* boulder up and right to climb the line of 7 bolts to anchors.

35. **Ministry** (5.12b) Begin near the left end of a low roof and fire up past 4 bolts to low anchors.

36. **Sancho Belige** (5.11c) Pumpy and quite popular. Begin near the middle of the low roof, and crank up the center of the bulging face. 7 bolts to anchors.

37. **The Bicycle Club** (5.11d/5.12a) Just right of *Sancho Belige,* climb through the low roof at a crack and up past 5 bolts to anchors.

38. **Boing** (5.10d) Around the corner to the right of the *Sancho* wall, climb the left line of bolts up the slabby face. 6 bolts to anchors.

39. **Springer** (5.10b) Much better than the show. Climb the nice, less-than-vert face along a series of flakes to anchors below a huge roof.

40. **Lost Souls** (5.12a) A Steve Cater classic. About 50 feet right of *Springer,* climb a slightly overhanging, juggy face past 6 bolts to anchors.

41. **Flight of the Gumbie** (5.9) Long, moderate, and extremely popular. Beginning on the face left of a prominent arête, climb up and right along the nice arête. 9 bolts to anchors. **Warning:** Need 60-meter rope to lower from anchors.

42. **Bourbon Sauce** (5.11d) Begin at a short, shallow left-facing corner below a flaky roof. Haul through the low roof, then straight up the face past another 'hang to anchors. 4 bolts.

43. **Control** (5.12a) Begin as for *Bourbon Sauce,* but move right at the roof and crank up to the anchors on *Kaos.* From here, move back left and finish up the face to a high set of anchors. 7 bolts.

44. **Kaos** (5.12c) Short and powerful. Begin right of *Bourbon Sauce,* then power up through tiered roofs. 4 bolts to anchors.

45. **Mo' Betta' Holds** (5.11c/d) Big roof, big holds, big fun! Start at a short, right-facing corner with blocks at its base. Climb the 6-bolt line out the big roof to anchors.

46. **All the Right Moves** (5.11d) Begin in a left-facing corner about 15 feet right of a tall, dead tree. Start up the corner and around the right side of a low roof to the first bolt. Apply a diverse range of moves straight up through the bulging finish. 8 bolts to anchors.

47. **Hard-Core Female Thrash** (5.11c) Lots of really good climbing. Begin on a block at the right side of the face located just before the trail cuts off toward 7–11 Wall. Climb up the arête to a stance, then move up and left into a prominent dihedral and finish through a high roof to anchors. 6 bolts.

## 7–11 WALL

Follow the cliffbase trail roughly 150 yards downstream to the first route on 7–11 Wall.

48. **Squirrely Adventure** (5.10a) This first route on the wall begins just right of a hemlock tree. Climb past 8 bolts to anchors.

49. **Fearless Symmetry** (5.11d) Start on a small boulder 10 feet right of *Squirrely Adventure*. Climb the right side of a small arête, then up the tiger-striped face to anchors. 6 bolts.

50. **The Sting** (5.12a) Begin at a crack just right of a vegetated corner and work up the pretty face past 7 bolts. Watch for a wasp nest on the right.

51. **Tit Speed** (5.11c) Climb the white face past the left side of a low roof. 7 bolts to anchors.

52. **Tony the Tiger** (5.11c) Begin on a ledge just left of a left-facing corner. Climb up past a roof, then up the steep, tiger-striped face to anchors. 9 bolts.

53. **Scenic Adult** (5.11c/d) A truly great climb! Begin on a large block below a sharp arête. Send the prominent arête past 10 clips to anchors. **Warning:** A 60-meter rope is required to lower from the anchors.

54. **Bimbo Shire** (5.11b) Technical, sustained, and quite popular. Begin at a tall tree and climb up the line of 8 bolts to anchors.

55. **Mr. Hollywood** (5.11d/5.12a) Start at a crack on the left side of a blunt arête. Move up and right to the first bolt, and continue along the bolt line to anchors. 5 bolts.

56. **Slash and Burn** (5.12c/d) Classic, if you climb the grade. Start on a block and move out right to the first bolt. Power up the steep, cruxy face (somewhat reachy) past 8 more bolts to anchors.

*Doug Cosby leading Slash and Burn (5.12c/d), Kaymoor.* PHOTO BY TOM ISAACSON

57. **Buzz Kill** (5.12c) Thirty feet right of *Slash and Burn,* climb the right-arching line up the smooth face. 10 bolts to anchors.

58. **First Steps** (5.10c) A good 5.10 outing or warm-up route. Begin on top of a 20-foot-high block located just right of a nice 5.10 hand crack. Climb the arête and face past 6 bolts to anchors.

59. **Fuel Injector** (5.13b) Reachy, and, ahem, hard! Start right of the huge boulder and power up the face and 'hang to anchors. 8 bolts.

60. **The Butcher Man** (5.11a) Climb the short arête on the far right side of 7–11 Wall. 4 bolts to anchors.

# OTHER WEST VIRGINIA AREAS

Wild, wonderful West Virginia has more than its share of great crags, and it's possible that you don't know about all of them. In previous chapters, I covered the world-class areas of Seneca Rocks and the New River Gorge, as well as a few other quality crags such as Coopers Rock, Summersville Lake, and Nelson Rocks Preserve. Below I'll introduce you to a few more areas that, while not destination crags, do offer some excellent climbing if you live nearby.

## BOZOO

### OVERVIEW

If the miles of "endless" Nuttall Sandstone walls at the New River Gorge aren't enough for you, let it be known that there is another small stretch of quality rock about 50 miles upstream from The New. In this rare case, "upstream" means "south," and it's just above the Virginia–West Virginia border that you'll find Bluestone Lake State Park and a recently developed cliff known as Bozoo.

While it's hard to imagine anyone driving south from The New to climb at this modest area of fewer than fifty routes, Bozoo is a worthwhile day-trip destination for climbers coming from places farther south, like Blacksburg and Roanoke. The rock at Bozoo is identical to The New, with colorful, bullet-hard faces that average vertical to overhanging. The majority of the routes follow all-gear natural lines, and there are a number of climbs that, no doubt, would be classics at The New, including *Birth Canal* (5.9), *Gold Finger* (5.9+), and *Superchunks, Marge,* and *Homer* (all 5.11b/c).

A majority of the traditional lines were established by Paul Sullivan and friends in the early- to mid-1990s. Bozoo has recently seen a number of sport routes added as well, including the enjoyable *Barking Spiders* (5.9-), *Chuck's Route* (5.10a), *Lime House* (5.10c), and Swiss Andy's testpiece, *Revelation of Doom* (5.13c/d).

# BOZOO, WEST VIRGINIA
# (SHERMAN BALLARD RECREATION AREA,
# BLUESTONE STATE PARK)

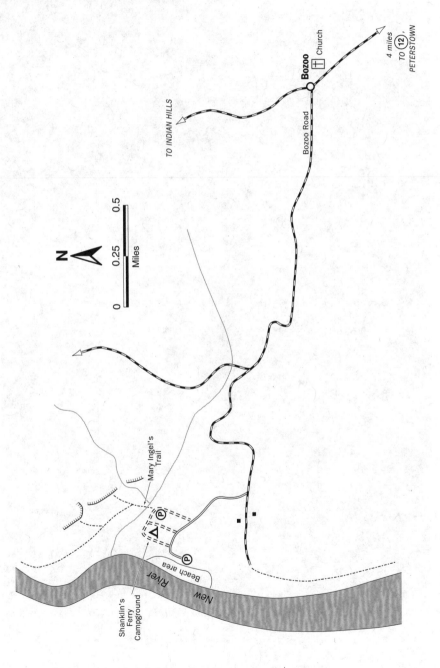

*Daniel Miller on Bovine Crack (5.10b), Bovine Wall, Bozoo.* PHOTO BY HARRISON SHULL

# TRIP PLANNING INFORMATION

**General description:** Clean, steep Nuttall Sandstone cliffs up to 60 feet high. The majority of routes are traditional or mixed-protection lead climbs, although there are several sport-style bolted routes.

**Location:** The crags are near the edge of Bluestone Lake State Park, along the New River in extreme southern West Virginia. This is about one hour north of Blacksburg, Virginia, and an hour-and-a-half south of the New River Gorge.

**Camping:** Shanklin's Ferry Campground is located adjacent to the climbers' parking area. There is a beach area along the river, but no showers. Cost is $8.00 per night for groups of six or fewer.

**Climbing season:** Year-round climbing is possible, although spring and fall are best.

**Gear:** A standard rack of traditional gear up to 4 inches, a dozen quickdraws, and a 50-meter (165-foot) rope.

**Restrictions and access issues:** The crags are located on the edge of Bluestone Lake State Park, and portions of the rock may lie on private property. At present, there are no restrictions.

**Guidebooks:** None.

**Nearby mountain shops:** Blue Ridge Outdoors (540–774–4311) in Blacksburg, Virginia, is the closest source of climbing supplies.

**Services:** Gas and food are available in Peterstown, West Virginia, just 8 miles south of Bozoo. All services are available about 30 miles to the west in Bluefield, West Virginia.

**Emergency services:** Call State Police at 304–466–2800. Hospitals are forty-five minutes to an hour away. Columbia St. Luke's Hospital (304–327–2900) is in Bluefield, West Virginia, and Columbia Montgomery Hospital (540–951–1111) is located in Blacksburg, Virginia.

**Nearby climbing areas:** The region's finest climbing area, the New River Gorge, is located just 90 minutes north, near Fayetteville.

**Nearby attractions:** Bluestone Lake Recreational Area offers boating, fishing, swimming, hiking, and camping within walking distance of the crags.

**Finding the crags:** From the town of Rich Creek on US 340 near the Virginia/West Virginia border, follow US 219 1.7 miles north to Peterstown. Take WV 12 North for 1.2 miles, then bear left on Bozoo Road and continue 4 miles to the small town of Bozoo (church on right). Turn left and go 2.2 miles to a fork in the road. Bear left and drive downhill to another fork at the park entrance. Go right along a gravel road to a large, open field on the right. Here, take the first right onto a faint dirt road across the top of the grassy field. Park at the far upper corner of the grassy field, near the sign to the Mary Ingel's Trail. The park ranger insists that you parallel-park with the front of your car facing the river. From here, follow the Mary Ingel's Trail a short distance until

# BOZOO—RIGHT SECTOR

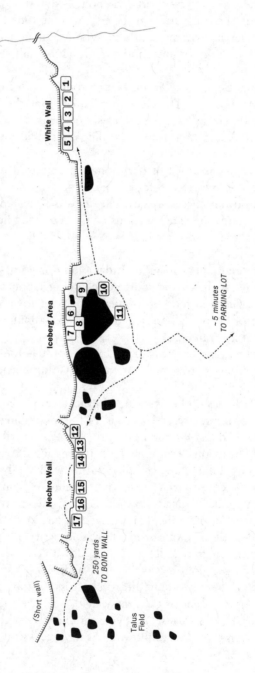

you cross a small stream. Beyond this, stay right at the fork in the trail and proceed uphill about five minutes to arrive at the Iceberg Area.

## WHITE WALL

This wall is located about 100 yards right of where the approach trail reaches the cliff at the Iceberg Area. **Descent:** Locate slippery downclimbs on either side of White Wall, or better yet, rappel from a tree above *Birth Canal*.

1. **Superchunks** (5.11b/c) Begin below a crack with pitons located on the far right side of White Wall. Climb the difficult crack to an overhang. Move right and continue up a seam and crack to the top.

2. **Chunks** (5.9) Start a few feet left of *Superchunks* and climb a right-facing, flaky corner up to the overhang. Traverse right about 10 feet and finish up the seam and crack per *Superchunks*.

3. **Bozooka** (5.9+) Start 12 feet right of the *Birth Canal* notch. Climb a left-facing flake to a small overhang at mid-height. Move right about 6 feet to gain a right-facing corner. Ascend this, then finish slightly left up easier rock. Variation: **Direct** (5.11c) From the mid-height overhang, continue straight up the thin face past a bolt to the easier finish.

4. **Birth Canal** (5.9) Classic all the way, and a great name to boot! Begin below the cool-looking "birth canal" notch about 20 feet up. Start up awkward moves to gain the "birth canal," then continue up a crack and flake to a nice finish (50 feet). **Gear:** Small to medium stoppers and cams.

5. **Wayne's Route** (5.9+) Start at an obvious crack system left of a large tree. Climb the crack to half-height, move right to a bolt, and fire straight up to coldshuts.

## ICEBERG AREA

Located at the top of the approach trail, just over five minutes from the parking area. Several topropes are possible on the Iceberg Block. Routes 6–8 are located in the corridor behind the block.

6. **Inflatable Forearms** (5.11d/5.12a) Often wet and generally green—the least desirable climb in this area. Zig-zag up thin, sustained moves on the green, right side of the corridor wall. 4 bolts to anchors.

7. **Barking Spiders** (5.9-) A great climb, and not as scary and run-out as it looks. Climb on great holds up the left side of the corridor wall. 2 bolts to anchors.

8. **Chuck's Route** (5.10a) Popular. This sport route is located opposite *Barking Spiders,* on the back side of the Iceberg Block. 3 bolts to anchors.

9. **Tip of the Iceberg** (5.10b/c) Start below the right side of a low roof on the Iceberg Block, at the entrance to the corridor. Climb up and left, then ascend a shallow corner to anchors.

10. **Icebreaker** (5.7) A good moderate route, but most often climbed to set up topropes on other routes. Climb the obvious, right-facing corner until you can exit left and finish up easy face moves to the top.

11. **Phat Back** (5.8) Begin on the right side of a low, triangle-shaped roof. Work left and up a ramp to a stance. Finish up the nice face past 2 bolts.

## NECRO WALL

From the Iceberg Block, follow the trail left through a few boulders and along a short, licheny face to Necro Wall.

12. **Cruella de Vil** (5.7) A nice, 35-foot corner. Climb the left-facing corner to a tree. Lower or rappel from slings.

13. **Tiers of Blood** (5.12c/d) Start up through a low roof and past a bolt, then climb up thin cracks and corners to the top (65 feet).

14. **Inject the Venom** (5.12a/b) Begin below a thin crack, then climb to a bolt about 20 feet up. Follow the crack past the bolt to finish up a left-facing corner (65 feet).

15. **Revelation of Doom** (5.13c/d) The Bozoo testpiece—steep and impressive. Start below a hole about 10 feet up and climb up the beautiful, overhanging wall to chains. 4 bolts.

16. **K.P. Corner** (5.10b) Start below a high roof and climb the right crack. Exit left to the top.

17. **Necromancer** (5.10d) Climb the left crack up to the roof. Head left to the top.

## BOND WALL

Follow the trail for about five minutes, passing a low wall and crossing a major talus field. You come to a wildly featured, basalt-like face with a couple of so-so trade routes. The three routes listed here are located on the left side of this face and just right of a few large blocks.

18. **Gold Finger** (5.9+) Nice! Climb the great-looking, left-facing corner and crack. Rappel, or lower from slings on a tree to the left.

19. **Dr. No** (project) 3 bolts up a short, blank arête.

20. **Detachable Penis** (5.10b/c) A popular toprope after climbing *Gold Finger*. Climb the flaky crack and corner to a roof and tree (with slings) on the right.

# BOZOO—LEFT SECTOR

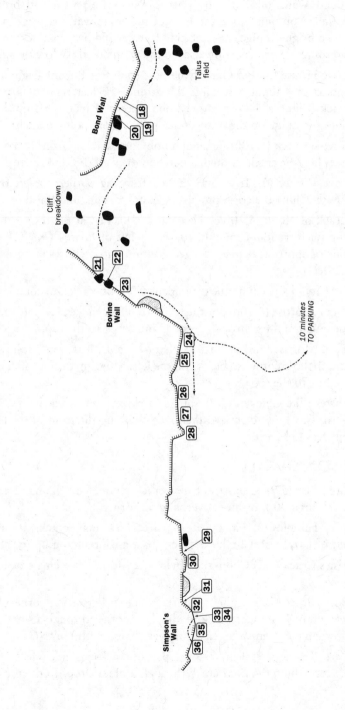

## BOVINE WALL

From Bond Wall, follow the trail a short distance past a cliff break to an orange wall. Continue along the base of the short wall, passing a few short routes, to a bright orange, 45-foot-high face capped by two blocky roofs. The first two routes described below ascend the wall directly below the high roofs.

21. **Lime House** (5.10c) One of the best routes at Bozoo! Begin at a large chockstone about 5 feet off the ground 10 feet right of a prominent crack. Climb a 5.6 crack (need one piece of 1-inch gear) up to the first bolt. Continue up the orange face past 2 more bolts to anchors.

22. **Bovine Crack** (5.10b) Begin at an obvious crack in front of a horizontal tree. Jam the crack through a notch in the roof (bolt) to the top (45 feet).

23. **Love Burger** (5.11b/c) Start at a left-facing corner 15 left of *Bovine Crack*. Climb the corner to a stance, move right, and finish up the arête.

24. **Crack of Noon** (5.10b/c) This route is located at the top of the far-left approach trail and roughly 100 yards left of *Bovine Crack*. Begin up a pair of short cracks to a ledge. Continue up a crack system to the top (50 feet).

25. **Fat City** (5.7+) Climb the prominent, 50-foot crack and chimney system.

26. **Rigor Mortise** (5.10d) Start up a short, left-facing corner and crack, then move left and up through a notch and crack to the top.

27. **Thru-Mortise** (5.8) Begin 5 feet left of *Rigor Mortise* and follow a crack and shallow corner to blocks on the left. Move up over a small roof with a crack to the top.

28. **Tastes Like Chicken** (5.7) Start at a short hand crack below a narrow buttress. Climb the crack, then face climb up the front of the low-angle buttress (50 feet).

## SIMPSON'S WALL

29. **Gold Fist** (5.9) A short but nice crack climb. Jam the hand-and-finger crack up a 30-foot-high, overhanging corner.

30. **Love Handles** (5.10a) Locate a pair of low-angle cracks about 20 feet left of *Gold Fist*. Climb the cracks past a roof and on up to the top.

31. **Lisa's Crack** (5.7) Climb the obvious, 25-foot, left-facing crack and corner.

32. **Bart Direct** (5.9) Begin at a dirty, shallow left-facing corner about 10 feet left of *Lisa's Crack*. Climb the flaky corner through a small, notched overhang and finish up easier moves shared with *Bart's Crack*.

33. **Bart's Crack** (5.9) Begin below a pair of cracks just a few feet left of *Bart Direct*. Climb the right crack through a blocky roof to the top.

34. **Lil Maggie** (5.8) Start as for *Bart's Crack,* but climb the left crack through the left side of the roof to finish at a pine tree.

35. **Homer** (5.11b/c) Start near the right side of a 15-foot-high, overhanging wall. Boulder up to a good jug and crank through the bulge along a crack to shared anchors (40 feet).

36. **Marge** (5.11b/c) Start on a block just left of *Homer.* Climb the crack through the bulge and up to anchors.

# FRANKLIN

## OVERVIEW
Midway between Harrisonburg, Virginia, and Seneca Rocks is a climbing area unique to the region. Located just west of the small town of Franklin, the area—some call it "Cranklin"—consists of several small limestone cliffs along the east side of the South Branch of the Potomac River.

Since about 1990, these crags have been quietly developed by climbers from both the Harrisonburg and Seneca Rocks areas as an alternative to climbing at the larger, traditional crags nearby. While certainly not a destination crag for climbers outside the local region, Franklin does possess a few dozen good lines up to 80 feet. A few of the better climbs are *Jumpstart* (5.8), *Blood, Sweat, and Chalk* (5.9+), *Decompression Sickness* (5.10b/c), and *Barnacle Bill* (5.11b). A number of harder routes are located at the less-popular River's Bend area (not covered in this guide) located about a twenty-minute hike downstream.

It's important to note that the Franklin crags are on private property and have been closed to climbing twice in the last decade. At present, the area is posted "No Trespassing" to minimize liability, but the landowner has been very gracious in allowing people to continue climbing. This is a similar situation to the Southern Pillar at Seneca Rocks, and one can assume the area will stay open as long as climbers recreate safely and remain good stewards of the land. Most importantly, if you show up and there is fresh evidence that climbing is no longer allowed, please respect the landowner's wishes and go climb somewhere else. If in doubt, talk to Kris Kirk at CMI (on Mill Street in Franklin) for the latest scoop on the area.

## TRIP PLANNING INFORMATION
**General description:** Rare Mid-Atlantic limestone sport climbing up to 80 feet.

**Location:** Along the South Branch of the Potomac River, 1 mile west of Franklin, West Virginia.

# FRANKLIN OVERVIEW

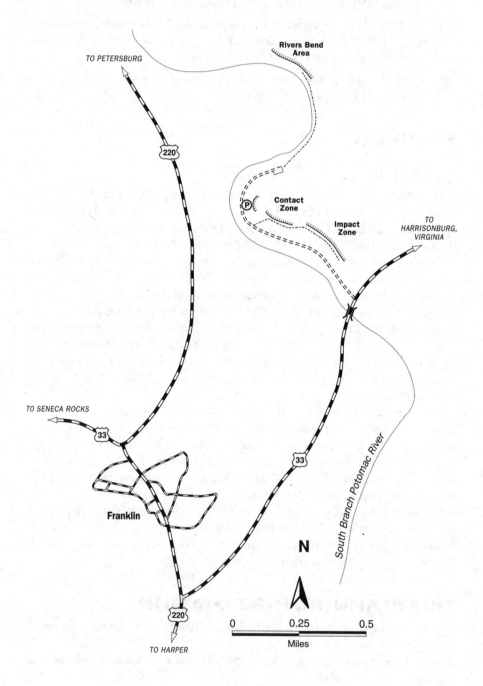

TO PETERSBURG

Rivers Bend
Area

220

Contact
Zone

Impact
Zone

TO
HARRISONBURG,
VIRGINIA

TO SENECA ROCKS

33

Franklin

South Branch Potomac River

33

N

220

TO HARPER

0      0.25      0.5

Miles

**Camping:** Camping at Franklin is not advised. Most persons day-trip from Harrisonburg or from the Seneca Rocks region.

**Climbing season:** Year-round.

**Gear:** A dozen quickdraws and a 50-meter (165-foot) rope.

**Restrictions and access issues:** This area is on private property and has been closed to climbing twice. Presently, the landowner has the area posted, but the area is open for recreational use, including climbing. As always, be a good steward of the land and exhibit your best behavior when visited by locals. Contact Kris Kirk at CMI in Franklin if you have any doubt about the current access situation.

**Guidebooks:** Numerous topos and mini-guides have been in circulation since the early 1990s. Information is occasionally available on the Internet, and supplementary topos are available at the CMI store in Franklin.

**Nearby mountain shops and guide services:** CMI (304–358–7041) is the local climbing shop, located just a few minutes from the rocks. At the main intersection in Franklin (with Mean Gene's Burgers), take US 220 South and turn left into the first street. Follow this to Mill Street, and you'll find CMI next to the community center and pool.

**Services:** All services are available less than a mile from the crag in the booming Franklin metropolitan area.

**Emergency services:** Call the Pendleton County Sherriff (304–358–2214) or the State Police (304–358–2214) in Franklin. The nearest hospital is Rockingham Memorial Hospital (540–433–4100) in Harrisonburg, Virginia.

**Nearby climbing areas:** Nelson Rocks Preserve and Seneca Rocks are just over a half-hour to the west. Good bouldering can be found about forty-five minutes east of Franklin at Rawley Springs, Virginia.

**Nearby attractions:** The South Branch of the Potomac River near Franklin is a popular fishing spot. Of course, there are countless recreational activities and tourist stops in the vicinity of Seneca Rocks.

**Finding the crags:** About 1 mile east of Franklin on US 33, turn north onto a gravel road that begins next to a bridge over the South Branch of the Potomac River. Follow the road along the river for almost 0.5 mile and park in a small pulloff on the right. If the pulloff is full, continue down the gravel road and park near the dam. Be careful never to block the gravel road—this would be a quick way to upset the locals who visit the area.

## PARKING AREA WALL

The small outcrop at the parking area has three routes.

1. **Left route** (5.10d) Climb the face past a series of small dihedrals. 6 bolts to anchors.
2. **Middle** (5.10b/c) Ascend the right-facing dihedral through a notch to anchors. 4 bolts.

3. **Right** (5.10a) Begin at spray-painted "Mike" at the cliffbase. Send the white face through a roof to anchors. 7 bolts.

## CONTACT ZONE

**Finding the cliff:** From the parking pulloff, hike back out the gravel road (south) about 60 yards to a trail on the left. Follow the trail uphill to the beginning of Contact Zone. The trail along the cliffbase continues right and up a short hill to the beginning of Impact Zone.

4. **Barney Rubble** (5.11b) Climb the middle of the downstream-facing, white wall to shared anchors on *Potential Energy*. 5 bolts.

5. **Potential Energy** (5.10b) Popular. Climb the arête just right of *Barney Rubble*. 5 bolts to anchors.

6. **Dynosaurus** (5.12a) Begin in a chossy, right-facing corner, move up and left to a white arête, then up through an overhang to anchors. 7 bolts.

7. **Roofasaurus** (5.11d) Start in the chossy corner and follow bolts that lead through a roof and up a hanging corner to anchors. 6 bolts.

8. **Hello** (5.10d) Start 8 feet right of a chimney and climb past 5 bolts to finish up a crack through a bulge. A mixed route—bring a few small- to medium-sized cams for the top.

9. **Lost Planet Airmen** (5.11c) Begin at a shallow, short, left-facing corner 10 feet right of the chimney. Climb up and through the right side of the overhang to anchors. 6 bolts.

10. **Bircham's Beach** (5.10a) Both *Bircham* routes are quite good. Beginning at a tree, send the line of 6 bolts up the bright white face to anchors.

11. **Bircham's Other** (5.9) Start at a shallow, right-facing corner just right of *Bircham's Beach*. Climb the corner, then move right around a roof to anchors. 7 bolts.

12. **Break the Chain** (5.10c) Beginning at a tree with two trunks, climb the white face past an overhang at mid-height to anchors. 8 bolts.

13. **Deeper Shade of Soul** (5.10a) Start just left of a large, left-facing flake and below a rusty coldshut. Climb past an assortment of bolt hangers, coldshuts, and a chain to finish through a roof to the top. Bring a few cams in the 2- to 4-inch range.

14. **Unknown** (5.10c) Begin on a ledge with loose rock and climb up through the large roof to finish up an orange face. 5 bolts to anchors.

## IMPACT ZONE

15. **Blood, Sweat, and Chalk a.k.a. Blood, Sweat, and Jeers** (5.9+) The best route of its grade at Franklin. Locate a tall, narrow, orange face above a short rise in the cliffbase trail. Climb good slots up to a broken crack,

# CONTACT ZONE

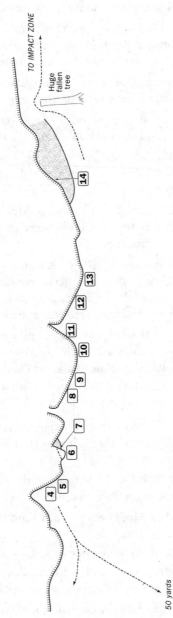

continue past a small overhang, and finish up a steep face. 9 bolts to anchors.

16. **Unknown** (5.9) Eighty yards beyond *Blood, Sweat, and Chalk* you'll find a face protected by coldshut "hangers." Climb the blocky face up through a small overhang and run it out to anchors. 5 bolts.

17. **Castaways** (5.8-) Good holds, good pro, and easy for its grade—probably the most-climbed route at Franklin! Send the center of the orange face with many nice horizontal cracks. 4 bolts to anchors.

18. **First Aid** (5.7) Start below a small, triangular roof about 12 feet up. Pass the roof on the right, then head up to a tree. 4 bolts.

19. **Unknown** (5.10b) Beginning on a blocky face just left of a chimney, climb past a low, square roof and up along a thin crack to a tree. 3 bolts.

20. **Captain Hook** (5.10d) Start below the right side of a 20-foot-high chimney. Follow the line of 4 bolts up and right onto the face above a roof, then up to anchors.

21. **Trident** (5.10a) Begin on a protruding block just right of a small "tunnel" through the buttress. Climb through tiny, tiered overhangs to anchors. 5 bolts to anchors.

22. **Decompression Sickness** (5.10b/c) An area classic! Start on blocks in front of a tall pine and below tiered roofs. Send the line of 9 bolts straight up past the roof to anchors. Variation: **The Bends** (5.11c) At the fifth bolt, move left and up a smooth, orange face to anchors. 9 bolts.

23. **Barnacle Bill** (5.11b) Steep, sustained, and quite awesome! Begin on the left wall of a short chimney "notch" and fire straight up the bulging face to anchors. 9 bolts. Variation: **Walk the Plank** (5.11a) At the third bolt, move out left and climb up through a roof on the front face to anchors. 9 bolts.

Note: Routes 24–27 begin from a ledge 20 feet above the cliffbase. To approach these routes, squeeze through a small tunnel in the buttress, just left of Route 21.

24. **Anchors Away** (5.9+) On the left side of the elevated ledge near the tunnel exit, climb the juggy face past 4 bolts to anchors.

25. **Super Amazing Sea Monkeys** (5.10d) Climb through the left side of the juggy roof to anchors. 6 bolts.

26. **Unknown** (5.10c/d) Start on the right side of the ledge, below a low, square roof. Climb up around the right side of the roof to anchors. 3 bolts—take care while clipping the second bolt.

27. **Belly of the Whale** (5.7+) A popular route with just one "hard" move. On the right side of the ledge, begin below the right wall of a 30-foot-

# IMPACT ZONE—LEFT SECTOR

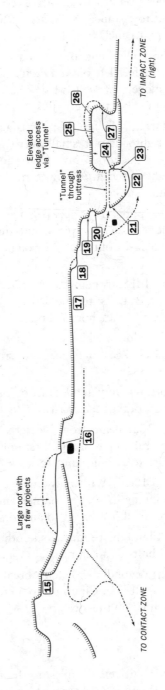

TO IMPACT ZONE
(right)

26

25

27

24

23

Elevated
ledge access
via "Tunnel"

22

"Tunnel"
through
buttress

21

20

19

18

17

16

Large roof with
a few projects

15

TO CONTACT ZONE

high alcove. Climb up and right along the juggy face to anchors. 4 bolts.

28. **Wasp Stop** (5.9) Start at a blocky corner 8 feet left of *Neptune*. Climb the face on the right to a stance. Now fire up the steep face (watch out for a huge wasp nest) to anchors. 5 bolts.

29. **Neptune** (5.10b) Nice climbing. Begin at a crack and juggy, shallow, right-facing corner 10 feet left of *Aqualung*. Blast up easy rock to the high first bolt and move past the left side of a roof. Trend right and up the steep face past a few small overhangs to anchors. 6 bolts.

30. **Aqualung** (5.9+) Start at a 15-foot-high, left-facing corner. Begin up the arête and past the right side of a small overhang to a stance. Work up the steep face above to anchors. 7 bolts. **Variation Start** (5.10a) Begin on large blocks just right of the *Aqualung* start. Face climb past 3 bolts to join the regular route.

31. **Shipwrecked** (5.9+) A popular voyage. Begin at jugs below a small overhang on the left side of a small cirque. Climb through the overhang and up a smooth face to ledge. Continue on through a few bulges to anchors. 7 bolts.

32. **Hidden Treasure** (5.11d) Start below a vegatated ledge about 25 feet up. Climb the face past 3 bolts to the ledge. Now fire up the steep, downstream-facing wall to anchors. 8 bolts.

33. **7–11** (5.11c/d) Begin below a white, convoluted face on the right side of a small cirque. Climb the short face and crank through a roof to anchors. 3 bolts.

34. **Jumpstart** (5.8) Short, but very good. Start on bucket holds under a low roof. Climb the bright orange face past 3 bolts to anchors.

35. **Early Retirement** (5.10a) Begin from blocks under the right side of a huge roof. Move carefully up to a high first bolt, then trend left and up a smooth, orange face to a stance and anchors. 3 bolts.

36. **Rock Your World** (5.10c/d) With only one hard move, this is a good "project" 5.10. Beginning in a large, orange-and-white, left-facing corner, climb past three small overhangs to anchors on the right. 3 bolts.

37. **Edgecation** (5.10c) Climb the beautiful, smooth face just right of a thin, zig-zagging crack. 3 bolts to anchors.

38. **Mean Gene's** (5.10a) Beyond a short cliff break, locate a downstream-facing wall with a 5-bolt line. Climb up to a crack and around the left side of a roof to anchors on the face above.

# THE MEADOW

The crags along the Meadow River, 10 miles north of the New River Gorge, have got to be the biggest, not-secret, "secret" area in the eastern United

States. Since the late 1980s, New River Gorge locals have explored and slowly developed the Nuttall Sandstone crags here, and world-famous climbers like Lynn Hill and Scott Franklin have established testpiece classics, such as *The Greatest Show on Earth* (5.12) and *Mango Tango* (5.13d/5.14a), respectively. You may have even seen photos of these routes or, possibly, the hyper-classic *Puppy Cow* (5.12c) in climbing magazines and catalogs. The fact is, The Meadow is a great area, but it is clearly overshadowed by the climbing at Summersville Lake to the north and the New River Gorge just to the south.

Another real problem preventing The Meadow from becoming a hit with the populace is the lack of safe parking and free access over public land. Tales of cars being broken into and climbers being shot at with buckshot are true. These types of incidents date back ten years and continue, though infrequently, today. But things are never as grim as they seem, and local activists are working to secure better access for climbers. However, given the less-than-ideal access situation at The Meadow, it is agreed that this area should remain low-profile and "third on the list" of areas to climb at in southern West Virginia. If climbing at The Meadow interests you, please stop by Blue Ridge Outdoors in Fayetteville first, and inquire about the latest access information.

# SENECA ROCKS/ NORTH FORK VALLEY REGION

While driving WV 28 down the North Fork Valley on a clear day, it's easy to see that Seneca Rocks is just one of many crags in the immediate area. While Seneca Rocks is the most dramatic and historic crag, good climbing does exist at other locations, such as Smokehole and Champe to the north and at Riverton, Judy Gap, and Nelson Rocks to the south. Of these five areas, Nelson is now the most active, though low-profile climbing has gone on for decades at each of these crags. In each case, the rock itself is on public land, but unfortunately, the shortest approach to the rock often crosses private property. This situation has caused some problems in the past, especially at Champe. If you want to explore some of these crags, consider visiting Judy Gap or Smokehole, as they are most directly accessible.

Last but not least, do not forget the miles of Tuscarora Sandstone along the ridge of North Fork Mountain. While a few mountain men have ventured onto the crags along the North Fork Mountain Trail, the approach is long and almost certainly requires an overnight stay. If you really want to escape the climbing populace, load up your expedition pack with overnight provisions, your climbing gear, and lots of water, and explore this wonderful, largely untouched wilderness area. Inquire at the climbing shops at Seneca Rocks for further beta on North Fork Mountain and the other climbing areas in this region.

# APPENDIX A: FURTHER READING

*Carderock: Past & Present,* Selma Hanel, Potomac Appalachian Trail Club, 1990.

*Climbers' Guide to the Great Falls of the Potomac,* James Eakin, Potomac Appalachian Trail Club, 1985.

*Gritstone Climbs,* Bill Webster, 1978. (out of print)

*New River Gorge and Summersville Lake,* Steve Cater, King Coal Propaganda, 1999.

*New River Rock,* Rick Thompson, Falcon Publishing, 1997.

*Rock 'N' Road: Rock Climbing Areas of North America,* Tim Toula, Falcon Publishing, 1995.

*Seneca Rocks: A Climber's Guide,* Bill Webster, Nippenose Books, 1980. (out of print)

*Seneca: The Climber's Guide,* Tony Barnes, Earthbound Sports, Inc., 1995.

*The Best Sport Climbs of the New River Gorge,* Roxanna Brock and Brian McCray, 1997.

*The Climber's Guide to North America: East Coast Rock Climbs,* John Harlin, Chockstone Press, 1986. (out of print)

*The Complete Great Falls Climbing Guide,* Marida Brinkworth, Dog Day Graphics, 1998.

*Virginia Climber's Guide,* Jeff Watson, Stackpole Books, 1998.

*Virginia's Shenandoah National Park,* Russ Manning, The Mountaineers, 2000.

# APPENDIX B: ROUTE RATINGS COMPARISON CHART

| YDS | British | French | Australian |
|---|---|---|---|
| 5.3 | VD 3b | 2 | 11 |
| 5.4 | HVD 3c | 3 | 12 |
| 5.5 | MS/S/HS 4a | 4a | 12/13 |
| 5.6 | HS/S 4a | 4b | 13 |
| 5.7 | HS/VS 4b/4c | 4c | 14/15 |
| 5.8 | HVS 4c/5a | 5a | 16 |
| 5.9 | HVS 5a | 5b | 17/18 |
| 5.10a | E1 5a/5b | 5c | 18/19 |
| 5.10b | E1/E2 5b/5c | 6a | 19/20 |
| 5.10c | E2/E3 5b/5c | 6a+ | 20/21 |
| 5.10d | E3 5c/6a | 6b | 21/22 |
| 5.11a | E3/E4 5c/6a | 6b+ | 22/23 |
| 5.11b | E4/E5 6a/6b | 6c | 23/24 |
| 5.11c | E4/E5 6a/6b | 6c+ | 24 |
| 5.11d | E4/E5 6a/6b | 7a | 25 |
| 5.12a | E5 6b/6c | 7a+ | 25/26 |
| 5.12b | E5/E6 6b/6c | 7b | 26 |
| 5.12c | E5/E6 6b/6c/7a | 7b+ | 26/27 |
| 5.12d | E6/E7 6c/7a | 7c | 27 |
| 5.13a | E6/E7 6c/7a | 7c+ | 28 |
| 5.13b | E7 7a | 8a | 29 |
| 5.13c | E7 7a | 8a+ | 30/31 |
| 5.13d | E8 7a | 8b | 31/32 |
| 5.14a | E8 7a | 8b+ | 32/33 |
| 5.14b | E9 7a | 8c | 33 |
| 5.14c | E9 7b | 8c+ | 33 |

Sources: *Mountaineering: The Freedom of the Hills*, 6th Edition; *Climbing* magazine, No. 150, February/March 1995.

# APPENDIX C: MOUNTAIN SHOPS, CLIMBING GYMS, AND GUIDE SERVICES

## Virginia

Alpine Outfitters
7107 West Broad Street
Richmond, VA 23294
(804) 672–7879

Blue Ridge Mountain Sports
1121 Emmet Street North
Charlottesville, VA 22903
(804) 977–4400

Blue Ridge Mountain Sports
10164 West Broad Street
Glen Allen, VA 23060
(804) 965–0494

Blue Ridge Mountain Sports
11500 Midlothian Turnpike
Richmond, VA 23235
(804) 794–2004

Blue Ridge Mountain Sports
1616 Laskin Road # 762
Virginia Beach, VA 23451
(757) 422–2201

Blue Ridge Mountain Sports
1248 Richmond Road
Williamsburg, VA 23185
(757) 229–4584

Blue Ridge Outdoors
125 North Main Street, Suite 100
Blacksburg, VA 24060
(540) 552–9012

Blue Ridge Outdoors
4362 Electric Road
Roanoke, VA 24014
(540) 774–4311

Eastern Mountain Sports
Tysons Corner Center
7954 Tysons Corner Center
McLean, VA 22102
(703) 506–1470

Highland Ski & Outdoor Center
I–81, exit 19
Abingdon, VA 24210
(540) 628–1329

Hudson Trail Outfitters Ltd.
11781 Lee Jackson Highway
#11743
Fairfax, VA 22033
(703) 385–3907

Hudson Trail Outfitters Ltd.
9488 Arlington Boulevard
Fairfax, VA 22031
(703) 591–2950

Hudson Trail Outfitters Ltd.
6701 Loisdale Road
Springfield, VA 22150
(703) 922–0050

Mountain Sports Ltd.
1021 Commonwealth Avenue
Bristol, VA 24201
(540) 466–8988

Mountain Trails
212 East Cork Street
Winchester, VA 22601
(540) 667–0030

Outdoor Adventures Ltd.
4721 Plank Road
Fredericksburg, VA 22407
(540) 786–3334

Outdoor Trails
4925 Boonsboro Road
Lynchburg, VA 24503
(804) 386–4302

Peak Experiences
11421 Polo Circle
Midlothian, VA 23113
(804) 897–6800

REI
3509 Carlin Springs Road
Bailey's Crossroads, VA 22041
(703) 379–9400

Rocky Top Climbing Club
1729 Allied Street
Charlottesville, VA 22903
(804) 984–1626
www.rockytopgym.com

Sportrock Climbing Center
5308 Eisenhower Avenue
Alexandria, VA 22304
(703) 212–ROCK
www.sportrock.com

Virginia Beach Rock Gym
5049 Southern Boulevard
Virginia Beach, VA 23462
(757) 499–8347

Wild River Outfitters Inc.
3636 Virginia Beach Boulevard
Virginia Beach, VA 23452
(757) 431–8566

Wilderness Voyagers
1544 East Market Street
Harrisonburg, VA 22801
(800) 220–1878

**Maryland**

Earth Treks
7125-C Columbia Gateway Drive
Columbia, MD 21046
(800) CLIMB–UP
(410) 872–0060
www.earthtreksclimbing.com

Eastern Mountain Sports
Annapolis Harbour Center
2554 Soloman's Island Road
Annapolis, MD 21401
(410) 573–1240

Eastern Mountain Sports
Towson Town Center
825 Dulaney Valley Road
Towson, MD 21204
(410) 296–1780

Hudson Trail Outfitters Ltd.
149 Annapolis Mall
Annapolis, MD 21401
(410) 266–8390

Hudson Trail Outfitters Ltd.
424 York Road
Baltimore, MD 21204
(410) 583–0494

Hudson Trail Outfitters Ltd.
10300 Little Patuxent Parkway
Columbia, MD 21044
(410) 992–3063

Hudson Trail Outfitters Ltd
401 North Frederick Avenue
Gaithersburg, MD 20877
(301) 948–2474

Hudson Trail Outfitters Ltd
8525 Atlas Drive
Gaithersburg, MD 20877
(301) 840–0650

Hudson Trail Outfitters Ltd
12085 Rockville Pike
Rockville, MD 20852
(301) 881–4955

Potomac Outdoors, Ltd.
7687 MacArthur Boulevard
Cabin John, MD 20818
(301) 320–1544

REI
9801 Rhode Island Avenue
College Park, MD 20740
(310) 982–9681

REI
63 West Aylesbury Road
Timonium, MD 21093
(410) 252–5920

Sportrock Climbing Center
14708 Southlawn Lane
Rockville, MD 20850
(301) ROCK–111
www.sportrock.com

Trail House
17 South Market Street
Frederick, MD 21701
(301) 694–8448

**West Virginia**

Adventure's Edge
137 Pleasant Street
Morgantown, WV 26505
(304) 296–9007

Blue Ridge Outdoors
101 East Wiseman Avenue
Fayetteville, WV 25840
(304) 574–2425

CMI Corporation
224 Mill Road
Franklin WV 26807
(304) 358–7041

The Gendarme
Behind Buck Harper's Store
Intersection of US 33 and WV 28
Seneca Rocks, WV 26884
(304) 567–2600

Hard Rock Climbing Services
131 South Court Street
Fayetteville, WV 25840
(304) 574–0735

Seneca Rocks Mountain Guides and
Outfitters
Intersection of US 33 and WV 28
Seneca Rocks, WV 26884
(800) 451–5108
(304) 567–2115

**Washington, D.C.**

Hudson Trail Outfitters Ltd.
4530 Wisconsin Avenue Northwest
Washington, DC 20016
(202) 363–9810

# APPENDIX D: CLIMBING ORGANIZATIONS

Blue Ridge Mountaineering Association
522 Highland Avenue Southwest
Roanoke, VA 24016
(540) 343–8391
www.geocities.com/Yosemite/Meadows/1069

Lynchburg Climbing Club
634 Baltimore Avenue
Bedford, VA 24523
(540) 586–5663
www.lynchburgclimbingclub.com

New River Alliance of Climbers
P.O. Box 145
Fayetteville, WV 25840
(304) 574–2425

Potomac Appalachian Trail Club (PATC)
Mountaineering Section
118 Park Street, Southeast
Vienna, VA 22180-4609
(703) 242–0693
www.patc.net/chapters/mtn_sect

The Access Fund
P.O. Box 17010
Boulder, CO 80308
(303) 545–6772
www.accessfund.org

# ROUTE NAME INDEX

# RATED ROUTE INDEX

# ABOUT THE AUTHOR

An active climber for twenty-five years, Eric Hörst has established more than 400 climbs at his "home crags" in Pennsylvania, Maryland, and the Virginias. Eric is also known as the author of the popular *Flash Training* (1994) and *How To Climb 5.12* (1997); both books have foreign translations available in parts of South America and Europe. His feature articles and photographs have been published in numerous national magazines, and he has written many articles on the subject of climbing performance for *Rock & Ice* and *Climbing*. Eric's Web site is www.TrainingForClimbing.com.

He currently lives in Mountville, Pennsylvania, with his wife, Lisa Ann, and his son Cameron.

*The author on Supernase, Frankenjura, Germany.* PHOTO BY MIKE McGILL

# ACCESS: It's every climber's concern

The Access Fund, a national, non-profit climbers organization, works to keep climbing areas open and to conserve the climbing environment. Need help with closures? land acquisition? legal or land management issues? funding for trails and other projects? starting a local climbers' group? CALL US!

Climbers can help preserve access by being committed to leaving the environment in its natural state.

• **ASPIRE TO CLIMB WITHOUT LEAVING A TRACE** especially in environmentally sensitive areas like caves. Chalk can be a significant impact – don't use it around historic rock art. Pick up litter, and leave trees and plants intact.

• **DISPOSE OF HUMAN WASTE PROPERLY** Use toilets whenever possible. If toilets are not available, dig a "cat hole" at least six inches deep and 200 feet from any water, trails, campsites, or the base of climbs. *Always pack out toilet paper.* On big wall routes, use a "poop tube."

• **USE EXISTING TRAILS** Cutting switchbacks causes erosion. When walking off-trail, tread lightly, especially in the desert on cryptogamic soils. "Rim ecologies" (the clifftop) are often highly sensitive to disturbance.

• **BE DISCRETE WITH FIXED ANCHORS** *Bolts are controversial and are not a convenience* – don't place 'em unless they are *really* necessary. Camouflage all anchors. Remove unsightly slings from rappel stations.

• **RESPECT THE RULES** and speak up when other climbers don't. Expect restrictions in designated wilderness areas, rock art sites, caves, and to protect wildlife, especially nesting birds of prey. *Power drills are illegal in wilderness and all national parks.*

• **PARK AND CAMP IN DESIGNATED AREAS** Some climbing areas require a permit for overnight camping.

• **MAINTAIN A LOW PROFILE** Leave the boom box and day-glo clothing at home.

• **RESPECT PRIVATE PROPERTY** Be courteous to land owners. Don't climb where you're not wanted.

• **JOIN THE ACCESS FUND** To become a member, make a tax-deductible donation of $25.

**The Access Fund**
*Preserving America's Diverse Climbing Resources*
PO Box 17010

# HARRISONBURG AREA CRAGS OVERVIEW

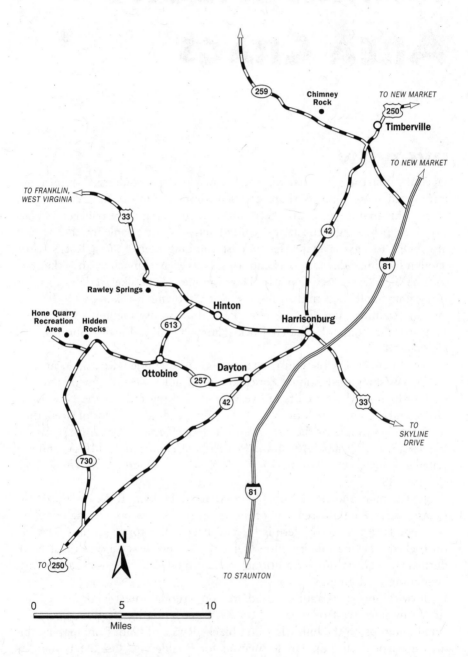